# Language *and* Learning
## Disorders
### *of the*
## Pre-Academic Child

73    5.00

# Language and Learning Disorders
## of the
# Pre-Academic Child:
### With Curriculum Guide

### Tina E. Bangs

HOUSTON SPEECH AND HEARING CENTER

Appleton-Century-Crofts

New York

DIVISION OF MEREDITH CORPORATION

# *Preface*

Medical scientists, psychologists, linguists, speech pathologists, audiologists, and others have made great contributions over the past decade in investigations concerned with oral and written language and the avenues of learning related to these communication skills: sensation, perception, memory-retrieval, attention, and integrative processes. The results of their efforts have played an important role in the development of assessment tools for school age children with communication disorders. Furthermore, the diagnostic findings have given impetus to a new management of preschool children predicted to be future academic failures.

The need for textbooks which translate and apply this scientific information to the educational needs of children is preeminent to teacher-training programs. Until such textbooks are written and curriculum guides are developed, the educational lag will remain between what is now known about children with communication disorders and how to educate them.

Children have suffered the consequences of school failure primarily because their language deficiencies were not detected at preschool ages, or if the deficits were observed, appropriate courses of action were not taken. The general purpose of this text is to approach this problem diagnostically and educationally at the preschool level.

Specifically, the text is designed: (1) to present a plan for early identification and assessment of a child's assets and deficits which are related to future academic achievement, (2) to present a *pre*-academic curriculum guide designed to strengthen a child's assets and/or deficits or find means of compensating for the deficits, (3) to present a means of adapting the curriculum guide to current classifications of children such as: deaf, mentally retarded, aphasic, aphasoid, brain injured, minimally brain injured, emotionally disturbed, perceptually handicapped, language disordered, underprivileged; as well as the normal and the gifted, and (4) to present clinical and educational materials to assist the teacher in the training program.

The author recognizes the importance of scientific studies related to human communication and has based her educational philosophy on much of the research that has been conducted in psychological, neurological, neurophysiological, audiological, and other scientific laboratories. It is not the purpose of this text, however, to present and discuss the scientific investigations, but rather to interpret results for the diagnostician or teacher who is concerned with understanding human communication and its disorders.

Furthermore the author presupposes that the basic principles of this text—*early* identification, assessment, and training—will not change, but newly published scientific data will continue to enrich the educational philosophy as it is herein presented.

To keep semantic problems at a minimum, the author has operationally defined the terms which give structure to the text. These definitions may be different from those used by the reading audience, but this should cause no difficulty. If the reader understands the author's use of these terms, better communication will result.

The reading audience may be as varied as the number of disciplines related to human communication and its disorders. Professors in elementary education, special education, and departments of speech pathology and audiology will observe that the material is suitable for a college textbook.

Trained nursery school and kindergarten teachers of normal and gifted children will find that the basic principles and the curriculum guide enrich their programs. Directors and teacher-clinicians employed in language development programs for children under the classifications of deaf and hard of hearing, blind or partially sighted, mentally retarded, aphasic, minimal brain dysfunction, or any of the current categories, will find in this textbook an eclectic, pragmatic approach to training children with handicaps.

In general, the book is directed to the reader who is interested in the assessment and pre-academic training of preschool children for purposes of improving language and learning skills. The ultimate goal for each child is academic success.

Although few direct quotations or references appear, the author is indebted to the many writers and lecturers who have contributed to her development of a basic educational philosophy for the training of young children with language disorders.

Special acknowledgment is given to Mrs. Anne Rister for her invaluable participation in the development of the curriculum guide. Her many years of teaching experience are reflected in the guide.

The author wishes also to recognize the contributions of the teacher-clinicians who in the past years have developed new teaching techniques and motivational materials: Mrs. Nancy Charters, Mr. Cal Foster, Mrs. Heddy Lee, Miss Catherine Solomon, Mrs. Nancy Sunkel, Miss Joan Williams, and Miss Lucinda Young.

Most important, however, have been the teachings, wise counsel, and encouragement given by my husband, Jack L. Bangs.

T.E.B.

# *Contents*

*Language and Learning*
*Disorders*
*of the*
*Pre-Academic Child*

# 1

# *Introduction*

Room 4, Fisher Elementary and Preschool: Blond, blue-eyed Debbie bends over a set of blocks her teacher has given her to help build number concepts. The four-year-old assembles the blocks, frowns, then says, "Me want some more. Me used down all the blocks, teacher!"

Room 5, Fisher School: Five-year-old Edward has been given a pair of scissors and a piece of paper with a circle drawn in its center. He is told to cut out the circle. Edward views the drawing from all angles, then wails, "But how can I cut out the circle when all this paper is in the way?"

Display case, Fisher School entry hall: Seventeen matchstick-drawings on bright orange construction paper depict the kindergarten class's assignment to "draw a house with straight lines." Sixteen of the drawings are composed of the sticks glued vertically and horizontally to form houses. But the seventeenth composition is a maze of matchsticks which fail to form proper angles, indeed, often fail even to meet. This drawing belongs to Terry, age five.

One school—three incidents, involving three children with no general intellectual deficit.

Is Debbie, the four-year-old who uses her blocks "all down," rather than "up," and who expresses her problem in language suited to a younger child, a mere lingual nonconformist?

Shall Edward's refusal to cut out a drawn circle "because all this paper is in the way" be categorized as stubbornness?

And what of little Terry's disorganized drawing, standing in jumbled contrast to the symmetric constructions of his classmates? Shall Terry's failure to carry out the assignment be attributed simply to lack of artistic ability—and forgotten?

Debbie, Edward, and Terry—and there are thousands of such chil-

1

dren in the United States today—have run up warning signals related to disorders of communication. These signals may be diagnostic of current or future oral and written language disabilities which will thwart the young student as his academic education gets underway.

## PARENT GOALS

Parents in our society will agree that the primary goal for their children is academic achievement. Years ago it was a high school diploma, but currently high value is placed upon a college degree and as much post-college work as can be accomplished.

Yet, relatively few parents recognize that language, oral and written, forms the very cornerstone of their children's education, and from the cornerstone of language skills, rises the multilayered framework that constitutes a modern education.

## LANGUAGE

**Language,** in a limited sense, is a communication system that includes the comprehension and usage of gesture, oral and written symbols. Oral and written language involves four linguistic systems each of which contributes to the development of acceptable words, phrases and sentences: phonological (sound features), semantic (meaning), syntactic (word order), and morphologic (tense, person, number, case).

### Oral Language Skills

In his preschool years, as well as in his first years at school, the child becomes knowledgeable primarily through auditory channels. He learns the meaning of words and a communication code which enables him to understand connected discourse and to use it appropriately. With continued listening experience he makes use of this oral language system to develop concepts of everyday living, to influence those persons about him, and finally become prepared for formal education.

Inability to use oral symbolization adequately, then, is a serious deterrent to academic success in its most elemental form.

### Written Language Skills

Written language, from an academic point of view, includes reading, writing, spelling, and arithmetic. Although reading aloud as well as the subjects of spelling and arithmetic may be included in the category of oral language, they are basically related to the read and written language.

Written language skills, the second great half of education's mighty cornerstone, do not normally become true tools of learning until the third or fourth grade. For this reason, the child with potential deficiencies in reading and writing will usually pass unobserved in his preschool years. There will be little recognition of his incipient difficulty until some time during the first through the third grade. This is relatively late if reading is a prime learning tool beyond third grade.

Certainly from the fifth grade upward, the child's opportunities to enlarge his scope of information are increasingly linked to his written language ability. History, geography, social studies, science, and much of mathematics actually become courses in reading.

It is understandable, then, why failure in reading is the largest single cause of school failures during the elementary education phase.

## AVENUES OF LEARNING

Knowledge of the dynamics of the acquisition of oral and written language and the disorders of each is not well understood. Scientists continue to study sensory-neural systems in animals and humans in an effort to better understand the mechanisms involved in human communication. From their scientific reports, diagnosticians and educators have found at least the following avenues of learning important to the acquisition of language: sensation, perception, memory-retrieval, attention, and integration. In addition, appropriate motivation, social maturity, social perception, and emotional stability are related to the ultimate goal of academic achievement and/or vocational accomplishments.

## ASSESSMENTS

Due to a paucity of scientific information upon which to build an academic program for children with language and/or learning deficiencies, State Departments of Education have been obliged to lean heavily on diagnosticians who used tools to measure sensory, motor, and intellectual impairment (IQ scores). These diagnosticians supplied labels for supposedly homogenous groups of children: *deaf, blind, mentally retarded, minimally brain injured, orthopedically handicapped, emotionally disturbed.* In theory these labels provided an adequate grouping of children for educational purposes. The teacher, however, was among the first to recognize the fallacy of placing children into such a wide variety of classified groups with nothing more than a label and an IQ score. She found individual differences among children in these specific groups so apparent that teaching was difficult, if not impossible, without a complete audit of each child's language, learning, and emotional status.

Taking into consideration the teacher's concern, diagnosticians began to search for tools which would assess the assets and deficits of school age children in the areas of language and the avenues of learning specifically related to academic achievement. Of even greater significance has been the contribution of persons who have developed assessment tools that assist in delineating language and learning deficits in children from birth to six years of age.

# PRE-ACADEMIC TRAINING

Over the years, teachers have observed that the older the child who has problems, the more difficult it becomes to cut through his compensatory mechanisms and to patch up the basic problems. The child who proceeds undiagnosed until a relatively late stage in his career is in severe difficulty. By the time the problem is pinpointed, the child, his parents, and his teachers are struck with a thorny, many-faceted dilemma.

The first facet of the problem is, of course, the child's frustrations in quest for additional knowledge. If grades must be repeated to correct his disability, the child is denied further pursuit of knowledge while he backtracks to remedy the deficit. If grades are not repeated, the deficiencies must somehow be corrected in order for him to make further progress.

In either case, the child is faced with emotional overlay; a keen sense of failure if he is retained a grade—or further frustration if he is expected to maintain a standard of scholastic achievement with classmates who do not share his difficulties.

Parental concern, then parental pressure, often adds to the child's increasing problems. And teachers are placed in a quandry as to the successful unthreading of the child's difficulties.

A solution to this dilemma is early identification of children predicted to be academic failures. And equally as important as early identification is a program for early training. Such a program involves a pre-academic curriculum guide designed to teach oral language; reading, writing, spelling, and arithmetic skills; and parent roles in the home training process. As this text is being written, only a few college education departments have developed curriculums for teachers that stress the development of language and learning skills of children between birth and five years of age. Yet, thousands of teachers are needed.

## SUMMARY

The identification, assessment, and training of children between birth and six years of age with language and/or learning deficits is a national concern. Unfortunately teachers have been asked to conduct classes for these children and their parents when basic training concepts related to the deficits have not been a part of their college curriculums.

Diagnosticians and teachers will find that the following chapters bring together a basic philosophy and an eclectic approach to training children who are predicted early in life to be academic failures. One thing is certain; if early training takes place, ultimately there will be a rapid decline in special education classes. Furthermore, less public money will be spent in the wrong places—trying to patch up weaknesses that should have been identified, assessed, and corrected before six years of age. Age six is too late.

# 2

# *Communication*

Human communication in its broadest meaning is the act or acts which produces some kind of a response between two or more persons.

Communication takes place through a system of arbitrary signs: oral language; written language; everyday gestures such as beckoning; elaborate sign language (developed for persons with severe hearing impairment); Morse Code; Balinese dancing; and flag signals, to name but a few.

## OPERATIONAL DEFINITIONS

If human communication is concerned with producing some kind of a response between two or more persons, then these persons must clearly understand one another, or the response may be far from what is expected. This is particularly true in written language, for the writer is seldom available to make explanations. It seems logical, then, that operational definitions of terms employed in this text will help eliminate semantic confusion.

Bridgman,[1] in his discussion of operational definitions, states, "Experience is described in terms of concepts, and since our concepts are constructed of operations, all our knowledge must inescapably be relative to the operations selected. Operational thinking will at first prove to be an unsocial virtue; one will find one's self perpetually unable to understand the simplest conversation of one's friends and will make one's self universally unpopular by demanding the meaning of appar-

[1] P. W. Bridgman, *The Logic of Modern Physics* (New York, The Macmillan Co., 1927), p. 25.

ently the simplest terms of everyday argument." Whatmough [2] wrote
". . . it is operational definitions which make science scientific, i.e., productive of verifiable and repeatable results, logically connectable and
communicable, provided that the conditions of investigation or experi-
ment are not changed."

There is a growing tendency in the study of language, intelligence,
and emotion to define terms operationally. Although the reader may
prefer different definitions than appear in this text, he can better understand the concepts set forth because the terms are operationally defined.

## ORAL LANGUAGE

### Definition

Oral language is a "structured system of arbitrary vocal sounds and
sequences of sounds that is used in interpersonal communication and
which rather exhaustively catalogues the things, events, and processes
of human communication." [3]

### The Study of Language

Interest in the origin, growth, and changes of language, and the
structure and differences among language, has led to the development
of the *field of linguistics*. The linguist has examined and continues to
examine language from a variety of viewpoints but for purposes of this
text, normal language development and its disorders are viewed primarily in terms of four linguistic systems: phonologic, semantic, syntactic, and morphologic.

The phonologic system has become a source of interest to both
linguists and speech scientists. In fact, the problems relating linguistic
units to the acoustical characteristics of speech have yet to be resolved.
In general, linguists are concerned with meaningful sounds that are
meaningfully produced, whereas speech scientists study the manner in
which speech sounds are perceived and produced.

**Semantics** deals with meanings, in particular the relationship between the sign (the word *chair*) and its referent (a real *chair*). Teachers
very often use the term vocabulary to refer to the semantic aspects of
language.

[2] J. Whatmough, *Language: A Modern Snythesis* (St. Martin's Press, 1956),
p. 104.
[3] J. B. Carroll, "Language Acquisition, Bilingualism and Language Change,"
from *Psycholinguistics: A book of readings,* S. Saporta, ed. (New York, Holt,
Rinehart and Winston, Inc., 1961), p. 332.

**Syntactic** features deal with the order in which words are put to-gether to form phrase or sentence structures.

The *morphologic* system includes rules for building words; the cor-rect use of tense, number, case, and person.

It is of interest to note that the linguist is the person most often concerned with analyzing the structure of the language, whereas the *grammarian* determines its social acceptability. Society makes the value judgment by applying an arbitrary set of rules for determining accept-able sentences, and the grammarians derive and rewrite the rules based on their observations of language in use.

Although every language changes with time, some of the systems are subject to greater shifts than others. In the study of semantics we find that new words are added, some words drop out completely, and that word meanings undergo much change. The syntactic and morpho-logic structures, on the other hand, remain relatively constant.

Descriptions of the developmental stages of language are being reported in the literature and researchers continue to present evidence to verify the hypothesis that language develops in an orderly fashion, far more orderly than has been earlier supposed. The answer as to *how* language develops, however, is only in elementary stages of research. In fact, the questions are not yet formulated clearly.

Linguists currently are working closely with psychologists, particu-larly in the areas of verbal behavior, language acquisition, and learning theory. In addition, research in genetics, molecular biology, speech sci-ence, audiology, and other specialized fields are providing a better un-derstanding of the communication process and its impairments. With a continued interprofessional approach, more will be known about the neurophysiological and/or observable aspects of normal and substand-ard language. Such efforts will yield new and improved theories to ac-count for language acquisition.

## Order of Development

### PRE-LINGUISTIC SYSTEMS

There have been numerous studies dealing with the developmental stages leading to the child's understanding and use of words. In general, investigators have observed that babies begin to vocalize early in life, usually starting with the birth cry. As weeks go by, gross noises become differentiated into recognizable sounds and at some time during the early months, vocal play emerges. The baby apparently finds pleasure in producing and listening to his own sound production. The relation-ship, if any, of this to language behavior is not clearly understood. The auditory feedback and exercising of the articulatory mechanism, however, is undoubtedly related to processes involved in the acquisition of language.

There is a period of time during this vocal play when the baby begins to match the sounds of others with his own. This echoic state or echolalia is pre-linguistic behavior. At this time the baby perceives auditory signals, repeats them, but does not yet attach meaning to the symbols. Furthermore, the repetition of words without fully grasping their meaning continues long after a child acquires language. School children repeat, "I pledge allegiance to the flag of the United States of America . . ." before they fully understand the broad concepts of allegiance, flag, or patriotism.

## LINGUISTIC SYSTEMS

Although the pre-linguistic stages of language have been described in the literature in a fairly concrete manner, such has not been true of the linguistic aspects. The psychological and physical attributes of language and how these elements relate to its development are topics of interest to many scientists.

We know that children must perceive words before they understand them, and understand them before they are used appropriately in spoken language. In other words, soon after a child begins to associate words with their referents he may attempt to say them. Subsequently through unknown processes he begins to generate phrases and sentences with these basic words.

It is obvious that little children do learn to make appropriate sentences without a grammar book, but it is hardly possible to believe that they store in their memory bank all sentences they have heard. It is more reasonable to hypothesize that they find a "system" for making sentences, or a set of rules that guides them to a sentence, such as "I want a drink," as opposed to "Drink a me want."

The comprehension and expression of oral language becomes an ongoing process with a finite number of words to be learned and an infinite number of sentences to be generated from the words. Researchers have demonstrated that many of the grammatical rules have been acquired between the ages of three and four, yet it is not unusual to find seven- and eight-year-olds who are still having difficulty with irregular verbs.

*Semantic Features (vocabulary).* When a child hears the word *run*, and makes an association with a boy, animal, or bird whose legs move in an alternating fashion at a fast pace, he has acquired a new vocabulary word. He has learned that a specific set of visually observed operations can be labeled *run*. Once he understands this meaning of the word, he may attempt to use it in this narrow sense for communicative purposes,

"I can *run*," or "The dog can *run*." But it is not enough to merely know these aspects of the word *run*, for other meanings occur if a different series of operations is observed. When a thread in a woman's nylon stocking is broken, he may hear her say, "My stocking is *running*," or "I have a *run* in my stocking." Children also learn that boards *run* in certain directions on the floor, that a car *runs* well, that a child's nose *runs* when he has a cold, and that people *run* for office.

In general, children learn concrete words before category. names for these words. For example, the meanings of the words *cars, blocks, dolls,* are acquired before the category word *toys*.

> Mother was concerned because her son would not put his *toys* away. Perhaps she would have had more success if she listed the kinds of toys, "Put your *blocks* in the drawer." *Toys* may have been a meaningless word.

As experiences of the individual multiply, vocabulary increases and words become more generalized. It is the meaning of words in isolation and in connected discourse, the semantics of our language, that forms the foundation for oral communication.

*Syntactic Features.* Phrase and sentence structure can be described in terms of the order in which words are put together. Children probably obtain their first basic words and phrases through an imitative process. They understand and say such stereotypes as BYE BYE, DADDY and CAR, CAR before longer combinations are uttered. This basic vocabulary apparently forms a large open class of words to which he can add indefinitely as he acquires the rules of the oral language code.

He learns, for example, to develop from the stereotype BYE BYE, a variety of phrases and sentences: DADDY BYE BYE, BYE BYE CAR, GO BYE BYE CAR, DADDY GO BYE BYE CAR, ME GO BYE BYE CAR. With each year of maturation he generates sentences that will eventually be grammatically correct. DADDY IS GOING TO LEAVE IN THE CAR.

*Morphologic Features.* Not only does a child somehow learn the rules of syntax but through a currently unknown process he also induces morphologic rules from the language he hears. In his early stages of development many errors of usage prevail: DADDY DRIVED THE CAR. THERE'S TWO MANS. Again, with maturation, the child learns a set of rules which makes his grammar acceptable to society.

*Concepts.* Children begin early to discriminate one set of elements from another. They are developing concepts of likenesses and differences. They learn that some things are edible and some are not, boys are different from girls, and that fruits and vegetables are in different categories.

Concept development may take place through verbal or nonverbal channels.

Julie, who has not heard language because of severe hearing impairment, and her brother Jim are in the kitchen. Jim reaches into the forbidden territory of the cookie jar. Mother, who has reprimanded him for doing this on other occasions, walks into the room. She scowls, shakes her finger, and slaps his hand. He hears the words "That's a *bad* thing to do." and the meaning of the word *bad* is formed. Sister, who does not hear the words and does not lip-read, develops, through visual cues, the concept that taking cookies without permission is not very rewarding. Furthermore she learns that little people who do such a thing are apt to receive some kind of punishment.

Jim, in the foregoing example, will learn later that this word *bad* may generalize into the word *stealing*. Both Jim and Julie will develop concepts of *rightness* and *wrongness* even though Julie may never learn the words *right* and *wrong*.

Children with total visual or hearing impairment may be taught concepts of *big* and *little* through sorting tasks using visual, or tactile cues. But as the concepts become broader or more generalized—*bigger, smaller, space*—these children may be handicapped by their impairments. With special instruction in concept formation, however, their language development need not be substandard.

## Disorders of Language

Children who do not follow an orderly pattern when learning the language code may be referred to as *language disordered:* those who do follow an orderly pattern but one not commensurate with chronological age may be referred to as *language delayed*. Attempting to use these terms definitively in a clinical situation is not always feasible because of limited knowledge of the developmental stages of the syntactic and morphologic systems. For purposes of this text, then, reference to disorders of language includes disordered and delayed.

### DISORDERS OF SEMANTICS: VOCABULARY

*Reduced Vocabulary Comprehension.* Standardized vocabulary comprehension tests (3, 35)* are available to determine an approximate age level at which preschool children understand concrete and abstract words when an oral response is not required.

A child is presented with a series of pictures, one of which is a *chair.* The examiner asks him to point to the picture that means *furniture*. He may be unable to do so but readily selects the appropriate picture when asked to "Point to the chair."

If the child is seven years of age, he is expected to know the mean-

* Numbers in parentheses refer to references in Bibliography.

ing of the word *furniture*. If three years old, he is performing as might be expected.

*Reduced Vocabulary Usage.*  One of the simplest ways for measuring the child's ability to tell the meaning of single words is to present him with a series of objects or pictures known to be identifiable by certain age groups. The ability to answer with a good association, yet be unable to name the object or picture may be an indication of a current language disorder.

> Johnny, at age four, looked at the picture of the coat and said, "Put it on." He looked at the stove and said, "Cook." His classmate of the same age looked at the first picture and said "Coat," and when shown the stove said, "Stove."

Children may learn the meaning of a word in one context only, hence use it inappropriately in another context.

> Melanie, with severe hearing impairment, was participating in a language reassessment. She was asked the question, "What sails?" Her reply, "Mrs. Lovenstein's garage." This appeared to be quite a bizarre answer unless one knew that Melanie's mother and neighbor had for the past week been collecting all their unwanted items of clothing and furniture for a neighborhood *sale* to be held in Mrs. Lovenstein's garage.

## DISORDERS OF SYNTAX AND MORPHOLOGY

*Comprehension Disorders of Connected Discourse.*  It is not unusual to find a child with normal hearing who performs quite well regarding his understanding of single words, yet performs below age level when the examiner uses these known words with function words to present the task.

> A series of objects, two of which are a spoon and a cup, is placed before a child. The examiner asks him to "Put the spoon in the cup." Although the child knows the meaning of the words *cup* and *spoon,* he is unable to comprehend the total message "Put the spoon in the cup."

The teacher is sometimes in a dilemma to know whether the child does not understand a word(s) in a sentence, or if he is unable to decode the message when several words are used.

> Mrs. Charters was presenting a lesson in number skills. She gave each child a piece of paper, a pencil, and a ruler. In order to make straight lines on which to write, the teacher said, "Use your rulers to draw a straight line." Karen picked up her ruler and attempted to use it as a pencil.

*Usage Disorders in Connected Discourse.*  Awkward sentence construction, improper sequencing or omissions of words, and incorrect use of morphological rules may contribute to language disorders depending, of course, upon chronological age.

> Karl, age five, in training because of severe hearing impairment, was asked to tell what he remembered of the Thanksgiving party which had been held in the classroom one week before. He related the following: "A turkey and food. Ready to go home. Eat and not the boys and girls. That's all."
>
> Five-year-old Gary with normal hearing caught the teacher's attention, and pointing to his mouth said, "Another one coming in back a tooth." Teacher looked in his mouth expecting to find a missing tooth. Instead a six year molar was just appearing through the gum.
>
> John, age four, with hearing impairment, put his ideas in improper sequence when asked what he did after school. His answer, "Buy toys and go store."
>
> Mathew, age five, with hearing impairment, was asked to tell what he remembered of the Thanksgiving party. His reply, "Teacher sit in the chair watching the children. The children all eating dinner. The children sitting down in the chair. Some of the children didn't ate all their supper. And the children went to get a drink of water in the cup and they was all quiet. And they came back in the room. Then they ate, and then they went back home. That sure is a long story."
>
> A group of six-year-old children without hearing impairment were drinking their milk. John finished, looked up, and noticed Kerry had also finished. Instead of saying "We tied." John commented, "Me him beat together."

Disorders of language, then, are concerned with a child's inability to comprehend the meaning of single words and connected discourse, and/or his faulty application of semantics and the syntactic and morphologic rules in his oral output.

# SPEECH

## Definition

Speech may be thought of as the process by which oral symbols are perceived and produced. This process involves the auditory pathways concerned with perception and the intricate coordination among several neuromuscular mechanisms including the respiratory, phonotory, resonatory, and articulatory systems.

## The Study of Speech

Persons interested in normal as well as abnormal aspects of speech development have come to be known as speech scientists, speech pathologists, and audiologists. Because the work of these specialists cuts across so many academic disciplines, it necessitates a close relationship with the structural and neuroanatomist, neurologist, otologist, psychologist, and more recently the linguist.

Speech must be considered a multidimensional process. Its primary components are auditory perception, articulation, and voice (including quality, pitch, time, and loudness). These components can never be thought of as functional entities. Rather, they work in a highly integrated fashion to receive and produce word symbols. Even though investigators may be looking at the specific acts, they are always aware of the interaction of the entire speech mechanism.

## ARTICULATION

*Order of Development.* Children must perceive distinctions before they can produce them orally. In general, these distinctions begin with gross differences that gradually become more refined. Contrasts between the high vowel *ē* (as in eat) and the mid vowel *ä* (as in arm), for example, may be perceived before the two front vowels, *i* and *e* that appear in m*i*lk and m*e*lt.

> Eighteen-month-old Judy consistently referred to her "Grandma" as "Ga-Ga." It may be postulated that her phonemic system had reached the stage of two series (ga-ga) with highly differentiated sounds (g and ä). The r had not yet been acquired in isolation or in blends, and she could not differentiate between the vowel ä and a, and selected ä because it had greater stress in the word "grammä" (grandma). Hence, Ga-Ga became the telegraphic word symbol for "grandma."

In addition to a perceptive mechanism that is capable of discriminating accurately among similar sounds, children also need a motor system capable of handling production of the various consonant and vowel sounds. Again, the development is from the simple to the complex. In general, sounds requiring gross movements of the articulatory mechanism, such as **p**, **b**, and **m**, are among the first to be acquired by the child. It is a simple motor process to open and close the lips in a manner required for production of labial sounds. Subsequently **t**, **k**, **d**, and **g** may appear. Others, however, which require an intricate coordination of the neuromuscular mechanisms may not be uttered until the child is physically capable of producing these sounds. Therefore, **s**, **j**, **r**, and blends such as **sw**, **bl**, **tr** generally appear later in the developmental stages of learning to talk.

> Two six-year-olds were engaged in play. Tommy, in a stern voice turned to Joyce and said, "Yoice, don't keep calling me 'ommy!'"

*Disorders of Articulation.* If a child omits, distorts, substitutes, or adds sounds as he talks, he is described as presenting a disorder of articulation, providing these errors are substandard for his chronological or mental age. Substandard articulation is determined currently by phonetic inventories that have been developed through normative studies (54, 106).

Because of the vast number of substitutions, omissions, and distortions of consonant and vowel sounds during the early language development period, the speech pathologist may not understand the child, hence find it difficult to separate a speech disorder from jargon.

When a child says "tee," is he just using jargon, or is he attempting the word "sit?" The t is substituted for the s, the ē for the i and the final sound t is omitted. Is it that his phonemic system is not ready for the word "sit," or is this sound of "tee" just jargon?

Some causes attributed to articulatory disorders are obvious; faulty anatomical mechanisms, inappropriate motor coordination, cultural deprivation, and perhaps emotional instability. Not all children with articulation errors, however, can be classified so simply. Their undiagnosed etiologies fortunately have become the concern of scientists who are currently investigating the mechanisms of sensation, perception, attention, memory-retrieval, and integration of auditory signals. Clinical research in these areas is directed toward better understanding of the acquisition and use of phonetic symbols, and appropriate teaching techniques to improve articulatory skills.

## VOICE

*Order of Development.* Equipped with an adequate functioning vocal mechanism, the newborn will begin to use it in an undifferentiated manner. During the first two or three months of life he will produce nonmeaningful sounds; yet ones that are *qualitatively* different. Subjectively, the sounds are judged to be of a certain pitch, loudness, or pleasantness. Objectively, the speech scientist, through spectral analysis, studies these subjective aspects of voice by investigating frequency, intensity, and time correlates.

Early in life a child differentiates meanings of words through intonation and stress. In fact the linguist may ask the question, "Does a child learn to *respond* to intonation and stress before he responds to the word symbol?"

When father says "No" to little Billy it may always be in a louder-than-usual voice and with no inflectional change. Billy immediately ceases his unacceptable behavior. Mother may say the same word, "No," but with a rising and falling inflection and not so loud. Billy does not cease his activity.

From birth to old age we find alterations in voice; alterations that cannot be thought of as discrete entities, but rather as a reciprocal relationship between frequency, intensity, and time.

*Disorders of Voice.* Terms such as hoarseness, huskiness, nasality, breathiness, stridency, and dozens of others are literally figures of speech. They are subjective terms applied by investigators who needed words to describe vocal disorders. Needless to say, speech scientists are attempting to objectify what is meant by these terms. Currently they have classified them into not more than five or six categories which are related to the attributes of frequency, intensity and time.

The basic etiology of voice problems is comparable to that of articulation disorders, namely, a faulty anatomical mechanism, inappropriate motor coordination, cultural factors, emotional instability.

# WRITTEN LANGUAGE

## Reading

### DEFINITION

The foregoing discussion of oral language, including phonology, semantics, syntax, and morphology provides a construct upon which a definition of reading can be developed. Reading is the ability to gain meaning from a structured system of written signs which are used to represent oral language. The oral symbol, then, becomes the referent for its written counterpart.

In order to learn to read, the student must be taught the meaning of specific written signs and their relationship to each other in words, phrases, and sentences. To make use of reading, he must be able to comprehend and store the written information, then retrieve it when needed.

### THE STUDY OF READING

The literature abounds with studies concerned with reading, primarily disorders of reading. Until recent years these reports have been descriptive treatises on what the teacher, reading specialist, and psychologist have observed in children who do not learn to read according to their grade placement.

Partly as a result of this descriptive reporting, investigators have looked for a single cause of reading failure and a specific method that will enable all children to learn to read. As a consequence, numerous books are available that contain overlapping methods of training, all of which purport to teach children to read.

The obvious facts are still with us. There are children who learn to read through any method—possibly even osmosis—and other children whose reading never becomes functional. In between are the good to poor readers.

Teachers continue to ask the same questions they have asked for years because answers have not been forthcoming.

1. How can the classroom teacher determine if a first grade student is failing reading because of a true neurophysiological disorder, or if his problem is one of slow maturation? Teachers are becoming more and more aware of the dangers inherent in the developmental lag concept. They found that a laissez-faire attitude resulted in first grade repeaters whose inability to read was something more than late blooming. Furthermore, those who were late bloomers suffered the consequences of failure; or the self concept, "I am not as smart as my friends."

2. Should methodology involve a phonetic or whole word approach or a combination of the two?

Present information is spotty. There is much need for bringing together such disciplines as neurology, psychology, and education; professionals that will work together in both clinical and research settings without preconceived bias.

DISORDERS OF READING

Reading disorders may become apparent in first or second grade. Certainly by fourth or fifth grade the disorder makes itself known. At this point in the child's educational career arithmetic, history, science, and geography become courses almost entirely dependent upon previously learned reading skills. Lacking the skills needed to comprehend written language, the child becomes an academic failure, branding him with an image of failure in life.

In general, standard reading achievement tests identify poor readers and aim to measure: (1) vocabulary level, (2) ability to retain the concepts read, (3) ability to interpret facts and draw inferences from them, and (4) ability to make one generalization or select one main idea with regard to what has been read. These are important assessments to make if a child is to be prepared for his future academic program, which, with each added year, requires more and more reading. Levels (1) and (2) often are met by normal readers and perhaps are adequate for primary grade reading. Levels (3) and (4) frequently are not attained because of poor instruction or limited experiences.

The discovery that a child cannot read takes no great amount of insight, but the reasons for his inability to read are often obscure and appropriate methods for training even more remote. Currently, reading disorders are thought to be attributed to one or more of at least the following conditions:

1. Reduced vocabulary
2. Substandard use of other oral language systems
   (phonology, syntax, and morphology)

3. Sensory deficits
4. Perceptual deficits
5. Memory-retrieval deficits
6. Poor attention
7. Integrative disorders
8. Poor instruction
9. Lack of opportunity

Teachers are asking reading specialists to help pinpoint the cause or causes of reading failures among their first grade students. If such becomes possible, the diagnostic information can be translated to preschool children in an attempt to predict future reading failures. Training programs will then be designed to help preschool children develop reading readiness skills needed in an academic program.

# Spelling

### DEFINITION

Spelling is a process concerned with the appropriate ordering of sounds or letters to form words. Although spelling may be an oral act, or originate as such, it is usually thought of as an integral part of written language.

> Children in the readiness class were being exposed to phonetics. They thought of words that began with the "d" sound (daddy, dog) and the "l" sound (leaf, light). As Elizabeth looked at some of her picture books at home one evening, she came across the word "doll." She asked her mother, "What does daddy-o-leaf-leaf spell?"

### THE STUDY OF SPELLING

Few investigators have published significant findings related to the subject of spelling. What has been written tends to indicate that the skills needed to spell words, oral or written, are varied and perhaps independent of each other. Consequently it has been postulated that both auditory and visual systems are important avenues for learning to spell.

### DISORDERS OF SPELLING

That a child has difficulty learning to spell is obviously apparent to the classroom teacher. The reasons for the difficulty are not clear, but may result from one or more of the deficiencies listed as causes for reading disorders (p. 17).

If a variety of avenues of learning is believed to be needed for accurate spelling, it is not surprising to find that two children with the same total spelling score present different types of errors. Some teachers are currently attempting to develop differential spelling tests to find the specific reasons why some students are poor spellers.

# Handwriting

DEFINITION

Writing is the process of transducing a linguistic message into a graphic form.

THE STUDY OF HANDWRITING

Teachers are aware that the movement for handwriting is a patterning process. There is a circular, up and down, and a forward movement with constant pressure changes. In addition there is horizontal as well as vertical and spatial organization. Children are taught, or develop on their own, a method that will produce the patterns necessary for written language.

Less than half a century ago children were taught to keep fingers still and let their arm guide the pencil across the paper. Although their writing quality was often good during the training period, something happened when training ceased. Students reverted to total or partial finger movement. For some reason the pattern was not retained and handwriting changed. The method obviously was not successful.

When a child is not shown a method for writing, he will usually use a tight and almost total finger movement. The side of the hand is planted in one spot and the fingers move. At short intervals the hand is lifted and placed a bit further to the right. The disadvantages are apparent; cramping of the fingers over a period of time, poor formation of letters, and a reduction in speed.

Currently a combination of the two methods is preferred. The child places his arm on the desk with his hand tilted slightly to the outside, resting on the fourth and fifth fingers. As he writes, his fingers guide the pencil, and his hand and arm slide across the paper.

Teachers have questions related to handwriting just as they ask questions related to reading and spelling skills.

1. Should manuscript or cursive writing be taught first? Proponents of manuscript writing say it is easier to learn, the letters are more like those the child will find in his reader, and movements are less complex because they are broken. Manuscript writing currently is the most popular method in first and second grades throughout the country.

Those who teach cursive writing from the start believe that because it is the chosen form for future writing, it should be taught before manuscript. Proponents of cursive writing also state that it is more easily mastered if the child does not have to effect the change from manuscript to cursive. The issue is not settled.

2. Should the writing be slanted in the time-honored tradition or may it be vertical? Teachers are inclined to say writing is better if it slants. Is this a value judgment, or is there a functional reason as to why slanted writing is better?

Some teachers in preschool programs are experimenting with methods that will teach prewriting skills; teaching proper holding of chalk or pencil and left-right progression. In addition, these preschoolers practice making the counterclockwise circles and line movements common to both manuscript and cursive writing. In general, this kind of training begins at a blackboard where gross muscular activity can come into play.

Motivation is easily obtained by making such things as faces with circles, and wagons with circles and lines. With the acquisition of these skills a child is better prepared to enter into a writing program. And writing truly is one of the first things he wants to learn to do.

How many times have we heard a child say, "Daddy, I can write my name," then observe the production?

A right-handed five-year-old child with no language or learning disorders printed his name from right to left. This is a common error for preschool children.

Research related to handwriting has been neglected. Reported studies generally have been poorly designed and poorly executed. Teacher's colleges have not stressed the subject, and elementary teachers have been more concerned with arithmetic, reading, and what is *said* in writing. As a result, school personnel and parents complain that the children of today have poorer handwriting than the children of yesterday. In-service teacher-training programs are currently being formed in many school districts to find solutions to the problem.

Investigators are sure of one thing; writing must become a unified product composed of movement and concepts. It becomes important then to teach the movement skills early so that subsequently the child will be able to think of *what* he is writing, not *how*.

DISORDERS OF HANDWRITING

If the ultimate purpose in handwriting is to express and communicate meaning, the teacher must be concerned with content, spelling, quality, and speed.

Assuming that content and sentence structure are adequate, disorders of writing become qualitative from the standpoint of legibility and attractiveness. The disorders are quantitative from the viewpoint of number of words per second and number of words misspelled.

Judgments as to the degree of excellence of handwriting are usually relative. The written work of the child who has cerebral palsy may be legible with no misspellings, but the form may be gross. For his neurological mechanism the writing is acceptable. The child who has no particular motivation to write well may demonstrate a writing product that is very poor.

Teachers follow certain basic rules in an attempt to help children write legibly. The paper is placed before the child parallel with the desk if manuscript is being taught, and parallel to the writing arm when cursive is introduced.

With regard to left-handed children, a few simple rules are followed:

1. If desk chairs are used, provide ones with left-sided writing space for left-handed children.

2. Turn the paper in such a direction that it parallels his left arm when doing cursive writing, then the child will see what he is doing and will not smudge the writing.

Left-handed children who are taught to write with the paper arranged for right-handed children are forced to use an awkward back hand position in order to view what they are writing. There is no need for texts teaching writing to left-handed children if the preceding suggestions are observed.

The importance of making written information legible should not overshadow the merits of accuracy in spelling or in writing information. Teachers must view these three aspects of written work in proportion to the purpose of an assignment. If the assignment is to present a composition on the concept of democracy and the student does so in a well thought-out and well constructed theme, he has fulfilled his duty. The fact that he has misspelled four words should not lower his grade point, for the original assignment had nothing to do with spelling. Perhaps all of this indicates a need for four merits: the ability (1) to write information, (2) to structure sentences appropriately, (3) to spell accurately, and (4) to write legibly.

The total writing process: presenting information, structuring sentences appropriately, spelling accurately and writing legibly is perhaps the result of an integrated neurophysiological mechanism and environmental factors.

## Numbers

### DEFINITION

Mathematics is a language of science that deals with measurement, properties, and relations of quantity. Problems relating to size, shape, form, structure, or location are best answered through mathematical concepts.

Arithmetic is the art of computing with numbers. It becomes the language for solving problems and communicating scientific facts. Arithmetic provides a foundation for mathematics.

It is easier to solve arithmetic problems with a set of symbols different from oral and written words. Hence society has a language of numbers, algebraic equations, and geometric signs for computation purposes. Children learn that $2 + 2 = 4$, and a $\times$ a $= a^2$.

### THE STUDY OF NUMBERS

Investigators over the years have probably contributed more to improving the teaching of numbers than of spelling and writing. Historically we read that in acquiring the processes of addition, subtraction, multiplication, and division, extensive drill was necessary. Primary grade children were introduced to rote learning of number facts; $6 + 2 = 8$ or $8 - 6 = 2$.

Teachers and investigators decided that this type of training was inadequate so they developed an incidental or activity type method. Children brought their milk money to school and were responsible for correct change. Play stores or field trips to real stores provided life situations for the teaching of number facts.

Not too many years ago, a "meaning" theory of teaching number concepts was introduced in the primary grades. This theory demonstrates the fact that we have a number system with a base of ten and a place value. For example, the numbers one through nine take one number and hold one place. The number ten, then, requires two numbers with zero as a place holder.

Teachers currently employ such devices as the abacus, chart slots, flannel boards, or coins to teach number concepts. Children learn, for example, that the number 432 is represented by four beads on the left (four one hundreds), three beads in the middle (three tens), and two beads on the right (two ones). Perhaps in the near future, third grade children will be able to explain in detail to parents why a computer usually employs a base of two.

Modern mathematics also includes drill and incidental types of training. Drill makes the use of facts automatic. Incidental teaching enables the child to solve everyday problems. Teaching the meaning behind our number system, hopefully will open the door to algebra, geometry, and higher mathematics.

Apparently children develop arithmetic and mathematical skill in an orderly fashion. They learn a basic oral vocabulary and a symbol system which leads them to the goal of mathematical competence.

*Vocabulary.* There is a need for acquiring a basic vocabulary for arithmetic computation, and most children learn incidentally many of the concepts which prepare them for their introduction to arithmetic. By first grade, they know the meaning of the words *more, one more, less than, not so many, below, above, under, first, last.* These are only a few of the words basic to understanding number facts and processes involved in mathematics.

*Rote Counting.* Although there is an overlap in the steps which children are thought to take in acquiring the use of numbers, rote counting probably comes early. This step is a mere repetition of number words with no meaning attached.

*Rational Counting.* When a child can point to each object as he counts, he has reached a stage of rational counting. In general, this skill follows rote counting.

*Number Concepts.* Looking at a configuration of five (such as is found on dominoes) and calling it five without the use of rational counting is the beginning of number concept development. The child knows that five chairs are not the same as five oranges but that these groupings have a common factor of "fiveness."

*Number Facts.* Perhaps the next step is concerned with the ability to see the relationships among numbers, and the similarity of the processes involved in adding and subtracting, in multiplying and dividing.

*Mathematics.* As vocabulary increases and an understanding of our number system unfolds, children acquire a foundation for quantitative thinking.

DISORDERS OF NUMBER COMPUTATION

Experts agree that there are multiple reasons for failure in arithmetic and mathematics, not the least of which is lack of basic vocabulary. Teachers may assume that their pupils have developed number concepts when actually the pupils are still on a rote counting level. Moving students ahead too fast may cause frustration and lack of motivation.

Consider the older child who does well with his addition facts on some days but not on others.

> Jimmy, in the third grade, took a test on Thursday which included addition problems, the majority of which started with the highest number, e.g., $8 + 2 = ?$ He made no errors. The following Monday he took another test where the reverse occurred—most of the problems started with the small number, e.g., $2 + 8 = ?$ Jimmy made many errors. Is it more difficult to add 8 to 2?

Problems in learning arithmetic skills may lie in the teaching method. Were the children taught answers by going to the appropriate number? For example, learning "plus one" would mean going to the next number. "Plus two" or $6 + 2$ would indicate two steps beyond 6 for an answer of 8. Was the child taught that $2 + 8$ means 8 steps beyond?

After acquiring the basic concepts of addition facts, some children still have difficulty. There is the child who can add two numbers but fails when given a column of numbers, e.g., $2 + 7 + 4 + 9 = ?$ Does this child have a short term memory deficit? When he thinks "two and seven is nine" he must hold that number until he thinks "and four is thirteen." Would it be better to have him omit the connecting words in his early addition drill so that he can later think 2, 9, 13, 22? Or should he be taught to write the number in the margin, instead of holding it, for example $2 + 7$, write 9; $9 + 4$, write 13, etc.?

The teacher continues to look for evidence that her method may be responsible for a child's inability to develop number skills. In addition to environmental influences, however, she should be aware that failure to learn mathematical concepts may lie in a faulty neurophysiological mechanism, an hypothesis proposed earlier in the discussion of reading, spelling, and writing disorders.

## SUMMARY

Scientists interested in human communication and its disorders are progressing toward an understanding of language systems and the processes which generate them. An urgent need is for better communication among the diverse scientific professions that currently are investigating bits and pieces of language. Even more urgent is the translation of scientific information into the language of the teacher who is responsible for the academic achievement of her children.

# 3

# *Intelligence*

What is **intelligence**? Is it problem solving ability? Motor skills? Memory? Perception? Language? Achievement? Or is it a combination of all or part of these? Is intelligence a unitary factor or is it multifactored?

Unfortunately, there is no single, universally accepted meaning for intelligence, and no one universally accepted means for measuring it.

The most standard measure has been the IQ or "Intelligence Quotient," an outgrowth of the writings of Binet (107), who believed that intelligence is a unitary factor, or a general ability to solve daily living problems. On the other side of the ledger, writers like Thurstone (109) suggest that intelligence is based upon specific factors, each of which plays an important role in academic success or in problem solving of everyday living. In between these viewpoints is the philosophy of Spearman (102) postulating that intelligence includes a unitary factor as well as specific factors of learning.

If a psychologist or the director of a special education program is looking simply for a number which categorizes a child for class placement; normal, educable mentally retarded, or trainable mentally retarded, an IQ score suffices. If the number is below 70, a diagnosis of mental retardation has been made. The teacher who receives such a score learns nothing of the child's assets and deficits in oral and written language skills. Only a score for class placement is revealed.

A numerical IQ score is of as much aid in determining training as a numerical thermometer reading is in determining treatment in illness. Consider these analogies:

### ANALOGY I

An Educational Problem
      Complaint:           A child is doing poorly in school.

|                    |                                                              |
|--------------------|--------------------------------------------------------------|
| Recommendation:    | An IQ test.                                                   |
| Results:           | An IQ of 67.                                                  |
| Recommendation:    | Enroll in class for the educable mentally retarded. |
| Type of Training:  | Same as for other children whose IQ's range from 50 to 70. |

A Medical Problem

|                    |                                                              |
|--------------------|--------------------------------------------------------------|
| Complaint:         | A child is not feeling well.                                 |
| Recommendation:    | The physician takes the child's temperature.                 |
| Results:           | A temperature of 102°.                                       |
| Recommendation:    | A diagnosis is not made at this point, but further tests are recommended to help discover the cause of the fever. |
| Treatment:         | Tailor-made for this child with his kind of problem.         |

## ANALOGY II

An Educational Problem

|                    |                                                              |
|--------------------|--------------------------------------------------------------|
| Complaint:         | Failing in school.                                           |
| Recommendation:    | An IQ test.                                                  |
| Results:           | An IQ of 120.                                                |
| Recommendation:    | Psychological counseling and a home visit because this child is a day dreamer, lazy, comes from a poor home environment, is uncooperative, etc. |
| Training:          | Repeat present grade placement.                              |

A Medical Problem

|                    |                                                              |
|--------------------|--------------------------------------------------------------|
| Complaint:         | A child is not feeling well.                                 |
| Recommendation:    | The physician takes the child's temperature.                 |
| Results:           | Normal temperature.                                          |
| Recommendation:    | The physician does not dismiss the child or say that he is malingering. Rather, recommendations are made for further tests to help determine the problem. |
| Treatment:         | It is related to the basic problems uncovered through specific type tests. |

At best, the IQ provides a numerical label which serves to place a child in a predetermined slot, but most importantly, the IQ concept ignores the teacher who is the key figure in developing the child's pre-academic and academic skills. Considering this relationship between intelligence and academic training, psychologists and teachers have become increasingly aware of a need to move beyond a unitary concept of intelligence. As a result they have attempted to list and define specific avenues of learning necessary for academic achievement.

## DEFINITION

Operationally, intelligence may be defined as the capacity to solve problems through the integration and interdependence of two systems, language and learning. Children with deficits in one or more (but not *all*) avenues of learning are described as having specific learning disabilities. Children with deficits in language and all avenues of learning demonstrate general intellectual retardation. Theoretically, the child with no deficits in language or learning has adequate learning potential.

## AVENUES OF LEARNING

Appropriate motivation, social maturity, social perception, and emotional stability are essential attributes for social and/or academic achievement. In addition, a child must have a neurophysiological mechanism which allows him to make use of his avenues of learning which include sensation, perception, memory-retrieval, and attention. The orderly intra- and inter-integration of at least this number of avenues from the sensorium is believed to be responsible for the acquisition and structuring of the skills needed for oral and written communication. In contrast to an IQ score, an audit of a child's specific avenues of learning presents a more meaningful approach to the exceedingly complicated topic—language. It is the detailed assessment of the avenues of learning that suggests the dynamics of language disorders.

In the hierarchy of the senses, audition and vision appear to be most significantly correlated with language development. The importance of other sensory avenues certainly is not to be ignored.

Sensation, perception, memory-retrieval, attention, and integration undoubtedly play a dynamic role in a child's ability to learn oral and written language—important keys to academic success. In general, the ability to assess these individual avenues becomes a complex problem due to the interrelated influences of one upon the other.

> The college student studies his assignments in a noisy dormitory. Conversations buzz around him, and when asked if he heard the joke told, he replied, "No." Did his visual intake mechanism in some way attenuate or eliminate the auditory stimuli? Or is there a brain mechanism of attention that interacts with all stimuli and serves as a sorting device?

Studies of the brain and its function are part of current research in human communication. Bits and pieces of these investigations are beginning to tell something about the great network of neurons. Yet, the relationship between learning and the functioning of these networks is still not clearly understood. Perhaps it is more important to find what human behavior is like before trying to explain how it is produced! And until scientists can point the way to better assessment and educational techniques than are now available, the clinic, school, and home will remain the primary observation laboratories.

In order to relate the various avenues of learning to pre-academic training, the teacher needs operational definitions. Even though it is dangerous to fractionate these abilities through definition, because they apparently do not function as entities, there must be a starting point and the definition route is a good choice. Such definitions may change as new discoveries in brain function and the effect of environment on learning are brought to the foreground. In the meantime, educators need answers because children with learning disabilities are in school *in far greater numbers than we thought ten years ago.* Investigators can help teachers pull together basic educational philosophies, diagnostic tools, and principles of training which will meet the individual needs of children. A look at the specific avenues of learning is a logical beginning.

## Sensation

**DEFINITION**

Sensation is dependent upon a stimulus or an agent that acts upon appropriate receptors. If the receptors are intact, sensation, which may be thought of as the immediate physiological correlate of the stimulus, is created. The stimulus is received.

*Auditory Sensation.* The question is asked, "Did you hear it?" If the answer is "No," the first hypothesis may be that the problem is one of sensory hearing impairment.[1]

*Visual Sensation.* The question is asked, "Did you see it?" If the answer is "No," the first hypothesis may be that the problem is one of sensory visual impairment.[2]

---

[1] Sensory hearing impairment as used in this text refers to any impairment of audition associated with dysfunction of the auditory transmissive system.

[2] Sensory visual impairment as used in this text refers to any impairment of vision associated with dysfunction of the visual transmissive system.

# Perception

DEFINITION

Perception is the process of attaching structure to sensation. In order for a stimulus to be perceived as it was received, there must be sensory exitation, an intact sensory end organ, and adequately functioning neural systems.

*Auditory Perception.* When the activity of listening becomes integrated with the sensation of hearing, auditory perception takes place. "What do we hear when we listen?" If the auditory image in the child's brain does not match the auditory stimulus, he is said to have an auditory-perceptual disorder. The stimulus was not structured appropriately.

Perceptual studies in all sensory modalities indicate developmental patterning and scientists continue to make inroads into the understanding of the auditory pathways concerned with perception. (See Chapter 2, the section on Speech). To date, however, few diagnostic tools are available to measure auditory perceptual deficits (discimination loss) in children. We know that if they understand and use oral symbols on an acceptable chronological age level, there is no significant auditory perceptual deficit. But if they demonstrate disorders in any of the speech and/or language areas, we only postulate with the use of limited assessment tools as to where we might look for the problem.

Disorders of auditory perception may occur as a result of past experiences, immediate set, physiological experience during the discriminatory process, condition of the auditory pathways, and nature of the message. Deciding which interference causes an inappropriate reply is not always possible. Is the following an example of a distorted intake of speech due to past experience and immediate set?

Julie brought a bird nest to school for "Show and Tell." She had much to say about the mother bird, the eggs, and the babies. Later in the morning the teacher presented a unit on health. One of the vocabulary words the children had been taught was "ache." To test Julie's concept of "ache" the teacher asked, "Julie, do you have any *aches?*" Whereupon Julie replied, "No *eggs* in nest now."

We know that children with certain types of sensory hearing impairment experience a reduction or a distortion of the speech signal. It is not unusual, then, for a child with sensory hearing impairment to give an inappropriate response to a statement which was slightly unintelligible. The classical example is the student who excells in all subjects except spelling. If he does not have time to watch the teacher as she dictates the spelling words, he must rely on his faulty listening mechanism. Therefore he misspells because he mishears.

Some children may have difficulty perceiving speech in the presence of noise or a competing message, which in turn may be the cause of delay in the acquisition of oral language. Auditory tests for adults have been designed to measure the ability of one ear to attend to a signal while a competing message is presented to the nontest ear. Significant breakdowns in the ability to understand the primary signal have been found to exist in persons with 'certain acquired temporal lobe lesions. Although these types of tests are not yet applicable to preschool children, it is feasible to believe that certain temporal lobe pathologies occurring later in life might well be present at or shortly after birth.

A teacher of normal hearing children with language disorders posed the following questions to a scientist. "Is it possible for the senory end organ to be intact, yet the auditory signal perceived as noise? If so, is there a retrocochlear lesion which causes the change in the patterning of the input signal? In such an event may the signal be so poorly structured that there is not enough information for the child to decode the message into meaningful word symbols? Should he be described as having an auditory receptive disorder? If so, could such a disorder be confused with receptive aphasia? Or, are auditory perceptual disorders and receptive aphasia more closely related than the literature implies?" The scientist answered, "Such hypotheses can be made, but evidence for support is meager."

The correlates of audition; past experience, immediate set, sensation, and perception as they affect the intake of the signal have been discussed briefly. Certainly the temporal factor or rate at which the signal is transmitted to the auditory mechanism, localization of sound, pitch, loudness, and other psychological factors are important. All of these facets of audition are under investigation and much is being learned regarding auditory discrimination in adult populations. Unfortunately, additional time will be needed to relate this information to preschool children with language and/or learning deficits.

*Visual Perception.* When the activity of looking becomes integrated with the sensation of seeing, visual perception takes place. "What do we see when we look?" If the visual image in the child's brain does not match the visual stimulus, he is said to have a visual-perceptual disorder. The stimulus was not structured properly.

As with audition, there appears to be developmental patterning in visual perception. Some scientists, for example, believe that the ability for gross segregation of the figure from its background is present at birth but perception of form requires a fairly extensive period of learning. Children may be expected, therefore, to discriminate between an oval and an angular object before they can make a finer discrimination between circles and ovals. Children under six years of age may have greater difficulty with discrimination of mirror images than upside-down figures. In reading-readiness tests they will recognize the one which is different if it is upside down, but may fail the task if the figure is facing to the left when all others face to the right.

Babies are not born with knowledge of distance and direction, they see the moon and reach for it. Only through maturation and hundreds of trials and errors does distance become meaningful to them. Apparently there is a general type of developmental sequence related to the acquisition of spatial concepts and their word symbols. Children, for example, seem to learn the meaning of the words "in," "on," and "under" before they discriminate between "right" and "left." The developmental concepts related to space, and word symbols for these concepts, appear to be closely associated with the acquisition of written language. Reading and writing, of course, are dependent upon concepts of *top, bottom, left,* and *right.*

Varying degrees of impairment of the visual systems may effect discriminatory processes. The child with limited or no peripheral vision may fail to match large pictures because he does not see the outer portions of the picture where the differences appear.

The visual end organ may be damaged or its pathways to the cortex may be disordered. As a result, a child may demonstrate an inability to discriminate the parts of a whole or spatial relationships. The inability to recognize and make use of the whole and its parts is probably one cause of reading failure. The good reader can respond to the total printed word, at the same time being aware of the individual letters and their significance. In addition, he is capable of looking at parts of the letters and through a process called "closure" coming up with meaning. In fact, he may read a sentence successfully if either the top or bottom half of each word is covered!

As with audition, visual-perceptual *disorders* may be related to past experience, previous set, physiological experiences during the discriminatory process, condition of the visual pathways, and nature of the message. Textbooks in psychology present demonstrations with adults, illustrating the fact that perception changes because of past experiences and previous sets. One has only to visit a nursery or kindergarten program to find evidence of the same behavior in children.

The teacher drew a  ✝  on the board and asked the children to tell her what it was. They answered, "Like when you bury someone." "A sword." "You wear it." "The church has it on top." "Like telephone poles." "An ambulance has it." When the teacher connected the four points with a solid line, however, and added an appropriate kite tail, each child immediately said it was a kite.

As Louise left the classroom to run an errand, Johnny noticed that she had something in her pocket which made it bulge. He immediately identified it as a box of matches and called the teacher's attention to it. Mrs. Rister, he said, "Louise has a box of matches in her pocket and she is going to burn something!" "Do you think so? Let's not worry about it. Let's wait and see." Louise returned and was asked, "Do you have a box of matches in your pocket?" to which she replied, "No." She reached into her pocket and retrieved a piece of heavy folded paper. "You have learned a lesson, children," said Mrs. Rister, "sometimes your eyes play tricks on you."

Visual-perceptual disorders are not easily identified because of the complicated intra- and inter-networks of the central nervous system, and the crudeness of the tools available to measure such disorders.

Karl, age nine, can look at a drawing of a diamond and call it by name. He is unable to copy it accurately. Does he draw it as he perceives it? Or does he have an accurate visual image, yet lack the ability to convert the image into a motor skill?

Studies of visual perception are being conducted, in general, by psychologists concerned with visual discrimination. The literature abounds with reports of investigations about localization, brightness, shape, depth, form, space, and illusion, each of which is felt to be related or interrelated in some way to visual perception. The great need is to translate the data obtained to the areas of assessment and training of children with language and/or learning disorders.

*Tactile, Olfactory, and Gustatory Perception.* These senses are seldom discussed in relation to oral communication. Yet, in view of language development, it is important to know how well a child can structure what he feels. Perhaps he fails to learn the concepts of soft, hard, and rough because he cannot perceive or feel the differences. By the same token, he may use inappropriate word symbols when describing how something tastes or how it smells.

*Self Perception (Body Image).* The prick of the diaper pin, the warmth of the bath water, the feel of his body in an upright position, grasping the object, learning to walk upstairs, localizing a human voice, and the hundreds of other sensations received by the baby as he matures all help him develop an awareness of his physical self, commonly referred to as body image. The study of body image has become a popular topic in the field of psychology where an attempt is being made to relate disorganization of body image to the various inappropriate responses of certain adults and children. Such information adds to the differential diagnosis of psychoneurological problems.

## Memory—Retrieval

### DEFINITION

Memory is a facet of learning that may be thought of as the ability of sensory storage systems to hold perceived events. These memories, whether in planaria, rats, or men, are stored and retrieved through some kind or kinds of processes currently incomprehensible. Certainly the process is only a piece of the integrated activity of all avenues of learning and does not function alone. Without memory, however, it is inconceivable that learning could take place.

## AUDITORY AND VISUAL MEMORY

Investigators use a wide variety of terms to label their memory studies: immediate, recent, short term, long term, and past memory; recall; memory trace; perceptual storage; retention; sequential learning; and others. The terminology is meaningful only if operationally defined in the context of the specific investigation. Short term and long term memory, however defined, appear to be dependent upon the variety of ways in which a stimulus is presented, the condition of the central nervous system and the mode of action requested of the subject.

1. Through which sensory avenue were the stimuli received, auditory or visual? That is, was the subject asked to remember a series of digits that were read to him or were those digits flashed on the screen? How did the subject report what was remembered? Did he recall the numbers orally, write them on paper, or did he select the correct ones from another series of numbers?

2. Was the subject asked to remember meaningful or nonmeaningful material? For example, were the stimuli nonsense syllables or meaningful sentences? Were the visual tasks related to unidentifiable shapes or to printed words?

3. How many practice periods were allowed? Does the subject actually learn to remember; to do better with each successive trial? At what point does he level off? And the question which remains unanswered, can neural networks be *taught* to remember, or is memory simply a developmental process?

4. With regard to temporal factors, at what rate were the stimuli presented? For how many minutes, hours, or days after presentation is the subject asked to recall the material? In other words, how does the investigator differentiate between short term and long term memory?

5. Is the subject given credit for the number of correct responses or is the factor of sequence important? In a test of memory for numbers, can he repeat all the digits, but not in sequential order?

6. How much redundancy is in the information which the subject is asked to remember and retrieve? Oral and written language is built upon a system of redundancy. One sentence, for example, may contain phonemes and words which have no semantic values. "I thred needle," is a meaningful sentence in spite of the fact a letter and a word have been omitted. It is redundancy that helps reduce errors and makes it possible to guess what one has heard or read.

Telephone numbers are a subsystem of language with no word redundancy. If you do not hear or remember one of the digits, you cannot make the telephone call. Perhaps it is the lack of redundancy in rote counting and number concepts which makes arithmetic difficult for children.

7. Was the material presented to the individual child or to groups of children? It is not uncommon to find a child who remembers better with a private tutor than in a classroom with other children. Perhaps with a tutor he is able to attend to the tasks at hand. Or, the tutor may enhance learning through rephrasing, repeating, or simplifying the language used.

8. How much noise interference was present? Does a child remember better when in quiet surroundings?

9. How loud was the investigator's voice when he presented the material? There is some evidence to indicate that messages which are hard to hear are hard to remember. Were the visual stimuli in printed or manuscript form; in color, black, or white?

10. In a test of short term auditory memory, does a child fail to remember the sentence because he has not mastered for himself the language code? Perhaps the child who uses substandard sentences ("Buy mamma candy."), has difficulty remembering a sentence ("We are going to buy some candy for mother."), because he does not yet know the language code.

Experiments with animals and humans with brain lesions reveal important information to diagnosticians and teachers. The temporal lobe, probably the left, appears to be the focus for making use of oral symbols. Furthermore, the temporal lobe is believed to be the central area for both auditory and visual memory activities. Is it conceivable, then, that if brain aplasia or damage is present at birth, particularly in the temporal lobe areas, short term memory may be a deficient agent? Is there a specific kind of damage to the temporal lobe area of infants which results in disorders of oral communication?

Scientific reports demonstrate that short term memory, visual and auditory, is one of the first avenues of learning to subside in adults when the aging process affects brain tissue. Current events are quickly forgotten whether they were presented visually or auditorially. Details of childhood are well remembered.

Perhaps homes for the aged in some instances are a favorable retirement spot. Senior citizens can tell their childhood stories over and over to one another for neither he nor the listener will remember from day to day what has been told.

If information learned early in life is remembered, are we dealing with two mechanisms—short term memory now out of order, and long term memory probably intact? If so, is it logical to postulate that the processes related to short term memory are the first to disintegrate in some adults and the last to function in some children?

Memory status of children often must be assessed through case histories and listening to the responses of children.

> Mr. Farrington asked the teacher, "What do you mean when you say that my son has poor auditory memory?" Said the teacher, "When I asked the children to put their work books in their desks, take out their crayons and paste jars, then wait until I pass out sheets of paper; your son is lost. He starts to get the paper I have in my hand, then looks at the other children, then reaches in his desk, and never does accomplish what was requested of him auditorially." "Isn't that strange," said the father. "When I was in grade school, I couldn't remember what the teacher said in class so I learned very early to write notes to myself. Even today my wife laughs at me in the evening when I empty my pockets of all the notes I have written to myself during the day."
>
> Karl knew the meaning of the word *numbers* but could not rote-count past three. In class, the discussion centered around parachutes and the detailed procedure of leaving the plane and getting the chute open. "Would you like to be a parachuter, Karl?" asked the teacher. "No, Mr. Foster, cause I can't count."

Some children age five or older cannot repeat digits or sentences any better than three-year-olds. In addition, their oral sentence structure is poor. Can a child construct a plan for a sentence if he cannot remember the sequence of words that make up a sentence?

> David was presented with a picture of two cars that had crashed into each other at an intersection. He was asked to tell a story about the scene. There was a pause and then his answer, "Two green lights."

Is a child sometimes reprimanded by his parents because he does not perform what they call a routine act? Does he fail because he does not remember the sequence of motor acts?

> Mother tells her four year old son. "Take your bath." He does not accomplish much in the line of bath taking. Perhaps if mother were to give step-by-step auditory instructions, her son would learn the motor sequence of taking a bath. "Take off your clothes and put on your robe." Next, "Go to the bathroom and call me." When this is accomplished, she meets him at the designated spot and says, "Now I will fill the tub for you." Next, "You get into the tub and put soap on the wash cloth." Done enough times, this sequence of events will be remembered and "Take a bath" will bring appropriate action.

## Attention

**DEFINITION**

Attention is the ability to focus appropriately on the object or task at hand.

AUDITORY AND VISUAL ATTENTION

The efficiency of a human system in receiving and storing information depends upon the intactness and appropriate integration of sensation, perception, and memory. In recent years, investigators, primarily in animal studies, have found evidence that there is a mechanism in the brain with a basic function called *attention*.

With reference to auditory and visual attention we may ask, "How well can you attend to what you hear?" and "How well can you attend to what you see?"

The child who does not attend well is described as having poor attention, short attention span, or as being distractible or hyperactive. Such terminology is often misleading, for a child's short attention span does not mean that he cannot attend; quite the reverse, he may attend to too much.

> Miss Williams seats Mary in the front of the class by the wall which has no window. Here she is not so apt to attend to the movements of the other children, furnishings of the room, or activities outside the window.

Attention may vary from intermittent to fixated. When fixated, we say that the child is unable to shift. He cannot move along to another task.

> The diagnostician was administering a battery of tests to John. The telephone in the adjoining room rang three times and ceased. This was a rule instigated to avoid numerous rings while testing was in progress. John fixated on the fact that no one answered the phone. He could not shift to another test until the examiner went to the phone and pretended to talk with someone.

In the classroom the child's brain is not waiting in a vacuum for the next statement or question from the teacher. On the contrary, the brain is busily occupied with either past memories or future plans. When the teacher speaks, the child with an intact alerting and attention system shifts quickly from his inner thinking to what the teacher has said. This seems to be almost an instantaneous shift. But because the child with a disordered mechanism may be unable to make such a rapid shift, he cannot attend to the teacher's comments. He may be said to have internal noise which is affecting his reception of the message.

External noise and competing messages are other modes of distorting the message. Investigators in the field of audition are studying the effects of external noise on a message. Using a speech audiometer, subjects are asked to repeat verbal material that has been distorted through filtering of certain frequency bands or changing of temporal patterns. Although information obtained from this kind of experimental design is usually studied under the category of "speech perception," there is evidence to indicate that the mechanism of "attention" may be reacting with the noise.

Studies have been designed which require the subject to listen to two messages simultaneously, but to attend to only one message. Is the second message attenuated or blocked out?

Further studies have been concerned with developing sentences that range from meaningful to meaningless (Small boat with a picture has become). In the presence of noise, subjects apparently can perceive and/or attend better to meaningful messages. Do we inhibit listening activities if we do not know the meaning of what is being said? And is this process related to the mechanism of attention?

> A common statement among parents of generally retarded children runs something as follows: "It is hard to believe that he is retarded, because he has such a keen memory. We have only to take him to a new park a couple of times and he can anticipate the landmarks along the route. In addition, if we have not been to a friend's house for two years, our son will anticipate accurately all of the landmarks."

In the preceeding example, may we hypothesize that the retarded child does not understand the conversation of the other passengers in the car, therefore inhibits what to him is mere auditory noise? Does he attend primarily to the landmarks? Perhaps visual memory in generally retarded children is more highly developed than other avenues of learning.

## Integration

### DEFINITION

The mechanisms of sensation, perception, memory, and attention are of little use without some system of retrieving and integrating ideas and experiences as needed. That such a system exists is acceptable, but the neurophysiological mechanism which activates a response is poorly understood.

We can assume from careful studies of the human brain that it is divided into semiautonomous areas. Each has a unique specialization, but to function adequately, must work in harmony with other areas. It is this orderly interrelationship and interplay that we call integration.

### INTEGRATION STUDIES

The diagnostician's task is to check the various sensory systems that may be related to the problem at hand. The more central the problem becomes, the more difficult the task of pinpointing the deficit. Sensory impairment of vision and audition are generally easy to detect with appropriate instruments. But tests for perception, memory, attention, and integration are far from pure. The inability to obtain valid assessments is due to the extremely complicated neurosensory network. Perhaps the majority of children who have undefinable communication problems are those who have impairment of the integrative mechanism(s).

Is it possible to have intact sensory, perceptual, memory, and attention mechanisms yet a disordered system of integration?

> For an exercise in teaching the concepts of *on top,* and *underneath,* Mr. Foster gave the children a piece of paper with an identical picture on the front and on the back. After the pictures had been colored he said that they were not to be taken home. Alice raised her hand and said "But Mr. Foster, can't I take this one home?" She turned the paper over, pointed to the second picture and said "I'll leave this one at school."

# Learning

**DEFINITION**

Learning is referred to as the process of developing a skill or acquiring information. Learning is measured by the change between pre- and post-incidental and/or intentional instruction.

**LEARNING STUDIES**

Learning theorists are forever searching for answers to the multitude of questions asked.

> How does a child with intact modalities of sensation, perception, memory, attention, and integration learn to read, write, acquire information, and make use of it in a socially acceptable way? How does learning take place? Is the infant born with an organized neurologic structure which develops independent of experience or is this logical structure not present at birth but emerges as a result of an equilibrium between the organism and its environment? Are some skills acquired and others learned?

Theories in response to these questions have been developed and researched over the centuries. Application of these theories, however, has been made primarily on animal and human adult populations. The teacher has been given few guidelines as to which theory or theories she should follow. Most likely she has been taught a method which supposedly applies to all children.

Because one method has never met the needs of all teachers or all children, new techniques continue to be developed. We have only to look at the literature on the subject of "Reading Disorders." No one knows which of the many methods is appropriate for remedial reading instruction because no scientific studies have provided an answer. It is the abundance of pseudoscientific publications that has misled teachers.

# SUMMARY

In reality, we are all in the field of learning. We are trying to modify behavior, to keep it moving appropriately or to get it going when it is not going well.

Numerous texts have been written on the theories of intelligence and learning and perhaps the most significant thing about the theories is the wide disagreement which prevails among psychologists. As diagnosticians and teachers, however, we cannot wait until scientists agree on theories. We must develop our own basic educational philosophy from the knowledge at hand. As more acceptable assessment and training procedures develop, we will adapt them where needed.

# 4

# Assessment Tools

> Kurt is four years of age. He is a clumsy child who always manages to be in someone's way. Mother describes his language and speech as "baby talk." He is a difficult child to discipline and has many tantrums.

Kurt exhibits manifestations of cerebral palsy—emotional disturbance—language or speech delay—mental retardation—hearing or visual impairment—poor home management—or a combination of one or more of these conditions. But these descriptive terms do not spell out the specific physical, emotional, language, or learning assets and deficits that should be known in order to plan for everyday living and future academic needs.

A complete audit is essential and must be obtained through the collaborative efforts of parents, teachers, and the various professions concerned with the child's growth and development. No longer can one person cover the ever broadening field of differential diagnosis if consideration is being given to the total child.

## PURPOSE OF ASSESSMENTS

### Early Definition of the Problem

The time to make an appointment for a language assessment is when a parent, physician, relative, or friend suspects the child has a problem. True, some children talk before others and those who lag behind often catch up with their peer group. Notwithstanding the validity of the developmental-lag concept, there is more often than not a tendency to wait too long for this catching up period. During this time the child with something more than a maturational delay unwittingly may be neglected; sometimes beyond remediation.

Investigators report that biologic readiness for learning language begins at birth. With each added year of disregard for appropriate language stimulation, the child's opportunities for normal communication are decreased.

Although all deviations in behavior are not related directly to an organic problem, such abberations can be predicted to occur with many children who have specific language and learning problems. Lack of parent understanding often leads to poor child management. The result —a child with inferior communication skills plus an overlay of emotional instability.

If early assessments are not made, the child attempts myriads of ways to protect himself from his inadequacies: he gains attention by disturbing others, hitting, pinching, pushing; he withdraws from his peer group and becomes engrossed with specific toys; or he is disobedient when requests are asked of him, sassing or refusing to comply. To cut through these compensatory mechanisms at the age of five or six is a much more difficult diagnostic, assessment, and training task than it would have been at an earlier age.

Listen to mothers:

"Karen isn't talking as well as other children in the neighborhood, yet her Aunt Helen was late in talking and is now a college graduate." "Bill can't color and cut like his older brother could, yet my friends say to give him time." "I told my physician I was worried about George, my two-year-old, because he was not talking. I was afraid he did not hear. I was afraid to say this to my doctor but I did. I was advised to wait until George was three and then bring him back for another check."

Parents, particularly mothers, are notorious for their concern over developmental milestones. Their uneasy states of mind are real and should not be dismissed with a "Be patient; your son will be all right." Children should be referred for appropriate assessments whenever parents express anxiety over what they feel is a problem. To be told early the child is in difficulty enhances the chances for success in a training program. To be advised that a problem does not exist releases parent tensions.

Too many parents of children with handicaps are suffering from feelings of guilt because they did not follow their hunches or were willing to accept the developmental lag concept. Parents' observations of their children should not be ignored.

## Provide a Baseline for Remediation

Appropriate assessments provide the teacher with a baseline for training each child in the areas of language and learning. The delineation of assets and deficits informs her at which level each child is functioning in the skills needed to progress in the pre-academic program. With this information daily teaching activities can be planned.

## Grouping

Skilled teachers with thorough assessments of each child will be able to determine appropriate grouping of children in a training program. One misplaced child in an otherwise compatable group retards his progress as well as the achievement of his classmates.

## Measuring Progress

Once a baseline has been established, periodic reassessments must continue. Only through this routine can the teacher, physician, and parent be apprised of each child's progress or lack of progress. Only then will plans for continued training and treatment be meaningful.

## Predictions

To predict which children will be future academic failures is a more tenable concept than waiting until the problem becomes apparent. This point of view is being taken by many professional people who are searching for predictive tools that will locate in supposedly normal populations of children, those who will have academic problems and thus need early training. The fact that the latent abilities in very young children are difficult to measure accurately does not preclude trying.

Predictive tests will be a reality. Techniques for testing the hearing and vision of newborns are being developed. In addition, nation wide projects are concerned with the adequacy of the central nervous system during the first twelve months of life. This kind of research means that the diagnoses of high risk children will be obtained in infancy making it possible to plan for early preventive or remedial treatment.

In the not too distant future, physicians and personnel in places such as well-baby clinics will be administering screening tests. Information gained will predict in the first year of life those children who will have problems: physical, language, learning, and/or emotional.

As another means of locating children for early training, form letters are sent home with children in kindergarten through third grades.

Upon receipt of requests for children to be evaluated, the secretary makes appointments and diagnosticians administer a battery of tests designed to predict future academic failure. Children with problems are enrolled in a pre-academic program in one of the public schools of that district.

Date:

Dear Parents:

The Pasadena Independent School District in cooperation with the Houston Speech and Hearing Center has developed a preschool training program for children who have language or speech problems or who can be predicted to have difficulty learning to read after entering school. We believe that preschool training will accelerate progress of these children giving them greater opportunity for academic success from first grade on.

In order to locate the youngsters who will benefit from a preschool training program, staff from the Houston Speech and Hearing Center will be available to assess your child sometime during the month of March. You will be advised shortly after that time whether or not preschool training is indicated.

If you are interested in having one or more of your children between the ages of three and five and one half assessed, please read the following questions. If your answer is "Yes" to one or more, call now the person listed below for further details regarding an appointment.

1. Do you have a child (or children) who has a language problem, i.e., poor sentences, limited vocabulary?
2. Do you have a child who has a speech problem so severe that you and others have trouble understanding what he says; i.e., poor articulation, poor voice quality?
3. Do you have a child who has had trouble learning nursery rhymes, prayers or what you ask him to do?
4. Do you have a child who seems to be clumsy with his (her) hands or tends to fall or stumble a great deal?
5. Do you have a child who seems to have a hearing loss?

Mrs. Bernier
JA 4-3136

## Criteria for Developing and Using Assessment Tools

In our existing culture, assessments are based primarily on normative data. The diagnostician develops a systematic procedure for making two types of comparison: (1) the behavior of the child being studied with a normal population, and (2) the behavior of the child being studied over a given period of time.

When developing and using assessment tools, the diagnostician asks himself many questions regarding validity, practicability, and reportability.

## Validity

Is the information obtained valid? Do the assessment tools measure what they purport to measure?

A ten-year-old is asked to tell what is foolish about the following statement: "In an old graveyard in Spain they have discovered a small skull which they believe to be that of Christopher Columbus when he was about ten years old." [1] The child was unable to provide an answer. Is it because he does not recognize *verbal absurdities?* Does he fail the question because of a deficit in *short term memory,* inability to *attend* to words, or does he lack information?

On a standardized test a child passed all tasks which were thought to measure short term memory. The teacher, however, found that he could not follow directions in the classroom. Is this incompatible behavior due to an inability, for reasons unknown, to follow group instruction as opposed to receiving instructions in a one-to-one relationship?

The validity of any test must always be questioned. Seldom does the total score, percentile rank, or mental age of a single test tell what determinants are related to the deficits. It is better to approach the validity of a problem through a battery of tests, inter- and intra-correlating of sub-tests, and keen observations of the manner in which the subject performed.

## Practicability

Will the assessment tools provide useful information, yield findings for treatment and training?

Pedro demonstrated good work habits during testing but received an IQ score of 78 on a vocabulary comprehension test. The diagnostician studied the words Pedro did not know and found many to be foreign to his environment: electric stove, propellers, firecracker, newspaper.

Diagnosticians must evaluate their assessments, study, and find reason for errors. Only then will the tools become practical implements for training.

## Reportability

Can the results of the assessment be reported in a language that is meaningful to the recipient?

A teacher received the following summary of a total assessment: "Billy is a *minimally brain damaged* child with perceptual difficulties." What did this mean to her in light of teaching techniques? Little if anything.

[1] L. M. Terman and M. A. Merrill, *Stanford-Binet Intelligence Scale* (Boston, Houghton Mifflin Co., 1960), p. 93.

A good reporter is one who can translate his professional language into the language of the person receiving the results of the assessment. The findings are solely for planning treatment and/or training.

## ASSESSMENT TOOLS

The psychologist, speech pathologist, audiologist, and teacher cannot predict which individual test will be crucial in assessing a child with language and learning problems. Each must turn to a battery of assessment tools which will provide the kind of information that leads to an appropriate recommendation for treatment and/or training.

### Case History Forms

In general, two types of case history questionnaires have been designed to serve somewhat different functions. The first is given to the parent to be completed before an interview takes place. The second is for the examiner to obtain further detailed information from the parent.

#### FORM FOR PARENTS

The *questionnaire for parents* to be filled in by them (p. 337) is a guideline for the ensuing interview. First, rapport is easily established because the examiner, giving a seemingly cursory review of the parents' answers, may make an appropriate comment, "You did have a difficult time with labor." or "I see you have five other children. What a nice family." or "So your child likes TV commercials too? It seems that most do."

In addition to gaining the parents' confidence, the questionnaire may be used as a starting point for the detailed case history. "I notice that under the heading *What do you feel is your child's problem?* you have written, "He doesn't get along with other children." Perhaps it is because he doesn't talk plainly. However, before we talk about his not getting along with other children, tell me more about his speech. When were you first concerned about it?"

Sometime during the interview, the diagnostician reads in detail the answers on the parents' questionnaire sheet. Such scrutiny will reveal any discrepancies between written and oral reporting. Furthermore, the quality of handwriting, accuracy of spelling, grammar, and sentence structure will be observed for diagnostic significance.

#### FORM FOR DIAGNOSTICIAN

The *General Case History Form* (p. 341) is to be used by the examiner, and includes under general headings, key words which serve as a guide during the interview. Appropriate use of symbols before each key word clearly delineates significant and nonsignificant information as well as areas where information is lacking. The final case history report is written in essay form.

Much time is consumed interviewing parents and summarizing and recording the pertinent data. In order to make this time profitable the examiner must ask himself "Why do I want this information?"

## Importance of Case History Data

### BIRTH HISTORY DATA

*Birth history data:*

1. *are important to proper diagnosis.* Parents often request an appointment for their child at a Speech, Hearing, and Language Center before obtaining a medical examination. Any information the diagnostician can obtain that will assist the physician should be recorded and forwarded to him.

Certain pre- and post-natal conditions of the infant are known to correlate highly with language and learning disorders. Illness of the mother during her first trimester of pregnancy may affect normal fetal development. Medical scientists continue to report a high incidence of central nervous system dysfunction in children whose records show abnormality in one or more of the following: gestation period, length of labor, and birth weight. Furthermore, cyanosis, jaundice, and convulsions are known to be related to problems in newborns.

2. *indicate areas of parent anxieties.* Parents of children with handicaps often suffer from many anxieties. The birth history may reveal that a child was the living one of four pregnancies. Parents may become oversolicitous for fear of what could happen to their only child. Or, a mother reports that her son had several seizures during his first year of life. The question "Will he have more?" continues to haunt her.

Appropriate parent counseling by the physician is indicated when the diagnostician finds medical information which is causing parent anxiety.

3. *assist the teacher.* Teachers will have better rapport with parents if there is a mutual understanding of past events which cause current anxiety.

4. *are important to clinical research.* Scientists in the professions of speech pathology, language, audiology, and psychology are interested in correlating certain types of behavior with medical and developmental data. If appropriately obtained and coded, case history data may be retrieved for purposes of investigation.

## MOTOR DEVELOPMENT DATA

*Motor development data:*

1. *are important to proper diagnosis.* Has the patient always been delayed in gross motor development? If true and this information correlates with slowness to acquire language, speech, and social maturity, a diagnosis of general retardation may be hypothesized.

Some children who are late in acquiring adequate speech reveal a history of eating problems; difficulty with sucking and chewing solid foods, and persistent drooling. This information may indicate fine motor incoordination of the articulatory mechanism, possibly associated with articulatory disorders. Such a diagnosis is helpful in planning a training program for this child.

2. *indicate areas of parent anxieties.* The fact that children do not walk when their peers walk, or are still wetting their beds long after others have stopped gives parents good cause for anxiety. Attempts to bring about walking skills and bladder control before the child was ready have contributed to poor parent-child relationships and further anxiety. No one should be blamed. Parent problems must be understood and alleviated by appropriate counseling.

3. *assist the teacher.* If the teacher knows that a child still wets or soils himself, she will ask the mother to stay within a short distance from the classroom, to be called when needed.

Knowing that a child's deviant gait is the result of an orthopedic problem will indicate to the teacher a need for working closely with the orthopedic surgeon and/or physical therapist. Much that is done in the classroom may be geared to improve the orthopedic problem.

4. *are important to clinical research.* Many questions concerning motor development remain unanswered. Specifically, the speech clinician is still in need of an answer to the question, "Will maturation take care of Joe's articulation disorder or does he have a permanently faulty articulatory mechanism?"

## MEDICAL HISTORY DATA

*Medical history data:*

1. *are important to proper diagnosis.* Careful questioning of parents may point up pertinent diagnostic information.

Two-year-old Melissa was being assessed because she was not talking. The examiner asked mother, "Does she understand anything you say?" "Oh yes," replied mother, "but only when she wants to understand. I know she hears because when her back is turned to me she understands "Bye-bye" and can point to her nose and eyes on request. But some days she will not do this."

The examiner has a clue that this may be a child with **hearing impairment.** The words that have been said loudly enough and close enough are recognized, but only when spoken at this same distance and loudness level. Audiological and otological studies would be indicated to determine the presence or absence of hearing impairment.

2. *indicate areas of parent anxieties.* Parents often retain feelings of guilt if they were responsible for the car accident which caused their son's head injury, or if they were not at home when he suffered a severe convulsion. A father may have a difficult time accepting his son because of his dysplastic features: malformed ear, misshapen head, club feet.

3. *assist the teacher.* It is important for the teacher to be apprised of a child's propensity for seizures and how they should be handled in the classroom. If he is on medication or medication is changed, he needs to be observed in view of any behavior differences. The qualified teacher keeps records which will assist the physician in his program of drug therapy.

Which children have allergies and to what? Pets? Foods? Flowers? Teachers can control the classroom environment for children with allergies but must have access to the medical histories to do so.

4. *are important to clinical research.* Currently there is no valid way of predicting which drug will continue to produce acceptable behavior in children. There is every reason to believe that teacher and parent observations of children under drug therapy may give clues to investigators who are searching for answers. Teachers play an important role with a research team.

LANGUAGE HISTORY DATA

*Language history data:*

1. *are important to proper diagnosis.* Parents may report that their child performs on age level in all modalities of learning yet uses mostly gesture and jargon to communicate. Sensory hearing impairment may be postulated.

When hearing is normal and opportunity has been plentiful, yet there is a lateness in a child's language development, **central nervous system dysfunction** will be considered.

2. *indicate areas of parent anxieties.* If a child is cerebral palsied, blind, or a polio victim, his handicap is visible. Not so with all language delayed children. Parents often are subjected to and become disturbed by such questions as "Does the cat have your tongue, son?" "Why don't you deny him his food or toys if he refuses to ask for them?" A child who does not communicate adequately is a frustrating problem to parents.

3. *assist the teacher.* The teacher will want to know if the parents have punished a child for not talking, or have overrewarded him when

he did say something. Such information suggests discussion topics for group parent conferences.

Knowledge of previous methods used in training is helpful. Conversations with former teachers is often enlightening.

4. *are important to clinical research.* There is a paucity of developmental data in the area of language. Pertinent language information as recorded from case histories may be of subsequent value in research studies.

## SPEECH HISTORY DATA

*Speech history data:*

1. *are important to proper diagnosis.* Some children can be understood only by their siblings who often are used as interpreters. This information leads the diagnostician to believe that the child has at least some functional language, but masked by severe articulatory problems.

2. *indicate areas of parent anxieties.* Stuttering, high pitched voices, or unintelligible speech causes great parental concern. Friends and relatives are quick to offer suggestions and "cures," none of which seem to alleviate the problem. The result is extreme anxiety in both parents.

3. *assist the teacher.* If a new student stutters and is embarrassed by his nonfluencies, the teacher will avoid asking him to perform orally before the class until she feels he is ready. Or, she will prepare the class appropriately for acceptance of the deviant speech.

4. *are important to clinical research.* Nonfluencies and severe articulatory disorders are usually *described* in research literature. Investigations which discover *causation* will be welcomed by clinicians who are seeking a rationale for training.

## INTERPERSONAL RELATIONSHIP DATA

*Interpersonal relationship data:*

1. *are important to proper diagnosis.* Aggressiveness, hyperactivity, distractability, and perseveration are characteristics of some children with language and learning problems. This descriptive behavior is meaningless by itself, but studied with the total case history may become an important part of the differential diagnosis.

2. *indicate areas of parent anxieties.* When children are subjected to undue stress, primitive activity may come into being. If they have many failures during the day, they tend to build defenses against further failure. These may take the form of tears, daydreaming, tantrums, or extreme affection. Parents cannot accept the deviant behavior, yet have no answers as to how it may be controlled.

3. *assist the teacher.* A teacher can avoid many classroom casualties if she knows the child's fears, his play habits with peers, and his general disposition. Anticipating behavior problems in the classroom and cir-

cumventing them may mean the difference between an adequate and inadequate learning milieu.

4. *are important to clinical research.* There is some research evidence to indicate that unacceptable behavior in children; inability to cope with unstructured environment, inadequate peer group relationships, poor social perception, and tempers which can be turned off as quickly as they are turned on, is organically based. Such children may demonstrate convulsive equivalents with no known cause; stomach aches, leg cramps, headaches, fever. There is currently some electro-encephalographic information that points to such behavior as being organic in origin. If scientifically verified and appropriate treatment is discovered, parents and teachers will have many child rearing problems solved.

FAMILY DATA

*Family data:*

1. *are important to proper diagnosis.* There is evidence in the literature to indicate that some of the problems of children are hereditary; hearing impairment, general retardation, reading disabilities. Inquiry into familial problems may be the only clue to etiology.

2. *indicate areas of parent anxieties.* What parents would not be filled with anxiety if they had an invalid grandparent and five children in the home, and an income which could not adequately care for the family—yet were faced with bringing one daughter to special classes each day? The diagnostician records such pertinent data and often refers the family to a social worker who can study the home situation and provide appropriate care and treatment.

3. *assist the teacher.* It is often a slow process to teach a child with learning disabilities the skills needed for oral and written language. Teaching problems are multiplied if the parents are bi-lingual and speak mostly their native language at home.

If the parents work, or if the child lives part time with the father and part time with the mother because of marital separation, responsibility for the home training must be decided upon.

4. *are important to clinical research.* Is a disturbed parent-child relationship caused by parents, or is it a by-product of the child's deviant behavior? This is a moot question and needs to be researched.

SCHOOL DATA

*School data:*

1. *are important to proper diagnosis.* If a child has attended a nursery or play school, he will have demonstrated many of his language and learning skills to the teacher. Relating current abilities to previous behavior helps determine learning rates.

2. *indicate areas of parent anxieties.* Parents want their children to succeed with their peers. To be told that a child can no longer stay in a play school because he is too undisciplined is a family tragedy. Mothers tend unwittingly to blame themselves, and by so doing become extremely anxious over disciplinary procedures.

3. *assist the teacher.* Teachers will be grateful for any previous information about a child in a play school, pre-academic, or academic program. The subject matter he was exposed to, what he learned, from whom and where, and at what time are all important pieces of information.

4. *are important to clinical research.* As this text is being written, no scientific research has demonstrated that children with specific learning disabilities do better in academic subjects if they have had pre-academic training. The clinical judgments of many teachers favor pre-academic training. Research is still forthcoming.

## Speech Assessments

Because numerous books have been written on the subject of speech diagnostics, it does not seem appropriate to review them in this text. The reader is referred to the APPENDIX for references each of which has its own bibliography.

Scientific research in the area of speech disorders, as in the field of psycholinguistics, is greatly needed. Until the etiologies of stuttering, undiagnosed dysphonias, and treatment-resistant articulatory disorders are explained, the teacher-clinician will continue making educated guesses when developing her training techniques.

## Psychometric Tests

A variety of psychometric tests are available for measuring the general or specific aspects of intelligence. During the standardization of these psychometric measures, the researcher finds some children who perform poorly, some who do well, and some who do very well. Those who score poorly do so, in general, because of language or learning deficits and/or emotional instability.

In order to assess children with a chronological or mental age of six years or under, the examiner must select tests which have a basal age well below the fifth year. Few such tests are available and those currently on the market have one or more of the following disadvantages: (1) only a single score is obtained, as for the comprehension of single words, (2) tests measuring the accuracy of syntax and morphology have yet to be standardized for this age group, (3) sub-test items are seldom designed for children with specific language and learning disabilities; (tests for short term auditory memory, such as digit span, and repetition of sentences, cannot be administered to children with severe expressive language problems), and (4) the raw score or mental age of a sub-test item is often misleading for it is doubtful if any test measures a pure language or learning modality.

In order to *develop* or assemble a battery of tests which attempts to assess language and learning levels necessary for academic success, the diagnostician follows several basic principles: (1) operational definitions are formulated for the language and learning units to be assessed. These definitions keep pace with current psychoneurophysiological research, (2) standardized tests or sub-test items which best fit each definition are created or selected from available tests, (3) the total battery of tests is designed to obtain a language and learning assessment with a reasonably cooperative child in one hour or less. The results give the teacher a baseline for the child's general functioning level before enrollment in the training program. The teacher continues to assess while teaching, (4) qualitative as well as quantitative information is recorded, and (5) the battery of tests is fluid; as new, appropriate, standardized items are developed, less acceptable items are deleted.

Diagnosticians formulate basic principles for testing but are handicapped because appropriate test tools are not available. A further dilemma occurs when diagnosticians do not have the time and/or the skill to develop new tests. Yet—many children must have language and learning assessments before they are placed in pre-academic training programs. The answer to the diagnostician's problem has been to combine and utilize available standard psychometric measures. Such a battery of tests, *Language and Learning Assessment: For Training* has been assembled by the author. The purpose of the assessment is twofold: (1) to locate children who have language and/or learning deficits, and (2) to provide the teacher with information essential to her training program—information that will delineate the assets and deficits of each child enrolled in pre-academic or academic classes.

## ASSESSING LANGUAGE SKILLS

### Problems

Scientific inroads to understanding, assessing, and teaching skills for oral language are being made, but much is left to be learned. Linguists have long been studying the semantic and structural components of language. Teachers, for just as long a period of time, have been seeking appropriate methods for training children with language disorders.

Only recently has the linguist teamed with the psychologist and speech pathologist in an effort to obtain developmental data in the age group from birth to adolescence.

Complete developmental data· on the syntactic and morphologic aspects of sentence structure are not available as this text is being written. A generalized statement such as "By age four a child's syntactic and morphologic structure is fairly complete and by age eight is quite complete." does not lend itself to psychometric measurement. At present the diagnostician is making an educated guess when he reports that a four-year-old child is delayed in the syntactic and/or morphologic aspects of language.

Research is under way in the combined areas of linguistics and psychometric measurement. Experimental psycholinguistic batteries are being field-tested. Currently the most widely used is the Illinois Test of Psycholinguistic Abilities (75). A break-through in methods of measuring the structure of language is forthcoming.

The component of language which has been given a great deal of attention is semantics. Standard vocabulary tests of word recognition and definition have been available for many years. These tests have been a boon to teachers because semantics is an important linguistic area in the educational process. Words are an indispensable tool for broadening concepts.

While researchers continue their efforts toward the development of tests to measure the structural aspects of language, the diagnostician must not deter the use of what is on hand, namely semantic tools.

## A Design for Assessing Language Skills

Language assessments are basic to lesson planning for children in pre-academic programs. Test scores plus subjective comments regarding the child's approach to the test items provide answers to the many questions the teacher asks: Does a child understand single words better than connected discourse? Does he comprehend on age level but have no functional expressive language because of a severe motor involvement of the articulatory mechanism? Is defining words a difficult task? Does he lack certain vocabulary words needed to develop pre-academic skills? Is his language comprehension and expression level commensurate with his mental age in all avenues of learning which have been measured?

### THE FACE SHEET

Four scores from the items measuring language comprehension and expression are entered on a face sheet which accompanies the total battery of tests.

Richard, age five, received the following mental age scores (see Table 1):

### TABLE 1[a]
### SPEECH, HEARING, AND LANGUAGE CENTER
### LANGUAGE AND LEARNING ASSESSMENT: For Training
### (LLAT)

Name: ...... Richard ......　　　　　　　　　　Age: yr. 5　 mo. 0

| ABILITIES ASSESSED | TESTS | M.A. Scores |
|---|---|---|
| LANGUAGE SKILLS | | |
| *Comprehension* | Single Words (3) .................... | 3-11 |
| | Connected Discourse (44, 107, 108) .................. | 3 - 1 |
| *Expression* | Connected Discourse (44, 107, 108) .................. | 2 - 7 |
| | Defining (108)........................ | *4 - 0 |
| | Sentence Structure (poor, fair, adequate) ...... | poor |

[a]Numbers in parentheses refer to sources in Bibliography.
*Test Ceiling

Information of this nature apprises the teacher that Richard (1) comprehends the meaning of single words better than connected discourse, (2) names single pictures better than gives an oral response to a question, statement, or sentence completion, (3) understands better than he expresses himself.

The shape of this profile of language development is generally typical of children whether they are accelerated, normal, or delayed in language. Developmentally they understand words before they use them appropriately in sentences.

*Comprehension of Single Words*

Test item: *Ammons Full-Range Picture Vocabulary Test* (3) or any comparable test.

The Ammons Vocabulary Test contains a series of plates with a sampling of words according to chronological age. The examiner speaks the word and the child points to the picture which best represents the stimulus word. No oral response is required. The total of correct responses is converted into a mental age score.

*Comprehension of Connected Discourse*

Test items: Sub-tests from Gesell (43) and the old and new forms of Binet (107, 108) are arranged in developmental age levels (pp. 190-194, 198-199, 229-230, 262-263).

This collection of tests purports to obtain an average mental age level at which a child, through nonverbal performance, can answer questions and follow commands. For example, "Which one is longer?" The child selects the longer of two sticks. Or, the child in answer to "Put the spoon in the cup," follows the directions by manipulating the objects before him.

*Expression: Naming or Defining Words*

Test items: Sub-tests from Gesell (43) and the old and new forms of Binet (107, 108) are arranged in developmental age levels (see above).

This collection of tests purports to obtain an average mental age level at which a child is able to name objects, answer questions, complete statements, describe pictures, and make sentences with specific words.

THE WORK SHEET

A comparison of chronological age with average mental age scores is helpful in identifying children with language delay. These scores, however, do not delineate for the teacher specific deficits in the pre-academic areas of learning which are in part dependent upon oral language. The fact that Jenny can identify objects by name but is unable to identify pictures is not revealed through the mental age scores. All of Andy's scores are close to age level, but the fact that he failed items related to number concepts is not known.

Certain vocabulary words must be acquired and generalized before pre-academic skills can be taught. Teachers who have a sampling of this kind of information for each child are ready to meet individual needs. Teachers who do not have it must spend valuable time in trial and error assessments with each child as he participates daily in the group. The *Worksheet* (p. 343) helps *delineate* specific language deficits.

On this work sheet each sub-test from the comprehension and expression section of the battery is forced into a category related to pre-academic training: *recognizing objects* by name and by function; *recognizing pictures* by name and by function; *naming and defining; categorizing; numbers; spatial relationships; serial directions; sentence building.* Under each category is a space for entering the child's faulty or correct responses to the test items, a number which refers to the number of the sub-test item, and the mental age range for each item. In addition, the work sheet provides the examiner with cue words;

*jargon, echolalia,* and *gesture* in the event he wishes to make appropriate comments under such headings.

Three additional sub-tests from Hiskey (57) have been included under categorizing: *Pictorial Identification, Pictorial Associations* and *Pictorial Analogies.*

## Qualitative Interpretations of the Assessment

Skilled diagnosticians knowing that psychometric tests do not always measure what they purport to measure, look for qualitative aspects of a child's performance which may give insight into why he passed or failed a test item. Sometimes the reason is not revealed. In such instances the teacher may be the one who will seek the answer as she diagnoses and teaches in the classroom.

The following examples are the kinds of subjective impressions a diagnostician may make while assessing a child.

### RECOGNITION OF OBJECTS

*by Name.*

1. Which objects does he fail to identify? If it is the thimble and the button, has he had experience with them?

2. Does he demonstrate an inability to shift? Once he sees his favorite toy—the train—is he unable to listen further to the commands of the examiner?

*by Function.*

1. When asked "Which one do we drink out of?" the child points correctly to the cup. When asked, "Which one do we cut with?" he points again to the cup. Is it that he does not know the word "cut" or the object "knife" or is there other evidence during the testing that he cannot make fine phonemic discriminations?

2. A child cannot point to "Which one do we cook on?" Is it because the toy stove does not look like the "built in" hot plates and oven that mother and her friends have in their kitchens?

### RECOGNITION OF PICTURES

*by Name.*

1. Is the child uninterested in looking at pictures? What experience has he had with them? Does mother read picture stories to him? If the child is significantly below age level in all modalities of language and learning, he may not recognize pictures because pictures are meaningless stimuli for him.

*by Function.*

1. A child misses the items "Which one has the longest ears?"

and "Which one tells us the time?" In other parts of the assessment does he not know the concept of long and short nor the concept of time?

2. Does the four-year-old child score on age level when administered the Ammons Picture Vocabulary test, yet fail two or three items such as finding the picture for the stimulus word "Crying?" Perhaps the child does not see the tear on the face of the girl in the picture. Visual impairment should be ruled out.

### NAMING (OBJECTS, PICTURES, SELF)

1. When presented a toy car and asked to name it, does the child say nothing? Upon further observation does he push the car in a functional manner, does he drop it on the floor, or does he put it into his mouth? Such observations by the examiner give insight into interpretation of the total assessment.

2. When asked to name words from the picture vocabulary test, does he gesture the answer? The case history may reveal that this child's parents have pressured him to "say words." Because of his inability to be understood he prefers to gesture.

3. A child may fail the item which tests ability to name coins. If he fails other items in the battery related to number concepts, he will not be pressured by the teacher to learn the names of the coins. First, he will acquire a basic vocabulary for rote counting and number concepts.

### ACTION AGENT

The Action Agent Test (43) is scored very liberally. However, much information about the child's language may be obtained by recording his responses.

1. Does the child give all answers in gesture language? If this has been true in other parts of the test, the case history may reveal an emotional block when oral communication is involved.

2. Are answers to the following questions due to vocabulary deficiency or phonemic imperceptions? "What melts?" Answer, "Milk." "What aches?" Answer, "Eggs."

3. Is a child unable to shift? When asked "What scratches?" he responds, "Skeeters." The same answer to all successive items is given. Has this inability to shift been reported in other parts of the test?

4. Does the child give function answers rather than naming the thing that represents the function? "What scratches?" Answer, "Scratch my hand." "What sleeps?" Answer, "Sleep in a bed." "What flies?" Answer, "Fly in the air." The examiner will make note of the fact that this child names by function. Perhaps he knows the name but cannot retrieve it at that moment.

DEFINING

When a child is defining words, describing a picture, or volunteering conversation, direct quotations of what he says are recorded by the examiner. Until standard tests are available to measure adequacy of sentence structure of children under six years of age, diagnosticians will make subjective judgments of these linguistic attributes.

1. When asked, "What is a ball?" does the child repeat the question rather than answer it? Echolalia may indicate that the question had no meaning for him.

2. Does the child fail to define most of the words? The inability to define on age level is common among children with language disorders.

CATEGORIZING

*Pictorial Identification* (57). This item provides a child with an opportunity to demonstrate his ability to match pictures.

1. Does a child fail this test yet perform matching tasks with objects? Has he rejected other picture test items?

2. A score far above the child's chronological age level may be attained. Perhaps case history will reveal that he has had an abundance of this kind of training at home and in school. The score does not necessarily indicate superior performance, but rather an ability to learn a task when taught or to learn the method.

*Pictorial Association* (57). This item provides a child with an opportunity to demonstrate his skill in finding a picture which is most like the other two. For example, pictures of two different hats are placed before him. From four additional pictures, he must select the only one which is correct, another hat.

1. Are his responses erratic; missing concrete tasks yet succeeding in more abstract items? Has there been other evidence that this child is distractible and has difficulty attending to the task before him?

2. At age four a child succeeds at the six-year level. At age six he has made no gains. By observing the nature of the tasks beyond age six, the examiner notes that they become more abstract. In other areas of assessment, has this child appeared to function well in a concrete realm but poorly with abstraction?

*Pictorial Analogies* (57). This item provides a child with an opportunity to demonstrate his skill in forming analogies with pictures. Before him is a picture of a shoe and a foot, a hat and a blank space. From four pictures he must select the correct one, a head of a girl.

The responses a child makes to this item are similar to the ones described under *Pictorial Associations.*

ITEMS FROM BINET AND GESELL (107, 108, 43).

1. A child is shown pictures of two faces, one ugly and one pretty, and is asked to select the one which is prettier. He identifies correctly. The examiner cannot always assume that the meaning of the words "ugly" and "pretty" have generalized, for the child may have selected the correct picture because the lady or man had hair that was combed neatly. The teacher will test his understanding of this concept in the classroom.

2. The child is presented with a card which has three similar pictures and one that is different. The examiner says, "See these crosses that are just alike? Here's one (pointing) that is not like the others. Put your finger on the one that is not the same as the others." [2] He fails to respond correctly on the trial card even when the examiner demonstrates. Standardization of the test does not allow for further demonstration. He fails the second card but the examiner decides to explain again. The child succeeds and completes the remainder of the series. Although the child did not receive a quantitative score, the diagnostician may report. "Perhaps this boy did not know the meaning of the language involved in my directions. When I demonstrated items one and two, he was able to complete the others without oral directions." Did he somehow learn the method without the oral symbolization?

3. A child may be able to separate a group of birds from a group of dogs, but is unable to answer the question, "Tell me the *difference* between a bird and a dog." The diagnostician writes a qualitative judgment. "Perhaps this child does not know the meaning of the word *difference*."

NUMBERS

1. Does a child correctly hand the examiner three blocks, but not three beads? Perhaps he has not generalized the concept of "threeness," because mother has worked only with blocks at home.

2. Thirteen pennies are placed in a horizontal row before the subject. He is asked to "Count them out loud and tell me how many there are. Count them with your finger this way, one (pointing to the first one on the examiner's right). Now go ahead." [3] Some children will add extra numbers, or skip pennies. They are unable to touch and count. Perhaps rote counting is intact, but the skills for rational counting have not yet developed. Or, is this an indication of no number concepts, fine motor incoordination, or inability to perform and to verbalize a task simultaneously?

[2] L. M. Terman and M. A. Merrill, *op cit.*, pp. 89-90.
[3] *Ibid.*

SPATIAL CONCEPTS

1. When shown a picture of a large and small ball and asked, "Which ball is bigger?" he may fail the test. During refreshment period teacher asks "Do you want a big cookie or little one." To check the adequacy of the children's responses, the teacher on some days may present a large uninteresting cookie and a small, attractive one. A child may know the concepts of big and little in relationship to circles representing balls, but not cookies. Transfer of learning has not taken place.

2. The teacher will want to know if a child understands the meaning of *in, on,* and *under,* as well as *in front of, beside,* and *behind.*

SERIAL DIRECTIONS

1. The child is asked to put a thimble on the block. Perhaps he does not perform because he has never seen a thimble. He missed a preceding task which asked him to identify a thimble.

2. A child may be able to remember the three commissions because the directions include visual as well as auditory cues. The teacher will design classroom procedures which will test his ability to follow auditory directions without visual cues.

SENTENCE BUILDING

If three words are provided *boy, fell, leg,* can a child generate a sentence?

1. Does he repeat the three words indicating he does not understand the task?

2. Perhaps he does not understand the task and remembers only the last word. To provide a response, he points to his leg. Is this a short term memory deficit?

JARGON

1. Is the child's performance below twelve months in all avenues of learning measured, and his expressive language nonfunctional? Perhaps his oral output is jargon.

2. Is the two-year-old child's performance in all avenues of learning close to the two year level, yet his comprehension and use of language below six months? Hearing impairment should be ruled out.

3. Does the three-year-old comprehend on age level, demonstrate normal hearing, yet present inarticulate speech? The case history may reveal excessive drooling and difficulty in chewing solid foods. Fine motor incoordination of the articulatory mechanism may be responsible for the speech disorder.

ECHOLALIA

1. When the examiner gives a simple command "Sit in the chair," does the child echo, "Sit in the chair?" If so, the interpretation may be normal sensory, perceptual, memory, and speech mechanisms, but no understanding of the words.

2. Does the five-year-old child follow concrete, short commands, yet echo the end of a lengthy statement?

The examiner presents the item "In daytime it is light, at night it is——?"[4] The child responds, "It is night."

Does he remember only the last portion of the statement indicating a short term memory deficit? Is it difficult for him to remember because he has not completely acquired the language code? Was he attending? Some children cannot attend to or organize the connection between phrases. They can take in only one unit at a time.

3. Does the four-year-old child repeat radio and television commercials, yet is unable to answer only the most concrete of questions? Can he rote-count but give no indication of number concepts? If other areas of learning are depressed, this child may be demonstrating poor conceptual development.

GESTURE

1. Does a child comprehend what is said to him yet choose to use simple gestures for a response? The case history may indicate a reticence to talk as a result of being ridiculed for poor speech patterns.

2. A child does not comply when asked, "Show me how you comb your hair." Does he know the meaning of the words comb, and hair? If he does, is there other evidence of an inability to *gesture* a function?

3. For the child who requires gestures to interpret a command or question, hearing should be assessed.

## ASSESSING AVENUES OF LEARNING

### Problems

The hypothesis that intellectual behavior is largely independent of oral language requires two categories of assessment: (1) the previously discussed areas of language and (2) the avenues of learning. Just as the diagnostician finds problems in measuring oral communication skills, so does he find difficulties in assessing avenues of learning.

Psychometric tests related to the specific modes of learning are

[4] L. M. Terman and M. A. Merrill, *op. cit.*

designed primarily to reveal a quantitative score for each item. The experienced diagnostician is aware, however, of many artifacts that make for a child's incorrect answers to standard tests: past experience, previous set, poor attention, motivation, and motor incoordination, to mention but a few. In addition he is well aware that few, if any, test items measure a pure modality of learning.

The fact that valid tools are unavailable should not discourage the diagnostician from developing a battery of tests. He can make use of available instruments, but will be cognizant of their limitations.

## A Design for Assessing Avenues of Learning

Operational definitions of sensation, perception, memory-retrieval, attention, and integration have been presented in Chapter 2. In order to measure these avenues of learning or at least some aspect of each avenue, sub-tests from standardized psychometric tests were selected.

### THE FACE SHEET

On the same face sheet that lists items for assessing language are suggested tests for assessing specific avenues of learning: *Memory-Attention* and *Perceptual-Motor*. Information related to *Social Maturity* is also obtained.

Five-year-old Richard received the mental age scores shown in Table 2.

Information of this nature apprises the teacher that Richard: (1) has a severe deficit in short term auditory recall, (2) is probably close to age level in the picture memory task, and (3) is somewhat below age level in tests that involve remembering a motor task. A review of his performance on these items revealed him to be closer to age 4 years-6 months than 5 years, (4) at or above age level in perceptual-motor tasks (no memory involved), and (5) close to age level in self-help skills.

### TEST ITEMS

*Memory-Attention (short term).* It is sometimes difficult to know whether a child fails an item because he cannot remember or because he cannot readily attend to it. For this reason memory and attention appear as a hyphenated term on the Face Sheet of the battery of tests.

*Auditory.* How well can a child remember what he has just heard? Standardized tests for short term auditory memory are limited in their use. The two most common, repetition of digits and repetition of sentences, require that the subject can talk intelligibly. Until new tests are

## TABLE 2

### SPEECH, HEARING, AND LANGUAGE CENTER
### LANGUAGE AND LEARNING ASSESSMENT: For Training
### (LLAT)

Name ....... Richard ............................ Age: yr. _5_ mo. _0_

| ABILITIES ASSESSED | TESTS | M.A. Scores |
|---|---|---|
| AVENUES OF LEARNING<br>*Memory-Attention (Short term)* | | |
| Auditory | Digits (108, 118) ..................... | 2 - 6 |
| | Sentences (108) ........................ | below 3 - 6 |
| Visual | For Pictures (57) ..................... | 4 - 6 to 5 - 6 |
| Visual-Motor | Tapping (6) ............................. | below 4 - 6 |
| | Tapping (4) ............................. | 4 - 0 to 6 - 0 |
| | Paper Folding (57) ................... | 4 - 6 to 5 - 0 |
| | Draw-A-Man (47) ..................... | refused |
| *Visual-Motor-* | Form Board (108) .................... | dna |
| *Perception* | Block Patterns (57) ................. | 5 - 6 to 7 - 0 |
| (no memory) | Block Patterns (118) .............. | dna |
| | Copy Forms (108) ................... | 5 - 0 to 7 - 0 |
| SOCIAL MATURITY | Social Maturity Scale (47) ........ | 4 - 9 |

dna - Did not administer

developed the following are included in the *Language and Learning Assessment.*

Tests:  Digits (108, 118)
        Sentences (108)

A series of digits are said to the child. He repeats them in sequence. By the same token a sentence is spoken and the child is asked to repeat it just as he heard it.

*Visual (for pictures).* How well can a child remember a picture or groups of pictures he has just seen?

Test:  Visual Attention Span (57)

Fifteen pictures are placed before the subject in three rows of five each. They are covered with an appropriate size cardboard while the subject is exposed to a single picture (man) for a designated period of time. The picture and cardboard are removed and the subject finds the matching picture (man) among the fifteen cards. An additional picture is added until a group of six has been presented. No penalty is given for incorrect sequencing.

*Visual (no word symbols).* How well can a child remember a visual-motor pattern when no word symbols are required?

Test:   Knox Cubes (6)

A series of four blocks is placed before the subject. The examiner taps the blocks in a specified series: 1-2-4. The subject is required to re-member the pattern and duplicate it.

Test: .  Ontario Tapping (4)

A series of six blocks is placed before the child. Two different types of tasks are required. One involves tapping the block and then tapping the table in front of the block (designated as t). Example: 1, t 2, tt 3, t 4, tt etc. A second task involves remembering whether the block was tapped in front of or behind the block (designated as T). The sequence would be 1, t 2, T 3, t 4, T, etc.

Test:   Paper Folding (57)

The examiner folds a square of paper in a certain pattern. The child is given another square and asked to fold one like the examiners.

Test:   Draw-a-Man (47)

How well can a child draw a man or person? There are so many ways to interpret children's drawings that diagnosticians are cautious with the impression they write in their reports.

*Perceptual-Motor.* It is difficult to measure a specific avenue of learning such as visual perception. In fact, no tests are available for very young children which distinguish between the ability to perceive the image accurately and the ability to integrate it into a motor pattern. Until such tests are available for young children, the category visual-perceptual-motor is a better choice than visual perception.

How well can a child perceive a pattern and reproduce it when memory is not involved?

Test:   Form Board (108)

The child is expected to match a solid form to an identical space.

Test:   Block Patterns (57)

A black and white three dimensional drawing of blocks arranged in a specific pattern is shown the child. He reproduces what he sees with a set of blocks that have been placed before him.

Test:   Copy Forms (107)

How well can a child copy with pencil and paper a circle, cross, square, and diamond?

*Social Maturity.* Social maturity scores are provided to give an indi-cation of the child's self-help skills. The average score, however, is not as important as the specific details of the test indicating areas in which the child is not performing on age level: ambulating, dressing, eating, and/or relating to peers.

Test: Vineland Social Maturity Scale (34)

*Handedness.* The literature abounds with studies related to handedness. Little of the scientific research is applicable in the classroom. Teachers are interested in knowing a child's hand preference, primarily for helping him execute hand-skill tasks.

# QUALITATIVE INTERPRETATIONS OF THE ASSESSMENT

## Sensation

Ruling out auditory and visual impairment in young children is made possible through the efforts of the physician, the audiologist, and the language-speech pathologist. A diagnostic label must not be used until thresholds of these two sensory modalities are known.

On occasion the diagnostician may be asked to assess a child before hearing and vision tests are administered. In such an event the following qualitative judgments may help determine the sensory status.

1. A child who tips his head to view the test items or holds them close to his eyes may be suspected of having visual impairment.

2. A child may attend immediately to the sound of a snapper held under the table, yet never respond to the sleigh bells. He may have a severe high frequency impairment. Thresholds would not be known, of course, until audiometric tests were obtained.

3. The examiner names the appropriate pictures on the Ammons test. Periodically in a soft voice he asks the child to point to nontest pictures. Hearing impairment may be suspected when the child has no visual cues from the examiner's face and ignores the request or asks to have the word repeated.

### MEMORY-ATTENTION
*Digits and Sentences* (108, 118)

1. It is not uncommon to find children who perform well with the digit task but fail the sentences. Is there other evidence that they can remember a few words or syllables but not several words? For example, three digits are repeated successfully in sequence. This scores at an age level four to four and one half years. The nine word, twelve syllable sentence is missed. "We are going to buy some candy for mother." This scores between the three and one half to four year level.

2. Another child may repeat the sentences on age level but not the digits. Does he make use of redundancy or, are number words meaningless, therefore, difficult to remember?

3. One girl was sporadic with her responses on both items. The notation appeared, "Can she remember if she can attend?"

4. Jim repeated digits on age level. He failed the sentences only because he omitted function words. The content was correct. Has he learned to comprehend the meaning of a sentence even though he cannot remember all the words? Does his oral communication evidence substandard syntax and morphology?

*Visual Attention Span* (57)

1. Items one, two, four, and six were correct. This child remembered six pictures but failed the third and fourth. The examiner made the following notation, "It appears during testing that he could remember if not distracted."

2. The mental age score was higher than the child's chronological age. It was noted that this child repeated aloud the names of each picture. The question, "Did auditory reinforcement seem to help in other portions of the assessment?"

3. With a chronological age of three-years-six-months, Gary failed all items. The lower limits of the test are also at this age level, therefore not much can be said about his performance.

*Knox Cubes* (6)

1. One child reverses the starting point. The examiner checks for reversals that may have appeared in other test items.

2. Those who are sporadic in their performance may remember, providing they are able to attend.

3. Other children may attend very well, but score far below age level. Is this truly poor memory for a hand-eye-motor activity?

4. A six-year-old child may score below age level on all tasks administered with the exception of Knox Cubes on which he scores two years beyond age level. The reason is not revealed because this item may measure a skill not measured by any other test.

*Ontario Tapping* (4)

1. The starting point is reversed. Were reverses in other test items noted?

2. Lisa scores on all items that proceed from left to right. She is unable to complete items that require motion in front of and behind the blocks. Does she have a different spatial orientation problem than Jack who can complete them but reverses? If school age, does she have difficulty getting her written work on paper?

3. If a child is sporadic in his performance, can he remember if he can attend?

4. Would it be advisable to make the blocks out of sponge rubber

to eliminate the auditory cues while tapping? Would such a standard-ized test reveal different results than the Ontario which utilizes wooden blocks?

*Paper Folding* (57)

1. Bill can fold all the patterns except those which require the formation of a triangle. His teacher may use auditory cues to help him learn this skill.

2. A grossly retarded child will be more interested in tearing or crumpling the paper than folding it.

3. One child does not score on this sub-test but attempts diligently to complete the first item. The examiner demonstrates once or twice how to fold and the child is successful on his third trial. The diagnostician records "Appears to have potential to learn if given adequate cues."

4. A child scored on age level but his work habits were poor and his finished product was "sloppy." Did he demonstrate problems of fine motor incoordination with other tasks?

*Draw-a-Man* (47)

1. Henry places many of the body parts on the paper, but in a random arrangement. The examiner must look at the total assessment to find meaning for this performance.

2. A five-year-old does not score on age level with this task but does on most other test items. The first question to ask, "Has he had experience with drawing figures on paper?"

3. A six-year-old leaves out parts of the body. It is difficult to know through this single test whether the problem is related to one or more of the following: poor body image, memory deficit, emotional disturb-ances, or lack of opportunity.

4. Shaky movements while drawing may indicate fine motor incoor-dination.

PERCEPTUAL-MOTOR

*Form Board* (108)

1. If a child fails this item yet is taught the task, does he remember it at a later time?

2. Does he drop the pieces on the floor or place them in his mouth? If so, his level of functioning may be quite low.

*Block Patterns* (57)

1. Only those items that required placing one block behind another were failed. Is this a problem of depth perception?

2. All items were completed on age level, but the examiner noted hand tremors while the child was constructing the pattern.

3. One child did not score on some of the tasks because he had an incorrect number of blocks. His design was well formed. The diag-

nostician checked other portions of the battery to determine if he performed poorly with numbers.

*Copy Forms* (107)

1. A four-year-old boy cannot copy the circle or cross. He holds his pencil in an immature fashion. He does not know what to do with it. The case history may indicate slow development in all avenues of learning, or it may suggest a lack of opportunity.

2. The score is on age level but the performance is clumsy and work is "sloppy." This may exemplify fine motor incoordination.

3. A five-year-old girl refused to pick up the pencil and draw. The case history revealed that both parents had spent many hours trying to teach her to print her name. She never experienced success because her parents always insisted she could do better. Now she rejects pencil and paper.

# DIAGNOSTIC TEACHING

Teachers have an on-going testing-training program. They attempt to discover how each child learns, and how he makes use of what he has learned. Because individual standardized tests are not commonly used in the classroom, the teacher must take an heuristic approach to her diagnostic program.

Six-year-old Mark could not remember his telephone number long after the other class members had memorized theirs. The teacher observed that he could read the numbers with no problem. A chart with the phone numbers of the entire class was placed on the bulletin board. When phone number drill took place, Mark was permitted to read his. The suggestion that his mother make an identification card for his billfold was carried out and Mark was delighted to use this means of answering the question, "And what is your telephone number?"

During "Show and Tell" Annette was relating a story about her friend, "Doth." Knowing she substituted "th" for "s" the teacher asked, "Is her name Doss?" "No," said Annette, "it has—" and she tapped her thigh twice which was the original class cue for counting syllables. The teacher was correct in guessing the name to be "Doris." Annette feels comfortable with her speech problems now that she can indicate how many syllables a word has.

Many behavior traits of children can be assessed to a better advantage in a classroom milieu than in a standard test environment. A child's social perception is described more readily by the teacher who sees him with his peers, parents, strangers, and herself. She is quick to find the child who is insensitive to the kind of behavior to which other people are sensitive, or the child with fears, jealousies, and shyness.

Criticism has been aimed at teachers who "teach to a test." For this reason some diagnosticians do not inform classroom teachers or parents as to the kinds of errors a child makes. Qualified teachers are capable of interpreting test scores and do not teach to a test.

Molly failed the test items, "Put the spoon *in* the cup." "Put the thimble *on* the block." "Put the ball *on* the box, *in* the box, *in back of, in front of,* and *under.*" Because the teacher knew the test items she avoided using the same objects to teach the concept. There wasn't much need to teach "Put the thimble *on* the block." or "Put the ball *on* the box." Instead Molly was given many meaningful experiences to reinforce learning of these concepts and provide transfer of training. She was taught to hang her coat *in* the closet and *on* the hook, put the paper *on* the teacher's desk, her handkerchief *in* her pocket and her chair *beside* John's.

Even though diagnostic teaching is in progress each day, the teacher knows that she can measure a success in one situation yet see this same skill turn to a failure in a different activity. She is ever aware that a child's retention of a specific skill in a specific task is transient; it may be here today and gone tomorrow. In order to measure the stability of a learning situation or transfer of learning to a new situation, the teacher continues to make daily observations.

## REASSESSMENTS

Have the changes hoped for really occurred or have the parents and teacher been misled by a child's gains in but a few areas? Reassessments are an answer to the question.

Generally, the diagnostician administers the same battery of tests at the end of the school year. The quantitative and qualitative judgments are given to the teacher. Any disagreement between diagnostician's impressions and teacher's judgments on any child's performance are studied at a staffing which includes all professional people who have been working with the child during the year. Out of the staffing come impressions, recommendations, and important specific information for parents as well as teachers.

## SUMMARY

Many psychometric tools are available for measuring intelligence by means of an IQ score. But too many of these psychological reports tell nothing of the child's specific assets and deficits in the areas of language and learning needed for academic success.

"In summary: Joe has an IQ of 95. Although he is capable of learning, his hostility toward school is interfering with academic achievement. Play therapy is recommended."

Surely there is a basic reason for the hostility. Current clinical evidence often reveals the cause to be related to specific language and learning disorders.

Standardization of assessment techniques is necessary, but too much attention is being directed to the statistical interpretation of the data. Diagnosticians need to take a look at the operations employed by the test maker in obtaining his data. From these observations new, more meaningful assessment batteries can be developed—tests which will reflect teaching techniques to be applied in a pre-academic program.

The battery of tests *Language and Learning Assessment: For Training* found in the APPENDIX is incomplete, but is a starting point. It has proved clinically useful in the hands of qualified diagnosticians and teachers who are preparing children for an academic program. Improvement and expansion of the battery will come as research in the area of language and learning adds to current knowledge of these skills.

# 5

# Techniques of Assessing and Reporting

## TECHNIQUES OF ASSESSING

A group of children with language, learning, and/or emotional disorders have little more in common than the fact that they are children. Every child, then, becomes a new challenge to a diagnostician. Tools for assessing may be the same, but skill in administering and interpreting the tests becomes an art.

Assessments are made in order to obtain as complete an audit as possible of a person's assets and deficits. Once this has been accomplished a diagnostic label is selected to provide a brief description of the problem. The labels should be definable and functional for physicians, parents, and teachers. *Hearing impairment, specific learning disabilities* or *mental retardation* are acceptable terms that apply to children who may need special education. Labels such as *minimal brain dysfunction* or *brain injured* are undesirable because they fail to reveal the educational nature of the problem which confronts the teacher.

Etiology is sometimes difficult to determine even though detailed medical, language, and learning assessments have been made. Educated guesses are often recorded in lieu of anything better. A continued search for the cause (but not at the expense of treatment or training) will be certain to benefit parents who are anxious to know "Why," as well as physicians and teachers who will be better equipped to plan their treatment and training program.

A diagnostician must keep in mind that the assessment and tabulating of results does not conclude his assignment. He is responsible for conveying all meaningful information to appropriate persons who will be able to interpret the results and do something constructive for the child.

71

An assessment without thought for what may be done about the problem is an unworthy project.

## The Manual

Remembering the standard procedures for administering numerous sub-test items within a battery of tests may be a difficult task for new employees or diagnosticians who assess infrequently. To assist these persons as well as to provide a diagnostic philosophy for all staff examiners, a *Manual for Assessment Procedures* is helpful. The table of contents may include:

  I.  General Principles
      A.  Qualifications of the examiner
      B.  Physical aspects of the room
      C.  Rapport
      D.  Scoring (quantitative and qualitative)
 II.  Suggested order for administering the battery
III.  Administering the test items
      A.  What is the mental age range of the test or sub-test items
      B.  May errors be corrected by the examiner
      C.  When is the test terminated
      D.  How are quantitative scores obtained
      E.  Standard procedures with each test item
 IV.  Writing the report
  V.  Appendix
      A.  IBM coding instructions
      B.  Conversion tables of raw scores to mental age for each test item
      C.  Conversion table of years and months, to months
      D.  References for all tests

## Physical Aspects of the Room

The appearance of the assessment room is such that the child finds test materials the most interesting objects in view. This means a fairly sterile room. All materials not in use are out of sight and far enough away that the subject cannot reach them. The examiner is thoroughly familiar with all the test items and their location so that he may select them immediately. (Time is often an important factor when children are being appraised.)

When assessing an active, mobile child, the examiner will find it advisable to sit between the subject and the exit!

## Rapport

Knowing that no two children are alike, the examiner adapts his materials and techniques to each one's needs. Although it is customary to sit across a table from the examiner, some children will not conform. One child may prefer to participate in the examination while standing. Another may sit by the table but only on mother's lap. It is not the examiner's responsibility to modify this behavior, only to observe and record it. Children should not be reprimanded for unacceptable behavior so frequently that the assessment becomes a lesson in discipline. Inflexibility in assessment techniques is a primary cause of incomplete testing or failure to obtain any usable results.

Children often associate persons in white coats with painful experiences; immunization shots, or dental care. Audiologists, speech pathologists, and psychologists avoid this kind of apparel to lessen the chances of frightening a child. By the same token, those who hold Ph.D. degrees seldom introduce themselves as "doctor" in the presence of the child.

Rapport with mothers and fathers is also essential. Parents who bring their children for an appraisal of their problem have many concerns. "Will Ted talk for the diagnostician? Will he cry? Will he have a temper tantrum? Will I have to talk about my marital problems? Will I be blamed for the many things I have done wrong in rearing my children? How much will the assessment cost? What will the diagnostician recommend? If it is training, I do not drive. What will I do?"

The diagnostician's attitude and conversation during the first five minutes with the parents and child can help to alleviate the tensions that are known to exist. A warm greeting, sitting for a minute or two with them in the reception room, or providing an opportunity for questions may circumvent what might have been a stressful relationship.

## Should Parents Observe the Assessment?

There is no rule as to whether parents should or should not observe the assessment. The examiner will know which is advisable through previously obtained reports and clinical judgment at the time the parents are greeted. In general, the flexible and experienced diagnostician will find many advantages in having parents observe testing procedures.

Parents *should* be permitted to observe their child in the test room under the following conditions:

1. *If the child appears immature and fearful.* If he clutches mother, hides his head in her lap or begins to cry, the chances are he needs his parent. Children may fear the unknown. Taking them away from mother to an unfamiliar room may be a traumatic experience. Is it any wonder

that tears and tantrums prevail? To avoid a rebellious scene, one or both parents may be invited to accompany the child to the test room. Usually the parents sit quietly and the child becomes so engrossed in the "games" that he ignores all but the examiner and the materials.

2. *If the examiner wishes to demonstrate the child's performance to the parent.* Such a demonstration may become the basis for a successful conference on the results of the assessment. For example a parent may be surprised to see that her child does not point to the picture *chair* when the stimulus word *furniture* is said, but may quickly point to it when the stimulus word *chair* is given.

> "Did you notice, Mrs. King, that David knows many concrete words such as chair, but not the category word to which it belongs—furniture?" "Yes, and I was not aware of it."

Assessments are made to help parents and teachers obtain a better understanding of their children; their assets and deficits. Knowing some details of the problems leads directly to remedial action. If parents have observed the assessment, home training suggestions become meaningful, and often benefit the entire family.

> "Mrs. King believed that David's inability to remember two or more directions was due to inattention or not wanting to do the tasks asked of him. She observed during the assessment his failures on short-term auditory memory items. The examiner discussed what is currently known about memory and provided home training suggestions. One month later Mrs. King reported the following: "I decided to help David by enrolling all of the children, we have four others, you know, in a household memory game. I started by giving each child two directions. 'Elaine, clear the table and stack the dishes.' 'Bill, make your bed and hang up your clothes.'— As the days passed sixteen-year-old Ruth was following eight directions which were closely checked, by the others. David could follow four. It was surprising how quickly errors of sequence or omission were picked up by the siblings." Mother knew the children were having fun with the game, and, to her advantage, dozens of household chores were being completed.

3. *If the child's speech is unintelligible.* Parents often understand their child's language when an examiner cannot. For this reason the parent, who is the best interpreter, will be needed in the test room.

When a parent or any observer comes to the test room, he should be asked to sit somewhat behind the child and instructed to make no comments or corrections. If mother or father attempts to rephrase the question, answer for the child, or hint at the answer, the examiner might say laughingly, "Be careful, or I'll be obtaining a test on you!"

Parents *should not* be permitted to observe their child in the test room under the following conditions:

1. *If the referring source has asked that no results be given the parents.*

2. *If the parent appears to be an overly anxious person who wants to observe, yet the child is willing to go along with the examiner.*

3. *If the parent has accompanied the child and it soon becomes obvious that he would perform better alone.* Parents are usually the first to sense such a situation and are not reluctant to leave.

## Creativity

When the diagnostician first confronts a child for purposes of a language and learning assessment, quick decisions must be made. Can testing begin immediately or is there a need for a short play period? Which toys should be given to him? Which test should be introduced first?

Hypotheses are formulated and tested as the assessment progresses. Wrong guesses are made, and new ones continue to be created. Within a relatively short period of time a skilled diagnostician observes and records what has been heard and seen. These quantitative and qualitative judgments will form a profile of the child's assets and deficits.

## Listen to Parents and Child

With few exceptions parents are good reporters. They desire to present an honest chronology of their child's behavior in an effort to secure the counsel and advice of the persons who are assessing. Parents can furnish needed information if diagnosticians will listen.

Four-year-old Kay did poorly on all test items related to hand skills. Mother later reported that she had never allowed her daughter to paint, cut with scissors, or color. Home training suggestions were carried out and within a short period of time, Kay developed hand-eye-motor skills commensurate with her age. Mother's comment was "Kay was not low in hand skills, she was low in 'mothering skills!' "

Children often diagnose their own problems:

Bob passed all of the paper folding items except those which involved a triangle. As he attempted to place the appropriate corners of the square into position he said, "I can't do that. That's hard. That isn't right. This way. No, this way. I can't do that one." Bob probably perceived the shape of the triangle but was unable to integrate the image into a motor pattern.

Melanie was asked on Thursday what she planned to do on Sunday. "Sleep—wake up, sleep—wake up, sleep—wake up; go to church." Certainly she had concepts of time but not the vocabulary to express the concepts in acceptable form. The teacher knew from this one experience what Melanie needed in vocabulary development.

## Time Allotment

It is unrealistic for an examiner to expect the majority of young children to maintain a high level of attention over a long period of time. The examiner must be so familiar with the materials and the manner of testing, that he can administer the language and learning battery in less than sixty minutes for young children and within sixty to ninety minutes for school age children.

### OBSERVATION CLASSES

The purpose of an observation class is to obtain subjective and objective information about a child who did not respond in a more formalized testing situation. The examiner selects a room in which the child may move freely about. Pictures and toys are presented him in a variety of ways. His responses to the stimuli are recorded.

Many children, originally not testable, begin to relate well to the examiner after a few days in a one hour observation class. Formalized testing may be possible on the second or third day.

A few youngsters will not be ready for an assessment with standardized tests for several months. Under no circumstances should they be kept for this length of time in the observation class. A subjective report of the child's performance should be given to the training supervisor who will make a probational class assignment where diagnostic teaching can transpire.

## Scoring

Each task completed is scored with an appropriate symbol to indicate a correct, incorrect, questionable, or no response. All test items are scored on their own merit. Some children because of their charming manner or attractiveness, immediately appear more capable than they are. Conversely, the textbook physical appearance of some children creates a false hypothesis of severe intellectual retardation.

Throughout the testing the examiner never assumes that because a child has performed poorly on one section of the battery he will continue to score in like manner. Few children demonstrate flat profiles of their language and learning skills.

Many older children, especially those who are in an academic program, will be curious about the symbols used for recording right and wrong answers. Frequently they will ask, "Is that right? What are you marking?" The response may be that the marks help the examiner remember what was said. Score sheets must be kept from the view of these inquisitive children. If a child persists in asking about his responses, the examiner may say, "It's against the rules to tell answers," or "Yes, you gave one of the correct answers. There are several that might be right."

Some children are quite perceptive of their own errors and are disturbed by their failures. When the examiner senses this, he may comment, "That was a hard one. I would guess that you haven't studied that in school yet." or "I know these are hard, but I want to find how many you can do." During a series of failures, a task that will bring success is introduced.

At times a child's response may be ambiguous and impossible to score. The examiner may say, "Tell me what you mean. Tell me more about it." Some directions for administering specific tests, however, are quite rigid. The examiner notes in the manual how many times a question may be repeated. If questioning beyond the requirements is needed, the item is marked a failure. If the child scores correctly with additional cues, a qualitative note should be entered beside the test item.

The examiner endeavors to praise the child's efforts, not his correct responses. In fact, the examiner gains as much if not more information when a child fails a task as when he succeeds in a performance.

## Order of Item Presentation

The face sheet of the *Language and Learning Assessment: For Training* (p. 53) is arranged in an order that will be meaningful to those persons who can interpret psychometric test scores. The items are *not* arranged in the order for presentation to a child.

### SUGGESTED ORDER FOR CHILDREN WITH NORMAL HEARING

Rapport and an immediate feeling of success for the child must be fostered. Since many children referred for an assessment will present an oral language deficit, they will feel more comfortable with nonoral test items in the initial period of testing.

1. The Hiskey Block Designs item (57) is a good choice for starting the assessment. Young children are familiar with blocks and like to play with them.

2. When a ceiling on performance with the block designs has been reached, comprehension of number concepts may be tested. Before putting the blocks away the examiner will ask the child to select the appropriate number as requested in the language comprehension section of the *Language and Learning Assessment: For Training.*

3. No child should be threatened with the thought that he will have to answer questions. If he has been criticized many times for his poor language and speech, he may resent talking in the initial part of the assessment. Therefore, it may be necessary to intersperse some of

the language expression items among non-oral tasks. "What did you say your name was?" "Are you a boy or a girl?" "What do you do when you are thirsty?" may be asked while test materials are being put away or new items are brought out.

4. Close attention is required for all of the memory tests. It is important that they be administered at an optimum time during the assessment; when the child is interested and enjoying the "games."

SUGGESTED ORDER FOR CHILDREN WITH HEARING IMPAIRMENT

While there is no basic change either in the test battery or in the method of presentation, the examiner takes cognizance of certain specific factors.

1. Children with impaired hearing who are expected to be educated with normal hearing children should be compared test-wise with a population of children with no hearing impairment.

2. If a child wears a hearing aid, the examiner makes certain that it is functioning properly during the assessment.

3. The examiner provides maximum auditory and visual cues throughout the assessment. It may be advisable to communicate orally with the child before testing and between test items. These conversations give the child practice in "lipreading" the examiner.

The skilled examiner is almost intuitive in his approach to selecting test items in an order that will maintain a child's cooperation. The first signs of unwillingness to perform are immediately apparent. Before the child withdraws, the task is discontinued and presented subsequently. More successes than failures are provided by inserting an easier item among difficult ones. Assessments, more often than not, can be obtained during a first visit if the diagnostician is sensitive to the behavior changes of children.

## Interpretation of the Assessment

Language disorders may be accompanied by other deficits. What are they? Case history studies, standardized tests, and a diagnostician's experience and insight uncover the facts. But isolated facts do not become meaningful until placed in perspective. Only when patterns begin to form does the total assessment become meaningful.

Scoring the battery of tests is usually the first step toward bringing the total assessment into focus. The raw scores and mental age ranges are recorded on the *Face Sheet*. A breakdown of the language comprehension and expression items is tabulated and entered on the *Worksheet* (p. 343). Relevant qualitative information accumulated during the testing is reported.

Because unequal intervals often appear among sub-test items, con-

Fig. 5 - 1
LANGUAGE AND LEARNING ASSESSMENT PROFILE
OF CHILD WITH NO LANGUAGE
OR LEARNING DEFICITS

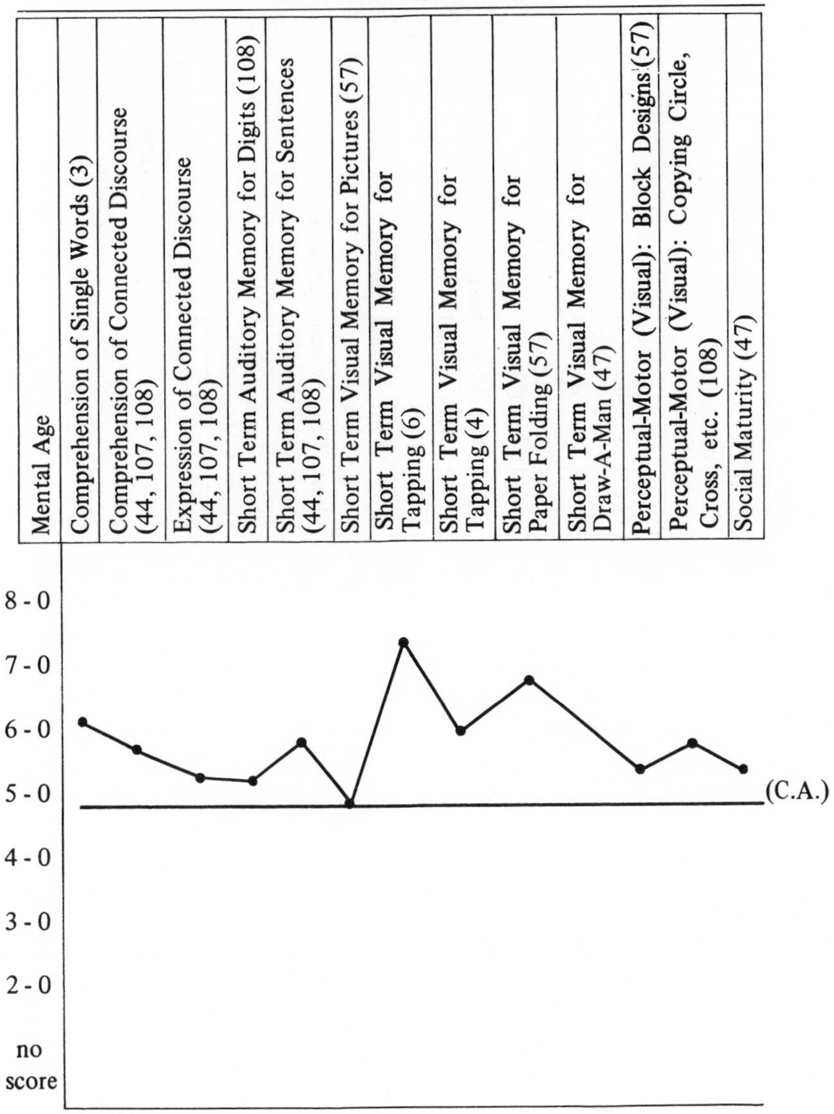

79

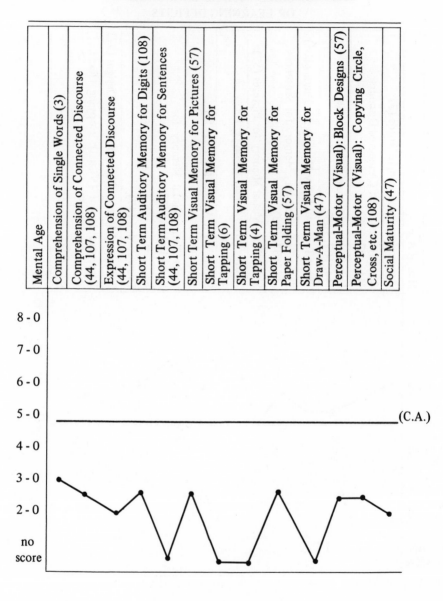

Fig. 5 - 2
LANGUAGE AND LEARNING ASSESSMENT PROFILE
OF CHILD WITH GENERAL RETARDATION

Fig. 5 - 3
LANGUAGE AND LEARNING ASSESSMENT PROFILE
OF CHILD WITH LEARNING DEFICITS
BUT NO ORAL LANGUAGE DEFICITS

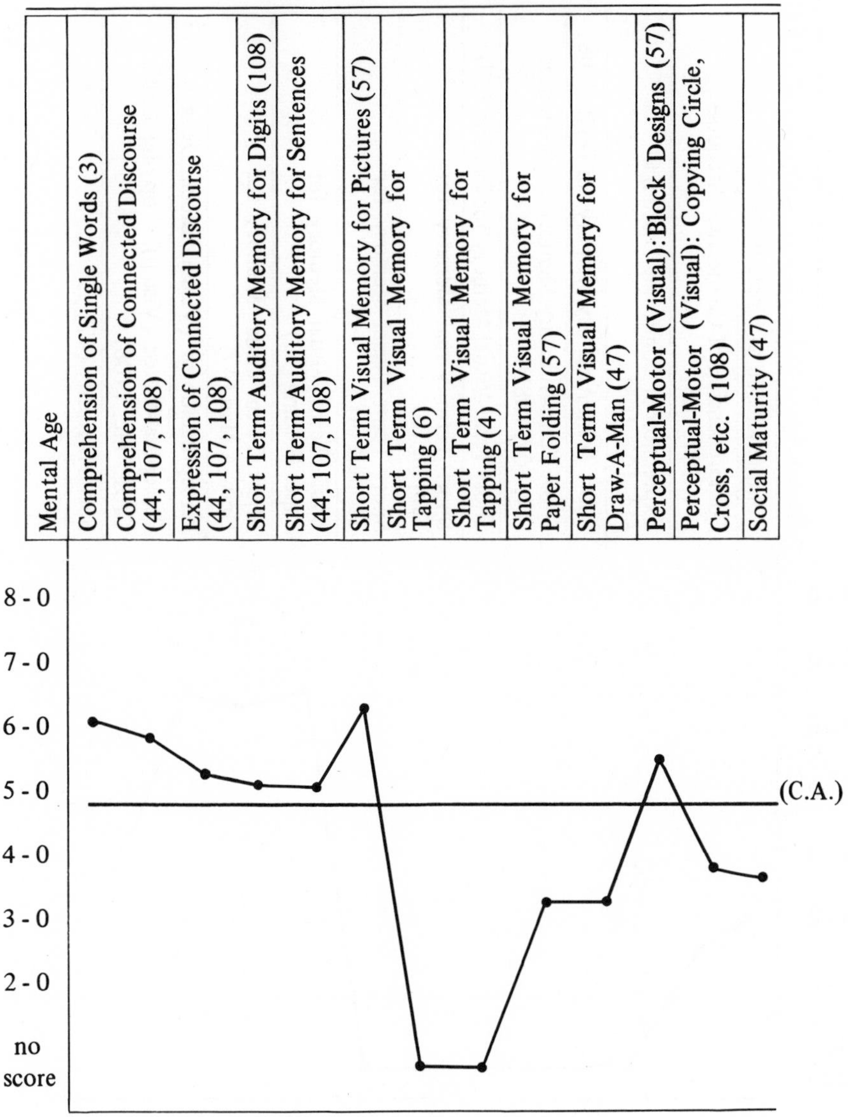

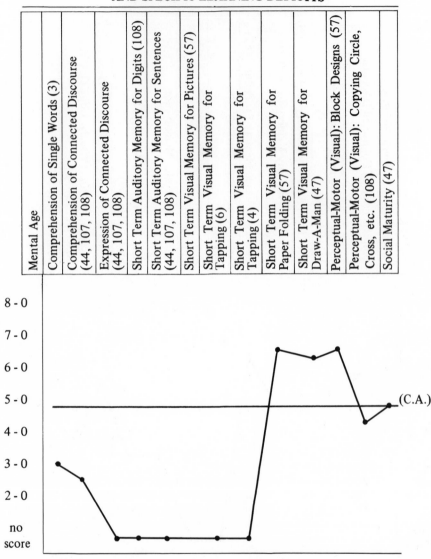

**Fig. 5 - 4**
**LANGUAGE AND LEARNING ASSESSMENT PROFILE**
**OF CHILD WITH LANGUAGE DISORDER**
**AND SPECIFIC LEARNING DEFICITS**

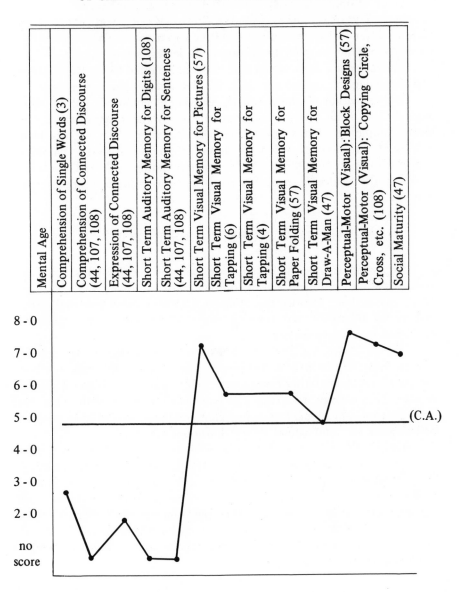

Fig. 5 - 5
LANGUAGE AND LEARNING ASSESSMENT PROFILE
OF CHILD WITH SENSORY HEARING IMPAIRMENT

sistency in recording the mental age scores must be maintained. Raw scores for example, may be converted to an age range of 5 years-6 months to 7 years-0 months. The examiner does not always know if the child is closer to age five and one half or seven years. The decision will be made whether to plot the mean or the lowest score.

When mental ages for all test items are plotted along the abscissa and chronological ages on the ordinate, five distinct profiles emerge.

Interpretation of the language assessment continues with a thorough review of all information accumulated by the diagnostician: case history, audiological assessment, phonetic inventory, and reports from individuals or agencies. All observations begin to fall into a pattern— a diagnosis is made, etiology is known or hypothesized, and pertinent results of the total assessment are ready to be translated to appropriate persons.

## THE DIAGNOSTICIAN'S REPORT

Reporting the results of an assessment of a child with language and/or learning problems serves four purposes: (1) to provide a diagnosis, (2) to help identify the etiology, (3) to present essential information for treatment and training, and (4) to demonstrate gains as measured by a reassessment.

The diagnostician first asks himself, "Is the report to be oral or written and for whom is it intended?" The parent, physician, teacher, insurance agent, or father's employer usually require different kinds of reports. Terminology may vary and emphasis on details shift. (For reports to professional persons; physicians, teachers, audiologists, speech pathologists, see the General Report Form outline, p. 361).

During the oral reporting to parents or while writing the results of the assessment, a second question is asked, "Am I reporting anything that will attach a stigma to the child—a mark that may influence professional persons to make inappropriate choices in future treatment and training?" Statements about a child's performance must be related to the place and that period of time in which he was assessed. Terminal diagnoses often lead to unworthy predictions and subsequent inadequate treatment and training.

### Reporting Assessments to Parents

REPORT TO BOTH PARENTS

Parents are anxious to receive the findings of their child's assessment. Often because of anxiety they hear only the desirable aspects, sometimes the less desirable, or they leave the session in utter confusion. A mother may come alone and leave with a clear understanding of the report but be unable to find words that translate the information to her husband.

Not always is it possible for a father to leave work to attend a conference, but usually special appointment hours can be made. Both parents need an explanation of their respective roles in helping their child. Most fathers want to be a part of the team and when included, function very well.

### ESTABLISH RAPPORT

In general, parents expect a conference to reveal the defect they hope did not exist. With this psychological set, they are apt to hear few of the opening remarks. To help them become socially comfortable and focus on the important facts, the diagnostician may open with trivia. "I had a pencil a moment ago—and here it is. One day my desk drawer has ten or fifteen then suddenly it seems to have only one or two. Guess I'm careless about leaving them elsewhere."
Parents may become better listeners if they hear good things first.

> I was pleased with Helen's responses. Even though she sat on your lap she did try to do all the things I asked her to do. The shyness didn't affect the test results. Weren't you pleased at her sometimes successful attempts to correct her errors? She was a joy to assess.

### USE LAY TERMINOLOGY

Too often the important factors of a report are ensconced in professional language which is not meaningful to parents, for example:

> "The psycholinguistic battery of tests which I administered revealed behavior that is common to children diagnosed as having minimal brain damage. The assessment of his avenues of learning is not indicative of mental retardation. He demonstrated perceptual problems which will interfere with learning if not corrected early in his life. Much of his current behavior is due to the minimal brain dysfunction which was reported to you by your neurologist. We will enroll him in our training program next week."

*Minimal brain dysfunction, perceptually handicapped, not retarded.* Is this good news? Initially the parents believe it is. Then a relative asks for an interpretation and receives a confused answer. Parents, while their children are in class, begin to discuss the terms among themselves —in the waiting room or over coffee. They feel someone in the group will clarify these currently acceptable yet mysterious labels. Confusion mounts. One parent hears of another training program which is different and promises a rewarding future for the child. Inquiries are made and some children are transferred.

Parents are still not satisfied. They become distraught and feel a need for doing something other than what they consider is being done; they organize a parent group. Other uninformed, confused parents with no basic understanding of their children's problems join together and begin a crusade for better medical attention and better training programs. They raise money to bring in speakers who hopefully will provide an answer to their dilemma. Professional people either add to the confusion by failing to define the terms adequately or fraudulent lecturers propose a "new technique" and cults develop almost overnight.

Why do parent-pressure groups form? There are several reasons, but, in general, the answer is directly related to poor communication among the parents, diagnosticians, and teachers. When parents are satisfied with their understanding of the problem, can verbalize it to others, and are given something acceptable to do about it, they do not have a need to join a parent group sponsored by the community designed to seek quick or sure "cures."

The skilled diagnostician is one who can translate professional terminology into meaningful language. Without this skill he confounds his diagnosis and recommendations.

DEVELOP A PROFILE

Profiles depicting the results of the *Language and Learning Assessment: For Training* battery are plotted during the parent conference. The names of the specific tests are labeled in functional terms across the abscissa as noted on Fig. 5-6.

A line representing the child's age is drawn half way down the ordinate and parallel to the abscissa. All assets are marked at or above the line that depicts chronological age and all deficits appear below the line. Specific mental ages are seldom provided. As with IQ scores, parents tend to retain a number and often out of context.

"Mrs. Bartell, let's take a look at what is meant by all of the games Richard and I played. (See Fig. 5-6.) I think it will be clear to you if I draw a picture of the things he does well and those things which he does not do so well. Across this line I am going to write the different abilities that I tested. These are the abilities which are related to Richard's future success in school. In the middle of the picture or graph, I will draw a heavy line which will represent how old he is. And today he is 3 years and 11 months. Now we are ready to take a look at his test scores. In this first slot I will write *Understands what is said to him*. As you already know and have reported to me, he probably understands little if anything that is said to him. So, I will place a minus sign far below the heavy line. Next I will write, *Talking*. If a child does not understand what is said to him, he will not answer in functional oral language. Far below the heavy line we will place another minus. Even though he attempted to repeat after me, it was really an echo of what I was saying. This, of course, is like 'parrot talk.' In the next slot I have written *How well does he remember what he hears?* Because our tests in auditory memory require that he talk, I could not obtain a score—another minus. Next, *How well does he remember what he sees?* He could not perform on this test which begins to measure at three years and six months. All we know now is that he did not perform on this item. Let's assume from what you have told me that he is someplace between thirty and forty months. This is still a minus score but better than the language scores. Next, *Hand Skills*. This means, *How well can he perform with his hands when you do not have to give him oral directions?* Remember when he looked at the picture of the block design and then constructed what he saw? This he did close to age level so we will give him a minus sign but close to the heavy line. The next item is *self-help*. Remember when I asked you about feeding, dressing, and playing with other children? This is a sort of social maturity score which you gave him and it was about the 3 year level so we will place the minus sign here. Now, does that look like Richard's profile? When he is enrolled in the training program, he will be given work to do in these better areas which will make him feel successful. The teacher will find the lowest level at which he can perform in these areas and begin to move him toward the solid line. Do you have any questions? You may have this profile to take with you—At the end of the school year we will reassess Richard and add his new profile to this one."

## SUMMARIZE THE RESULTS

When a child has deficits which do not show physically but result in deviant behavior, relatives, neighbors, and friends are quick to blame the mother and father for the unacceptable conduct. For lack of a cause of the problem the parents too often assume the blame, and feelings of guilt and remorse develop. When summarizing an assessment for parents, a diagnostician is careful not to blame them for the child's problem.

"Blaming yourself, Mrs. Bartell, for Richard's problem is ridiculous. He was born with a body that just didn't run like the bodies of your other children. And when something doesn't operate properly it is different. The fact that you brought him in early for an assessment was the best thing you could have done. Let's not worry about placing the blame, let's get to the business of helping Richard. Your physician and our staff are eager to get started."

Not only does a diagnostician refrain from placing blame, but also from making predictions.

"You asked me, Mrs. Bartell, if your boy would ever be ready for college. I can't answer that question any better than you could answer it for other parents. I have made too many mistakes predicting, so I have learned the

## Fig. 5 - 6
## LANGUAGE AND LEARNING ASSESSMENT PROFILE
## AS PRESENTED TO PARENTS

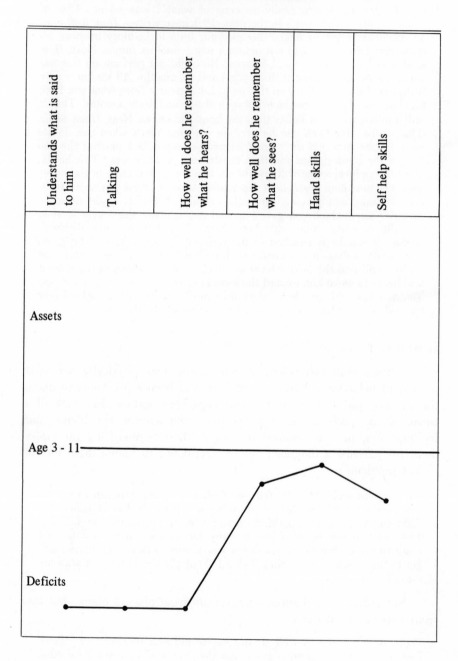

hard way to observe progress as it comes along and plan for the future in small steps. I believe that you will be more comfortable if you will try to think of Richard in the present, not the future."

The final summary of the total assessment should leave the parents with a clear understanding of at least the basic problem, an ability to explain the problem to others, and the promise of the best training program available. If the diagnostician is a part of the training program, he may wish to discuss fees and introduce the parents to the supervisor of the training division. She will describe the classes and allow for observation if feasible.

"In summary then, Mrs. Bartell, let's look at Richard this way. He is a little boy who is more like other little boys his age than he is different. He can hear and see, has arms and legs, can think, and many more similarities. The way in which he is different is his inability in understanding what people say to him and making people understand him. This is why you brought him to us. This, you knew. He will be enrolled in a program which is designed to develop oral language and the skills which will be needed for reading, writing, spelling, and arithmetic. In addition, you and your husband will be provided with many suggestions which will help you in a home training program.

### REASSESSMENTS

It is not uncommon to meet a parent who takes the original language and learning profile from her purse at reassessment interviews. Often the profile shows the wear of having been studied and shown to other persons. If feasible, the second assessment should be added to the first. If, as usually happens, the child can accomplish more tasks, new headings will be needed across the top of the profile. The original scores, then are added to the new profile.

If a child is enrolled in a pre-academic program, reassessments are interpreted to the parents by the supervisor of the training division. She is knowledgeable about the child's performance in the classroom, hence can relate the findings to pre-academic or academic placement.

## Reporting Assessments to the Physician

### ORIGINAL ASSESSMENT

When reporting to the referring physician, the diagnostician follows two general procedures, (1) he writes a brief report which communicates its intent and (2) invites the physician to request detailed information if desired (p. 351).

On occasion a child may reside in a distant community where the referring physician will be responsible for redefining and reinforcing the impressions and recommendations of the language assessment. In some instances he may be the one who locates the appropriate training program. Under such circumstances reports must give a detailed account of quantitative and qualitative judgments which ensued from the assessment (p. 352).

### REASSESSMENTS

After the parents have received a report of the reassessment, they should be asked to whom they would like to have the summary forwarded. The same principle of reporting initial findings to physicians should be followed.

## Reporting Assessments to the Teacher

### ORIGINAL ASSESSMENT

From a training point of view, original assessments indicate appropriate class placement for the child. Furthermore, the teacher has a baseline for each child in the areas of language and learning which provides the framework for her lesson plans.

### REASSESSMENTS

Reports of the reassessment are comparable to the original. Teachers compare current performance of the child with any previous performance.

## Special Requests for Reports

The Carlton family lived 300 miles from the closest city which could provide an appropriate training program for their child. The diagnostician inquired as to the possibility of the family changing their residence. The idea was feasible to them and Mr. Carlton checked areas with educational facilities which might also have employment for him. A letter recommending transfer was sent the employer with successful results (p. 357).

Reports for insurance companies, court trials, social workers, or family friends are often requested. No matter from whom the request comes, the diagnostician obtains parental consent to send the report, then summarizes an appropriate description of the assessment.

## The Teacher Reports

Diagnostic teaching continues each day in the classroom. Specific gains made in the areas of language, learning, and social adjustment are recorded by the teacher. Her cumulative record is studied at the end of the school year at which time a final report which follows a general outline is prepared (p. 361). The purpose is to provide the next teacher with basic information for each child in the areas of language and learning necessary for academic success.

## SUMMARY

Many children may be classified under the same medical or educational diagnosis and many will present a common etiology. Few will have the same assets and deficits, but if they do, the mental age ranges will differ among the sub-tests.

Most important is the selection of suitable techniques of assessing and reporting the language and learning status of children for the ultimate purpose of providing the teacher with a framework for structuring her training program.

# 6

# Developing a Pre-Academic Program

Reading, writing, arithmetic, spelling, and oral communication are requisites for school success. In our American culture, acquisition of these subjects is not left to chance. Children are enrolled in educational programs around the sixth year, for at this period in life they are expected to be ready for formal training.

Six-year-old children, however, differ in their abilities to grasp formal educational concepts. The average students become the pacesetters at the expense of the children who fall below or above the average. The fate of slow and gifted children is apparent to educators.

The concept of enrolling children with or without handicaps in a nursery school or kindergarten program *is not new*. In the school placement of children with handicaps, the focus has been on the *descriptive* aspects of the problem; deaf, blind, mentally retarded, cerebral palsied. Little attention has been given to the basic skills needed for future academic achievement.

The *concept* of pre-academic training programs, one that precedes the formal education usually beginning at age six, *is new*. The classwork in a pre-academic program is structured and emphasizes training in the specific areas of language and learning needed for academic success. Such programs are designed to utilize assets to either improve or circumvent deficits.

The first *hazard* in organizing a pre-academic program for children with or without specific learning disabilities is in giving insufficient regard for details. A stable program needs both a system and flexibility— a system for teaching groups of children and flexibility which provides for individual differences within the groups. Such a notion implies that staff members establish basic educational philosophy and school policy.

92

# EDUCATIONAL PHILOSOPHY

## Early Training

ENVIRONMENT

Though a child may have the kind of protoplasm needed for future academic success, his performance is not likely to be good if the crucial years from birth to four years are not utilized. During this span of time the child's infinite number of neurological networks have not been subjected to the variety of stimuli and interference as has been in the older child's brain. In addition, the new brain has remarkable resilience. Early pre-academic training is essential, particularly for children with handicaps.

MATURATION

Investigators are convinced that there are individual differences among newborns and that these differences continue to be apparent throughout life. One child may begin to say words at eight months and another at thirty months. Yet, through different maturational processes both children may be talking on age level by their fourth birthday.

READINESS

Children are ready to learn a task when they have the ability to make use of what is to be taught. But who knows when this readiness period will occur? Or, will it ever occur with or without specialized training? Should we assume a laissez-faire attitude or should we launch into a training program as soon as there is evidence that a problem exists?

Diagnosticians and educators cannot risk the chance that a child's language and/or learning disorder is due to slow maturation alone. A diagnostic training program should be instigated for if it becomes apparent that the problem is one of maturation, nothing will have been lost. Indeed, much may have been gained in the areas of language and learning. If maturation was not the significant factor, early training may have saved the child from future educational and/or emotional casualties.

## A Professional Staff

Special education programs are not available in all communities. Parent groups, therefore, often play a leading role in demonstrating the need for organizing special classes for their children. Once the need is recognized, publicity, fund raising, and classroom facilities follow with few problems encountered. Recruitment of qualified teachers, however, is too often given last consideration. The result is a parent-run program until such time as qualified teachers can be obtained.

Once an appropriate educator has been hired, however, she may find that the parent group is reluctant to allow her to design the program as she views it professionally. Parent-teacher clashes result at the expense of the children enrolled.

Pre-academic classes must be organized, supervised, and taught by qualified persons.

# A Curriculum Guide

## PURPOSE

A curriculum guide is not considered a final treatise on what, how much, or how children are to be taught. It merely serves as a directive for the teacher's course of action. In general, a curriculum guide includes basic vocabulary, methods for teaching the skills needed to develop oral and written communication, and levels for expected achievement.

A curriculum guide does not replace a qualified teacher. On the contrary, only a skilled teacher knows how to use a guide for expansion of its basic principles into broader concepts.

## ONE MULTIAPPLICABLE PRE-ACADEMIC CURRICULUM GUIDE

The labeling of children—deaf, perceptually handicapped, cerebral palsied, mentally retarded, brain damaged—is a common practice. Various curriculum guides have been developed to meet the needs of children in these specific groups. Publications abound with such titles as *Arithmetic for the Deaf, Speech for the Deaf, Language for the Deaf, Basic Mathematics for the Retarded Child, Readiness and Reading for the Retarded Child,* and *Teaching the Retarded Child to Talk.*

The implication? *That the education of one category of children with handicaps is quite different from the training of youngsters in some other category.* This is false reasoning. The goal for each child is having him reach his full potential so that he may function as a contributing member of society. The education of the retarded or hearing-impaired child is not significantly different from the education of any other child, although the quality and quantity of what is learned will vary among categories.

The great need is for one multidimensional, pre-academic curriculum guide designed to assist the teacher in her efforts to develop pre-academic skills among all children, regardless of their handicaps. The dissimilarity in training children with a variety of handicaps lies in understanding individual differences, and application of teaching techniques and motivational materials as they apply to the functional level of the child.

The teaching techniques and motivational materials may differ among the categories of blind, mentally retarded, normal, or gifted, but the need to improve vocabulary, syntax, morphology, and skills for written language remain the same.

The basic principles for helping children attain their potential school success should be the core of a pre-academic curriculum guide.

# SCHOOL POLICY

## The Staff

Teaching staffs working in a pre-academic language building program must function within the framework of a basic educational philosophy. They must participate in coordinated planning toward the future of each child. And, all important, the staff must be able to communicate among themselves—to speak a professional language based upon operational definitions.

Studies of desirable personality traits of supervisors and teachers have not been very revealing. The time-worn standards of an appropriate teaching certificate, personal integrity, patience, and dedication are still universally acceptable.

Academic qualifications for a supervisor or teacher of a pre-academic program for children with language and/or learning disorders are not clearly defined. Few colleges and universities have made decisions in regard to which departments should certify these special teachers. Few courses of study have been laid out for the person who wishes to do full-time supervising or teaching in a pre-academic program.

THE SUPERVISOR

*Certain basic qualifications* for a supervisor are needed. (1) An elementary teaching certificate. The pre-academic curriculum guide is designed to teach the skills needed for reading, writing, spelling, and arithmetic. Understanding the principles involved in the formal teaching of these subjects is necessary, if children are to be prepared for them. (2) Appropriate background in the area of normal and abnormal child growth and development. (3) Clinical experience with children from birth to six years of age. (4) Course work in learning theories. (5) Academic work and experience in administering and interpreting psycholinguistic type tests. (6) Courses of study in communication; audiology, language, speech, and the disorders of each.

*The responsibilities of a supervisor* will vary with the institution but in general will include the following:

1. Administration of all language and learning assessments unless the staff includes qualified speech and language diagnosticians. In such a case, the diagnostician would discuss the test results with the supervisor before class placement.

2. Scheduling of classes for children entering the program for the first time. This job is often inappropriately given to the diagnostician. It is the supervisor, properly trained, who is familiar with the structure of the classes and openings in the classes.

3. Reassignment of children to other classes when indicated. Based on the results of reassessments and/or teacher judgments, a child may be ready for a more advanced class. Or, the child may have been improperly placed and must be shifted to a more appropriate group. On rare occasions it is realistic to recognize that teacher-child relationships are such that the child would profit from another instructor.

4. Dismissal of children when indicated. If a child is no longer profiting from the training program, he should be given an appropriate referral. Perhaps he has reached a plateau and would perform just as well at home or in a play school. Dismissals should also be considered if a parent or responsible person does not attend parent conferences, or if a child has numerous days of absenteeism and another child is on a waiting list.

5. Counseling with parents when the need arises. Results of the original language and learning assessment should be given by the supervisor unless administered by a diagnostician. All reassessments given by the supervisor should be interpreted by her.

6. Responsibility for listening to and evaluating criticism that may center around a teacher or the program.

Mrs. Carsten made an appointment with the supervisor to register a complaint. "You moved my child to another class last week and I am most unhappy. His present teacher is not nearly as competent as the first one."

Usually the comment, "Please give yourself six weeks before you decide the new teacher's adequacy" is a starting point for a discussion of competency among teachers. It is pointed out that teachers may not use the same techniques but that their educational philosophy and goals are the same. Parents must never be led to believe that one teacher is superior to another within a given program, for in the course of three years, one child may be taught by all teachers on the staff.

7. Knowledge of other programs in and out of the city. Some parents need the information because they are moving to a new vicinity. Others are "shoppers" for a program that will provide a "quick cure." If a supervisor believes in her own program and knows it is up-to-date,

she will find little difficulty in selling it to parents. Parents should be encouraged to talk over their problems with the supervisor, who must be astute enough to analyze the cause of the problem and plot the course of action which will relieve pressures from the teacher as well as the parents.

8. Planning and presiding over weekly teacher meetings which are designed for keeping up with current literature, discussing unusual diagnostic and training findings, and revising the curriculum guide when indicated.

9. Reviewing progress reports submitted by the teachers.

10. Disseminating information regarding the training program to those who request it.

## THE TEACHER

*Qualifications* for teachers are the same as for the supervisor. The only requirement which might be disregarded would be experience in administering the battery of tests. Certainly the ability to interpret the tests is desirable.

*The major responsibility* of the teacher is to provide an environment conducive to teaching children the skills that will be needed for their future academic program. In addition and in conjuction with this objective the teacher must:

1. Arrange for and conduct group and individual parent-teacher conferences.

2. Keep cumulative records up to date.

3. Arrange and plan for all class field trips.

4. Administer such assessments as the Vineland Social Maturity Scale (34) when the child enters the program or when he is reassessed. This responsibility will help establish parent-teacher rapport and provide the teacher with further insight into parent attitudes and home environment.

## THE COUNSELOR

Counseling of parents in a pre-academic program is provided by the teacher and a social worker or psychologist. The purpose of the counseling is to help parents accept intellectually and emotionally the specific problems which face them.

In addition to training the children, the teacher has a threefold counseling task: (1) defining normal language and learning skills and deviations as they unfold in the classroom, (2) providing and clarifying teaching procedures to be carried out at home, and (3) motivating parents to carry out a home training program. The teacher, basically, is counseling on an intellectual and educational level.

Trained counselors in social work or psychology are concerned with improving family relationships. Have the parents accepted their child's problem intellectually, but not emotionally? Do they tend to say, "Now we will become educated parents because we have our child in a training program which also trains us," yet ignore the emotional side of the picture?

> Mrs. King attended several group sessions with the social worker. Her statement revealed the progress she had made as a result of the counseling sessions. "I don't want to cry now every time I think about the future."

Are the parents working together for their child's daily successes? Does father attend the sessions? Adding fathers to the counseling group provides another dimension—an approach which views the total family.

Are there specific factors which cause problems among the siblings? Are these problems that a counselor can unravel and rethread?

> Five-year-old Henry came home from school most every day with a star or some other kind of merit from a class activity. His work would be considered poorly done as compared with the work of a normal five-year-old. For him and the teacher it was considered a "job well done." Eight-year-old brother received C's in reading and never brought home a gold star or other merit. Why should he be denied reward when little brother, who continues to receive nothing but praise from mother and daddy, brings home what older brother views as a "job poorly done?"

For economy of personnel and time and for the value of group interaction counseling by a social worker or psychologist can be carried out in groups. Some parents need to listen in a group. They are not ready for individual work which may be threatening to them. They are unable to shift from the intellectual level to the feeling level. In a group situation the counselor is able to verbalize the feelings of many parents—feelings which parents are afraid to say out loud.

Parents who read extensively know about disagreements among professionals. This creates anxiety. Interaction with the group of parents and the counselor helps relieve tension.

Counseling by a social worker or psychologist should reinforce the teacher's conference, and help answer the problems that cause emotional stress. Parental acceptance of the problems is a process that rarely ends.

## Residential vs. Day School

The basic principles underlying the training of preschool children or school age children in an academic program are the same whether they are carried out in a residential or day school. The need for residential schools becomes apparent when: (1) no acceptable day school facilities are available within the community where the child lives, or (2) parents must travel and wish to start and continue their child in a specific program. Normal children can make school changes; perhaps others cannot, or (3) parents for one reason or another cannot or do not wish to accept the responsibility of reinforcing at home what is learned at school.

> Three-year-old Gary was enrolled in a day school program which met five days a week for two hours. His mother along with the six other parents of children in the class was given home assignments to enhance the school training. In addition she was given an opportunity to demonstrate her ability to teach the children as the other parents and the teacher observed through a one way vision mirror. Constructive criticism was given. Gary's mother was so constituted that she could not carry out any of the assignments. A residential school was recommended and Gary stayed there until he was ready to enroll in a public school classroom. The teacher and the other parents were not critical of Gary's mother. They were understanding.

## Selecting the Children

### THE NEED

There is only one criterion for judging the need for a child and/or his parent to be enrolled in a pre-academic training program. It is that point in time when the assessment of the child reveals a problem that will interfere with future academic success. Language and learning readiness begin at birth.

### AGE

> The parents of a six-month-old retarded child were advised to attend group lectures and conferences. They were guided in such areas as how to provide an environment conducive to learning language and what milestones to expect from their child. After ten months of participation in such a program they both agreed that much of their anxiety had dissipated.

Some parents, usually through no fault of their own and at the urging of their well-meaning physician, wait for the magic day when their child will outgrow his problem. Because this magic day never appears the child may not be properly assessed until he is four or five years of age. At this time he may be found to have a sensory hearing impairment. The time to begin training? Immediately, without long discussions of "Who was to blame for not finding the problem earlier."

Taking a look at preschool programs for children with hearing impairment, we find that more and more children are being accepted at age three. This is a step in the right direction, but why should a child be denied the opportunity of learning language during his first three years of life? By the same token, why should a child spend two years in a physical fitness program designed to improve his motor patterns without attention to assessment and training in language and other pre-academic skills?

Commissioners and administrators of some State Education Agencies are beginning to see the need for critical evaluation of many current school policies: i.e., (1) children must be six years of age as of a certain date to qualify for enrollment in public school first grade programs. Should the gifted child be denied formal educational opportunities just because he does not meet an age deadline? (2) Children should repeat a primary grade if they fail in reading and/or arithmetic. If a child is not promoted because of failure in arithmetic, should he be subjected to the same reading program in which he was successful the year before?

What is the answer? Forward looking educators find the answers in pre-academic and nongraded classes with early emphasis on prevocational assessments and vocational training when indicated.

Children, specifically those with language and/or learning difficulties, should be enrolled in educational programs before the age of six. Pre-academic programs should also accommodate the older child who did not have early training and/or cannot function in academic subjects.

The answer to child and parent problems related to repetition of grades is found in school systems that have developed nongraded programs. Children progress from one level to another with only limited regard to age or grade placement. Susan may be on level four in reading but only level two in arithmetic.

Not every child can achieve standard requirements of many high school programs; a foreign language, geometry. But many of these children can become productive citizens if prevocational assessments are made early (age 12 or 14) and academic efforts are guided by what the child will be *capable of doing*—not what he *cannot* do. The result is vocationally trained students at the completion of high school making less need for vocational training programs after high school.

Habilitation or rehabilitation, children should be enrolled in an appropriate program when their needs are revealed.

### TOILET TRAINING

Enrollment criteria varies whether it be in a normal play school, or classes for the hearing impaired or mentally retarded. Too often the first rule states, "The child must be toilet trained." He either must indicate his bathroom needs to the teacher or better yet be able to take care of his own. Such a rule is paradoxical to those educators who believe remedial training must commence as soon as language and/or learning problems are noted.

The fact that a child is not toilet trained may not correlate with his readiness to learn communication skills. Posing such a standard creates an emotional overlay to the basic problem, because anxious parents try to force a child into a physiological pattern for which he may not be ready.

> Mothers of children under two years of age with severe hearing impairment were enrolled with their children in a language building program. A title of one of the parent-teacher conferences was "How much language can emerge from a wet diaper?"

The solution to accepting children who are not toilet trained is simple. Parents are required to stay within the proximity of the classroom. When an "accident" occurs, the mother is called to remedy the situation.

## PARENT ATTENDANCE

A child's pre-academic success in a training program is dependent upon home reinforcement. Parent attendance at conferences and class observations is imperative. Even though the parent problems may be real, such as lack of transportation or both parents working, enrollment of a child should not be considered unless provisions can be made for a responsible person's attendance. The problems are seldom unsurmountable.

> Mrs. Stevens did not drive a car, but joined a car pool, paid her share, and never missed a conference.
> A working mother and father employed an excellent full day baby sitter-housekeeper who served as a mother substitute in the training program. Home suggestions were discussed and demonstrated by the housekeeper when parents returned from work.

## PHYSICAL HANDICAP

Should a child with cerebral palsy and hearing impairment be refused enrollment in a class for hearing impaired children because he cannot move about like the others? If he is the only orthopedically handicapped child in the vicinity should he be denied training because there are not enough of his "category" to constitute a class? Or, if a child is hyperactive and current medication is not solving the problem, should he be barred from training?

The answers to the foregoing questions are obvious to the teacher who believes that a child should be enrolled in a pre-academic program when he has demonstrated a problem which needs to be alleviated. Just as a mother can be called in to change a diaper, so can a teacher-aide assist in moving the orthopedically handicapped child about the classroom or help manage the hyperactive child who disturbs his classmates.

# Grouping

## GROUP VS. INDIVIDUAL TRAINING

Society is made up of groups: the family, the neighborhood, the country. Within these groups information is shared and new concepts are developed.

The obvious advantage of teaching children in groups is that they learn from one another in a natural setting. Reinforcement of a skill is possible because of the number of times it may be repeated by classmates. In addition, more successes than failures are possible. If one child is known to have extreme difficulty with an activity such as drawing a circle on the blackboard, he may be given the last turn. After he has observed six or eight children perform, he may find the task much easier. In another assignment this child may excell, hence is asked to be the first to perform in order to set the pattern for the remaining children in the group.

Norika, hearing impaired, age 7, arrived from Japan with limited native and no English language. The teacher challenge was to develop Norika's look and listen skills so that she could acquire the Japanese language (both parents spoke it at home) in a three year period at which time the family would return to their country. English, as a second language, obviously had to be introduced. Norika, an intelligent child and older than her classmates, excelled in many nonverbal skills. She was selected first for demonstrating drawing activities and visual sequence stories. She was one of the last to be asked to respond to verbal activities. It was easier for her to give correct answers when she had the advantage of listening to and watching the others. She communicated in Japanese on age level at the end of the three year period.

Working with groups of children in a pre-academic setting provides an environment for teaching the basic concepts that will be needed for future independent study. A total class, for example, can learn the simple concepts of likenesses and differences through such games as follow the leader, matching pictures to objects found in the classroom, aligning the girls on one side of the room and the boys on the other, or listening for the noisemaker that is different. When children can perform in this kind of group activity, they will be ready for seatwork: "Draw a circle around the two that are alike."

No matter how large the group, there may be a need for individualized training. But when should a child be isolated from the class for private instructions? For children below kindergarten with language or learning disorders, regardless of the etiology, there seems to be little or no need for individual tutoring. When a child is ready for seatwork, the advisability of special individual attention will be evidenced. At this point, tutoring may be helpful.

The place for individual training of the very young child is the home. Here he learns through the experience of helping mother make cookies, the names of various dishes, the concept of mix, and basic arithmetic vocabulary (one cup, two teaspoons). He is being trained to attend and remember what is said to him because mother asks him to bring her a cup, to keep mixing while she gets the vanilla, and to measure one teaspoon of vanilla.

## INTER- AND INTRA-GROUP DIFFERENCES

There is a growing need for recognition of and allowance for individual differences. The teacher knows that she must focus on individual differences for it is impossible to form homogenous groups.

The specific deficits found in a group of children with learning difficulties are probably no more numerous than those found in a group of children who are able to succeed academically. The differences lie in the severity of the deficits. The solution is to assign children to pre-academic class levels: *Beginning, Pre-Kindergarten, Kindergarten, Readiness.* Instruction is aimed at individuals as they work in a group.

The following suggestions have been found useful in grouping children during their early years of training.

1. As much as possible, children whose social maturity and intellectual levels are somewhat commensurate should be grouped together.

2. Children with like sensory deficits should be together if they are not multiply handicapped. Some visually impaired must acquire the ability to learn to move about in an environment which cannot be seen. They must develop basic skills that will be needed to learn Braille. Children with hearing impairment must learn to make maximum use of amplification, to care for their hearing aid, and to develop look and listen skills needed for the acquisition of oral language.

3. Multiply handicapped children may move from group to group. One with hearing impairment, cerebral palsy, and global retardation may receive initial training with a group of hearing impaired children. During this period of time, he may also be receiving physical therapy. At a later date when language begins to emerge, education may continue in classes for the retarded with continuation of physical therapy.

4. Children with specific learning disabilities may be grouped together in spite of the great number of intra-group differences in how they learn. The skilled teacher quickly learns to know the assets and deficits of each child; just as she learns to know their names, hair color, and personalities.

## NUMBER OF CHILDREN IN THE CLASS

In years past, educators of the deaf developed a concept that six deaf children was a maximum number for a class, and six became the standard number for many remedial classes. Currently preschool teachers have found no magic in numbers.

Children are placed in classes on the basis of their needs and their ability to conform to group activity. Only five may be enrolled in a class if two of the youngsters are extremely hyperactive or destructive. On the other hand a group of nine four-year-olds may be ideal if all are manageable. Fifteen children with hearing impairment who have had previous training may constitute a group if the primary goal is to prepare them for a regular public school classroom where the numbers often exceed twenty. The ability to learn with a group of fifteen classmates is very different from receiving class instruction with only six peers.

## Class Hours

Rules governing the number of hours children should spend in school are not static. The amount of time is dependent upon how many teachers and classrooms are available, and the needs of the children. Most important is to make certain that these hours are utilized by the teacher in pre-academic learning situations. Free play periods, frequent field trips, and many other activities become parent responsibilities.

Many children are in need of pre-academic training. Few qualified teachers are available. The solution is a structured training program with groups of children in shorter time intervals. One teacher may have twenty-nine children enrolled daily: five in the Beginning Language Class, nine in Kindergarten, and fifteen in her Readiness group.

The goals of the Beginning Language development program for children three years of age or younger are to lay the foundation for future academic skills, and to demonstrate to parents how to reinforce these skills outside of school. Such a class can be successful even though it meets only one hour a day, five days a week. The success, however, is dependent upon parent cooperation which is usually easily obtained, but occasionally not obtained.

Three-year-old Brenda had a severe hearing loss and was enrolled in an excellent one hour daily program. Mother was required to attend tri-weekly group conferences to learn how to teach her daughter at home. This was more time than mother could tolerate so she withdrew Brenda from the class, and enrolled her in a half day program which included bus service. This three-year-old spent three hours in class and two on the bus. No home assignments were required. Mother was content; she had free mornings and was able to shift the responsibility of developing Brenda's language to the new teacher. Without a coordinated school-home program Brenda was at a disadvantage and subsequently demonstrated poor progress.

Four- and five-year-old children enrolled in a Pre-Kindergarten or Kindergarten class are able to attend for longer periods than their younger cohorts. Yet there is a limit to the length of time a teacher may hold their attention. A two hour class which meets five days per week including parent training is adequate.

Five- and six-year-olds in a readiness class are introduced to seat work with work books, paper, and pencil. They profit from a half day program if parent education is included.

# Record Keeping

### MASTER FOLDERS

One master folder including all diagnostic, assessment, and progress report information should be available in a central location such as the admission clerk's or principal's office.

A continuing services sheet stapled to the inside back cover provides a brief chronology of events that does not warrant a standard written report. Dates and summaries of telephone conversations, significant parent comments, and other pertinent information provides a quick reference for the supervisor or principal. Teachers must, of course, be responsible for getting their entries into the master folder.

### TEACHER FOLDERS

No longer does protocol demand that children's cumulative records be locked in a drawer in the principal's office, unavailable to teachers. Educators know that if a person is qualified to teach she must be expected to be equally qualified to make use of professional information. Assessments are made for the teacher and should be readily available to her.

Teacher folders are a duplicate of the master folder with pertinent additional information: samples of a child's language, hand skills, or his behavior on a certain day. This information will assist the teacher when writing her final progress report at the end of the school year.

### ENROLLMENT INFORMATION

A specific day for enrollment of children in classes helps keep records up to date and answers many parent questions (p. 359). At this time the parents: (1) sign, if agreed, releases for photographs, field trips, and requests for information about their child, (2) receive an information sheet on fees, attendance, and reassessments, and (3) receive a handbook of information concerning school policies.

Parents feel more secure if they know what is expected of them.

PROGRESS REPORTS

A progress report written by the teacher (pp. 366-371) is completed for each child at specified dates. If the classes meet during a school year, September through May with an additional summer session, suggested report months are December, May, and the end of the summer session.

TEACHER COMMENT SHEETS

A lined form sheet in the teacher's folder is used to record information that may be helpful for subsequent teachers; additional units that were presented, specific sounds stressed in phonics or articulation training, and the number of reading charts introduced.

Personal data inappropriate for the continuing services sheet in the master folder may also be recorded.

May 12, 1965: Mrs. Collins is very reluctant to work with the group of children while being observed. She teaches much better when demonstrating an activity with one child.

When the child leaves the program, such pertinent data may be transferred to the master folder, labeled CONFIDENTIAL, or it may be relayed to the next teacher.

ROLL BOOKS

As in any organized school program, attendance books (for each class) should be kept by the teacher.

## Physical Attributes of the Room

AVERAGE VS. STERILE ENVIRONMENT

It was visitors' day at Fisher School and three out-of-town teachers observed a group of four-year-old children with specific language and/or learning disabilities. Some children had abnormal EEG records, some did not. At the close of class a discussion of the pre-academic program ensued. One visitor's opening comment was "The brain damaged children we teach are not like your brain damaged children." "Tell me more," said the Fisher School teacher. "Our children cannot learn in your kind of classroom with bulletin boards, children's work displayed on the peg board, flowers on your desk, and one wall with windows. We painted our walls grey and constructed cubicles of the same color for each child. We could not conceive of a child attending to what was asked him if the teacher wore a flowered blouse like yours and colorful jewelry."

Two questions were asked of these teachers who believed in a sterile environment. (1) "How old are your children?" The answer was

"Eight through fourteen years." (2) "Did they have any preschool training?" The answer was, "No."

Unfortunately some children who are inclined to be hyperactive are allowed to become undisciplined, are denied enrollment in preacademic or early academic programs and often do not receive adequate medical attention until they are eight years of age or older. At this stage in their life they may need the sterile type teaching environment but they need a great deal more. What they needed was early identification, assessment, and early pre-academic training.

Knowing that hyperactive distractible children have difficulty learning in regular classrooms has led several investigators to conduct pilot studies. They have attempted to demonstrate whether or not there is a need for a sterile environment. To date no scientific research has isolated sterility of a classroom environment as the prime ingredient for the successful teaching of hyperactive, distractible children.

Clinical experience of the author has demonstrated that children (other than schizophrenic-autistic) under five years of age, and who have exceedingly short attention spans do adjust to the kind of environment that is normal for any nursery or kindergarten student. The fact that they are placed at early ages in a situation where they are accepted, experience more successes than failures at school and at home, benefit from continued care of a physician, and are instructed by qualified teachers is probably reason enough, to the casual observer, why "they are not like other brain injured children."

DESKS, TABLES, OR CUBICLES

The manner in which children are seated in a classroom is dependent upon many factors; age of the students, size of the room, behavior of the children, physical problems, and most of all the teacher's judgment of what she knows is best.

One teacher may choose to have tables which measure approximately eight feet by two and one-half feet. They are arranged in an L or U shape or distributed to various areas of the room.

Another teacher may find that individual desks with separate chairs are a more satisfactory arrangement, so that the children may be less distracted by classmates. In addition she may approve of storage space in the desk, and the ease with which desks may be moved about the room.

Certain attached seat and desk combinations have not proved particularly satisfactory. The surface space of the desk top is too small and is often made to slant toward the child. Such a design, though it may provide better vision and posture, allows pencils and crayons to roll to the floor or child's lap. The storage space under the chair is not adequate and the individual chairs are inconvenient to move for activities in other parts of the room.

Cubicles are probably not warranted for children in most pre-academic, preschool programs. At this stage of development children must learn to conform in groups and to make use of their skills within the group. To isolate them at this age is not normal, because it deprives them of the opportunity to learn to develop self-discipline with peers and adults.

In readiness, first grade or non-graded class, the need for cubicles may be very realistic for some children. At this level they are beginning to do independent seat work that requires them to attend to tasks for a longer period of time. Three or four cubicles at one end of the room probably will be adequate for a class of eight to fifteen children. Only those who need to develop powers of concentration, or who, apparently are unable to study except under conditions of minimal visual and auditory distraction, will require isolation. The use of a cubicle, then, becomes not much more than what it means to the adult who prefers to study in a quiet library or in a carrel within the library.

## Teaching Materials

### TEACH CHILDREN NOT MATERIALS

To provide an environment conducive to learning, a teacher will need motivational materials to hold the child's interest. What is more, she will have no problem locating games and toys that will command attention during a learning situation. It is important to note, however, that some teachers may become so carried away with new table games, party favors, hand puppets, and puzzles that they forget they are to teach children and not materials.

Motivational materials in school are used to assist the development of new skills or to impart information; they are not primarily for entertainment. Hours outside of school should be spent in the kinds of amusements that help a child gain satisfaction through the repetition of tasks he has already mastered.

During conference hours parents are told which games the children can play well. Suggestions are also made as to the best kind of instructional and creative toys and materials parents may purchase.

## Teacher Aides

Scheduling teacher-parent conferences during class time is desirable, so that parents need not make arrangements for transportation at a different hour. A substitute teacher will be needed to carry on the activities with the children while the regular teacher is in conference. The substitute may be a paid teacher-aide or a volunteer aide.

To assure that the children will be given constructive work in the absence of the teacher, an appropriate "Handbook of Information for Teacher-Aides" should be prepared. The aide must have an opportunity to read the handbook, discuss its contents, and observe the class before taking over her responsibilities.

## Student Teaching

Children with specific learning disabilities must be taught by qualified teachers. Student teachers on their own are not qualified. Without daily guidance they may err in one or more teaching principles which means they may perpetuate and practice their errors.

Student training programs include appropriate course work, observation of teaching techniques, attendance at parent conferences, and practice teaching. Most important is supervision by the qualified teacher.

## SUMMARY

Modern educators no longer debate the implications of such arbitrary dogma as "Children are not ready for school until age six," "No more than six children shall be enrolled in a class for the deaf," or "Day schools are superior to residential schools." The emphasis is placed on early training in pre-academic programs which include a sound educational philosophy, appropriate curriculums and material, and qualified teachers. Furthermore, the development of these kinds of programs will provide a more controlled environment for scientists interested in researching the efficiency of various educational training techniques.

# 7

# *Pre-Academic Curriculum Guide*

I am not really unhappy with your training program, but it disturbed me yesterday when Paul brought home the neatly colored picture of the balloon man and proceeded to name the colors of the various balloons. He could count them, too. Now, you know that Paul has been in your program for two years, but what you probably do not know is that I have saved most of his school work. He now has a collection of five pictures of the same balloon man.

The parent had said enough. The need for a curriculum guide utilizing various levels of achievement with specific motivational materials for each level was clearly indicated.

## PURPOSE

The pre-academic curriculum guide is designed to teach the skills needed for academic success—oral and written language, good work habits, and appropriate social living relationships. These skills become the foundation for formal education as defined by a first grade curriculum guide.

Proficiency in oral and written language is basic to academic success. This means translation of the skills needed for first grade subject matter to a pre-academic level.

To insure appropriate use of the dexterity needed for academic success, good work habits must be acquired. Careful listening, proper use of time, recognition of errors, and working independently in groups are pertinent to academic achievement.

To develop acceptable interpersonal relationships with people, chil-

110

dren must be guided toward developing self-confidence, accepting responsibility, sharing ideas and materials, conforming to social rules of the group, maintaining neatness, cleanliness, and respect for the rights of others.

The pre-academic curriculum is a systematized guide which provides a structured approach to training. Children make better use of their potential when learning is not left to chance. The integral parts of the guide are open-ended, allowing the teacher to develop additional teaching techniques and to create new materials.

The first requisite of the pre-academic curriculum guide is to meet the needs of any child for whom basic instruction for future academic success is desirable. It must accommodate children with hearing impairment, aphasia, specific learning disabilities, cerebral palsy, mental retardation, blindness, and multiple handicaps, as well as the normal or gifted child.

## LEVELS

The curriculum guide covers a four year period, each year representing a specific class level; *Beginning, Pre-Kindergarten, Kindergarten,* and *Readiness.* Pre-training classes are offered to parents before their children are enrolled in a class.

Children entering a training program are placed on a level as compatible as possible with their chronological age, social age, and abilities. Advancement in various pre-academic subjects is based on individual progress. This means that a child may be ready for a kindergarten class in all but number concepts, but he is not held back a year because of this deficit. On the contrary, a promotion is given because the kindergarten teacher will be cognizant of his arithmetic readiness level. He will continue to acquire new information through new units of study, yet progress at his learning rate in arithmetic.

## Pre-Training Class

Pre-training classes are designed for parents whose children demonstrate deficits in oral language, speech, and/or learning. The objectives of these classes which meet one hour for five days are: (1) to define and explain normal and abnormal language, speech, and learning development, (2) to outline a home training program if the child must be placed on a waiting list or if he is not ready for classroom instruction, (3) to discuss the basic philosophy of the training program if the child is a candidate, (4) to compare and contrast the philosophy and methods of this program with others, (5) to provide each parent with a *Hand-*

*book of Information* which describes the school policies, activities, and parent participation, and (6) to answer parents' questions.

At the completion of the Pre-Training Class all parents enrolling their children in the pre-academic program will have comparable information which will prepare them for future teacher-parent conferences. They will be ready to follow the teacher's instructions for reinforcing at home the language and learning skills taught at school.

## Beginning Level

The beginning level includes suggestions for teaching pre-academic skills to children who function like three-year-olds. The motivational materials, games, and nursery rhymes also are common to this level.

In general, children with specific learning disabilities and no auditory sensory impairment enroll at the Beginning Level sometime in their third year of life. Children with auditory sensory impairment or global retardation should be assessed and placed in an appropriate program prior to this age. (See Chapters 9 and 10.)

With appropriate selection of motivational materials, the teacher of older retarded children may find that the Beginning Level is a good starting point.

Nursery school teachers of normal or gifted three-year-olds begin at this level. Because of the intellectual prowess of these youngsters there will be a rapid need for added vocabulary and broadening of concepts.

> It was cookie and juice time in a nursery school composed of children well endowed intellectually. Three-year-old Joan took a bite from her round cookie and said, "Look, Miss Young, a half moon."

## Pre-Kindergarten Level

The assumption is made that children entering the Pre-Kindergarten program will have been taught and/or exposed to the vocabulary and pre-academic skills presented in the curriculum of the Beginning Level. If this level has been by-passed, the teacher provides the parent with three sections from the Beginning Level curriculum guide: vocabulary, games, and home training.

## Kindergarten Level

Kindergarten is an extension of Pre-Kindergarten.

## Readiness Level

The readiness level expands into a school year that which is taught in the first nine weeks of a beginning academic program (first grade).

The advantages are two fold: (1) Clinical experience has identified a need for many youngsters to have an added year of pre-academic training. This year allows for maturation and reinforcement of skills needed for first grade achievement. (2) Children with specific learning problems and hearing impairment will have a head start. They will feel more secure and begin their first academic year with successes.

## ORGANIZATION OF THE GUIDE

The Beginning Level and the levels that follow include: (1) descriptive behavior of children in the various age groups, (2) activities related to oral language, (3) activities related to avenues of learning, (4) activities and goals for teaching pre-academic subjects, (5) proposed calendar for presenting new units, (6) a sample lesson plan for each level, (7) a variety of units for each level including, (a) classroom activities adapted from specific motivational materials, (b) basic vocabulary, (c) games, stories, songs, and nursery rhymes, and (d) home training hints for parents.

### Descriptive Behavior

Developmental data is itemized according to chronological age and forms the introduction to each level. Teachers use this information to help select appropriate toys and games as well as a baseline for the growth and development characteristics of the children in her class.

### Language Skills

The same outline that appears on the Worksheet (p. 343) of the *Language and Learning Assessment: For Training* has been adapted to this section of the curriculum. Techniques are presented to help children develop the four language systems; phonemic, semantic, syntactic, and morphologic.

### Avenues of Learning

The primary senses involved in learning oral and written language skills are audition and vision. Within these modalities are sensation, perception, memory-retrieval, attention, and integration. Other senses—tactile, olfactory, and kinesthetic are not specifically treated in this text but general references do occur, particularly in the curriculum guide.

It is not uncommon for a teacher unwittingly to stress one modality at the expense of another. She may become engrossed in matching pictures, telling stories by placing specific scenes in sequence and hiding one object from a group of objects for the children to guess what is missing (all good training techniques to strengthen the visual modality). However, she will be reminded through periodic reference to the guide that the auditory avenues must also be strengthened.

Goals and examples in the areas of memory-retrieval, visual motor perception, and social maturity are included. As the teacher develops her total program, she will add many of her own ideas to this section.

## Teaching Pre-Academic Subjects

Academic success is measured not only by a child's oral language but also by his reading comprehension, writing, arithmetic, and spelling aptitudes. Vocabulary and the skills needed to accomplish these subjects are acquired without special training by some children in their preschool years. Others reach first grade unprepared because of learning disabilities and/or lack of opportunity.

Each level in the curriculum guide provides a section titled *Pre-academic Subjects* and includes: suggestions for teaching reading, spelling, writing, and number readiness.

## Proposed Calendar for Teaching Units

Units in the curriculum guide are arbitrarily assigned topics that fit both age level and teaching needs. Suggestions are made, relative to the length of time spent on a unit and the month of the year in which the unit is introduced.

The addition or deletion of units is at the discretion of the teacher. Geographic locations, cultural differences, and chronological age may alter the choice of units. For the new teacher, however, the basic format aids in structuring her program for the year.

## Sample Lesson Plans

For additional structuring of her program, the new teacher has access to a sample lesson plan for each level.

## The Unit

Learning is more efficient and retention better when the materials to be learned are meaningful and based upon experience. Presenting units such as family, workers, and transportation provides experiences, motivation and structure in a pre-academic training program.

Teachers have specific reasons for using the unit approach to lesson planning:

1. School activities; a trip to the pet shop; slides, movies or pic-

tures of the students' pets; and story books about kittens, dogs, and horses, are easily developed around a unit.

2. Classroom learning is carried over into the home in a functional yet organized manner.

3. Permanent acquisition of materials is possible for individual units and may become a project of parents as well as teachers. Packing the games, books, toys and written suggestions in appropriately labeled boxes makes for organized storage.

4. Because all materials related to a specific unit are stored together, they will not be utilized in any other unit unless for review purposes.

Each unit includes sections on: (1) classroom activities, (2) vocabulary, (3) games, stories and songs, and (4) home training.

## CLASSROOM ACTIVITIES

Motivational materials and techniques are important tools in developing language and shaping learning, but teachers sometimes overlook the simple, inexpensive materials available to them. At the beginning of each unit the teacher is supplied with a section that lists ten items common to any classroom or school and how each may be used to teach a skill or skills to a specific age group.

## VOCABULARY

Each unit contains a basic vocabulary which relates to the unit and to the skills being taught. The teacher will add additional words of her choosing, but will find that a basic vocabulary has the following advantages.

1. When a child moves from one level to another, the teacher will know which basic words he has been taught and/or exposed to.

2. If a child first enters a program at the Kindergarten level, his parents will be given the basic vocabulary that was presented on the Beginning level and Pre-Kindergarten level.

3. Once a child learns the meaning of a concrete word, the concept can be generalized to words not in the basic vocabulary—from "light" to "light bulb" to a "plant bulb."

> Miss Williams was explaining to her class the process of planting a bulb. She showed them a tin can and said they would go outside and find some dirt. Then they would plant the bulb. She turned the container upside down and asked the class why it had little holes in the bottom. Debbie answered, "To let the light shine through." A new meaning for bulb (plant) had not yet been learned.

## GAMES, STORIES, SONGS, AND NURSERY RHYMES

The fact that a child cannot talk or perform motor-wise on age level makes him stand out from his group as different. If parents or teachers allow his disability to interfere with peer play, he will become even more deviant.

Children with language and/or learning difficulties should be taught or at least exposed to the same songs, nursery rhymes, circle games, poems, and stories that are common to their age group. They will be rewarded by being able to participate in a game of Drop the Handkerchief at their cousin's birthday party, or by chanting "Three Blind Mice" with the children in the neighborhood. Knowing how to participate in some of the things their friends do will allow them to develop a self concept of being like others rather than always somehow different.

It is hoped that in memorizing songs and poems, saying them aloud, and benefiting from the auditory feedback, children will be aided in acquiring the language code. There is no current research to contraindicate the possibility.

In this section of the curriculum guide the teacher should select games, songs, and nursery rhymes that are applicable to each unit.

### HOME TRAINING HINTS FOR PARENTS

Reinforcement of skills learned and enrichment of concepts must be a continuing process between home and school. The teacher cannot do it all.

Oral and written instructions as to how the total family can participate in home training activities are necessary. Most parents do not consider themselves teachers, hence need guidance and specific suggestions as to how they might help their children out of school hours.

> Parents were asked to write the different ways in which the concept of *up and down* could be taught at home. Just a few of their suggestions were: (1) Go *upstairs* and get my purse. Go *downstairs* and see if baby sister is all right. (2) Brush your teeth *up* and *down*. (3) While child is swinging, parents call out *up—down* to the appropriate action.

## SUMMARY

The effects of a planned pre-academic program for children with language and/or learning disorders has not been researched. Until contraindicated we must assume that systems related to learning can be re-ordered. Furthermore, we need qualified teachers to develop new methods of teaching as well as to activate the methods we now have. One thing is clear—teachers must have a systematized program if they are to be efficient and at ease in a teaching situation. The curriculum guide provides this kind of program with an eclectic system and a basic philosophy.

# 8

# Teaching Principles and Techniques

## USING THE CURRICULUM GUIDE

How language evolves or how learning takes place are moot questions. The fact that answers are not readily available does not deter educators from developing training programs to meet children's needs. Over the years the author, with the help of many teacher clinicians, developed a pre-academic curriculum guide primarily for children wtih language and/or learning deficits.

The curriculum was designed to help the teacher shape children's learning in skills which are prerequisite to formal academic training. Basic questions repeatedly were asked as the guide developed: What are the skills needed to succeed in oral and written language as taught in the first grade? How can these skills be translated to lower chronological or mental age levels?

Specifically, what vocabulary will prepare a child for modern mathematics? What eye-hand coordination is needed for cursive writing? What perceptual-motor and/or memory skills are basic to learning to read?

Although originally designed for preschool children with language and/or learning disorders, the curriculum guide in the hands of a skilled teacher can be used in any training program; Head Start, nursery schools for the normal or gifted, or day care centers. If the teacher is cognizant of basic teaching principles and techniques, she will be able to adapt the guide to any preschool or pre-academic environment.

## Know the Entire Curriculum Guide

Full use of the curriculum guide is attainable only if the teacher knows what has gone on before, that which is going on now, and what is ahead.

117

For the unit on pets, Anne brought a parakeet to class for Show and Tell. The teacher, familiar with the total curriculum guide, remembered the preceding units of home, clothing, and family. This was an opportunity to assess the children's retention of previously learned concepts. "How many legs does a bird have?" "How many legs does a man have?" "What does a man wear that a lady does not wear?" Because the teacher is familiar with subsequent units in the guide she may lay ground work for future study of color shades. "Children, look at the beautifully colored feathers on this bird. Some are light blue and some are dark blue. Let's remember this bird because some day we will be talking about these shades of color."

# Know Each Child

The teacher is responsible for the academic achievement and welfare of the children during school hours. This is a large injunction unless the teacher is aware of each child's assets and deficits. Without adequate assessments a teacher will find herself spending days—weeks—months in an attempt to find each child's level of functioning in specific modalities of language and learning. Costly time is lost in light of concept and skill development.

Every teacher will have specific assessments on each child: language levels, assets and deficits in sensation, memory-retrieval, attention, and integration. Case history studies will furnish additional information: Is the child sensitive to punishment? Is he afraid of dogs or other animals? Does he have any food allergies?

Knowing details of each child's behavior provides the framework and starting point of pre-academic instruction.

# Collecting Materials

The listing, purchasing, classifying, and storing of materials to be used in a pre-academic program is a time-consuming project. Selection of sturdy equipment and subsequent care of all items will be a saving for each year's budget.

In addition to ready-made motivational materials, the teacher will find unlimited use for a picture and materials file (p. 391).

# Developing a Lesson Plan

The particular stimuli which a teacher selects to bring particular behavior under control is predetermined before the class meets. She is able to develop lesson plans which serve as a guide for day-to-day teaching because she knows what the children have been taught and/or exposed to.

Some children who come to school for the first time are fearful of the new surroundings. Careful planning of the room decor and activities during the first week of school will help allay the anxiety. Motivational materials familiar to the children are in conspicuous places throughout the classroom. There may be large pictures of pets, paper cups and a can of juice in full view, a doll, and small cars.

Children are comfortable in familiar surroundings but also like the thrill of something new. A film strip, a phonograph record, or a unique hand puppet puts them at ease. When the class is over, they are pleased to take something home; their art work for the day, a note to mother and daddy, or a gold star pasted on the back of their hand.

## THE UNIT

The teacher begins her daily or weekly lesson planning by selecting or continuing to use the appropriate unit. For purposes of the following discussion, the Clothing Unit from the Beginning Language Level is described.

### MOTIVATIONAL MATERIALS

Motivational materials which are collected by teachers over the years are stored in boxes appropriately labeled as to class level and unit. Each teacher is acquainted with the toys and games available in the storage area, and how they can be used to improve language, learning, and social skills.

When the clothing unit is introduced, the teacher may select a doll's trunk filled with duplicate clothing, a family of dolls, and a box of real-life dress-up clothes. The usual paper cups and can of juice or milk are available if refreshments are served.

### VOCABULARY

The basic vocabulary words which the children will be taught and/or exposed to are selected. The first lesson includes the noun words *clothes, shoes, socks, coat, dress, shirt, pants, zipper, button, hat, slip, petticoat, jacket,* and *purse;* basic phrases, *Put it on, Take it off, Hang it up;* review words, *one, two, three, four, five;* and the children's own and each other's names.

### GAMES, STORIES, SONGS, AND NURSERY RHYMES

Under the appropriate heading in each unit, games, stories, songs, and nursery rhymes should be selected by the teacher. To reinforce vocabulary learning in the lesson plan under discussion, the teacher may select the acting-out song, "This is the way we put on our dress, put on our dress . . ."

### MODALITIES OF LANGUAGE AND LEARNING

To insure teaching the appropriate semantic and structural features of oral language and to insure utilization of techniques to improve learning skills, the teacher refers frequently to the sections *Language Skills* and *Avenues of Learning* which accompany each level.

### PRE-ACADEMIC SUBJECTS

Techniques for teaching reading, writing, spelling, and arithmetic readiness skills are found in the section of the curriculum guide labeled *Pre-Academic Subjects.* The teacher uses this section not only for general suggestions, but also for setting the goals to be met by the children in her class.

# PARENT PARTICIPATION

Teaching parents techniques and providing them with information related to language and learning is accomplished primarily through group and individual conferences.

## Group Conferences

Conferences, early in the school year, lay the ground rules for the teacher and parents:

1. Conferences are scheduled at a specific time on certain days. In general, the younger the children and the shorter the class session, the greater the number of weekly conferences. For the Beginning Language Development Class the teacher may plan three fifteen minute sessions the first week, two for the remainder of the month and only one or two fifteen to thirty minute blocks of time per week for the rest of the school year. For older children in a half day program, a one half hour period per week may suffice.

2. Parents or the person who cares for the child must attend the conferences or their respective children will be placed on a waiting list.

3. Further reasons for dismissing a child from the program can be listed: excessive absence from class when other children are on a waiting list, readiness for another program.

4. A volunteer or teacher-aide carries out a prepared activity while the teacher is conducting parent conferences. Parents are assured that their children are in a learning as opposed to a baby-sitting environment when the teacher-aide is conducting class.

5. Parents who have children with seizures or children who are not toilet trained must remain in the waiting room where they can be reached for emergencies.

6. Schedules of school holidays are circulated.

7. In some instances parents may be asked to furnish the refresh-

ments. The teacher usually chooses the food and drink which is applicable to her lesson plan, for instance, animal cookies may be served for review of units on farm and wild animals.

8. The teacher and/or parents should provide answers to the following questions:

a. Are the children allowed to have their birthday parties at school? Are presents to be given?

b. Are parents allowed to give teachers gifts at Christmas time or the end of the school year?

c. Are parents to call the teacher by the first or given name? (A good policy is to stay professional and avoid the use of first names for teachers as well as parents.)

d. Does the teacher accept phone calls at her home, or can she provide the parents with a time schedule when she can be reached at school?

A child's academic success depends upon the teacher's ability to find the child's functioning level in his language and learning skills and to keep him moving ahead. Furthermore, his success is dependent upon the teacher's ability to translate her teaching techniques to parents who reinforce learning at home. Each parent conference, then, is structured to meet the needs of the week. For example:

1. Announcements. Dates of field trips, costumes for the Halloween party, or dates school will be closed.

2. Assignments. (a) A list of basic vocabulary being used in class. For example, a request that parents write all the ways in which the concept of "cold" could be generalized. They may decide to do this as a group activity in the coffee shop while waiting for their children to be dismissed from class. (b) Outside reading. (c) The date and place of an important lecture for parents. (d) Home training suggestions.

3. Topics for Discussion (p. 360). The teacher defines and discusses terms: language, speech, short term memory. She informs parents about other programs in the vicinity, what is expected of a child when he enters first grade, or what parents should do when they cannot understand their child.

4. Question and Answer Period. Some of the questions may be carried over to the next conference.

Each parent was asked to write a brief report of the value of group teacher-parent conferences.

Dear Miss Solomon: Since Herbert started to school I have noticed much progress in his speech. He is talking more voluntarily. Before, he would only say what he was told to say. About his pronunciation of words— before you had told us in group conference not to correct but to accept, I was always correcting him. When I corrected him, he would appear to be confused, have hurt feelings or at times even become angry with me . . .

Since I have stopped correcting him, his pronunciation is improving. There are times I cannot understand and I will say, "Herbert, Mommy doesn't know. Will you show me?" and he will say "Yeah" (not yes) and take me by the hand. When I cannot understand what Herbert says, I try to get the word interpreted so next time I hear it I will know what it is . . . Also at our individual conference I want to discuss with you about getting records for him. That is one thing he will "stay with" for any length of time . . .

I hope I have included in this letter what you wanted and that it will be helpful to you.

Sincerely, Mrs. Hazel Boone

Parents need guidance in carrying out at home the teaching principles used at school. Some parents need to be "spoon fed" while others develop their own techniques and plans for action. Success of the pre-academic program is dependent upon cooperation and insight of parents.

## Individual Conferences

The behavior of parents in a group conference often varies as much as the behavior of children in a classroom. One parent may need more detailed information than warrants the time in a group conference. Some may need constant support for their efforts or they may need answers to questions that apply only to their children. For these reasons individual conferences are held at the discretion of the teacher. She may decide to schedule a specific number for each parent during the school year and/or at the parent's request.

## Parent Observations

Language is a day-long activity and not meant to be taught to a child one hour a day, five days a week. Parent-teacher discussion groups serve as one medium for helping parents become teachers in the home. Other media are observations of classroom activities and actual participation in the training program.

Neither visitors nor parents should be allowed to observe a classroom procedure without a competent person to explain the basic educational philosophy and the purpose of the activities being observed. Without such explanations, observers may view the program as a glorified nursery or play school or misinterpret the teacher's purpose underlying each activity.

An observation booth large enough to accommodate as many as sixteen persons and separated from the classroom by a one-way vision mirror is desirable. In this booth parents are asked to observe specific aspects of teaching which may be helpful in planning home training programs as well as gaining a better understanding of their children.

On the assigned day for observation, each parent is given a sheet of paper with specific questions to be answered.

1. What new vocabulary word was introduced today?
2. In how many different activities was it presented?
3. How can you reinforce vocabulary learning at home?

or:

1. What successes did your child have today?
2. What were his failures?
3. How did the teacher handle the failures? (Because the teacher knows each child's functioning level, she can easily demonstrate successes and failures.)

The answer sheets are collected following which the parents and teacher may meet to discuss the observations. If time is not available, the comments can be presented at the next group conference.

## Parents Teach

Some parents are reticent about demonstrating their teaching skills before others. Fear of failure may be very real because mothers do not normally work with seven or fifteen children at one specified time or while under observation. The astute teacher will allow a parent to choose the number of children and the activity to be demonstrated. As the parents gain more confidence, the teacher can provide more difficult assignments.

> Mrs. Barnette chose an activity which would develop new concepts with already known words and phrases: *buttons, cut, roll, eyes, nose, mouth, pretend, Put it in, It's hot, It's cold.* She brought two boxes to class. In one was prepared gingerbread dough. The children rolled it out, *cut* with the cookie cutter, and appropriately placed raisins for *eyes, nose, mouth,* and *buttons.* The children discussed whether the dough was *hot* or *cold* and then the gingerbread men were placed in a *pretend* oven. In the second box, Mrs. Barnette had gingerbread men that she had previously baked. A discussion of the finished product followed.

At the conclusion of the activity, the other parents and the teacher discussed successful teaching techniques and offered constructive criticism.

## SHAPING LEARNING

A child's abilities to reason and solve problems develop as he matures, but his inadequate environment and/or language and learning skills may accelerate or slow him down. Teachers and parents have a responsibility to help children achieve and maintain their learning rate. Such is accomplished only if basic principles of how we learn are observed.

# Motivation

Performance occurs because of a need or inducement (intrinsic or extrinsic) to perform—motivation. Some teachers assume that motivation transpires only with extrinsic or tangible rewards: a smile, a gold star, a piece of candy. Intrinsic rewards, as a means of inducing children to learn, are frequently ignored.

## EXTRINSIC REWARDS

Adults are motivated to work for direct rewards in life: a pay check, vacation, new car, or praise. We assume that little children also want something tangible for their efforts: their names on the blackboard, a flower seal on their written work, or praise.

> Mrs. Rister found that a quick reward maintained motivation. In activities which required class participation in giving appropriate responses she would have the children sit on the floor when they answered correctly and stay in their seats if they failed to answer correctly. Or, they all stood in a line and those who failed moved to the end of the line.

It is not unusual to find children who are apparently motivated just by the presence of the teacher. What are the penalties if the teacher is the primary source of extrinsic reinforcement? The children may become so dependent upon her that future independent study skills will be acquired with difficulty. Furthermore, with some children, responses to specific motivational techniques—praise or a gold star—quickly become extinct. Because of the dilemma, teachers often spend too many hours searching for new rewards. Extrinsic motivational techniques are desirable but should be used sparingly.

## INTRINSIC REWARDS

To succeed in independent study, children must become intrinsically motivated. This is accomplished through a method of self discovery which leads to satisfaction and an inducement to try the next step.

> Jamie places the horse in the appropriate place in the form board and looks to the teacher for some extrinsic reward. With each successive trial he asks for approbation. George, with the same form board, selects an animal and after the third error succeeds in correct placement. He smiles, picks it up, looks it over and replaces it. Another animal is selected. This time George looks for a cue to help him make the correct response. When the board is complete, he asks the teacher for another one.

George is gaining intrinsic recompense from learning the basic principles underlying the problem to be solved. He is preparing himself for independent study. Jamie is still immature in his motivational needs, but with the help of the teacher and parents, his inner satisfactions will develop.

> Mrs. Sunkle assigns seat work to her class of seven and announces that no discussion will take place until each child has finished his assignment. She walks by every desk and stops by Jamie who is making an error. She points out the clue to the correct response, but no more is said. Jamie sees the relationship, smiles and moves on to the next problem.

What techniques can be employed to help a child obtain satisfaction from his own discovery?

1. He should be provided with more successes than failures. An assignment should begin at his functional level and stop just short of his tolerance level.

2. Teachers often intersperse the sandwich method of teaching; a failure between two successes. Billy, in a lesson stressing short term visual memory, recalls two pictures, is tested with three and fails. He has another try with two which ends in a success.

3. If a child has not learned to hop on one foot, he should not be forced to demonstrate his failure every day. He can jump on two feet and hop on one with the help of the teacher.

4. Some children's manuscript and cursive writing deteriorates as they move across a page. The insightful teacher will cut the paper in half and give credit for half a page well done. With time and practice the width of the paper is increased.

5. When papers are graded, an X is placed by the correct response leaving the errors blank. With more correct responses the number of X's increases.

6. Teachers and parents make every effort to understand what a child says. Failure to communicate his needs leads to a lowered verbal output.

7. Allowing a child justifiable time may lead to the completion of an otherwise unsuccessful assignment. Children can not work at the same rate in a classroom any more than unselected groups of boys can finish a race in the same length of time.

8. The teacher who presents tiny steps each day toward a distant goal will find her children demonstrating the value of intrinsic reward. Giant steps are meant for a limited number of children, and those left behind soon pall because they cannot succeed when bits are omitted. Motivation from within is built upon sequential successes.

## Decrease or Circumvent Deficits

Whether a deficit in an avenue of learning, such as memory, can be identified and trained is unanswerable. But until psychoneurophysiological research produces an answer, the teacher must provide diagnostic training techniques in her classroom.

Armed with the results of language and learning assessments and her own judgments, a teacher can recognize children who demonstrate greater deficits in some areas of learning than in others. If the liability lies in short term auditory memory, the teacher discovers the kind and amount of information a child can remember. Through teaching techniques, she attempts to improve the child's memory for auditory events. The success of these techniques and/or maturation is revealed in future reassessments as well as classroom observations. If inadequate gains are made, the teacher continues her attempts to improve auditory recall, but gives out information in short phrases and sentences; apparently the only way in which some children retain information.

## Repetition

### DRILL

Repetition of the stimulus is a basic tenet of learning and one of its simplest forms is drill. In learning to rote-count a child says his numbers in sequence over and over again. The artful teachers and parents do not expect a child to sit for fifteen minutes or longer until he learns to count to a certain number. Instead, a method of distributive teaching is applied wherein drill is interspersed with other activities. Furthermore, rote counting is carried out in real life situations.

> Miss Young has her children count those present during roll call and recount to test their accuracy. The room chairman for the day counts the sheets of paper to be distributed, the number of cups needed for juice or milk, and the number of match sticks needed to construct a house on paper. The class drills on numbers by referring to the calendar; the number of days in the month, the number of days past, and the dates that are to come.

### SAYING IT IN A DIFFERENT WAY

Group teaching has the advantages of allowing a child to hear one concept or one story expressed in a variety of ways. Repetition in such a situation enhances learning.

> Mrs. Rister selects three or more pictures which in sequence tell a story. Each child develops one oral sentence per picture then names the story. Children who have difficulty generating sentences or finding words are chosen last. They will have a variety of words and statements from which to choose.

OVERTEACHING

For lack of another activity, or because children like to play the same game over and over, a teacher may say, "Yes, you may play musical chairs." Although the children may gain additional information incidentally, they could learn more if the teacher would add something new.

Games and activities should not always happen the same way. Even if the rules or the goals of the activity are changed, the children view it as the same game.

Miss Solomon introduces new language concepts every time the children play musical chairs. In the beginning stages of language development they may be told to "Listen to the music. Walk, but sit down when the music stops." As the children acquire more language the directions may be, "Who will be first? Second?" Then. "Walk to the *rhythm* of the music until it stops. Sit on the *vacant* chair closest to you." At the completion of the game the teacher may ask, "Who won?" "Who was last?" "How do you know that everyone played fairly?"

Mrs. Lee's children like to play picture lotto. The first goal may be comprehension of the names of the pictures; second, the function of the objects; third, making a sentence; and fourth, a lesson in phonics. "This picture of *corn* starts with the same first sound in *cabbage*."

## Intentional vs. Incidental Learning

The teacher asked John to define a barn. He said he couldn't, but teacher kept insisting he try. When the pressure seemed too much for John, she asked Louise to define a barn and received a suitable description. It was the teacher's intention to help John learn the definition by listening to Louise. But John was so embarrassed with failure that he didn't listen to Louise. Incidental learning, however, did take place, for from his point of view he decided that teachers are mean, that girls are smarter than boys, and school is not much fun.

Incidental learning occurs throughout the day, frequently without the knowledge of teachers or parents. Not all of it is undesirable, much is good.

Because Bill had such difficulty learning new vocabulary words, his mother introduced three new words each day. When the diagnostician was assessing ability to define, he presented the word *puddle*. Bill was quick to respond, "My mother didn't teach me that word yet." Bill knew from incidental learning that new words were being taught by mother.

Rhonda with severe hearing impairment was enrolled in a second grade class. The teacher noticed that she never responded to the dismissal bell, so asked her if she heard it. "What bell?" asked Rhonda. "And who rings it?" The teacher replied, "The class bell that is rung from the principal's office." Not knowing that there was a bell in the classroom and thinking the teacher meant that it sounded only in the principal's office, Rhonda replied, "Oh, I couldn't hear it that far away." Rhonda had learned on her own the importance of distance to hearing.

Intentional and incidental learning are extremes of one dimension, the latter occurring under minimal conditions of reinforcement. In general, low motivation is better for incidental learning and high motivation for intentional learning.

Sometimes it is not the child's inability to learn, but his inability to learn what we want to teach him. This may be indirectly a result of the teacher's manner in presenting the material. To fortify intentional learning she must gain the attention of the children. This may be accomplished by a change in the rate, pitch, or loudness of her voice. Or, attention may be gained by means of a shift in activities.

## Discipline

Discipline, in the form of punishment; a spanking, social isolation, oral reproval, or a mouthwashing with soap has been used through the ages. Why one or more forms of such punishment are appropriate for some children and not others, and appropriate only some of the time, is unanswerable. The danger of administering such punishment lies in the abnormal states of fear or anxiety some children exhibit.

The best methods of helping children conform to rules is to attempt to avoid situations which provoke unsociable behavior. If a child is given more successes than failures in daily activities, is kept busy, and is satisfied with himself, he is not likely to become incorrigible. The following list of "Do's" points to ways in which a child's social conduct and work habits become acceptable:

1. Speak to a child with words he understands.

2. Give only as many oral directions as he can remember.

3. Shift activities when signs of rowdiness appear. The teacher observes that Stephen, on new medication, is becoming restless at his desk. She introduces a running or hopping game for all the class. In a short period of time Stephen is ready to do his seat work.

4. Set rules for home and school which must be adhered to. Consequences for disobeying the rules should be clearly understood and faithfully carried out.

5. Take a positive approach and talk in positive terms. "Everyone is to walk down the hall." Not, "Everyone is to stop running down the hall." When the teacher said "Don't take your chairs back to the table," all the children carried them to the table. Next day she said "Leave your chairs in the circle." Perhaps children sometimes fail to hear "Don't."

6. Avoid giving a child a choice when a decision has already been made. "Get ready for bed." Not, "Do you want to go to bed?"

7. Look for signs of physical illness when a child is misbehaving.

8. Avoid ridicule of a child from yourself or other children.

# TEACHING LANGUAGE PRINCIPLES

Throughout the text the reader will find basic principles of how children may acquire oral communication skills, and teaching techniques designed to improve language-comprehension and usage. A summation of these suggestions aids the teacher in preparing her lesson plans and parent conferences.

1. *Natural language.* Research evidence is accumulating to indicate that children make use of a built-in set of rules for developing language patterns, and that they deduce these rules from the language they hear. It seems logical, then, that parents and teachers should speak a natural language that is correct in all the language systems; phonemic, semantic, syntactic, and morphologic.

2. *Comprehension.* Language begins at birth, therefore, children must always be in an environment conducive to learning language. Simple but important rules relate to comprehension of language which is the precursor to expressive language.

Unwittingly parents may stop talking to children who cannot talk back. Or the child's expressive language level becomes the level on which parents talk to him, not realizing that comprehension is better than his expression. On the other hand teachers may advise parents, particularly of hearing impaired children, to "Talk, talk, talk to your child all day long." Such a system is more apt to repel language learning than enhance it, because the young child cannot absorb so much verbal input.

If a child does not understand what is said to him, three courses of action may be taken: (a) Select a different vocabulary. He may not obey the command, "Don't climb on the *furniture*," but obeys, "Don't climb on the *sofa*." In general common nouns are taught before collective nouns; *shoes, socks, coat,* and *hat* before the category word *clothes*. Through incidental learning they acquire the meaning and use of the word *clothes* because the teacher says "It's time to put the *clothes* back into the trunk," and Mother says, "Madge, help me bring in the *clothes*, please." (b) Shorten the phrase or sentence from "I surely would like to have you put your toys away before Grandma comes," to "Put your toys away." Then, "Grandma is coming." (c) In some instances it may be better to make a statement, show or demonstrate it, then say it again in a short phrase or sentence.

3. *Expression.* Apparently between two and three years of age children make great strides in acquiring the language code and putting it into use. Vocabulary increases and the syntactic, morphologic, and phonemic systems improve. This is the time to provide high quality listening experiences and opportunity for trying to express ideas in phrase

and sentence form. Children should be heard as well as seen for they need opportunities to "play" with sentence structure through their own talking and auditory feed-back mechanisms.

Four suggestions are offered to help children use appropriate vocabulary and sentence structure: (a) If a child uses an inappropriate word, he may not have generalized the meaning. The obvious example is the child who calls all women "mamma." The remedy is helping him define the word "mamma." (b) Teach children to use functional language by supplying them with functional language. Help them learn to respond to "Where is it?" "Tell me." and "What kind of sandwich do you want?" before teaching rote counting and color names. Too often parents of a child with language disorders teach rote counting as a device for proving he can talk. (c) One motivational activity such as Show and Tell may be utilized to develop single word responses, phrases, or a variety of sentence types.

> Dan brings a ball to school for Show and Tell. His expressive language consists of single words so the teacher asks "What did you bring, Dan?" to which he replies, "Ball." She responds, "A ball. A big ball. Dan brought a big ball." (Such a procedure allows him to listen to ways of developing phrases and sentences from a single word.)
>
> Donnie, who has difficulty defining, brings a baseball to Show and Tell. The teacher asks, "What do you do with a baseball?" "What is it made of?" "Is it hard or soft?"
>
> Karen who cannot formulate questions well brings a golf ball. Her assignment, with the teacher's help, is to ask the class questions about her ball. "What kind of ball do I have?" "Is it bigger than a baseball?"

(d) To help children practice oral sentence structuring, teachers avoid asking questions which always require "Yes" or "No" answers. They ask, "Do you want orange juice or milk?" in place of "Do you want orange juice?" "What do you want?" not "Do you want a pencil?" For the child with more language, "What did you do at the park?" not "Did you have fun at the park?"

An additional suggestion relates to the morphologic and phonemic systems. Correction of grammar or articulatory errors should wait until a child is using language fairly fluently. There is some evidence to indicate that the phonemic and morphologic aspects of talking follow a somewhat predictable developmental process and should not be interfered with until a qualified teacher recognizes the need for corrective measures. A five-year-old child with hearing impairment may be saying "goggy" for "doggy" but her language level may still be that of a three-year-old and "goggy" is not considered an articulatory problem at age three. Likewise "Me go too" may be appropriate for her language level.

4. *Motivation.* A child should be taught when he is eager and his attention has been gained. This may be while he is watching or helping

mother make a bed, bake a pie, use a dust pan, or answer the door bell. Too often teachers unwisely utilize a fifteen to thirty minute period twice weekly across a table to develop a preschool child's language. Furthermore, parents are advised to do the same; twice daily. What about the mother who has other children each needing special attention? Does she sacrifice their needs at the expense of one child? No, she does not create time consuming, artificial situations across a table, but uses natural, every day activities to help all of her children.

## DIAGNOSTIC TEACHING

A systematic program of instruction must include methods and materials for imparting information to children and, equally important, a continuing diagnostic study of each child. Children who fail to meet the teacher's goals for the first week are often required to attempt next week's goals. These children fall behind the others from the start of school and continue to fall further behind as the months pass by.

The teacher attempts to find a reason for every incorrect response given by each member of her class, and a means of correcting errors. In essence she diagnoses as she teaches.

### Questioning the Children

Mr. Foster said to his class, "I'm going to tell you something. Can you remember?" "Yes," answered the class. "Richard, how do you remember?" His answer, "With my hands."

The teacher's challenge was to find the basis for such an answer. Did the child give an inappropriate response because he was not attending to what was said? No, because when the teacher repeated the question, the answer was the same. Was this a semantic problem and the child did not know the general meaning of *remember?*

"Richard, do you remember where we went yesterday?" His correct response, "To the zoo."

Did he form a specific category from a previous experience for the word *remember* (numbers) and use his first cue (hand)?

"Richard, give me an example of how you remember with your hands." His reply, "Well, this morning when you put circles on the board (these are in configuration) and asked us to tell how many, I couldn't remember so I counted on my fingers."

Because of his extreme deficit in short term memory, Richard requires many exposures to retain information. (He has always been delayed in acquiring rote counting and number concept skills.) Mr.

Foster now knew more about Richard and his preoccupation with inability to remember the number configurations. The teacher also knew that the word *remember* had meaning for Richard. Home training suggestions were offered the parents to supplement his number work.

## Listen to Children

When students have limited verbal output, teachers are prone to increase the input to help take care of the silent periods. In essence, teachers often talk too much. If they wish to accomplish the diagnostic aspect of teaching, they are rewarded by listening to what the children have to say.

Miss Williams asked all the children to place their heads on their desks and listen for sounds. When someone heard three he was to raise his hand, come before the class and produce the sounds in sequence that he had heard. The sounds included crackling of paper, running water, closing a door, clicking scissors, and moving a chair. Gary had been able to remember only two sounds and not in sequence. He tried again. This time he was correct on the first then faltered. At this point he marched to the door, opened it and with hands on hips said, "Be quiet children so I can follow our noise." Gary was given another chance when all was quiet. He succeeded. He was telling the teacher that he could remember if he just wasn't distracted by noise.

The teacher was presenting a lesson on discrimination—finding those things in the classroom that were alike and those that were different. She listened carefully to their comments and was convinced that Kathleen had developed the concept of likeness. In the class were twin boys. The teacher asked, "How can you tell Dale and Neal are twins?" Kathleen replied, "Because they have the same face."

## Observe Nonverbal Skills of Children

When children demonstrate problems in activities which involve nonverbal skills, the teacher must listen carefully to their explanations and observe their performance. Failure may quickly be turned to success if the teacher recognizes basic problems.

In a writing lesson Johnny wanted to start at the bottom to make the letter *q*. He explained to the teacher that if he started at the top of the letter, he could not remember which way to go when he made the tail. He might make a *g* instead. The teacher became immediately aware that Johnny had directional problems.

Betsy, in activities of cutting, coloring, and pasting in her class was always far behind the other children. The teacher observed that Betsy tried to be a perfectionist and could not make judgments about when to do an extra neat job and when not to. In order to keep the child from always being the last or having unfinished work, the teacher during each activity would make an appropriate comment, such as, "Betsy, you may cut these circles quickly. I don't care if some of the white shows after they are cut."

## SUMMARY

As this text is being written there is no one valid method for teaching pre-academic skills to all children. Newly developed unresearched "restricted systems" continue to be introduced throughout the country. These restricted systems which may have a high emotional appeal to parents of children with handicaps should be carefully reviewed before applied.

Teachers do not necessarily need new methods, rather should understand and apply some of the long standing fundamental doctrines of learning. Such an approach gives meaning to instruction, makes research more tenable, and helps the teacher feel comfortable in her teaching milieu.

Education is not left to chance. The teacher is aware of what every child is learning and the level of his performance in every pre-academic area. She is a diagnostician, an assessor, and a teacher.

# 9

# *Adapting the Curriculum Guide:*
# *Children with Hearing Impairment*

Over the years children with sensory hearing impairment [1] have learned language skills in a variety of environments including residential and day schools for the deaf, speech and hearing clinics, nurseries with normal hearing children, the home, or classes with private tutors. Teachers from each environment speak with pride of their students who did acquire the oral language code and now live comfortably in a normal hearing society. Unfortunately, from each environment come children who attempt to function orally, but are substandard in the phonologic, semantic, syntactic, and morphologic features of language. And for reasons often unknown, a few children do not learn to generate oral sentences well enough to make their needs known, hence find it necessary to communicate with a language of signs.

The environment in which a child is trained is not always a predictor of success in oral language. Nor can the nature or extent of the hearing impairment or the profile of assets and deficits in the areas of learning foretell a child's future development in oral skills. There is no single, time-proven training technique that succeeds with all children. There is no panacea for a population of children with hearing impairment regardless of the time-worn labels—*deaf* and *hard of hearing.*

---

[1] Sensory hearing impairment refers to any impairment of audition associated with dysfunction of the auditory transmissive system.

# DEFINITION OF TERMS

## Deaf or Hard of Hearing?

Each child represented by his audiogram and scores from his language and learning assessment had an audiological assessment before age three. Annual hearing retests revealed comparable audiograms. The mothers and children were enrolled in a three week *Pre-Training Class* (p. 372) during which time individual hearing aids were selected for each child and subsequently worn during waking hours. At the conclusion of the *Pre-Training Class* the children were enrolled in the Pre-Academic Program beginning at the Nursery Level and continued through the Readiness Level.

Sharon, Phyllis, and Donna had no functional oral language upon entering the class. Mathew understood a few basic words and phrases which he used orally, but his connected discourse was, for the most part, unintelligible. Although a hearing aid would seem contraindicated in view of his audiogram, amplification did improve his comprehension in and out of the classroom.

Each parent was fully cooperative in attending scheduled conferences and competent in carrying out home training suggestions.

## SHARON (See Fig. 9-1 and audiogram)

The etiology of hearing impairment is unknown. She is the older of two children. The brother also has a hearing loss at approximately 70 dB (ASA) [2] from 500 through 2000 Hurtz (Hz).

Sharon attended first grade in a private school for normal hearing children. She transferred to public school at completion of the second year and is currently in the fourth grade. Academic achievement is above average in all subjects and she is socially accepted by her peer group.

When in the third grade, Sharon remained in the classroom and read library books while the classmates received instruction in Spanish. Learning a foreign language was thought to be too difficult for her. One

---

[2] The new standard for audiometric zero was established by the International Standards Organization. In order to distinguish this new method from the old system, the symbol ISO-64 is used to indicate the new system as opposed to ASA-51 which represents the old system. The audiogram shows hearing threshold level ISO-64 on the left hand side of the audiogram, and, for convenience of comparison, hearing threshold level ASA-51 on the right hand side. The difference between ISO-64 and ASA-51 is about 10 dB although the exact amount differs somewhat according to frequencies.

## Fig. 9-1
### SPEECH, HEARING, AND LANGUAGE CENTER
### LANGUAGE AND LEARNING ASSESSMENT: For Training
### (LLAT)

Name:     Sharon                Age: yr. _9_   mo. _5_

| ABILITIES ASSESSED | TESTS | M.A. Scores |
|---|---|---|
| **LANGUAGE SKILLS** | | |
| *Comprehension* | Single Words (3) ...................... | 10 - 9 |
| | Connected Discourse (44, 107, 108)................... | 6 - 0* |
| *Expression* | Connected Discourse (44, 107, 108)................... | 10 - 0* |
| | Defining (108)................. | 10 - 0 to 12 - 0 |
| | Sentence Structure.................. | adequate |
| | (poor, fair, adequate) | |
| **AVENUES OF LEARNING** | | |
| *Memory-Attention (Short term)* | | |
| Auditory | Digits (108, 118) ...................... | dna |
| | Sentences (108) ....................... | 11 - 0 to 12 - 0 |
| Visual | For Pictures (57) ...................... | 11 - 0* |
| Visual-Motor | Tapping (6)............................. | 15 - 6* |
| | Tapping (4)............................. | 8 - 0 to 9 - 0 |
| | Paper Folding (57).................... | dna |
| | Draw-A-Man (47).................... | dna |
| *Visual-Motor-* | | |
| *Perception* | Block Patterns (57).................. | 8 - 6 to 10 - 0 |
| (no memory) | Block Patterns (118) .............. | 12 - 2 to 12 - 6 |
| | Copy Forms (108) ................... | dna |
| **SOCIAL MATURITY** | Social Maturity Scale (47)........ | dna |

day she said to her teacher, "I can read library books at home. Please may I go to Spanish class with the other children?" Permission was granted and a surprising amount of conversational Spanish has been learned.

Amplification was so beneficial that teachers in the pre-academic program found it difficult to teach Sharon lipreading skills. Daily activities were planned to impress her with the importance of looking as well as listening. Instructions and general comments were not repeated if Sharon failed to watch the speaker and appropriate forms of punishment were utilized.

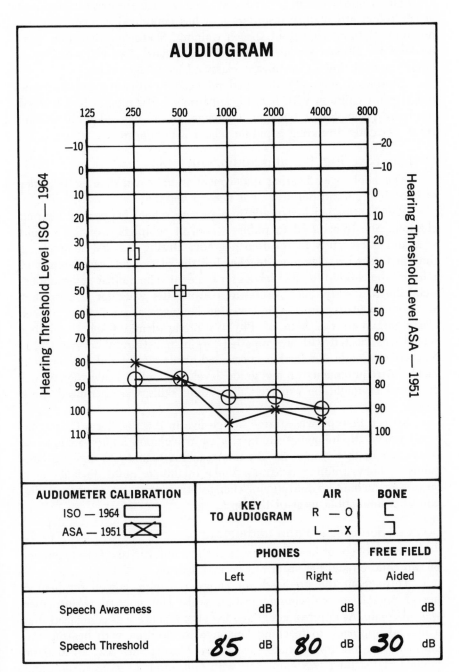

# AUDIOGRAM

**NAME** Sharon  **AGE** 7-0

| | 125 | 250 | 500 | 1000 | 2000 | 4000 | 8000 |

Hearing Threshold Level ISO — 1964

Hearing Threshold Level ASA — 1951

| AUDIOMETER CALIBRATION | KEY TO AUDIOGRAM | AIR | BONE |
|---|---|---|---|
| ISO — 1964 | | R — O | ⊏ |
| ASA — 1951 ⊠ | | L — X | ⊐ |

| | PHONES | | FREE FIELD |
|---|---|---|---|
| | Left | Right | Aided |
| Speech Awareness | dB | dB | dB |
| Speech Threshold | *85* dB | *80* dB | *30* dB |

Speech therapy primarily through phonics was started at age five in the Readiness Class and she was enrolled the following summer in an articulation improvement program. Mother learned the basic techniques of correcting articulatory disorders and has continued a home training program. Without consistent speech training, Sharon's articulation, particularly the sibilent sounds, becomes substandard. Her voice quality is mildly deviant, but by no means classified as a *"deaf* voice."

Sharon's younger brother had no need to attend a pre-academic program for children with hearing impairment. His mother had learned the basic principles of teaching language as she worked with Sharon. He is currently attending a public school Kindergarten.

### PHYLLIS (See Fig. 9-2 and audiogram)

The etiology of hearing impairment is unknown. She is the older of two children and her sister has normal hearing.

Phyllis attended first grade in a private school for normal hearing children. She transferred to public school at completion of the second year and is currently in the fourth grade. During the first semester of the third year her classroom teacher felt the placement was wrong and referred the child to the day school for the deaf. The mother never understood the reasons for such a referral, because her daughter at this point was communicating in oral and written language above average in her classroom. With the help of Phyllis's pre-academic teacher, another school was located with a sympathetic principal. Careful selection of a teacher was made. Phyllis has succeeded academically and continues to meet the requirements of her grade level. She relies heavily on visual cues and as might be expected, lipreading skills were acquired quite easily.

Speech therapy was started at age five in the Readiness Class. She was enrolled the following summer in an articulation improvement class where her mother gained insight into teaching techniques and has continued a home training program. Voice quality is quite deviant yet a surprising amount of inflectional change is present and connected discourse is intelligible most of the time.

### DONNA (See Fig. 9-3 and audiogram)

The etiology of hearing impairment is unknown. She is the younger of two children and her sister has normal hearing.

Throughout the pre-academic program Donna lagged far behind her classmates in oral communication skills. Her nonoral performance was adequate. At approximately age five, the teacher was convinced that a natural approach to teaching language to children with hearing impairment was not appropriate for Donna. During this year an analytic method of teaching was employed with only minimal gains in oral and

Fig. 9-2
## SPEECH, HEARING, AND LANGUAGE CENTER
## LANGUAGE AND LEARNING ASSESSMENT:  For Training
(LLAT)

Name:    Phyllis                                               Age: yr. 5   mo. 10

| ABILITIES ASSESSED | TESTS | M.A. Scores |
|---|---|---|
| LANGUAGE SKILLS | | |
| *Comprehension* | Single Words (3) ...................... | 7 - 6 |
| | Connected Discourse (44, 107, 108) ..................... | 6 - 0* |
| *Expression* | Connected Discourse (44, 107, 108) ..................... | 5 - 7 |
| | Defining (108).......................... | dna |
| | Sentence Structure.................. | fair |
| | (poor, fair, adequate) | |
| AVENUES OF LEARNING | | |
| *Memory-Attention (Short term)* | | |
| Auditory | Digits (108, 118) ..................... | 5 - 10 to 6 - 2 |
| | Sentences (108) ...................... | below 3 - 6 |
| Visual | For Pictures (57) ..................... | 7 - 0 to 9 - 0 |
| Visual-Motor | Tapping (6) ............................. | 5 - 6 to 6 - 6 |
| | Tapping (4) ............................. | 4 - 0 to 6 - 0 |
| | Paper Folding (57) ................... | 6 - 0 to 8 - 6 |
| | Draw-A-Man (47) ..................... | 5 - 6 |
| *Visual-Motor-* | Form Board (108) ................... | dna |
| *Perception* | Block Patterns (57).................. | 8 - 6 to 10 - 0 |
| (no memory) | Block Patterns (118) .............. | dna |
| | Copy Forms (108) .................... | 5 - 0 to 7 - 0 |
| SOCIAL MATURITY | Social Maturity Scale (47)........ | 6 - 5 |

written language. At six years of age she was referred to the day school for the deaf.

Although she continues to make minimal gains in oral communication, she lags far behind Sharon, Phyllis, and many others at the school for the deaf. Her comprehension and expression of oral language is not functional in a society of normal hearing persons. (To provide such children with a means of expressing themselves, to at least a limited population, a language of signs should be incorporated in the educational program.)

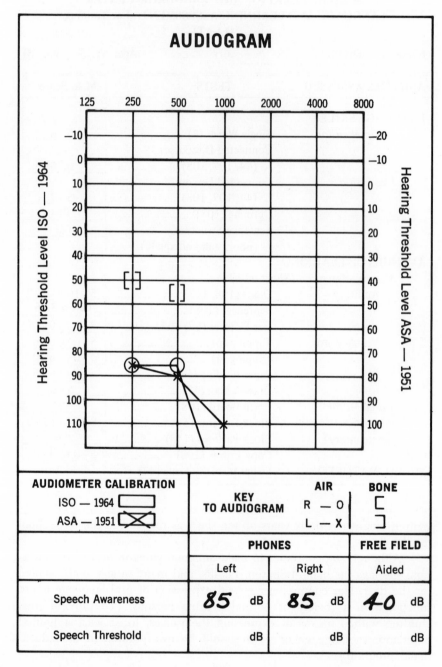

**NAME** *Phyllis*

**AGE** 9-11

# AUDIOGRAM

Hearing Threshold Level ISO — 1964

Hearing Threshold Level ASA — 1951

| AUDIOMETER CALIBRATION | | | |
|---|---|---|---|
| ISO — 1964 ☐ | **KEY TO AUDIOGRAM** | **AIR** R — O  L — X | **BONE** [  ] |
| ASA — 1951 ☒ | | | |

| | PHONES | | FREE FIELD |
|---|---|---|---|
| | Left | Right | Aided |
| Speech Awareness | **85** dB | **85** dB | **40** dB |
| Speech Threshold | dB | dB | dB |

140

## Fig. 9-3
## SPEECH, HEARING, AND LANGUAGE CENTER
## LANGUAGE AND LEARNING ASSESSMENT: For Training
### (LLAT)

Name:  Donna

Age: yr. 3  mo. 2   Age: yr. 5  mo. 11

| ABILITIES ASSESSED | TESTS | M.A. Scores | M.A. Scores |
|---|---|---|---|
| **LANGUAGE SKILLS** | | | |
| *Comprehension* | Single Words (3) ........ | no score | 2 - 8 |
| | Connected Discourse (44, 107, 108) ........ | no score | no score |
| *Expression* | Connected Discourse (44, 107, 108) ........ | no score | 2 - 4 |
| | Defining (108) ........ | dna | dna |
| | Sentence Structure (poor, fair, adequate) ........ | | poor |
| **AVENUES OF LEARNING** | | | |
| *Memory-Attention (Short term)* | | | |
| Auditory | Digits (108, 118) ........ | no score | no score |
| | Sentences (108) ........ | no score | no score |
| Visual | For Pictures (57) ........ | no score | 9 - 0 to 11 - 0 |
| Visual-Motor | Tapping (6) ........ | no score | 4 - 6 to 5 - 6 |
| | Tapping (4) ........ | no score | 4 - 0 to 6 - 0 |
| | Paper Folding (57) ........ | 3 - 0 to 3 - 6 | 6 - 0 to 8 - 6 |
| | Draw-A-Man (47) ........ | no score | 5 - 0 |
| *Visual-Motor-Perception* | | | |
| (no memory) | Form Board (108) ........ | dna | dna |
| | Block Patterns (57) ........ | 3 - 0 to 3 - 6 | 8 - 6 to 10 - 0 |
| | Block Patterns (118) ........ | dna | dna |
| | Copy Forms (108) ........ | 2 - 6 to 3 - 6 | 7 - 0* |
| **SOCIAL MATURITY** | Social Maturity Scale (47) ........ | 3 - 6 | 6 - 4 |

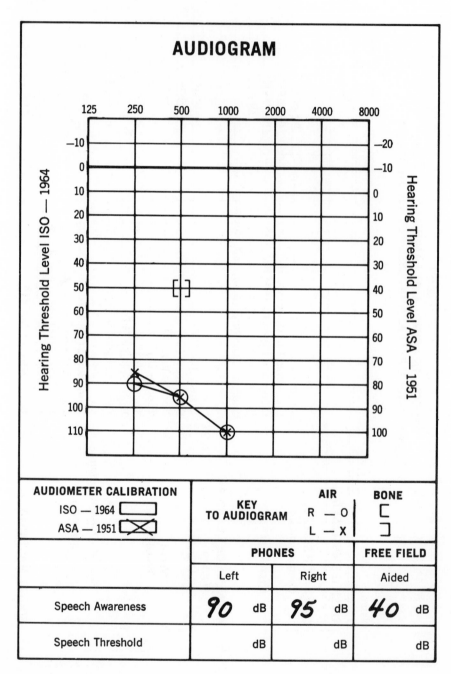

NAME *Donna*  AGE 7-2

# AUDIOGRAM

| | | PHONES | | FREE FIELD |
|---|---|---|---|---|
| | | Left | Right | Aided |
| Speech Awareness | | *90* dB | *95* dB | *40* dB |
| Speech Threshold | | dB | dB | dB |

**AUDIOMETER CALIBRATION**
ISO — 1964 ☐
ASA — 1951 ☒

**KEY TO AUDIOGRAM**

AIR
R — O
L — X

BONE
[
]

MATHEW (See Fig. 9-4 and audiogram)

Mother served as an X-ray technician during her pregnancy and although the etiology of hearing impairment is not definitely known, the physician questions the effects of the X-rays on the fetus. Mathew is the older of two children, the younger having normal hearing.

This child was referred to the Language, Speech, and Hearing Clinic because he was not understanding or talking on age level. A previous diagnosis of *childhood aphasia* had been rendered elsewhere. The audiometric assessment revealed bilateral hearing threshold levels common to children who hear much of what is said to them, but understand very little. The *Language and Learning Assessment: For Training* was also typical of a child with this particular pattern of sensory hearing involvement.

Because the parents had no understanding of the conditions under which their son must listen, they were invited into the test rooms to listen to the audiologist talk under filtered speech conditions. Subsequently in the Pre-training Class the mother heard tape recordings of speech signals attenuated, distorted, attenuated and distorted; and the quality of speech as he heard it through a wearable hearing aid (104). These two experiences helped them understand the listening problems their son faced.

Mathew at ages three and four was a fidgety child, had many tantrums at home, and was beginning to bite his finger nails. Although his emotional behavior improved immensely once he was appropriately diagnosed and a training program instigated, he was still somewhat difficult to manage. A referral for neurological studies was made and the results were negative with the exception of an abnormal EEG record. The physician recommended medication which apparently had some calming effect, for Mathew became easier to manage in class. Currently, he is completing first grade with better than average performance in a regular classroom.

It is interesting to note that this child received a "D" in reading on his first report card, yet was in the top reading group of his class. A parent conference revealed that reading grades were based upon phonics and, of course, Mathew could not hear many of the phonemes with high frequency characteristics. He could not for example, name a word that started like *sight*. Out of context the word *sight* may have been mistaken for *light, night,* or *kite*. An explanation to the teacher solved the problem.

There is every reason to believe that this boy will continue his education in regular classrooms.

Deaf or hard of hearing? The literature does not provide an answer because a variety of definitions have been submitted by a variety of

## Fig. 9-4
### SPEECH, HEARING, AND LANGUAGE CENTER
### LANGUAGE AND LEARNING ASSESSMENT: For Training
### (LLAT)

Name: Mathew    Age: yr. 3 mo. 10    Age: yr. 5 mo. 5

| ABILITIES ASSESSED | TESTS | M.A. Scores | M.A. Scores |
|---|---|---|---|
| **LANGUAGE SKILLS** | | | |
| *Comprehension* | Single Words (3) ........ | 3 - 4 | 6 - 9 |
| | Connected Discourse (44, 107, 108) ........ | 2 - 0 | 6 - 0* |
| *Expression* | Connected Discourse (44, 107, 108) ........ | below 2 - 0 | 5 - 8 |
| | Defining (108) ........ | dna | dna |
| | Sentence Structure (poor, fair, adequate)........ | | adequate |
| **AVENUES OF LEARNING** | | | |
| *Memory-Attention (Short term)* | | | |
| Auditory | Digits (108, 118) ........ | 3 - 0 to 4 - 0 | 5 - 10 to 6 - 6 |
| | Sentences (108) ........ | no score | 5 - 6 to 6 - 0 |
| Visual | For Pictures (57) ........ | 4 - 6 to 5 - 6 | 9 - 0 to 11 - 0 |
| Visual-Motor | Tapping (6) ........ | dna | below 4 - 0 |
| | Tapping (4) ........ | dna | 4 - 0 to 6 - 0 |
| | Paper Folding (57) ........ | 4 - 6 to 5 - 0 | 5 - 0 to 6 - 0 |
| | Draw-A-Man (47) ........ | 4 - 6 | 5 - 9 |
| *Visual-Motor-Perception* (no memory) | Form Board (108) ........ | dna | dna |
| | Block Patterns (57) ........ | 3 - 6 to 4 - 6 | 5 - 6 to 7 - 0 |
| | Block Patterns (118) ........ | dna | dna |
| | Copy Forms (108) ........ | 3 - 6 to 5 - 0 | 5 - 0 to 7 - 0 |
| **SOCIAL MATURITY** | Social Maturity Scale (47) ........ | 4 - 0 | dna |

144

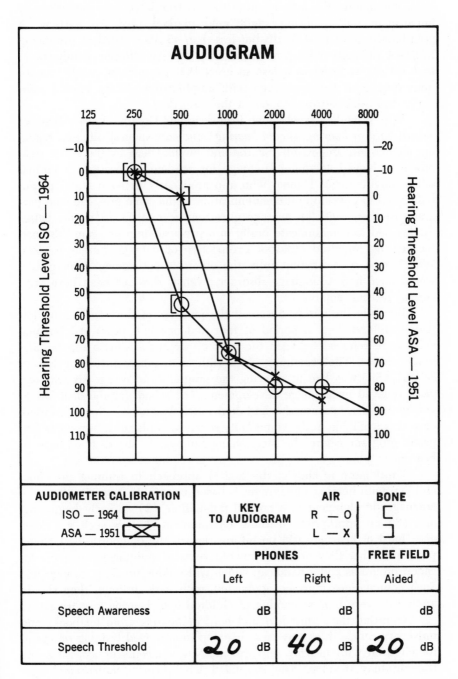

| NAME | Mathew | AGE | 6-11 |
| --- | --- | --- | --- |

# AUDIOGRAM

Hearing Threshold Level ISO — 1964

Hearing Threshold Level ASA — 1951

| AUDIOMETER CALIBRATION | | | |
| --- | --- | --- | --- |
| ISO — 1964 | | | |
| ASA — 1951 | | | |

| KEY TO AUDIOGRAM | AIR | BONE |
| --- | --- | --- |
| | R — O | ⊏ |
| | L — X | ⊐ |

| | PHONES | | FREE FIELD |
| --- | --- | --- | --- |
| | Left | Right | Aided |
| Speech Awareness | dB | dB | dB |
| Speech Threshold | 20 dB | 40 dB | 20 dB |

145

writers. A child in one community is labeled *deaf* if the average pure tone loss in the better ear is greater than 82 dB (ASA standard). In another community the average pure tone is translated into gradations of impairment; not significant, slight, mild, marked, severe, or extreme. A mild handicap, at least 30 dB but less than 45 dB is listed as producing frequent difficulty with oral communication. An extreme handicap, at least 80 dB, is listed as a loss so great that the person usually cannot understand oral language even with amplification. These graded categories were devised to circumvent the term *deaf*.

Why provide a label which is misleading? Do any of the categories —*deaf, hard of hearing, severe hearing handicap,* suggest different teaching techniques? Impossible. Sharon and Phyllis, deaf by the above definitions, achieved adequate language for academic success in a normal school environment. Donna, who appeared early to have equal potential, failed to develop oral communication in the same pre-academic program. Mathew, with an average pure tone loss of 55 dB on his better ear learned to communicate orally in a pre-academic program designed for hearing impaired children irrespective of average pure tone loss. Why Donna was different from the others is not known. Perhaps she would have had a language disorder, even if she had been born with normal hearing acuity.

Recently the author observed the progress of thirteen hearing impaired children over a period of four and one half years. All but one child were referred between the ages of six and seven to regular first grade classes. The remaining child with an average pure tone loss of 85 dB (ASA) was late in entering the program and at age six was two years delayed in language development. The school for the deaf would not accept her because she had "too much language." No appropriate class was available in the community so she was placed in a regular first grade program where she faces many failures. Is she deaf or hard of hearing?

Until more is known, the logical approach to training preschool children with hearing impairment is based upon: (1) known patterns of language development in a normal population, (2) an early beginning, and (3) an appropriate learning environment. Labels such as "deaf" and "hard of hearing" add no information to the diagnostic or training program. What they do is to connote years of training in special education programs and a handicap which will follow the child through life. Such connotations must be eradicated—with early training they should apply to a very limited number of children with hearing impairment.

Omitting the terms *deaf* and *hard of hearing* from textbooks and university course titles may be a first step to improved training programs for children with hearing impairment. New concepts of assessing and training may develop. The simplified label *hearing impairment* conceivably could come to mean an inconvenience, not a handicap.

# ASSESSMENTS

## Medical

All children need planned physical check-ups. Those with hearing impairment should be observed even more closely by the physician, in order to prevent further damage to the hearing mechanism. As with all children, teachers should require certificates of immunization before children are enrolled for training. An all-out effort to maintain health standards will permit good school attendance records so necessary for child and parent education.

## Audiological

### INITIAL ASSESSMENT

Certain conditions affecting the mother during the first trimester of pregnancy are likely to result in physical disabilities in the neonate. One of the most common diseases which affects a high percent of auditory problems is rubella during the early stages of pregnancy. Epidemics of this measle-type disease have occurred in communities to such an extent that post-rubella baby clinics have been organized for treatment, training, and research. The audiologist has become a part of the post-rubella diagnostic team with the commission to assess the hearing of children under twelve months of age.

Audiometric equipment and assessment techniques are being somewhat successful in identifying hearing impairments in infants. However, no valid techniques are currently available for obtaining hearing thresholds. Until a breakthrough occurs the audiologist must continue to use the classical conditioned response or startle type testing. A very simple approach for children under three years of age and as young as eight or nine months, conditions the child to look at a light source when he hears the auditory signal. A colored blinking light, mounted on the test room wall behind the subject's head, is activated through the circuitry of the audiometer in the control room. The very young child sits on the parent's lap while playing with appropriate toys. An auditory signal is introduced at varying intensity increments until the subject displays some kind of response (head raising, head turning, cessation of play). At this point, the assistant or parent turns the child's head to the point where he can view the blinking light. If the child is going to condition to the technique, he will do so within approximately three to fifteen signal presentations. As soon as the conditioning is established, the audiologist attenuates the signal and proceeds as in standard audiometry. For fear of early extinction of the orienting response, 500 and 2000 Hz are presented first. The remaining audiogram is completed if possible.

This same principle, with a few variations in materials and techniques, has been used by others. One audiologist [3] suggests the use of colorful toys, figures or cartoons in place of the blinking light. The inclusion of an electric light bulb and extension cord provides the clinician with a satisfactory distraction device which is reported to hold the child's interest over a longer period of time than an incurious light. With this method pure tone audiograms have been obtained with greater ease on children under twelve months of age than on three-year-olds using conditioned play audiometry.

## DIAGNOSTIC-TRAINING CLASSES

Multiple handicaps, immaturity, and many unknown factors contribute to the difficulty experienced in obtaining hearing thresholds from very young children. For this reason the audiologist may need to turn to a more subjective type assessment which can be found in a *Diagnostic-Training Program* for parents.

Classes are designed to: (1) provide supportive therapy for the parents, (2) obtain significant information from them regarding their child's auditory behavior in the home, and (3) offer practical suggestions for the child's pre-linguistic and linguistic development. Groups of parents attend one hour sessions one day per week.

For supportive therapy, parents are asked to bring questions to class. In general these inquiries center around the following topics: "If my baby has a hearing loss, will he ever learn to talk?" "Is there any surgical procedure that will improve his hearing?" "Will he always have to wear a hearing aid?" "Will he have to learn to talk with his hands?" "What are my chances of giving birth to a second hearing impaired child?"

Parents are asked also to make observations of the child in functional situations. Does he respond in any way to the ring of the telephone? If so, how far removed is he from the sound source? Does he respond in any way to other sounds, door bell or knocker, airplanes, car motors? Does he attend when spoken to: his name, "No, No," or "Bye-Bye?"

Parents are given suggestions as to how they may assist the baby in developing the looking and listening skills that will be needed for oral communication. He is bathed in such a position that his eyes can focus on mother's face and he is held while being fed, rocked, or entertained in a position that is conducive to learning lipreading skills. His oral language environment is comparable to that of any infant with no hearing impairment: simple phrases, short sentences, and singing.

[3] B. D. Kimball, "Audio-Visual Aids: Addendum to Previous Article," *Asha, A Journal of the American Speech and Hearing Association*, Vol. 6 (December, 1964), p. 500.

Audiometric assessments are attempted when the parents and teacher feel a measurement can be made. If hearing impairment is not present, nothing will have been lost. Parents will have had supportive therapy during a very stressful time of their lives and the information they learned about language development applies to all children. If a hearing impairment is found, the desirable early start will have been made.

### PRE-TRAINING CLASS

Whenever auditory impairment is strongly indicated a child is enrolled in a *Pre-Training Class* (p. 372) (his parents may or may not have attended the *Diagnostic Training Program*). This class will assist the audiologist in choosing a hearing aid with appropriate gain for the appropriate ear. In addition, the program will provide parents with basic information needed to understand and deal with the problem of hearing impairment.

In general the classes meet for three weeks with five, one hour sessions per week. The class procedure is directed toward preparing the child and his parents for a language development program which is orally oriented.

## Intellectual

Research related to differences between children with and without hearing impairment has been conducted in specified areas of "intelligence" or "cognitive thinking" and the most common factor resulting from these studies before 1960 was the disagreement among investigators. During the early 1960's more agreement has been realized to substantiate the hypothesis that the thinking processes of the *deaf* are essentially the same as for children with normal hearing (other developmental processes being equal).

In an editorial published in *Hearing* by the Royal National Institute for the Deaf, a person signing his name "Totally," writes:

> "As a totally deaf person, the more I think of it, the more ludicrous all this discussion on 'how the deaf think' appears to me. Surely your writers are not suggesting (or are they?) that God manufactured a special 'brain box' for the deaf alone? The way I see it the deaf appear to think differently only because of the lack of education as compared to a hearing person in the same social and age group . . ."

## Language

Psycholinguistic batteries for measurement of language acquisition are being developed and as linguists discover more detailed aspects of the language code, better assessment tools will appear. Until that time, batteries such as suggested in this text should be utilized to provide profiles of each child's assets and deficits in the areas of comprehension and expression of oral language and to establish a base line for training purposes.

## Speech

Speech and voice assessments are part of the total communication audit, hence phonetic inventories and tape recordings of voice quality are obtained as early as feasible. Annual reassessments provide a record of progress.

## Academic

The proof of a child's success in a pre-academic program lies in his ability to succeed in academic subjects. Teachers in an academic program must provide an environment conducive to learning and must avoid social promotions for the child who cannot compete with his peers. Achievement tests in academic subjects must be administered, preferably biannually. The scores indicate the child's educational progress or lack of progress and if adequate gains are not being made, special tutoring or a more suitable class placement is indicated.

# TRAINING

## Natural Language Approach

Natural language as a method of teaching children with hearing impairment is no different than the method through which normal listeners achieve linguistic competence. The fact that incidental learning of language is curtailed because of a hearing deficit, however, implies the need for a qualified teacher and a structured training program.

Do children with hearing impairment have the same inborn predispositions to develop language that have been postulated for children with normal hearing? The answer is "Yes" if we are to take a fresh approach to training. *We must assume that these children can learn the code needed to acquire the phonologic, semantic, syntactic and morphologic features of oral and written communication.*

Perception of phonetic distinctions is basic to learning oral language. *The knowledge that a child has a hearing impairment does not preclude his ability to perceive fine enough distinctions to develop language in a natural environment.* In fact, in a population of hearing impaired preschool children, the vast majority respond to one or more frequencies above 500 Hz. With appropriate hearing aid amplification supplemented with lipreading skills, such children can be expected to succeed linguistically when exposed to a natural approach to learning language. Granted, articulatory disorders related to hearing impairment may occur, but *language comprehension and usage can become commensurate with chronological age.*

Over the years, most research in "language of the deaf" has been conducted in residential schools and the experimental groups had limited if any preschool training. The findings among researchers have been much the same: the majority of high school graduates of schools for the deaf do not achieve in oral and written language beyond the third or fourth grade; sentences are short, vocabulary is reduced, and concept development, syntax, and morphology are substandard.

Reasons for poor achievement are becoming increasingly apparent. (1) The same teaching techniques instigated decades ago are still being used in too many institutions in spite of the knowledge that many *deaf* do not make acceptable academic progress under such methods. (2) Qualified training programs for youngsters under five years of age are uncommon—those for children under three are rare. (3) Use of hearing aid amplification is not clearly understood by many teachers of the deaf who have had few—if any—courses in audiology. (4) Educational philosophies with curriculum guides for pre-academic training have only recently been developed.

No scientific research is currently available to prove or disprove the adequacy of various teaching methods. We need a fresh look at teaching techniques and particularly at a new population of children with hearing impairment; those who have been enrolled in a structured pre-academic program from at least two years of age. Clinical evidence emerging from such programs shows promise. Careful academic follow-up studies of each child are needed.

*Teachers know that children do develop language through a natural approach even when the loss is greater than 80 dB at 500 Hz and no measurable hearing appears above this frequency.* Closely allied with this knowledge is the demonstration by audiologists and speech scientists that phonemic information can be utilized from a band width of 150 Hz through 500 Hz. Unfortunately children with islands of hearing are too often labeled *deaf,* underemphasizing the importance of amplification, and falsely emphasizing the need for artificial structuring of language principles.

Research is forthcoming. Much of it is placing great emphasis upon the number of phonemic distinctions that can be perceived with wearable hearing aids by children who have only a limited band of hearing in the low frequency range. The impact of such research in training programs leads scientists to investigate the validity of a natural approach to teaching language to *deaf* children. Old techniques need to be compared with newly developed ones, even for children who demonstrate no residual hearing as measured by standard audiometry. Educators want answers.

## Pre-Academic Classes

All children enrolled in a pre-academic program wear their own body type hearing aids. Neither group amplifiers nor induction loops are utilized. Clinical experience of the author and other teachers of hearing impaired children have demonstrated the adequacy of appropriate, wearable aids through children like Sharon, Phyllis, Mathew, and others. Until research demonstrates that group units or induction loops are a superior means of amplification for oral language development, wearable hearing aids could be the teacher's choice for hearing impaired children.

### NURSERY CLASS [4]

Classes meet one hour per week and are designed to instruct parents of children with hearing impairment who have not begun to walk. These group meetings serve the following purposes: (1) to demonstrate to parents the ways in which they can begin teaching their children good look and listen habits, (2) to help parents develop an environment conducive to the acquisition of pre-linguistic and linguistic skills, (3) to provide opportuniity to observe teaching techniques and activities in the pre-academic classrooms, and (4) to answer the many questions parents want to ask.

### TODDLER'S CLASS [5]

Structured group activities for children who have just learned to walk provide excellent opportunities to teach good look and listen skills. A class of four or five children meets one hour, five days per week. For the first month or two, frequent conferences are scheduled and parents observe teaching techniques which are applicable outside the classroom.

### TWO-YEAR-OLD CLASS [6]

Two-year-olds are a group unto themselves. They are no longer babies, yet do not have the skills or play activity of three-year-olds. Their

---

[4] The curriculum guide for the Nursery Class is not completed (see pp. 191-198).

[5] The curriculum guide for the Toddler's Class is not completed (see APPENDIX for suggestions, pp. 191-198).

[6] The curriculum guide for the Two-year-old Class is not completed (see APPENDIX for suggestions, pp. 191-198).

desire to be constantly on the move demands a wide variety of short term classroom activities. There is a need for the acquisition of a broad noun word vocabulary to supplement the basic phrases learned in the nursery class. This two-year-old group profits from a structured language program.

## CLASSES FOR CHILDREN BEYOND THREE YEARS OF AGE

The same class levels and curriculum guide described in Chapter 7 are appropriate for children with hearing impairment. *The language that is desirable for them to learn is no different from the language learned by children with normal hearing.* By the same token, pre-academic skills and acceptable social behavior must be learned by all children regardless of their handicap, if they are to succeed in a regular school program.

## Academic Classes

### STRUCTURE OF THE CLASSES

Currently, academic programs which include children with hearing impairment fall under two classifications, regular class and special education. The latter includes classes for the *hard of hearing* and *deaf.* Regular classroom placement is indicated when a child's language and learning assessment and social adjustment meet first grade requirements. Classes for the *hard of hearing* are designed for those youngsters who are developing oral language through natural methods, but due to a late start or poor attendance have not attained language and pre-academic skills commensurate with first grade requirements. Such classes could profitably enroll fifteen to twenty children under qualified tutelage. When indicated, regular classroom placement is made.

Special education classes for the deaf include: (1) children, who for reasons currently unknown, do not learn the language code and hence fail to profit from training in a natural language setting. These youngsters may be diagnosed at ages four or five by the skilled teacher who has been working with them in a pre-academic environment. (2) Children who receive no training until age five or older and demonstrate difficulty learning to communicate orally. In deaf education classes teachers attempt to artificially structure language for these children through analytical methods. Many of these children also learn the language of signs.

*Regular Classroom Instruction for Children with Hearing Impairment.* More than ever in the history of education of the *deaf,* children with hearing impairment are being enrolled in regular classrooms with normal hearing peers. The reasons are obvious. With the advent of modern electronic equipment, audiologists obtain near-threshold tests and provide the very young child with hearing aid amplification. Teachers have developed better ways of introducing language and coordinating that language with the curriculum of elementary subjects. In essence, pre-academic programs for hearing impaired children are based on the following premise: *potentially the deaf are capable of being educated with hearing children providing oral language is commensurate with academic placement.*

The teacher of the pre-academic program for hearing impaired children is responsible for the development of their language and learning skills. The elementary school teacher continues to make use of these skills for the accomplishment of academic subjects. Many regular first grade teachers, however, are not willing to assume the responsibility of teaching these children without some kind of guidance. Parents also ask for assistance when new hearing, language, and speech problems arise, therefore the following plan has been designed and successfully carried out; the supervisor or qualified person from the pre-academic program serves as: (1) consultant to the teachers who have accepted children into their classes, and (2) counselor to parents of these same children.

*Helping the Hearing Impaired Child in the Regular Academic Classroom.* Teachers have many questions to ask about the hearing impaired child in a classroom with hearing children. These questions, if answered early, or as they arise, may mean the difference between a child's success or failure in regular classes. A consultant serves as the intermediary.

Visits by the consultant during the school year may be scheduled one day per week for the first two months, biweekly during the following three, and one visit per month from then on. These visits are divided into two sessions: (1) at least an hour's observation of the child's participation in the classroom activities, and (2) sufficient time to answer the teacher's questions and discuss problems and progress of the child.

Before the consultant makes her first visit, she provides a list of instructions for the teacher which include the following hints for her:

1. The parents will talk with you about the child's hearing aid.

2. Seat the child close to your desk where he can see your face and turn to see the faces of the children.

3. Speak naturally. Do not exaggerate your mouth movements or speak too slowly.

4. Keep your hands and books away from your face while speaking.

5. Be sure you have the child's attention as you start to give assignments or make announcements. Remember that he may hear better on some days than others, so be careful about blaming him for being inattentive.

6. If the child misunderstands, restate once more. If necessary restate in a different way, as you may be using words that are difficult to lip-read.

7. When dictating problems or pronouncing spelling words, choose one place to stand and do not walk around while talking.

8. The child should participate in the same activities as the other children.

*Counselling with Parents.*    Three times during the school year parents meet as a group with the consultant to discuss various topics related to home and school adjustment problems of their children.

Not always is it possible, however, for a trained person to act as a consultant. She may not have the time or the schools may not wish to hire a consultant. Or, children may have been enrolled in regular school before a consultant was available. In the latter instance, upon request of a group of parents, Mrs. Rister invited twenty-nine parents from the local community and surrounding districts. The fifteen who attended had their children enrolled in first, second, third, or fourth grades. The parents' comments provided a framework for future discussions with classroom teachers as well as parent groups. Primary interest revolved around the following topics.

1. *Hearing aids:* All children were wearing their hearing aids. Some of the teachers had asked the children to demonstrate their aids to class members. One mother reported that her daughter arrived in the fourth grade the first day of school and walked directly to her teacher.

> "I'm hard of hearing. I have my battery and cord in my purse. Don't worry, I can take care of my hearing aid. Can I please sit close to the front?"

2. *Teachers:* The mothers agreed that teachers who are more sympathetic and understanding of the problem are the answer to whether their child succeeds or not. Parents had a tendency to blame the teachers for not trying to understand the child's specific problems, which, of course, were very clear to the parents. Many parents were happy with the teachers; others made the following reports:

> "In my boy's class the children do exercises like *listen for the missing letter.* He gets some but not others. My husband says the way the teacher screws up her mouth, nobody could get it."

> "My little girl is sensitive in class and the teacher doesn't seem to help her much. Linda is usually way behind in her seat work and that worries her. If these first graders don't finish their seat work, they are kept after school and that is severe punishment for a little one. She gets frightened and cries for fear of being left at school all night."

"Mary Grace's teacher does not believe that she has much of a hearing loss. I guess it's because she makes such good use of her hearing aid and lipreading. The teacher is continually turning her back when she asks Mary Grace a question. Mary Grace tells me everything so that teacher gets by with nothing."

3. *Discipline:* The majority of mothers stated that their children received good conduct grades. One mother had the following to say:

"Tommy made 3 B's and two A's but I won't tell you what he made in conduct. I would surely advise mothers of younger children to start right now to teach them to keep quiet in school. Tommy's behavior is such that if the room is quiet he causes some excitement . . . and he does cause plenty!"

"Sabrina was in a kindergarten class with all children who had discipline problems, and a very strict teacher. Every day Sabrina would come home just shaking because she was so petrified. She was having hearing problems and everything. I went to the teacher and before I could say anything, she threw up her hands and said, 'I have done everything I can for your child.' I said, 'I just wanted to find out why my daughter was being sent to the nursing station every other day for a stomachache.' The teacher said it was because Sabrina could not understand anything that was said to her so she just got upset. Now that isn't true, because she understands everything you say to her. Finally we got another teacher and in just two weeks Sabrina was a different child. She now makes a straight B report card and loves to go to school."

4. *Vocabulary building:* One mother asked the others what they were doing at home to develop vocabulary.

"I get together a list of 10 to 12 words daily and my son looks them up in the dictionary. After he thinks he knows the meaning, I ask him to use the words in sentences."

"Mine is in the 3rd grade. He made an A in arithmetic and B in everything else except a D in geography. He simply did not know what many of the words meant. So I have been going through his geography book and picking out words to teach him."

"My husband and I don't have much time to help Tom with his vocabulary at home, because we don't have much of a home life. But I work in PTA and spend my time buttering up those teachers, because that is the only way you are going to get anything for your child."

"Rhonda is in the third grade and we find that crossword puzzle books are a good source for vocabulary training. Don't get the picture type. Use the ones that require word definitions."

5. *Reading:* All mothers thought that the Weekly Reader (86) was the very best publication there was to help their children. Many found the local library a good source for reading material. Most of the discussion centered around teaching techniques and problems encountered in reading.

"My Don wants out of the first reading group to be in the third group with the little boy across the street. This boy has only half a book assigned for homework while Don has a whole book. Don just doesn't want to be different from his friend."

"Julia's teacher said that no child in the class can take a reader home, and that Julia is no exception. It seems to me that I could help her with new words if she could bring her book home. Well, I now go to the library and get books that are on her reading level."

"My daughter passes only the parts of the tests that relate to what she has read. When other children read paragraphs aloud, Charlotte doesn't always know what they have read. If only she were allowed to read the whole story herself."

"Instead of looking at his book, Randy watches the children as they read. The other day he was punished because it was his turn and he could not find the right page or paragraph." Another mother suggested that the children should be taught to keep their eyes on the page and try to read silently along with the child who is reading aloud. One mother suggested watching when the person next to him is turning pages.

A foresighted mother asked, "What will our hearing impaired children do when most of the academic subjects are taught by television? Visual aids are coming more and more into vogue, but will the persons programming the courses keep in mind our children who need lipreading cues?"

6. *Spelling:* There was some disagreement as to the need for so much phonics work. One parent reported that her child can spell any word given him because of his phonics training. Another disagreed that phonics helps because the English language is not entirely phonetic.

"Randy spells well and he surely does use his phonics. I took him to the eye doctor the other day and he was asked to read the letters on the chart. Instead of pronouncing them by name he read buh, kuh, and so forth. The doctor didn't know what was happening until I explained."

7. *Speech therapy:* Some of the children were getting speech therapy at school and others were being helped by parents at home.

"My daughter is in speech therapy class and the therapist uses the reading vocabulary and spelling lists as material for the correction of sounds."

"My son is getting it, but it's not doing him any good. He brings home such things as tongue twisters and has to draw pictures of the words he is supposed to be working on. I have never talked to the therapist."

"I asked Joe what he did in speech class and he said the speech therapist asks him what he likes on TV. Joe tells her, then she tries to guess what he says. Yes, he tells me all of this."

"I think the children miss a lot in class by taking time out for speech therapy. Billy misses reading class when he goes, and I think his reading is more important than the few faulty sounds he has."

8. *Television:* One mother brought up the question "Do many of

the children watch TV?" At home, most of the parents reported that only cartoon-type programs were watched. At school some Spanish and science classes were being presented on television. The sound apparently is difficult for most of them to decode, and the speaker's face is not always visible.

## Teaching the Semantic Aspects of Language

Teachers and parents concentrate on ways in which their children with hearing impairment can be taught to generalize their concepts through the use of words.

## Generalizing Concepts

All children in a kindergarten class knew how to use the word *catch* in a sentence providing the word *ball* was also used. (The boy can *catch* a *ball*.) After reviewing the unit on Pets, the teacher generalized the word *catch* to things which do not have hands. "A dog can *catch* a *ball*. The fish can *catch* a *bug*." The next step was to teach a new concept such as "Don't go near David. He has the chicken pox and you might *catch* it from him."

Eight year old Sharon, with hearing impairment, visited the school where she received pre-academic training. She stopped by her former classroom and peeked in. Here were a group of children with normal hearing. Sharon, observing that no one was wearing a hearing aid, turned to her mother and said, "These children must be 'hard of talking' not 'hard of hearing.'" Sharon's mother had a new concept to teach her daughter.

### WORD CONCEPTS OF EMOTION

Words which express emotions are an important part of early vocabulary development. Often children do not learn incidentally the meaning of contrast words such as *happy* and *sad* or gradations of emotions; *very happy*, *happy*, and *not so happy*. Parents are not aware of the need for reflecting feelings back to their children. It is not natural, for example, for a parent to say to his hearing impaired child who just hit his friend, "I know how you feel. You were angry when he wouldn't give you a turn." *Planned instruction for children with hearing impairment is necessary if we expect them to understand their emotions as well as feelings of others.*

### WORD CONCEPTS OF MORALITY

Concepts of morality are taught and reinforced often through punishment, but accompanied by word symbols. "That's *naughty*." "Tell the *truth*." "Don't *tattle*." and "Be *honest*." These words are difficult to define, hence the use of them is avoided long past the time they should have been taught. Appropriate words for right and wrong conduct must become a part of the vocabulary of hearing impaired children early in life.

## WORD CONCEPTS OF SOUND

The meaning of words which connote concepts of sound—*voice, noise, sound, loud, soft* are important parts of oral and written communication. Children with hearing impairment can develop concepts of sound even though they do not always hear what others hear.

> Ron, with an island of hearing at 500 Hz attended the rodeo parade with his class. As the band passed by playing a muted tune, Ron turned to his teacher and asked, "Miss Solomon, can you hear that?" She answered "Yes," and he immediately replied, "I can't."

All children who have some measurable hearing and use a hearing aid can develop concepts of sound. Early in the training program the teacher provides, in a functional situation, sound stimuli which can be heard by all the children irrespective of their aided thresholds. Once the concept of the presence and absence of sound is learned, the teacher introduces auditory stimuli that some of the children cannot hear. She asks, "Did you hear it?"

Words connoting sound are best taught in functional situations.

> John came to school with a severe cold and a hoarse voice. "Your *voice* is *hoarse* this morning. Do you have a cold?" asked the teacher.

When words are comprehended in functional situations they are used meaningfully.

> It was visitor's day in Mrs. Sunkle's class. Each child brought an object in a paper bag which was closed. The game was designed to teach the children how to describe an object without naming it. Rhonda with greater than 85 dB (ASA) impairment used an incorrect word, so Mrs. Sunkle, with hand hiding her face (so the audience could not lip-read) and in a louder than usual whisper, provided the correct word. Rhonda said, "Don't you know the mothers can *hear* that kind of *whispering?*"

If children with hearing impairment have acquired a vocabulary of words connoting sound, they will have advantages in a reading readiness class. Many, because of amplification, will be able to hear differences between phonemes and participate in such activities as "Tell me a word that sounds like (and later rhymes with) *boot.*"

## COLLOQUIAL LANGUAGE

Associating with normal hearing children provides a good environment for acquiring the colloquial language of the community. Further experience is gained when parents read comic strips to the child with hearing impairment.

DICTIONARY

The use of a dictionary should begin as soon as feasible. The ability to define their own words makes hearing impaired children more independent of the family.

## Teaching Sentence Structure

Most research related to sentence structure of children with hearing impairment has been conducted in schools for the *deaf* using samples of their written material. Common findings have been omission of function words: articles, prepositions, auxiliary verbs.

> The following are writing samples of a residential school for the deaf graduate employed as a typist. She was asked, "Do you want a doughnut?" Shaking her head she wrote, "I'm very gain fat." Asking about a forthcoming holiday she wrote, "Does you think we got off Wednesday?" A note left to the staff before resigning her job for marriage: "To all of you, I love you and I miss you. I will coming to see all of you sometime. Marie."

Common reasons attributed to poorly structured sentences in a *deaf* population are inability to attach meaning to words such as *the, have, as,* and difficulty encountered in lipreading these words in connected discourse. In order to overcome the omission and misuse of function words, analytical approaches to structuring language have been used. Yet, the *formal structuring of sentences has not been the answer because the majority of deaf students graduating from State Schools for the Deaf demonstrate substandard oral and written language.*

A more realistic reason for failure to structure oral and written sentences lies in: (1) lack of early amplification or no amplification, (2) a late start in oral communication training, and (3) ignoring maturation levels.

If a child wears a hearing aid, is enrolled in a training program at two years of age or younger, and a natural approach to teaching language is employed he stands a good chance of acquiring the oral language code and developing appropriate oral communication skills. Although the children may not be able to hear and/or lip-read all phonetic elements in a sentence, *they do receive more usable auditory information than was ever suspected two decades ago.*

Equally important is the fact that these youngsters go through many of the same developmental stages of language as normal hearing children. Attempting to force hearing impaired children into an adult pattern of speaking before they are ready may account for a good bit of their poor sentence structure. "Go bye-bye car," at a language age of 2 years is just as acceptable a phrase for a hearing impaired child functioning at this language age as for the child with no hearing impairment. Attempting to force a structured sentence, "I want to go in the car with Daddy," before a child is ready, is a deterrent to the acquisition of language.

Consider another aspect of normal language development. Children with normal hearing first make negative sentences in a primitive form, "No eat tatos, mamma." This primitive form gradually develops into "I don't care for any potatoes, thank you." Does the hearing impaired child who says, "No eat tatos, mamma," have faulty sentence structure because of his hearing impairment or because he is at that developmental stage in language expression? *The qualified teacher observes the child's language behavior in light of developmental linguistics.*

The outstanding morphological errors made by children with hearing impairment are with verb tense and plurals. With regard to tense, the child said, "I walk home yesterday." The word "walked" became "walk." Perhaps the sound of *ed* (t) which changes present to past tense was never heard or seen through lipreading cues. With regard to plurals, phonetic inventories of children with hearing impairment may reveal omissions or substitutions of phonemes for all sibilent sounds. For example, *s* and *z* may not be heard and therefore are omitted on such plural nouns as hats, shoes.

## Teaching Speech Patterns

### PHONEMIC PATTERNS

Correct pronunciation of consonant and vowel sounds are taught by some teachers before the child has "discovered" oral language. Early training in phonetic placement, in theory, is practiced to avoid subsequent articulatory errors. Although this concept may be valid, it does not always work in a clinical situation.

The exact developmental order in which a child distinguishes phonemes is not known. Clinical evidence, however, does demonstrate common factors in the acquisition of the phonetic elements of speech. If a hearing impaired child appears to be following the general pattern of children with normal hearing, then speech therapy is contraindicated.

Jenny, age five, with a speech reception threshold of 85 dB (ASA) had been in a pre-academic program for three years. Her oral communication level approximated that of a four-year-old. A phonetic inventory revealed the following substitutions common to children this age: "sork" for "fork," "dirl" for "girl," and "lellow" for "yellow."

Children with hearing impairment must be placed in an environment conducive to learning oral language. Vocabulary building and concept development at early ages are vital to comprehension and expression of language. Incidental teaching of articulatory skills during this time is warranted but not at the expense of causing confusion between the language and speech aspects of communication. The teacher, through interpretation of periodic phonetic inventories, is aware of errors and determines when speech therapy should start. With some, it may be when language is approximately at the four-year level. With the majority, speech therapy and phonics are combined with reading-readiness instruction.

### STRESS PATTERNS

With modern, electronic, wearable hearing aids, children demonstrating only islands of residual hearing develop appropriate syllable stress. Though they hear limited portions of the word, they incidentally acquire stress patterns. It is unlikely that the word elephant would be pronounced as elephánt.

Limited pitch variation leading to monotonous voice quality is still common among children with only islands of hearing. Techniques to help them monitor their voices have been relatively unsuccessful. New methods are needed.

## Lipreading and Auditory Training

Lipreading (or speechreading) refers to the visual skills that assist a person with hearing impairment to develop comprehension of oral language. Studies related to the acquisition of lipreading ability tell little if anything not already known through clinical observation. Teachers have long been aware that if placed in an ideal environment, persons with hearing impairment have better understanding of what is said to them. Important to this environment is maximum use of amplification, angle and distance from the speaker, adequate lighting on the speaker's face, facial expression, jaw, lip, and tongue movements of the speaker, and content of what is being said.

Auditory training is frequently defined as the process of making sound meaningful and forming habits of attending to sound. To accomplish this process, children are provided with maximum benefits in hearing aid amplification and are taught to make use of their aided thresholds. Amplification and listening skills become the basis for their acquisition of oral communication. Theoretically a child may hear the sentence, "Throw it away" in such a distorted fashion that it approximates "oh i a ey." If amplification allows him to consistently hear "oh i a ey" for "Throw it away," then what is jargon to persons with normal hearing becomes symbolic for someone with hearing impairment. The added visual cues or lip-reading skills make the phrase "Throw it away" distinguishable in meaning from "Give it to me." A combination of listening and looking are important to the development of oral communication.

Teaching the skills of lipreading, auditory discrimination, tactile, and kinesthetic awareness as separate entities in a beginning language development program is unrealistic. At least four different systems of communication would be presented to the child.

Learning to identify the sentence, "Throw it away," through visual cues alone, involves the identification of certain lip, tongue, and jaw movements. Learning the same command through an amplifier without visual cues is another form of symbolic language. At this point the child has learned two means of communicating, a visual and an auditory language.

With no visual or auditory cues he is asked to place his hand on certain portions of the speaker's neck or face. The command "Throw it away," is spoken and the child without auditory or visual cues feels some vibratory movements which he is expected to convert into something meaningful. Once the specific senses, auditory, visual, and tactile have been "trained" a combination of look, listen, and feel are offered simultaneously—a fourth form of learning the verbal command "Throw it away."

It is doubtful that any teacher drills on separate sensory modalities to the extent described above, particularly in the child's early attempts to acquire oral communication. There is every reason to believe, however, that many children are subjected to unnecessary hours of lipreading without amplification, auditory training without visual cues, and tactile stimulation with or without the other sensory modalities. One has only to visit classes in residential and day schools for the *deaf*, or special sessions with speech and hearing clinicians to observe such practices. Pictures still appear on magazine covers which show a child wearing earphones and his hand on the teacher's face or the sounding board of a piano. If he is hearing, it is doubtful that he needs the added tactile stimuli.

Appropriate amplification and knowledge of skills employed in lipreading become the teacher's tools in a program for children with hearing impairment. She teaches look-and-listen skills simultaneously in the presentation of oral material. The majority of children somehow learn to piece together the auditory and visual bits into a meaningful whole. Once language emerges they recognize the importance of listening and looking.

Ron had no measurable hearing above 500 Hz but had been enjoying the Christmas songs. He knew the meaning of the words *music, sing,* and *songs.* With the benefits derived from hearing aid amplification he had developed good rhythm and stress while singing. Pitch variation, as could be expected, was poor.

The teacher asked the children which song they would like to sing and
Ron was quick to raise his hand. With permission to reply, he answered,
"Let's sing that 'Ho, Ho' song so I can look and learn the words."

## Language of Signs

The language of signs consists of natural gestures such as pointing, waving, beckoning, posturing of fingers, hand(s), and arm(s) in
sequential movements to represent concepts of daily living, and finger-
spelling (forming letters with the fingers to spell words). The nonoral
language learned by many children in academic programs for the deaf
includes a combination of the three forms of symbolism.

The fact that a child is taught to sign is not so tragic. But the
knowledge that he has been taught to sign in lieu of a chance to develop
oral communication gives him an unnecessary handicap—inability to
communicate with persons who use primarily oral language. Some
teachers recommend a combination of oral language and signing for
children in pre-academic programs.

Preschool children even with appropriate training initially are
slow to acquire oral language concepts if their auditory discrimination
is poor. It would seem a double burden to expect them to learn simultaneously two languages. Until scientific research demonstrates the advantages of teaching preschool children signing in combination with
oral language, teachers are advised to begin with an oral approach.

*The language of signs should not be looked upon as one of the
teaching evils of training programs.* On the contrary, signing has its
place with certain hearing impaired persons. Failure to develop a means
of communication may have a serious impact of a psychological nature
which far exceeds the language impairment, therefore teaching a sign
language is indicated under many circumstances: (1) the child who fails
to develop oral language because of a late exposure or inability, for
reasons unknown, to generate oral sentences, (2) signing as a second
language for the hearing impaired person who may wish to communicate with nonoral persons, (3) signing as a language for the cerebral
palsied child who will never be able to make his wants known through
oral communication because of a seriously impaired speech mechanism,
(4) signing as a second language for normal hearing persons who wish
to communicate with parents or friends who do not comprehend oral
symbolization, and (5) signing as a second language for purposes of
serving as an interpreter.

## PSYCHOLOGICAL FACTORS

In an effort to improve the language skills of children, adults often
lose sight of a child's need for acceptance and praise. Constant repri-

manding or correction of the child's faulty language or speech patterns may lead to frustration and withdrawal from communicative situations.

Children, especially those with hearing impairment, must be able to look upon language as a pleasurable and rewarding experience. Parents and teachers help them accomplish this goal by knowing the language and learning level of each child as he progresses through the various phases of oral comprehension and expression.

## SUMMARY

There is increasing recognition that the training of children with hearing impairment requires a multiprofessional approach. No longer can the traditional curriculum for training educators of the *deaf* meet the needs. Departments of education, audiology, speech pathology, and psychology are combining their efforts to plan pre-academic and academic programs that will assist hearing impaired children to develop adequate oral and written language skills. The results should yield fewer schools for the *deaf* and fewer children enrolled in special education classes.

# 10

# Adapting the Curriculum Guide: Children in a Pre-Academic Setting

Basic assessment and training principles, in the areas of language and learning, have been presented on the preceding pages. In Chapter 9 specific application of these principles has been applied to children who manifest varying degrees of sensory hearing impairment. Techniques as they apply to this particular group are relevant, with the exception of electronic amplification, to any group of children enrolled in a pre-academic program.

The fundamental approach is identical: locating, identifying the etiology of the problem if feasible, obtaining medical and/or prosthetic care when indicated, assessing language, learning, and emotional behavior, development of a curriculum guide, starting the child at a level where he can succeed in the modalities to be trained, knowing when to circumvent deficiencies that do not respond to training, and keeping the child moving at his maturational pace.

## LABELS FOR CLASS PLACEMENT

Labels for class placement are often necessary in planning school programs: hearing impaired, visually impaired, mentally retarded, blind, multiply handicapped, normal, and gifted. Careful observations and descriptions of children, however, are far more meaningful to the teacher than labels, because individual differences within labeled groups are becoming increasingly apparent to the teacher and researcher. Both are interested in finding the level at which each child can function in the areas of language and the avenues of learning needed for academic success and emotional stability. Other pertinent information includes each child's rate of learning, motivation, and family background.

## Labels That Are Nonfunctional

BRAIN INJURED

There is a group of children, who, because of their hyperactivity, distractibility, and variability in behavior have come under the rubric *Brain Injured* (BI), the *Strauss Syndrome* or *Minimally Brain Injured* (MBI). Strauss and Lehtinen's publication (103) was a distinct contribution to the understanding and training of some children with brain damage. However, because readers frequently misinterpreted the text, diagnosticians and teachers were quick to label children *Brain Injured* even in the absence of data to prove neurologic deficits.

Following the Strauss publication, numerous scientific and observational studies appeared in the literature setting forth many hypotheses but few scientific conclusions regarding children with brain injury. There was and still is an attempt to answer many questions. Do all brain injured children as compared with non-brain injured children do poorly in sorting tests? Are all brain injured children hyperactive and distractible? Can they think only in concrete terms? Do they demonstrate deficits in only specific modalities of language and learning or in all modalities? Is it necessarily true that every brain injured child displays one or more deficits which will hinder academic achievement? Which aspects of a child's language, learning, emotional stability, and social perception are related to brain damage, and which are the results of the secondary effects of a child trying to cope with his environment?

"A major conclusion to be drawn from these studies is that brain injury can result in a bewildering array of behavioral symptoms, no one of which is common to all children. The variety of symptoms is not surprising when one considers the immense diversity in nature, site, timing, extent, and source of lesions in the central nervous system; rather, it is somewhat surprising that any similarities emerge at all." [1]

The variety of symptoms which may result from brain injury do not necessarily relate to language, learning, and emotional problems. The obvious example is a cerebral palsied child who, because of brain injury, demonstrates motor difficulties in one or more of his extremities, yet is a successful student and has a good chance of becoming a successful citizen.

Selection of the category *Brain Injury* as a label for class placement in educational institutions was a horrendous mistake. This label became

[1] H. B. and N. M. Robinson, *The Mentally Retarded Child* (New York, McGraw-Hill, 1965), p. 264.

a frightening and meaningless term to the teacher who was hired to shape language and learning skills of brain injured children. Somehow she was led to believe that these children were so deviant from the normal, because of brain injury, that a total new approach to management and training must be developed. Lack of information, misinformation, and sheer fright kept her from accepting the position of teaching brain injured classes. She was within her rights; the label was a poor choice. Because of this dilemma hundreds of children with theoretical or proven brain injury were placed on waiting lists because of teacher shortages.

In pre-academic programs, brain injury is considered part of the physiological and behavioral syndrome, but not a label which determines class placement or techniques for teaching. Training is based upon careful assessments, objective and subjective, of language and the avenues of learning necessary for academic achievement.

### LANGUAGE DISORDERED

And suddenly there were children in the schools who had language problems but no evidence of brain injury. They were somehow different from other children who did not achieve academically. Psychometric tests demonstrated a twenty point difference between oral and performance type tests in favor of the latter. Or, low scores on vocabulary comprehension tests did not seem commensurate with other learning skills. Said the educators: "We must develop a new label—a new category of classes. And we will call them *language classes.*"

The discovery of this nebulous group of children, their labeling and placement in full day or part day language classes was not as simple as the passage above portrays. Numerous meetings of decision-making groups were held before the label was acceptable. Only then, in addition to classes for children with *brain injury,* were classes for children with *language problems* opened and teacher recruitment instigated.

Who would teach these children? Educators were and still are in a quandary as to whether teachers should be drawn from regular classrooms, special education, or if the services of a speech clinician might not suffice.

If academic achievement is dependent upon language, oral and written, then why do schools need a special type teacher? The *basic task is not in recruiting teachers,* but in finding the level upon which each child is functioning in specific language and learning skills. With this information, insightful teachers group children and begin to teach them at their functioning level.

Separating children with language disorders into groups distinct from classes for brain injured children only confounds the academic picture.

As in academic settings, pre-academic programs are designed for children with oral language disorders, as well as children who through psycholinguistic type tests are predicted to have future problems in written language. The assessment and training techniques are essentially the same as for any group of children with communication problems regardless of such labels as *Brain Injured* or *Language Disordered*. Perhaps a better label for these children would be Specific Learning Disabilities.

## Labels That Are Functional

Significant labels are those which include the greatest possibility of homogeniety in grouping children; hearing impairment, visual impairment, mental retardation, specific learning disabilities (including aphasia), emotionally disturbed, multiply handicapped, normal, and gifted.

### MENTAL RETARDATION

Bill was jaundiced at birth and cyanotic for several days after birth. He was subject to Jacksonian-type seizures early in life but they were later controlled through medication. All developmental milestones were late and there were no observable periods of especially rapid development in any areas.

An assessment for this boy was first made at age six years, five months. The reason for referral read "He is not talking well and does not seem to be able to learn." An assessment with such items as form boards, bead stringing, block building, and developmental data revealed a mental age at approximately three years. His behavior was extremely immature. The recommendations were concise: enrollment in a class for trainable retarded children.

The *Language and Learning Assessment: For Training* was administered when Bill was thirteen years, four months of age. He had learned only minimal readiness work for academic subjects. His performance on the battery of tests demonstrated abilities that measured below the six-year level. Bill had subaverage intelligence so severe that by his thirteenth year of life he was still unable to profit from an academic program. He is currently living with his widowed mother and attending classes for educable retarded children. No future plans for Bill have been considered.

Would Bill have made greater gains had he been assessed and trained at an earlier age? Would he then be a better candidate for vocational training?

There is no answer but there are implications. Mentally retarded children must be studied and helped from the time they are born. Parent readiness classes and preschool, pre-academic programs must be pro-

## TABLE 3
## SPEECH, HEARING, AND LANGUAGE CENTER
### LANGUAGE AND LEARNING ASSESSMENT: For Training
### (LLAT)

Name:    Bill                              Age: yr. 13 mo. 4

| ABILITIES ASSESSED | TESTS | M.A. Scores |
|---|---|---|
| **LANGUAGE SKILLS** | | |
| *Comprehension* | Single Words (3) | 8 - 0 |
| | Connected Discourse (44, 107, 108) | 5 - 6 |
| *Expression* | Connected Discourse (44, 107, 108) | 5 - 0 |
| | Defining (108) | no score |
| | Sentence Structure | fair |
| | (poor, fair, adequate) | |
| **AVENUES OF LEARNING** | | |
| *Memory-Attention (Short term)* | | |
| Auditory | Digits (108, 118) | 3 - 0 to 4 - 0 |
| | Sentences (108) | 4 - 0 to 6 - 0 |
| Visual | For Pictures (57) | 7 - 0 to 9 - 0 |
| Visual-Motor | Tapping (6) | 4 - 6 to 5 - 6 |
| | Tapping (4) | 4 - 0 to 4 - 6 |
| | Paper Folding (57) | 4 - 6 to 5 - 6 |
| | Draw-A-Man (47) | 4 - 6 |
| *Visual-Motor-* | Form Board (108) | dna |
| *Perception* | Block Patterns (57) | 5 - 6 to 7 - 0 |
| (no memory) | Block Patterns (118) | No Score |
| | Copy Forms (108) | 3 - 6 to 5 - 0 |
| **SOCIAL MATURITY** | Social Maturity Scale (47) | dna |

vided. Appropriate training including prevocational and vocational training at appropriate ages must be instigated. Only then will follow-up
studies of mentally retarded children become meaningful.

*Definition.* "Mental retardation refers to subaverage general intellectual
functioning which originates during the developmental period and is associated with impairment in adaptive behavior." [2] Heber's definition suc-

[2] R. F. Heber, "A Manual on Terminology and Classification in Mental
Retardation," *American Journal of Mental Deficiency,* Vol. 64 (Monograph
supplement, 1959. Revised Edition, 1961), p. 3.

cinctly defines a group of children who will not be able to achieve with children of average intelligence.

There has been in the past and currently is a tendency to continue to dichotomize mentally retarded children into labels of *educable mentally retarded* (EMR) and *trainable mentally retarded* (TMR) or classifications of *borderline, mild, moderate, severe, or profound retardation.* Very little information is transmitted to the teacher through such dichotomizing.

Before a training program can be planned for a child with generalized intellectual impairment, an audit must be made of his assets and deficits in the modalities of language and learning. Because these children are more often than not retarded in social maturity, careful assessment of self-help skills and social perception is required. It is conceivable that many mentally retarded children, age six through adulthood would have made better educational gains had they been started in a pre-academic program that was designed to attempt to bring them up to academic levels. Too often the label mental retardation creates a misconception of the child's potential. A low IQ score does not necessarily mean that this level is fixed. On the contrary, it means the child needs help—help through appropriate assessments and appropriate training programs.

## COMMENTS

1. As compared to normal children, the mentally retarded learn in smaller and slower increments. Many repetitions of skills to be learned may be necessary before moving on to a slightly more difficult task.

2. Some mentally retarded children demonstrate twelve month gains on many of the test items after their first year of training in a pre-academic program. Cautious diagnosticians and teachers will not encourage parents to believe that their child will be normal. Parents should be advised that perhaps their child was not working at this potential before enrollment and the training provided a catching-up period. During the next year the gains may not be so great.

3. Before entering a training program a mentally retarded child usually has a history of many failures. Parents have wanted him to do better than he was capable of doing, hence placed him in impossible performance situations. As a result he finds it difficult to attempt even a previously known task for fear of further failure. As with all children the mentally retarded should experience more successes than failures from day to day.

4. Objective tests do not measure creativity, motivation, social perception, and other abilities important to learning and interpersonal relationships. A subjective awareness of the levels of these abilities and ways to capitalize or improve upon them is an essential part of training mentally retarded children.

5. Because of his subaverage intelligence, the retarded child is too often deprived of experiences basic to the development of language and learning skills. Parents must be encouraged to expose their retarded children to the many experiences that are provided outside as well as inside the home.

6. The training goal for mentally retarded children is economic usefulness.

## SPECIFIC LEARNING DISABILITIES

Debbie at age five years, four months was referred to a Speech, Hearing, and Language Center with the complaint that she was *deaf* and could not communicate orally.

Although pure tone audiometric studies were difficult to obtain on this child's ears, she did give evidence of normal hearing when speech signals were presented. These results were verified the following year when her responses to standard audiometry were reliable at normal threshold levels.

A language and learning assessment revealed a severe deficit in oral communication and specific deficits in some areas of learning. Debbie was enrolled in a pre-academic program.

Because a complete physical evaluation had never been made, she was referred to Children's Hospital where among other medical work-ups, a complete neurological study with EEG was given. Abnormal EEG findings were studied by the pediatric neurologist who decided to attempt medication for purposes of improving language function.

Within two weeks after medication was started, Debbie's oral communication began to emerge unbelievably fast. Seven months later she scored at the four and one half year level on oral comprehension items and at the three year level on usage items. This little girl remained in the pre-academic program until she was seven and was then transferred to a nongraded class for academic work. Her performance at age eight demonstrated continued deficits in oral communication, but some assets in the areas of learning which were assessed. Although Debbie could perform better than age levels on some skills, her deficits were great enough to warrant continuation in special education.

*Definition.* As distinguished from the mentally retarded, children with specific learning disabilities demonstrate subaverage intellectual functioning in one or more avenues of learning, but not in all. They are like the retarded in that they demonstrate intra-group differences, and in many instances are unable to achieve on age level academically. From a medical point of view some of these children demonstrate neurological problems while others do not. Some respond to medications and others apparently receive no benefit.

## TABLE 4
## SPEECH, HEARING, AND LANGUAGE CENTER
## LANGUAGE AND LEARNING ASSETS:  For Training
### (LLAT)

Name:  Debbie ...............

Age:  yr. 5 mo. 4    Age:  yr. 9 mo. 0

| ABILITIES ASSESSED | TESTS | M.A. Scores | M.A. Scores |
|---|---|---|---|
| **LANGUAGE SKILLS** | | | |
| *Comprehension* | Single Words (3) ........ | 3 - 0 | 6 - 6 |
| | Connected Discourse (44, 107, 108) ........ | 2 - 0 | *6 - 0 |
| *Expression* | Connected Discourse (44, 107, 108) ........ | below 2 - 0 | 5 - 4 |
| | Defining (108) ........ | below 2 - 0 | 4 - 6 to 5 - 0 |
| | Sentence  Structure (poor, fair, adequate) ........ | poor | poor |
| **AVENUES OF LEARNING** | | | |
| *Memory-Attention (Short term)* | | | |
| Auditory | Digits (108, 118) ........ | 2 - 6 | 3 - 0 to 4 - 0 |
| | Sentences (108) ........ | below 3 - 6 | below 3 - 6 |
| Visual | For Pictures (57) ........ | 4 - 6 to 5 - 6 | 7 - 0 to 9 - 0 |
| Visual-Motor | Tapping (6) ........ | below 4 - 6 | 7 - 6 to 8 - 6 |
| | Tapping (4) ........ | below 4 - 0 | 6 - 0 to 7 - 0 |
| | Paper Folding (57) ........ | 6 - 0 to 8 - 6 | *8 - 6 |
| | Draw-A-Man (47) ........ | 6 - 3 | 9 - 3 |
| *Visual-Motor-Perception* | | | |
| *(no memory)* | Form Board (108) ........ | dna | dna |
| | Block Patterns (57) ........ | 5 - 6 to 7 - 0 | 10 - 0 to 11 - 6 |
| | Block Patterns (118) ........ | dna | 6 - 6 to 7 - 2 |
| | Copy Forms (108) ........ | 3 - 6 to 5 - 0 | *7 - 0 |
| **SOCIAL MATURITY** | Social Maturity Scale (47) ........ | dna | dna |

In the classroom, teachers describe children with specific learning disabilities in one or more of the following ways: inability to follow individual or group instructions, difficulty in remembering such sequential events as two or more commissions, seasons, days of the week, or rote counting; telling time; limited attention to the task at hand, and concrete thinking. Many are falsely suspected of having hearing impairment.

These same deficits are described by parents as: "He doesn't pay attention to what I ask him to do." "He could not learn to say his prayers." "He is scatter-brained." "He is stubborn." "He uses words like my three-year-old." "At times he doesn't seem to hear me. I think he is *deaf*: he's not retarded though."

Steve, a child with specific learning disabilities, described his problem in a little different way.

> Kenny was discussing what he brought to class for "Show and Tell." During his monologue six-year-old Steve raised his hand and kept it up until Kenny was finished. "Do you have a question?" asked the teacher. Steve struggled to remember what he wanted to say but couldn't. His reply, "When I raised my hand, Kenny was talking—I forgot—sometimes my head gets all mixed up: sometimes I can remember."
>
> Miss Williams was reading a story to the class during a period of time when there was some confusion and noise outside the classroom. At the conclusion of the story she asked a question of Molly, who replied, "I don't know. I take in what I can. I only heard the noise."

Many confusing terms describe children with language disorders and specific learning disabilities: central auditory disorders, dysacousis, perceptual disturbance, minimally brain injured, aphasoid, and childhood aphasia to name but a few. Some writers have attempted to link these terms with retro-cochlear damage, and to stress the need to assess *central* auditory problems. As a consequence, many diagnosticians have lost sight of the importance of pure tone and speech audiometry in ruling out sensory hearing impairment. Rosenberg,[3] in an abstract of a paper delivered at the 1964 American Speech and Hearing Association convention, presented the issue. "A disturbing trend has been apparent recently in the early diagnosis of auditory disorders in children. This trend concerns the concept of auditory disorders which are not peripheral in origin and the terms 'aphasia,' 'congenital aphasia,' 'central auditory imperception,' 'central dysacousis,' 'auditory scramble,' 'neurological deafness,' and 'central deafness' are widely used. Although such entities may exist, the use of such diagnoses is absurdly out of proportion to the possibility of their existence in the general population. The Audiology

---

[3] P. E. Rosenberg, "Modern Trends in Auditory Misdiagnosis," *Asha, A Journal of the American Speech and Hearing Association*, Vol. 6, No. 10 (October, 1964), p. 411.

Department of Temple University Medical Center has seen a large number of children labeled with one of these terms. The majority of these children, both in early and later tests, have been found to have peripheral deafness. The indiscriminate use of these diagnostic labels may be due to ignorance on the part of the examiner, to uncertainty in examination interpretation, or to a desire to keep up with the current trend. I feel that a reassessment of diagnostic direction is indicated. The primary responsibility of the audiologist is to make a statement concerning hearing. When he goes afield into areas served by other professions, he does himself and the patient a disservice. Incorrect early diagnosis has led to educational problems. Children are being placed in educational settings completely unsuitable for them; requisite amplification is being postponed for years and valuable rehabilitative time is being irrevocably lost. Standard audiometric procedures can frequently be used with young children—some children are, in fact, deaf."

The use of labels in an academic environment is dangerous, if complete assessments are not made. Labels can be applied and used for grouping children in classrooms if appropriate assessments are made.

COMMENTS

Parents of children with specific learning disorders were asked this question: How do you think you have changed since you and your child were first enrolled in the pre-academic program? A compilation of their answers stated that they had learned to:

1. Talk more slowly and use shorter phrases and sentences.

2. Become more encouraged with vocalizations and attempts to talk and not be discouraged with substandard language and speech.

3. Use much more repetition when teaching a new idea.

4. Talk in more detail and expand on each idea.

5. Separate activities into individual steps. "I would have taught my child to write and mail a letter to Santa all in one day. Now I know to take more than one day."

6. Make better use of my time in teaching my child. "Instead of saying 'Get out of my way while I'm cooking' I make use of my work for building language. Now I don't have to sit down for certain periods with my child in a stereotyped situation. I teach him while doing the dishes, putting him to bed, or when driving the car."

7. Become more aware of what my child does not know. "I don't skip over these things like I used to."

8. Apply what I learned in parent class to my other children. They have benefited a lot.

9. Observe my child and listen to what he says. This tells me what he does and doesn't know.

10. Keep encouraging my child until he gets "over the hump."

APHASIA

Dear Speech Pathologist:

We have been employed to represent Jay for personal injuries sustained on April 11, 1963. Our client has advised us that you have been treating him and we are enclosing a written authorization signed by Mrs. M. which authorizes you to furnish us information concerning her son's condition.

At your earliest convenience, will you please furnish in triplicate a medical report containing the entire history including examinations, diagnosis, treatment, and prognosis. Please bill us for preparing the report and we will remit payment. Also furnish us with an itemized statement of Jay's account with you.

Very truly yours,
Signed by the attorneys

TO WHOM IT MAY CONCERN:

This will authorize you to furnish to my attorneys, Brown and Jones, any and all information which they may request concerning injuries suffered and sustained by myself or any member of my family, including full information as to history, condition, diagnosis, treatment, and prognosis. Please do not furnish such information or give medical reports of any nature to anyone other than the above designated attorneys.

Signed by Jay's mother

September 11, 1963
Gentlemen: RE: Jay

Following a traffic accident sustained by the above named child, on April 11, 1963, he was admitted to Fairview Hospital where he received a medical diagnosis of cerebral contusion. (Please write to Dr. RKG for medical information.) On May 29, 1963, the present examiner was consulted to provide a speech, hearing, and language assessment and to make subsequent disposition of this portion of the boy's problem. At the time of the examination this six-year-old male had normal hearing but oral communication in only rudimentary fashion. He smiled at appropriate times and registered unhappiness when his mother left the room. He did not talk. He was able to select a spoon and comb from among several objects presented him, but it was felt that this was probably due to coincidence since he missed several other items of equal difficulty. The speech mechanism appeared to be adequate, but it was noted that the boy's tongue was almost continually in a sucking motion, being thrust slightly forward. At this time our impression was severe receptive-expressive aphasia from an acquired lesion.

I saw Jay for reassessment on June 12, 1963. He was cooperative but demonstrated very substandard performance. During the examination a great deal of perseveration and considerable distractibility to all auditory stimuli was noted. It was observed, however, that he could profit from instruction as demonstrated by his ability to learn a form board task and to match pictures. He comprehended little if any oral language and used no meaningful words or phrases during the assessment. A few weeks later Jay was enrolled in a pre-academic program which met for two hours five days a week. At the end of July he was reassessed again and his

## TABLE 5
### SPEECH, HEARING, AND LANGUAGE CENTER
### LANGUAGE AND LEARNING ASSESSMENT: For Training
(LLAT)

Name: Jay

| ABILITIES ASSESSED | TESTS | Age: yr. 6 mo. 9 M.A. Scores | Age: yr. 7 mo. 7 M.A. Scores |
|---|---|---|---|
| **LANGUAGE SKILLS** | | | |
| *Comprehension* | Single Words (3) | 6 - 9 | 7 - 3 |
| | Connected Discourse (44, 107, 108) | 4 - 10 | *6 - 0 |
| *Expression* | Connected Discourse (44, 107, 108) | 4 - 7 | 5 - 0 |
| | Defining (108) | 4 - 0 | 6 - 0 |
| | Sentence Structure (poor, fair, adequate) | Fair | Fair |
| **AVENUES OF LEARNING** | | | |
| *Memory-Attention (Short term)* | | | |
| Auditory | Digits (108, 118) | 2 - 6 to 3 - 0 | 5 - 6 to 7 - 0 |
| | Sentences (108) | below 4 - 0 | 5 - 0 to 6 - 0 |
| Visual | For Pictures (57) | 5 - 6 to 7 - 0 | 5 - 6 to 7 - 0 |
| Visual-Motor | Tapping (6) | 4 - 6 | 4 - 6 |
| | Tapping (4) | 4 - 0 to 6 - 0 | 4 - 0 to 6 - 0 |
| | Paper Folding (57) | 3 - 6 to 4 - 0 | 4 - 6 to 5 - 0 |
| | Draw-A-Man (47) | 4 - 6 | 4 - 6 |
| *Visual-Motor-Perception (no memory)* | Form Board (108) | dna | dna |
| | Block Patterns (57) | 3 - 6 to 4 - 6 | 5 - 6 to 7 - 0 |
| | Block Patterns (118) | dna | dna |
| | Copy Forms (108) | 3 - 6 to 5 - 0 | 5 - 0 to 7 - 0 |
| **SOCIAL MATURITY** | Social Maturity Scale (47) | dna | dna |

177

language comprehension for single words was at age level. Comprehension of connected discourse, however, was approximately two years below age level, as was his ability to answer questions, complete statements and define words.

Tests for short term auditory memory demonstrated scores at about the three year level.

Currently Jay is enrolled in a Readiness Class at the Speech, Hearing, and Language Center. He has made significant strides in language development in this short period of training. He is still considerably language delayed.

We do not feel that a prognosis can be made with certainty at this time. However, by looking at the gains already made and the favorable indications on the most recent test battery, it is the examiner's impression that considerable improvement in communication can be anticipated in an appropriate training situation.

We hope that this information will prove of value to you and that you will not hesitate to call on us if we may be of further service.

Sincerely,
Speech Pathologist

*Notes from Chart Rounds at Fairview Hospital, December 10, 1963.*
This patient's temper tantrums have continued with two incidents yesterday. It has been suggested that his explosive behavior be investigated from a neurological standpoint; treatments were also recommended. A neurological consultation will be requested. This patient's Thorazine dosage has been revised to alleviate some of the drowsiness during his language training classes. Apparently, the revision is adequate at this time.

The Speech, Hearing, and Language Center reports that he is having difficulty learning new material and will continue to need help. On discharge he will be referred to special education.

It is our endeavor to progress this young man to an ambulation program so that by discharge time prior to Christmas he will not need a wheelchair. Orders have been forwarded for the patient to ambulate to and from his therapies and about the ward area. The wheelchair will be used only to transport him to his classroom, but he will walk back from class. The wheelchair will continue to be used for disciplinary reasons. A conference will be held next Tuesday, during which the family will receive instructions.

Physician

*Report from classroom teacher in the Plains Independent School District.*
Jay is now nine years two months of age and has been enrolled in an orthopedic class in our special education program. He has been out of his wheelchair for many months and no longer wears his leg brace. His fine motor coordination is still very poor. He uses his whole arm for any motor tasks which, of course, interferes with writing skills. He is still using manuscript writing.

His performance in reading and arithmetic is on low second grade level. The results of the Stanford Binet, Form L, administered January, 1965, provided a mental age of six years two months with a chronological age of eight years two months. This yields an IQ score of 84 which the psychologist felt to be minimal.

Jay's primary problems are his inability to remember directions and information, and becoming upset when he cannot do what he wants to do.

Signed,
Jay's teacher

*Definition.* Aphasia is a symbolic disorder of language resulting from brain dysfunction, and may be accompanied by a deficit in one or more areas; intellectual, emotional, sensory motor.

Language and learning assessments for an aphasic child are no different than for any other child. The purpose is to provide information which will guide the teacher in her training program.

## COMMENTS

1. Spontaneous recovery of language probably occurs more frequently in a preschool aphasic child than it does in adults. Much harm can be done to the child, however, if parents are not properly guided. For a child to have had language and suddenly lose it through illness or accident is a baffling experience for parents. Carefully planned parent lectures, in lay language, are initially the most important part of the child's retraining program. Such classes should transpire as soon after the injury as feasible.

2. If there is paralysis of one or more of the child's limbs, parents should faithfully follow the suggestions of the physician for muscle retraining.

3. Retraining in language and learning skills follow the patterns discussed throughout this text: begin where the child can succeed and ·keep him moving toward higher goals.

4. Obtain a case history of the child's language and learning performance before the onset of his aphasia. He may have been a mentally retarded child before the cerebral insult. Without this information the label *aphasia* may be used long after it is diagnostically accurate.

5. Frequent reassessments keep the teacher apprised of progress which may be rapid in some patients.

6. Parents and teachers must keep in mind that everything an aphasic does is not necessarily due to his aphasia. Appropriate discipline and management of the aphasic child is just as important as with the normal child.

EMOTIONALLY DISTURBED

## TABLE 6
### SPEECH, HEARING, AND LANGUAGE CENTER
### LANGUAGE AND LEARNING ASSESSMENT: For Training
### (LLAT)

Name:     John                             Age: yr. 6   mo. 5

| ABILITIES ASSESSED | TESTS | M.A. Scores |
|---|---|---|
| **LANGUAGE SKILLS** | | |
| *Comprehension* | Single Words (3) | no response |
| | Connected Discourse (44, 107, 108) | no response |
| *Expression* | Connected Discourse (44, 107, 108) | no response |
| | Defining (108) | no response |
| | Sentence Structure | no response |
| | (poor, fair, adequate) | |
| **AVENUES OF LEARNING** | | |
| *Memory-Attention (Short term)* | | |
| Auditory | Digits (108, 118) | no response |
| | Sentences (108) | no response |
| Visual | For Pictures (57) | refused |
| Visual-Motor | Tapping (6) | refused |
| | Tapping (4) | refused |
| | Paper Folding (57) | 4 - 6 to 5 - 0 |
| | Draw-A-Man (47) | refused |
| *Visual-Motor-* | Form Board (108) | dna |
| *Perception* | Block Patterns (57) | 8 - 6 to 10 - 0 |
| (no memory) | Block Patterns (118) | refused |
| | Copy Forms (108) | 5 - 0 to 7 - 0 |
| **SOCIAL MATURITY** | Social Maturity Scale (47) | 4 - 0 |

SOCIAL MATURITY

Six-year-old John was first seen for an audiological study at age nine months. Audiometric testing was unsuccessful, so he was enrolled with his mother in a diagnostic-training program. It was soon apparent that this boy may have had a sensory hearing impairment but certainly had other problems as well.

In the case history record he was described as evidencing jaundice, edema, and breathing difficulties shortly after birth and required oxygen and a longer than usual stay in the hospital. He is said to have sucked quite poorly as a newborn. His motor development was slow; lifting his head at six months and sitting at eighteen months. He appeared to be totally without hearing and used no means of communication with other persons. Electroencephalographic studies were normal.

During his first two years of life he was not responsive to affection. At about age two he seemed to develop abnormal fears of new places and of going to sleep. These fears have gradually subsided but exist in limited situations. All of his play behavior was deviant.

In their post diagnostic conference, the physician and social worker were impressed with the parents and their relative degree of mental health. Mother was felt to be quite appropriate in her feelings and seemed to be a person capable of warm emotions, affection, and understanding. Father was also a warm person. It was felt that theirs was a close-knit family; good family relationships with John and three older normal siblings.

John was diagnosed by the psychiatrist as a "close fit with the primary autistic psychotic children described in Kanner." (63) However, quite in contrast to Kanner's children, are the serious and multiple early biological insults John received and the apparent normality of his parents.

The presence or absence of hearing impairment has never been established, for John ignores or does not hear any sound stimuli presented to him through audiometric testing techniques nor in his everyday environment.

Between the ages of nine months and the present time, the parents followed through with recommended training programs. Until John was four years of age he was kept in a fairly structured environment conducive to teaching children with severe hearing impairment. Subsequently he spent one year away from home in a psychiatric hospital which provides a great deal of permissive behavior. Upon John's return from the residential hospital, the parents were appalled at his regressed behavior—urinating and defecating where he desired, destroying any toys given him, and pushing food into his mouth with both hands.

A structured program was again initiated in a pre-academic type class and after two years, John regained what he had lost in the year spent at the residential hospital.

*The Language and Learning Assessment: For Training,* administered at age six years five months, revealed no functional oral or written communication, and only one asset—the ability to copy patterns when no memory was involved. The following notes were recorded at the time of the assessment. "Mother states that her son can do many things at home when he wants to. The examiner noted that John was eager to get started with the Hiskey Block Design subtest but completely ignored the WISC blocks when they were presented. It was difficult to know whether he was disinterested in some of the tasks presented him, or whether he knew he could not perform them. His hand skills were very poor. He could not hold a pencil firmly enough to do much with drawing. If mother holds his hand, he does better. He can trace his name, and crudely draw houses, cars, and other objects. When drawing cars, he appropriately places details such as door handles and the gas tank. He watches TV cartoons and laughs appropriately."

His means of communicating with people is to take them by the hand and lead them to his needs. As a last resort the speech pathologist recommended that the family use a language of signs at home and a reference was provided (55). Within six months the parents reported that their son could communicate with many of the signs they had taught him: It's time to eat. It's time for bed. Wash your hands. The parents have been encouraged to continue with the sign language and search for a class of young children who are being taught manual language.

John's prognosis for maintaining himself was poor in his early years and still is. Perhaps he has given many people a different look at parents and their autistic and/or emotionally disturbed children.

*Definition.* Emotional disturbance has come to be known as inadequate social perception and inappropriate participation in social situations. The most severe cases of emotional disturbance are likely to receive the label of schizophrenia, autism or schizophrenic-autistic syndrome, which in essence means a loss of contact with reality. The label, whether it be schizophrenia or autism, is a collective term for a variety of conditions, some or all of which might be present in an emotionally disturbed child.

The schizophrenic-autistic child ranges from almost complete withdrawal from his environment to borderline "withness." The label is given him only because he is not adequately in contact with his environment. His many other deviant performances may be characteristic of the child with hearing impairment, mental retardation, specific learning disabilities, or multiple handicaps.

Language may be completely absent as noted in the case of John or may be fairly adequate in some children having the same diagnosis of schizophrenic-autistic syndrome. Such was Paul who did not talk until four years of age, but who by seven and one half years performed on items of oral language comprehension and usage at the six year level. At age seven and one half he was capable of doing average first grade reading, writing, spelling, and arithmetic. In spite of academic achievement he remained relatively out of contact with people.

Severely emotionally disturbed children, in general, demonstrate faulty timing and integration of all learning skills. Some children catch up as they grow older, while others lag far behind.

As a group they elicit one or more of many inappropriate behavior patterns: phobias, panic, twirling, irrelevant conversation, resistance to change, compulsive activity with a particular object as a car, piece of string, or light fixture. They differ to a greater extent as to whether they are agile or clumsy, hyperactive or not, destructive or careful with toys. But as schizophrenic-autistic children, they all demonstrate poor contact with people.

Recognizing and describing autistic symptoms in children is a relatively easy task. Assessing their potential is difficult and how to train them remains an enigma.

There is another group of emotionally disturbed children who are in contact with their environment, but who demonstrate poor social perception. Their outstanding characteristic is not inability to learn or develop oral and written communication skills, but poor social relationships with people. Their behavior includes some but not necessarily all of the following: (1) *Antisocial behavior.* The child appears almost as if he consciously plans to annoy others, and by so doing becomes rejected by peers and adults. He plays with younger children best, yet, even they learn to avoid him. (2) *Distractibility.* Any sensory stimuli seems to demand the child's attention and he has difficulty attending to the task before him. (3) *Convulsive equivalents* of unknown etiology: stomachache, headache, leg cramps, fever. (4) *Frustration.* Stimuli, usually unknown to the observer, set him into temper tantrums or almost fits of rage. When he has recovered and others are still too upset to talk to him, he regains his status quo. (5) *Ignoring right vs. wrong.* Stealing, and lying, a phase that comes and goes. (6) *Anxiety.* Disintegration of learning and performance when unfamiliar, stressful, or unstructured situations arise. (7) *Ineffectiveness of punishment.* Parents report that any form of punishment they have tried has been ineffectual.

This lesser type of emotional disturbance may be observed in any population of children: gifted, normal, mentally retarded, or those with specific learning disabilities. The origin of these behavior disorders is felt to be organic in etiology, yet research has not clearly documented this hypothesis.

COMMENTS

1. Performance is better in a structured environment. The children need to be told what to do and when to do it. School age children often behave more acceptably in the classroom than in their home, which is difficult to structure.

2. Consistent discipline is desirable.

3. Teachers and parents can help prevent catastrophic reactions if they anticipate and avoid situations that bring on such reactions.

4. This child needs acceptance and praise from as many persons as possible. Because of his unacceptable social behavior he seldom experiences approbation.

## THE MULTIPLY HANDICAPPED

Through hindsight it is now known that Bob was a multiply handicapped child: cerebral palsied, hearing impaired, with specific learning disabilities and poor social perception.

### TABLE 7
### SPEECH, HEARING, AND LANGUAGE CENTER
### LANGUAGE AND LEARNING ASSESSMENT: For Training
### (LLAT)

Name:       Bob                                     Age: yr. __18__ mo. _2_

| ABILITIES ASSESSED | TESTS | M.A. Scores |
|---|---|---|
| **LANGUAGE SKILLS** | | |
| *Comprehension* | Single Words (3) | 5 - 9 |
| | Connected Discourse (44, 107, 108) | 4 - 0 |
| *Expression* | Connected Discourse (44, 107, 108) | too spotty to score |
| | Defining (108) | below 6 - 0 |
| | Sentence Structure (poor, fair, adequate) | poor |
| **AVENUES OF LEARNING** | | |
| *Memory-Attention (Short term)* | | |
| Auditory | Digits (108, 118) | 3 - 0 to 4 - 6 |
| | Sentences (108) | no score |
| Visual | For Pictures (57) | 5 - 6 to 7 - 0 |
| Visual-Motor | Tapping (6) | *15 - 6 |
| | Tapping (4) | *10 - 0 |
| | Paper Folding (57) | dna |
| | Draw-A-Man (47) | dna |
| *Visual-Motor-* | Form Board (108) | dna |
| *Perception* | Block Patterns (57) | *11 - 6 |
| (no memory) | Block Patterns (118) | *15 - 0 |
| | Copy Forms (108) | dna |
| **SOCIAL MATURITY** | Social Maturity Scale (47) | dna |

He was first seen at a Speech, Hearing, and Language Center at age five for audiological assessment and was found to have bilateral sensorineural hearing impairment, comparable to the reassessment at age eighteen. (See audiogram.) At age five a hearing aid was recommended and purchased. Bob was enrolled for two years at a residential school for cerebral palsied children. The primary goal to get this boy ambulatory was accomplished. At age 18 he walks with only a moderately deviant gait. No staff member in the residential school was acquainted with techniques for training children with hearing impairment. Bob was not encouraged to wear his hearing aid and little if any language training was provided.

At age seven he was enrolled in a public day school for the deaf where he remained until age sixteen. Every year he attended summer school. During this period of time he failed to develop any really functional oral communication other than comprehending simple words and familiar phrases. His language usage at age 18 was often unintelligible, lacked adequate sentence structure and was extremely limited in vocabulary. He could read words and a simple paragraph, but he could not comprehend their meaning. His writing reflected his poor oral language.

For a year after leaving the school for the deaf he worked for his father, loading trucks and serving as a general handy man. His social perception and inability to maintain rapport with his co-workers caused the parents to seek further help. They received an appointment at the Vocational Rehabilitation office where their son was again referred to the Speech, Hearing, and Language Center to determine if he could be taught oral communication.

After the *Language and Learning Assessment* and a current case study were completed, the diagnostician recommended that this boy learn manual language. (It was unfortunate that this was not accomplished many years before.) The parents invited a hearing impaired college boy who was oral yet could sign, to live in their home. In exchange for room and board he would teach the manual language to Bill.

The college student soon learned that the parents had been told for fourteen years that their son should never learn to "talk with his hands." Furthermore they should never use any kind of gestures with him for it would impede his development of oral communication. It was not surprising that these parents were unable to learn the manual language and were resistant about their son's adoption of a language of signs.

The college student finished school and left the home. Bill is still loading his father's truck and serving as handy man. Currently he is enrolled in a special reading class in spite of the recommendation that it was doubtful if such a class would be beneficial.

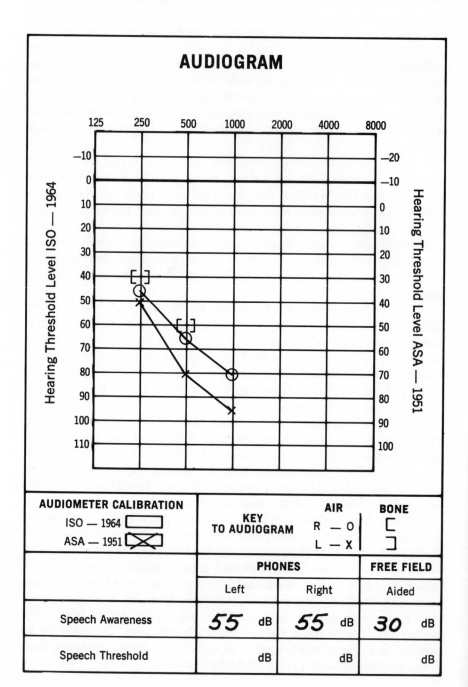

**NAME** *Bob*

**AGE** *18*

# AUDIOGRAM

|                    | PHONES | | FREE FIELD |
|                    | Left   | Right | Aided |
|--------------------|--------|-------|-------|
| Speech Awareness   | **55** dB | **55** dB | **30** dB |
| Speech Threshold   | dB     | dB    | dB    |

**AUDIOMETER CALIBRATION**
ISO — 1964 ☐
ASA — 1951 ☒

**KEY TO AUDIOGRAM**

|      | **AIR** | **BONE** |
|------|---------|----------|
| R — O | C |
| L — X | ⊐ |

186

COMMENTS

1. The cerebral palsied or otherwise crippled child should receive prostheses and physical therapy as needed, but not at the expense of pre-academic training. The two programs can be developed simultaneously, one enhancing the other.

2. The visually impaired child should receive glasses as soon as feasible and the hearing impaired child should have a wearable hearing aid when audiometric studies indicate the need. Few *blind* children are totally blind and few *deaf* children are totally deaf. Much more use can be made of their vision and hearing than was ever suspected a decade ago.

3. Parents of multiply handicapped children should receive home training instructions until their children can be enrolled in a pre-academic program. The combination of school and home training will provide academic and vocational opportunity for many multiply handicapped children.

4. It is conceivable that a child with *multiple handicaps* (hearing, vision, cerebral palsy, and mental retardation) with appropriate remediation may become a child with *several impairments* (hearing loss corrected with hearing aid, visual loss corrected with glasses, cerebral palsy corrected with physical therapy and bracing) but only one *handicap—* mental retardation.

NORMAL AND GIFTED

Children who perform at or better than age level in the areas of language and learning are often placed in nursery school programs because parents feel their child needs to be kept busy. Mothers often cannot provide a home environment which keeps a child performing at his potential level.

Unfortunately many nursery schools are baby sitting institutions where random free play activities occupy the child's time. It is conceivable that structured nursery school programs utilizing the basic concepts of training presented in this text could enhance the language and learning of normal and gifted children.

# SUMMARY

A modest approach to training children becomes a teacher at our present state of knowledge about children with language and learning disorders. She uses her best theoretical convictions, but is able to shift when scientists offer research evidence that contradicts or elaborates her theory.

# A
# Pre-Academic
# Curriculum Guide

# CHILD GROWTH AND DEVELOPMENT DATA

## 6 months to 1 year

Copies gestures as waving, nodding head, etc. (43)

Will locate source of sound, e.g., bell rung out of his sight. (43)

Vocalizes to toys and to his image in the mirror. Reaches to pat mirror image. (43)

Responds by raising his arms when mother reaches toward child and says "Come up." (31)

Moves toward or looks at family member when named, e.g., "Where is Daddy?" (31)

Says "Mama" or "Dada" during babbling, but not in relation to parents. (43)

Recognizes some words. (43)

Begins to put things in mouth. (43)

Begins to respond to strangers, e.g., crying, staring. (43)

Can sit unsupported. (34)

Weight: boys, 17-25 lbs.—girls, 16-23.5 lbs. (60)

Height: boys, 26-31 in.—girls, 25-30.5 in. (60)

Sleeps about 15 hours per 24 hour period. (71)

Average bedtime is 7:05 P.M. (71)

Generally has three to six deciduous teeth. (80)

Vocabulary of 0-3 words. (100)

## 1 year to 18 months

Imitates words. (43)

Suits actions to words. (43)

Gives toy on request accompanied by gesture. (43)

Accompanies verbal response with gesture, e.g., babbles while pointing. (43).

Uses jargon or inflected flow of connected sounds that seem like sentences. (43)

Says "Ta-Ta" or equivalent for "Thank you." (43)

Distinguishes between "You" and "Me." (43)

Cannot be reached by verbal discipline. Words mean too little. (43)

Mean length of verbal response is 1.2 words. (74)

Vocabulary of 3 to 22 words. (100)

The Curriculum Guide was prepared with the assistance of Anne Rister, M.Ed., Supervisor, Training Division, Houston Speech and Hearing Center.

Can stand alone. (34)

Walks alone. (34)

Throws a ball. (43)

Can build a tower of two blocks. (43)

Uses a spoon, but much spilling. May turn upside down before entering mouth. (43)

Pats pictures in book. (43)

Scribbles in imitation. (43)

Uses push-pull toys. (43)

Can open a closed door. (34)

Climbs up on chairs to reach. (43)

Removes socks and shoes. (34)

Weight: boys, 21-29 lbs.—girls, 19-27 lbs. (60)

Height: boys, 29-34 in.—girls, 29-33 in. (60)

Sleeps 13.5 hours per day. (71)

Has six to 13 deciduous teeth. (80)

Bedtime around 7:24 P.M. (71)

Repeats performance when laughed at. (43)

Indicates wet pants. (43)

Performs useful errands, such as bringing named objects. (43)

Resistant to changes in routine. (43)

Sudden changes are disliked. Avoids them by lying down. (43)

May pretend to read the paper. (43)

## 18 months to 2 years

Begins to claim "mine." (43)

Points to pictures of a car, dog, clock. (43)

Points to his nose, eye, hair. (43)

Waves "bye-bye" as sense of termination. (43)

Says "Eat" and "No" meaningfully. (43)

Carries out two directions with ball. (43)

Combines two or three words expressing two or three different ideas. (43)

Understands simple questions. (43)

Mean length of response is 1.8 words. (74)

Vocabulary of 22 to 272 words. (43)

Identifies one body part. (43)

Places three cubes one on another. (43)

Climbs stairs, without help at two years. (34)

Gets about house and yard. (34)

Eats with spoon from bowl and not too messy. (34)

Removes wrappers from candy. (34)

Has stiff, propulsive gait when hurrying. (43)

Pulls wheeled toys. (43)

Can throw ball. (43)
Scribbles but marks go off the page. (43)
Does more imitating as smoking, reading. (43)
Parallel play. (43)
Chooses between suitable and unfit food. (34)
Weight: boys, 24-32 lbs.—girls, 22-30 lbs. (60)
Height: boys, 32-36 in.—girls, 31-35.5 in. (60)
Sleeps 13.5 hours. (71)
Bedtime by 7:48 P.M. (71)
Has 13 to 17 deciduous teeth. (80)

## 2 years to 3 years

Likes simple sound patterns as Mother Goose. (43)
Likes stories about himself. (43)
Can formulate a negative judgment. A is not B. A fork is not a spoon. (43)
Loves to match words with objects. (43)
Recognizes self in mirror. May say "See the baby." or "It's me." (43)
Jargon begins to drop out being replaced by nouns and verbs. (43)
Repeats words compulsively. (81)
Gives full name. (108)
Names a number of pictures. (43)
Says "Peter slide" rather than "Me slide." (43)
Carries out four directions with a ball. (43)
Uses pronouns I, me, you, but not always correctly. (43)
Talks about immediate experiences. (34)
Beginning difficulty with syntax. (43)
Uses "a" before many responses. (81)
Understands "Just one block." (43)
Can repeat two digits. (108)
Gives full name on request. (43)
Shortens or telescopes words or phrases. (81)
Tendency to add sounds or syllables. (81)
Common expression, "I did." (81)
Mean length of responses is 1.8 to 3.4 words. (74)
Helps dress and undress self. (43)
Builds tower of six or seven blocks. (43)
One or more answers are expected to the question, "What do we do with
    it?" (43)
Personal identity is just beginning to emerge. (43)
Scribbles are confined to page. (43)
Uses blunt end scissors. (34)
Uses fork and eats solid food. (34)
Can get own drink. (34)

Can dry own hands. (34)
Can walk up to a ball and kick it. (43)
Can go up three steps alternating feet. (43)
Can go down long flight of steps. May mark time at each tread. (43)
Rough and tumble play. (43)
Turns pages of a book one by one. (43)
Strings beads with a needle. (43)
Can often hold glass with one hand. (43)
Places three cubes in a row for a train. (43)
Pushes chair to place as he needs it. (43)
Solitary or parallel play. (43)
Shows symptoms of pity, shame, modesty, etc. (43)
Dramatizes mother and baby, using dolls. (43)
Avoids simple hazards; rain, fire, broken glass. (34)
Looks for missing toys. (43)
Weight: boys, 26-37 lbs.—girls, 25-36 lbs. (60)
Height: boys, 33.5 to 39.5 in.—girls, 33-39 in. (60)
Sleeps 12.75 hours. (71)
Bedtime around 7:52 P.M. (71)
3.3% of children begin to bite finger nails at age three. (117)
Two-year-old usually repeats a sentence of from three to four syllables.
(43)
Vocabulary of 272-896 words. (100)

## UNDER THREE-YEAR-OLD LEVEL (UT)
### (Classroom Activities)

*Cardboard Box:* Obtain an extra large cardboard box, paint it, and cut a door and two windows that will open and close. The children *get in the box, open and close the door (and windows), look out of the window,* and hear or attempt to say, *I see you.*

Obtain a smaller box and teach the children to comprehend, *get in the box, push the box, I see you, get out of the box, pull it* (attach a string to the box).

Hide objects in a box filled with shredded newspaper. The children take turns finding the objects.

Place an interesting object inside a shoe box and cut a hole in the end of the box to simulate a "Peepshow." Have several boxes to pass among the children.

*Hand Puppet:* With the puppet on her hand the teacher gives such commands as *open your mouth, close your mouth, put your hand in, show me the eyes, put it on.*

*Flashlight:* The teacher demonstrates how the flashlight functions then asks the children to *turn it on, turn it off, look at the light.*

*Dolls and Stuffed Animals:* The teacher and children manipulate the toys to represent *walk, run, stop, turn around, walk fast (slow),* body parts and animal sounds are also introduced.

*Sandbox:* Phrases such as the following are taught *put it in the box, take it out, cover the shovel, find the boat* (hidden under the sand).

*Refreshments:* Children take turns giving out the cups as the teacher says, *give it to _____.*

Place a cookie or cracker under a bowl. A child with attention focused on the bowl is asked to *pick it up* (to find the surprise).

The phrase *shake it* may be taught when a new can of juice is brought out for refreshment period. (The same phrase may be taught with sleigh bells, Halloween noise makers, and marbles in a closed box).

A banana may be served to teach *peel it, eat it, throw it away* (the skin), *smell it.* When serving dry cereal or raisins as snacks ask the children to *hold out your hand, take one, eat it,* or, perhaps, *you dropped it.*

*Clothespin Bag:* Place objects in the bag and give each child a turn to feel them. Teach the phrases *look in the bag, feel it, open it, what's in the bag?*

*Clothespins:* The children drop clothespins into the jar. *Drop it in,* and *take them out.*

A parent brings a family pet to school and the following phrases are taught *drink the water, he spilled it, he walks, his tail moves, feel the dog, don't squeeze.*

*Playdough:* Teach the following phrases *squeeze it, make a ball, put it on your arm;* cut out a dog with a cookie cutter, *make him walk, open the can, close the can.* The teacher cuts gingerbread men with a cookie cutter and the children appropriately place the eyes, buttons, etc. at the teachers command, *put on the eyes.*

*Blocks:* Using large blocks the teacher builds a bridge by placing a piece of cardboard across two towers. The children *push the car under, crawl under.*

Smaller blocks are used to teach *stack the blocks, knock them down, pick it up, take it out, put it in the box.*

*Purse:* Fill an old purse with common objects. The children *look, open it, close it, take out the comb.*

*Dolls, Bed, and Buggy: Put her on the bed, pick her up, give her the bottle.* (Use the type of bottle that appears *full* or *empty.*) *Rock her, push the buggy.*

*Dishes:* Using toy or regular plastic dishes *put water in the cup, pour out the water.* Assemble tables, chairs, and dishes for a teaparty.

*Surprise Balls:* The children like to pull the crepe paper and discover the surprise. *It's a ring,* or *it's a doggie.*

*Paint Brush:* The children dip a paint brush into water and paint on the blackboard. *Dip it in, paint, it's wet.*

*Pull Toys:* Using a variety of pull toys the teacher reinforces understanding of *pull it.*

*Rocking Horse: Get on, get off, rock, ride the horse, go fast, go slow, stop, put it away.*

*Hats:* Using a variety of hats for the children to try on, the teacher reinforces the phrase *put it on.*

*Transportation Toys: Push the car, fly the airplane, it's broken* (the wheels have fallen off the car), *I'll fix it.*

*Water:* The children put boats or ducks in a small tub of water. Phrases such as the following are taught, *push the boat, push the duck, it's wet, it's dry.*

*Circle Games:* Children hold hands in a circle and the teacher gives such commands as *walk, run, fall down, stop.*

*Bean Bags:* While the children are throwing the bags into a box, the teacher says, *throw it, pick it up, give it to Judy.*

*Cardboard Tubes:* As the children look through the tube, they are taught to say, *I see you.*


## UNDER THREE-YEAR-OLD LEVEL (UT)
### (*Functional Words and Phrases*)

| | | |
|---|---|---|
| Hi | Close it | Go get the ___ |
| Bye-bye | Put it back | Fall down |
| Child's name | Put it down | Don't fall |
| Come here | Put it on | Family name |
| Come on | Put it in | (mamma, daddy) |
| Open the *door, box* | Get it | Move over, back |
| Close the *door, box* | Get down | Move it |
| Open it | Get up | Push it |

Pull it

Throw it

Shake it

Turn it

Up, down

Fast, slow

Fix it

Hurry up

Get in your chair

Push the chair

Don't touch it

Let's go

Let's go bye-bye

I see you

Stay there

Wait

Go around

Yes

No

Don't cry

Sit down

Stand up

Give it to ＿＿＿

Where is it?

Where's the ＿＿＿

Where's your ＿＿＿

Find it

Look for it

Look

Listen

Show me the ＿＿＿

Show me your ＿＿＿

Stop

Jump

Jump down

Hold my hand

Walk

Run

Ride the horse, car

It's broken

Blow it

Wash your hands

Dry your hands

Throw it away

It's wet

It's dry

It's mine

Where's your hearing
aid?

Drink it

Eat it

It's cold

It's hot

All-gone

Thank you

You dropped it

# UNDER THREE-YEAR-OLD LEVEL (UT)

## (Home Training Hints for Parents)

1. Use a variety of techniques to get the child to look at the speaker:
Say "Wait" then wait for the child to look up at your face before
talking to him.

Stoop to the child's level. It is easier for him to look straight
ahead than up.

Hold the object close to your face to draw the child's attention
in that direction.

If the child will look only at the object, hide it in back of you
in the hope that he will shift his attention to your face.

Make your face expressive and interesting. Be enthusiastic.

Certain activities draw attention to the face such as "Peek-a-
Boo."

If your child comes to you and gestures for you to do something, such as "Open the box," wait for him to look at you
before proceeding. You want your child to learn that he is
rewarded when he looks.

2. Use short functional phrases. Repeat the phrases many times
under different circumstances.

3. When a child has learned one phrase, say it in a different way.

"Sit down." is changed to "Sit in the chair." "Get in your chair." "Go to your seat." The concept of *big* is eventually generalized to *large, huge, enormous. Little* is generalized to *small, tiny, minute.* "Throw it away." becomes "Throw it in the wastebasket." "Put it in the wastebasket." "Get rid of it." "Throw the trash away."

4. Write ten ways in which you could teach "It's cold." Make a list of ten toys your child enjoys and write the phrases you could use with each toy. Write the phrases you use with your child on the subjects of eating, getting dressed, undressed, and bathing. Bring these to parent conferences.

5. Set aside short periods of time to create language activities for your child. It is important to initiate activities of interest to him as well as to take advantage of his initiative. Go for a walk outside. Pick flowers.

6. Paste a picture of a dog on the bottom of a glass of milk. When the milk is *all gone* the child will see the *dog.*

7. Call attention to the sounds in the child's environment; barking of a dog, car horn, jets. Begin with loud sounds and as they become noticed by your child, introduce less noticeable ones; ticking of a clock, buzzing of the bee, and the sound of the wind.

## BEGINNING LEVEL (B)
### (*Child Growth and Development Data*)

## 3 to 4 Years

Readiness to conform to the spoken word is outstanding feature of a 3 year old. (43)
Is learning how to listen and learns from listening. (43)
Responsive to in, on, and under. (43)
Often asks questions to which he knows answers. (43)
Can give two objects on request. (43)
On request he tells his sex. (43)
Repeats a sentence composed of 6-7 syllables. (43)
Knows a few rhymes or songs. (43)
Mean length of responses is 4.1 to 5.4 words. (105)
Pours from a pitcher. (43)
Runs easily and smoothly. (43)
Draws undifferentiated forms and will name them. (43)
Walks down steps one at a time. (34)
Can copy a bridge with three blocks. (43)
Can unlace shoes, take pants off. (43)
Can copy a circle and a cross. (43)
Dramatizes delivery boy, doctor, etc. (43)

He will sacrifice immediate satisfaction on a promise of later privilege. (43)

Will place milk bottles outside, run errands. (43)

Occasional outbursts are usually brief. (43)

Demonstrates fears, as of rubber boots, mechanical toy. Has some night terrors. (43)

Solitary and parallel play. (43)

Usually obedient. Gets over tantrums more quickly. (43)

Takes part in group activities as tea party, drop the handkerchief. (34)

Performs for others when requested. (34)

Will feed pets, dust, etc. (34)

Three year old more like four than a two year old. (43)

Will sit at the table in a test situation. (43)

Begins to wait his turn and will share toys. (43)

Weight: boys, 29-42 lbs.–girls, 29-41 lbs. (60)

Height: boys, 36.5-42 in.–girls, 36-42 in. (60)

Sleeps 12.25 hours. (71)

Bedtime around 7:53 p.m. (71)

Up to 20% of this age group bite finger nails. (117)

Vocabulary of 896-1540 words. (100)

## BEGINNING LEVEL (B)

### (*Language Skills*)

### I. COMPREHENSION OF ORAL LANGUAGE

A. RECOGNITION OF OBJECTS

    1. By Name

        a. An assortment of stuffed animals is placed before the class. Names of the animals are repeated in a variety of ways. "I have a dog." "Make the dog run." "Here is a rabbit." "Make the rabbit fall."

        b. After many repetitions the toy animals are placed in a box. Each child comes, one at a time, to select the animal named by the teacher.

        c. The children make a miniature sandbox from shoe boxes brought from home. Into each box the teacher pours sand. The children look at pictures of sandboxes and the word is repeated in a variety of ways. "Let's make a sandbox." "What do you want in your sandbox, Joey?" "Put a cup in your sandbox, Karen."

    2. By Function

        a. A toy bed, chair, and sink are placed before the class. In turn, each child demonstrates with a doll how to use the furniture and sink. Next the teacher says, "Show me where to wash your hands." "Go to sleep." "Sit down."

b. The teacher prepares to demonstrate a hand skill activity. In preparation for the activity she teaches the function of objects by requesting, "Bring me something we cut with." "Bring me something we write with."

c. One object such as a ball is used to teach several of its functions, as *bounce, roll, kick, throw.* Each child demonstrates these actions on request.

B. RECOGNITION OF PICTURES

1. By Name

a. Noun word pictures are placed before the class. In turn, each child selects the picture named by the teacher, then hides it in the room. After all pictures are hidden, children take turns finding one that the teacher names.

b. The teacher presents a large paper doll with appropriate clothing and says, "Here is the doll's dress. Show me your dress." Each child takes a turn finding the clothing named by the teacher and placing it on the doll.

c. A large drawing of a bedroom and precut furniture is placed on a table. The children select pictures named by the teacher and place appropriately. A review of naming all the furniture follows.

2. By Function

a. Pictures of toys are placed on the flannel board. The children find the one that spins, the one that cries, the one you can ride.

b. A large picture of a kitchen is placed on the chart rack. The children find the one we cook on, the one we sit on, the one we put dishes into.

c. A picture of a young child is placed in front of the class. The children point to appropriate body parts on request. What does the girl hear with? What does she see with? What does she wave goodbye with?

C. CATEGORIZING

1. Children sit in a circle. In the center of the circle are three objects. The teacher has duplicate objects in a sack. She removes one and asks a child to find one like it.

2. Two paper dolls, a boy and a girl with appropriate clothing, are assembled on a table. The directions are, "Find something the girl wears." "Find something the boy wears."

3. Pictures of a doghouse, birdhouse, and a people house are drawn on the blackboard. From a box of toys children select appropriate objects as the teacher points to a specific drawing.

D. NUMBER CONCEPTS

1. Valentines or another timely object may be used as a theme. The teacher demonstrates placing two valentines in the box. Each child is instructed to place the same number in the box.

2. During snack time the children are asked to take one or two cookies.

3. For the Thanksgiving unit, a large turkey with missing feathers is placed on a table. From a group of feathers each child selects one or two as directed by the teacher.

E. SPATIAL ORIENTATION

1. Utilizing a toy slide each child, upon request, moves a doll *up* the ladder or *down* the slide.

2. In functional situations the teacher asks the children to "Sit *on* the floor." "Put my pencil *on* my desk." "Put these papers *in* my desk drawer."

3. Outlines of a *big* and *little* house are drawn on the blackboard. With the aid of stick-tac, children place paper windows or doors on the *big* or *little* house as specified by the teacher.

F. SERIAL DIRECTIONS

1. Two simple serial commands are given during general classroom routine. "Go to the shelf and bring me the book." Take off your sweater and put it in the closet."

2. Objects are hidden in the room. Each child finds the two named by the teacher.

3. While decorating a Christmas tree, the teacher tells a child, "Take a bell out of the box and put it on the tree."

## II. EXPRESSION OF ORAL LANGUAGE

A. NAMING AND DEFINING

1. Naming

a. A picture of a girl wearing a red dress is shown to the children. Each child receives a similar picture and is asked to select an appropriate crayon to color the dress. Then they are asked to name red objects in the classroom.

b. The children take turns naming things they see in the room.

c. The scene is a clothing store. The teacher is the clerk and asks, "What do you want to buy?" The child may answer as best he can, by word or gestures.

2. Defining

a. Pictures are presented depicting simple actions such as a girl combing her hair. The children imitate the action. Then they attempt to answer the question, "What is the girl doing?"

b. During the refreshment period the children feel the juice can and answer the question, "Is it hot or cold?"

c. Household furniture is placed before the class and the teacher asks each child to define a piece, "What is a chair?" "What is a stove?"

3. Action Agent

a. Landscape scenes with sky and water are given each child. They paste pictures of things that fly or swim as the teacher calls out the action. At the completion of the activity the teacher asks, "What flies?" "What swims?"

b. Several pictures are placed on the flannel board. Children take turns naming "The one who cooks . . ." "The one that barks . . ."

c. Animal cookies are served for refreshments. The children are asked to name "One that hops." "One that meows."

B. CATEGORIZING

1. The children look at a picture of a house or a furnished doll house. They answer questions, "What goes in a bedroom?" "In a kitchen?"

2. Articles of clothing are spaced on the table. The teacher presents a hat and asks a child to find one that is like it. The two are placed side by side.

3. Pictures of a house, tree, and lake are placed on the flannel board. The teacher shows a picture of a boy and says, "The boy lives in a _____?"

C. NUMBER CONCEPTS

1. When playing musical chairs, the teacher and children count the number of chairs. They recount as one is taken away.

2. Drop pennies in a piggy bank to learn to rote-count to five or more.

3. The story of "The Three Bears" is told to the class using flannel board pictures. At the appropriate time the children count the bears, bowls, chairs, and beds.

D. SPATIAL AND TEMPORAL RELATIONSHIPS

1. Within the classroom the children answer the teachers questions. Tell me something that is *on* the wall, *on* the floor, *in* your school supply box.

2. The children make paper plate faces, some with long yarn hair and some with shorter hair. Each child in turn comes before the class and the teacher asks, "Is this hair *long* or *short?*"

3. Each child adds another pop-it bead to make the string *longer.*

E. SENTENCE BUILDING

1. The children are encouraged to imitate short phrases in the classroom routine, such as "I want a turn." "It's mine."

2. The teacher tells a simple sequence story such as one about a little boy getting dressed in the morning. The children are encouraged to imitate the action and relate it in short phrases or sentences.

3. The children are taught simple songs, games, or stories that have short repetitive phrases as in the song, "Here We Go Round the Mulberry Bush."

# BEGINNING LEVEL (B)
### (*Avenues of Learning*)

## I. MEMORY: SHORT TERM
### A. AUDITORY
Goal: To remember two auditory signals or commands not necessarily in sequence.

1. Noisemakers are placed on a table and a child turns his back to them. After the bell is rung and the whistle blown, he turns around and chooses the ones he heard. Using a matching set of noisemakers eliminates the possibility of selection through visual cues or a slightly misplaced bell.

2. Animal sound effects are played from a recording. The child listens, then waits until the teacher places several animal pictures or objects on the table. He selects the appropriate ones.

3. One child turns his back to the class. The teacher names two classmates. The child points to the two children she named.

Goal: To remember at least two auditory commands in sequence.

1. When it is time to go home, the teacher says, "Get your sweater and line up at the door."

2. At refreshment time a child is told, "Get the cups, then get the juice."

3. A short story is told. The children retell it using objects or pictures as needed. "Joyce went to the store. She bought some milk."

### B. VISUAL
Goal: To remember at least two visual events not necessarily in sequence.

1. At various places in the room, pictures are placed. One from a matching set is shown to the class, then turned over. A child finds the matching picture. Later the game is expanded to remembering two pictures.

2. One child hides his eyes while another leaves the room. The hider opens his eyes and calls the name of the child who is missing.

3. A picture of a boy running is shown to the class then taken away. A child is asked to do what he saw in the picture. The same may be done with "Jump," "Crawl," "Fly like a bird."

Goal: To remember at least two visual events in sequence.

1. Two sequential pictures are placed on the flannel board. For example, a picture of a wrapped gift and a picture of the unwrapped box showing the gift. These two pictures are removed and placed with

five unrelated ones. A child is asked to find the original two in the correct order.

2. Two pictures, a boy running and a boy jumping, are shown and then turned over. A child is asked to "Do what the first boy was doing." Then, "Do what the second boy was doing."

3. At refreshment time the teacher picks up a cup, napkin, and cookie. Each child must select his refreshments in the same order.

C. VISUAL-MOTOR

Goal: To remember motor acts in sequence when oral language is not involved.

1. A piece of paper is folded in a way that when opened provides two equal sections (boxes). The children fold one like it and stamp a picture in each box. (Stamp from left to right.)

2. On the blackboard the teacher draws a large circle then covers it. A child comes to the board and draws one like it. Next, the teacher draws the eyes, hides the picture, and a child imitates. She continues with mouth, nose, and ears.

3. The leader claps his hands and then pats his head. The children repeat the actions in the correct order.

## II. VISUAL-PERCEPTUAL-MOTOR

Goal: To perceive a visual image and reproduce it.

1. Each child is given a piece of paper with several kites drawn on it. The teacher illustrates on the blackboard that the cross inside the kite is missing. She demonstrates in two steps how to draw the cross.

2. Each child receives three different colored beads and a string. The task is to copy the teacher's pattern, step by step.

3. A bridge is built with three large blocks. The children construct more like it and play follow-the-leader by crawling under it.

## III. SOCIAL MATURITY

Goal: To teach work habits that are essential to learning in a group situation.

1. Simple, uncluttered pictures are used to help the children attend to the appropriate stimulus.

2. If a child has difficulty using the total surface of his desk to build a design, he is given a colored sheet of paper on which to concentrate the design.

3. Seating and desk arrangements may be changed about once a month to teach children to attend from various positions in the room.

Goal: To develop independence in self-help skills.

1. Self-care in the bathroom.

2. Removing and putting on coats.

3. Putting away his own materials after an activity.

Goal: To teach appropriate situational behavior.

1. Children must be told many times in positive terms to "Be quiet in the halls." "Eat your own refreshments." "Leave the teacher's desk alone." Or when shoving or hitting, "Put your hands down."

2. The teacher should vary classroom procedure—avoid letting games and activities always happen a certain way. The rules of the games can be changed.

3. Pictures are changed frequently in the room, as are plants and other objects. The children talk about them, but do not meddle with them.

## BEGINNING LEVEL (B)
### (Pre-Academic Subjects)

### I. LIKENESSES AND DIFFERENCES

Goal: To learn to match, proceeding from the simple to the complex.

1. Object to object (same object).
2. Picture to picture (same picture).
3. Object to object (different).
4. Picture to picture (different).
5. Object to picture.

### II. PHONICS TRAINING

Goal: Incidental learning of correct production of consonant sounds.

1. "I am going to tell you a story about a cat and a dog. All of you will be cats. Can you make a sound like a cat, f-f-f?"

2. Children are taught to say "thank you" when served cookies and juice. They are taught to listen and to watch the teacher's face while she talks, with the hope that imitation of visual phonetic clues will take place.

### III. WRITING

Goal: Writing readiness is limited to drawing crude forms.

1. Children make large circles on the blackboard and convert them to balloons by drawing lines to them. For seat work the children draw fairly large circles on paper. They cut them out, then scotch tape a string to the circle to form a balloon.

2. The teacher draws several pictures on the blackboard. As she names one a child is asked to draw a cross over it.

IV. NUMBERS
    Goals: Rote-count to five and number concepts through two.
    Teachers should be number conscious in all classroom activities.
        1. The children ask for one or two gummed stars for their sky
scene and select the appropriate number.
        2. Beanbags are thrown into a basket. The teacher requests them
to throw one or two.

## BEGINNING LANGUAGE DEVELOPMENT:
## PROPOSED CALENDAR

September:   School (B-1).
October:   Family (B-2); Halloween (B-3).
November:   Clothing (B-4); Thanksgiving (B-5); Toys (B-6).
December:   Toys; Christmas (B-6).
January:   Home (B-7).
February:   Review; Valentine (B-8); Yard (B-9).
March:   Yard.
April:   Easter (B-10); Easter; Pets (B-11).
May:   Pets; Review.
Extra:   Birthday (B-12).

# BEGINNING LEVEL (B)

## Unit: Clothing

SAMPLE LESSON PLAN

    I. Goals: To teach and/or expose children to:
        1. Their own and each other's names, basic vocabulary from the
           unit, and short phrases.
        2. Concepts of likeness and difference.
        3. Sounds that match.
        4. Rote counting through five.
        5. Number concepts through two.
        6. Drawing a circle on the blackboard.

    II. Activities
        **9:00–9:05** *Roll Call.* Each child is asked to raise his hand when his
name is called. When attendance is checked, the teacher asks, "Who is
absent?" For a different activity, one child may stand while the group

says his name or repeats it after the teacher. (Visual recall and memory for names.)

9:05–9:20 *Doll Clothing.* A doll's trunk is placed in front of the class. Each piece of clothing is removed and named by the teacher then the children. (Vocabulary building.) When one set of clothing is on the table, matching activity begins. The teacher reaches into the trunk and says, "Here is a dress. Ruthie, find one like it." All the children have a turn. (Concept of likeness.) A coat is put on one of the larger dolls and a jacket on another. "Button the coat, Jill." "Zip the jacket, John." (Comprehension of phrases and use of fine motor coordination.) Questions are asked. "What do you do with a hat?" (Defining by function.) While packing the trunk, the teacher may say, "I'll take off the coat. I'll hang it up in the trunk." (Sequence.)

9:20–9:35 *Dress-Up.* A box of dress up clothes is brought before the group. As the children choose the article they want the teacher and/or the child names it. (Vocabulary building.) When the children are appropriately dressed, they form a circle and sing the following song to the tune of "Here We Go Round the Mulberry Bush,"

> "This is the way we put on a hat, put on a hat . . .
> This is the way we take off a hat, take off a hat . . .
> This is the way we hang up a hat, hang up a hat . . ."

9:35–9:45 *Refreshments.* Children are seated for cookies and juice, and cups are placed on the table. The teacher counts as she points. (Rote counting.) Then, "Listen, children, do you hear the juice pouring into the cup? Does it sound the same in this cup? Does it sound like the paper on the cookie box?" (Matching and discriminating sounds.) One child turns his back to the table. As the teacher removes a cookie she says, "Listen!" Then he is asked to turn around and do what he heard. (Auditory memory.) The children count the cups with the teacher. (Rote counting.) Round cookies are offered each child with the question, "Do you want one cookie or two cookies?" (Number concepts.)

9:45–10:00 At the close of refreshment time, the teacher says, "Let's clean up and then bring our chairs to the blackboard." (Auditory memory for two directions.) Standing before the blackboard the teacher asks, "Who can show me with his hands how our cookies looked? Who can draw a cookie on the board?" Each child draws a cookie. (Circle.) Then the teacher draws a line downward from one circle to make a balloon, and asks, "What is it now?" (Perception changes.) The children take turns drawing lines to make balloons. "It's time to go home. Listen to me. Take your chairs back to the table and sit down." Then, "Get your coats and line up at the door." (Auditory memory for two commands.)

# BEGINNING LEVEL (B)

## Unit: School Routine (B-1)

CLASSROOM ACTIVITIES

*Picture File:* To teach the names of school supplies the teacher shows a picture of a jar of paste and the child finds the real paste jar from an assortment of items on a table. Comprehension and naming of the supplies is tested for each child.

To teach use of the items, she asks, "Show me how we cut." John demonstrates with the scissors. When finished he is asked, "Who cut with the scissors?" He replies, "I did." (Encourages use of pronoun *I*.)

*School Supplies:* Each child is asked to bring to school a cigar box which contains crayons, paste jar, scissors, pencil. The next day the teacher calls out the names of the objects and the children hold them up in the air.

*Roll Call:* Each child learns his own name by answering with his first and last name each day roll is called. He is allowed to see the mark the teacher makes when he is present (+) or when a classmate is absent (O).

For variety all girls are asked to stand and give their names. The boys do the same.

If the concept of sex has not been learned, a boy is asked, "Are you a boy or a girl?" When he gives a correct response, he stands on one side of the room. A girl is asked, "Are you a girl or a boy?" With a correct answer she stands on the opposite side of the room. This activity may be varied by asking the children to form a line in front of the table. The boys are to sit on one side of the table and the girls on the other as they call out their own names. To improve rote counting the girls are counted, then the boys.

*Peg Board:* The teacher holds a large peg board in front of the class. One child is asked to come before the group and place *two* pegs in the board. The next child may be asked to place only one peg.

Pegs may be used for matching and teaching color words.

*Refreshments:* During refreshment period each day, build new vocabulary based on what was learned before. "Do you want a cookie?" When he demonstrates comprehension ask, "What do you want?" Then, "Do you want a big cookie or a little cookie?" "A short or long cookie?" "One or two cookies?"

*Classroom Furniture:* The furniture in the classroom may be used to teach prepositions. A small desk, chair, and easel are placed in line.

One child is asked to crawl *under* the easel. Another is asked to walk *around* the chair or stand *by* the blackboard.

*Scissors:* The teacher demonstrates how to hold the scissors and each child is given practice in opening and closing them. (Use left handed scissors for left handed children.) Advance to simple cutting activities as fringing paper for placemats which may be used during the refreshment period.

*Blocks:* Use blocks to build a small bridge for a car to go *under,* a fence to keep miniature animals *inside,* and *tall* and *short* towers.

*Routine Class Activities:* Each day the children develop vocabulary and hear short sentences during daily routine. "Hang up your coat." "Go to your chair." "Get a kleenex." "Wash your hands." "Turn on the lights."

*Drawing Names:* From a box one child draws a name designating who will be *first* in line to go home. Another name is drawn for *last* in line. Or, *first* may hold the flag and *last* beat the drum while marching around the room.

### Basic Vocabulary (B-1)

| | | |
|---|---|---|
| bathroom | drink | how many |
| bell | dry | how old are you |
| big | eat | hurry |
| blocks | eraser | I |
| blue | fall | I did |
| book | find | inside |
| boy | fine | juice |
| box | first | jump |
| bye-bye | floor | kleenex |
| cabinet | flush | last |
| chair | four | lights |
| chalk | get | like |
| clock | girl | make |
| clothes | give | march |
| cold | go | me |
| come | good | milk |
| cookies | green | mine |
| counter | hang | more |
| cow | hat | no |
| cup | help | one |
| desk | here | open |
| door | hole | out |
| draw | horse | outside |

own name              room                  toilet paper
paper                 run                   turn
paste                 sat                   two
peg                   school                umbrella
peg board             scissors              wait
picnic                sheep                 walk
picture               sit                   want
pig                   snow                  wash
please                soap                  what
plurals               stand                 where
put                   sun                   window
rain                  table                 yellow
rain boots            teacher               yes
raincoat              thank you             you
record player         three
ride                  toilet

### Games, Stories, Songs, and Nursery Rhymes (B-1)

The teacher makes appropriate selections for this unit.

### Home Training Hints for Parents (B-1)

1. Refer to the Under Three Level (p. 197).
2. Stress the importance of getting to school on time.
3. Older brothers and sisters play with their younger siblings using the basic vocabulary of this unit.
4. Talk about what is seen while driving to school.
5. Out of school hours mention classmates by name and something about their dress, behavior, or accomplishment.
6. Talk in short phrases and sentences. If you are not understood, rephrase.
7. Obtain the child's attention then work with him while he is interested and eager. Do not create artificial situations; rather, use the most natural avenues possible.
8. Look at pictures of animals, trains, cars, etc. with him, naming them and imitating the sounds they make. Ask him to identify their sounds. Avoid using the phrase, Say ——.
9. Read stories, rhymes, and jingles. Begin with short, simple ones and progress to longer ones attempting to increase the length of listening time and concentration.

# BEGINNING LEVEL (B)

## Unit: Family (B-2)

CLASSROOM ACTIVITIES

*Flannel Board:* To teach body parts use a flannel backed paper doll which can be disjointed. The doll may be assembled, part by part, and then disassembled. One part may be omitted and a child asked to find what is missing. The teacher may place a body part on the flannel board and ask the children to point to their own.

*Potato Man:* The potato man or woman may be used for teaching body parts. Each child chooses which part he wants to stick into the styrofoam head. The teacher asks, "Where do you put the ear?" "Where does she wear her glasses?" Sort all the parts and place them in paper cups. Then the children may dress the potato people in different ways.

*Blindfold:* Learning the meaning of the word *see* may be accomplished by blindfolding the children. They learn that they can't *see* when the blindfold is on and can *see* when it is off.

Noisemakers are used to teach "I *hear* it."

The meaning of the word *smell* may be taught by bringing flowers, a bottle of perfume, and an orange to class.

Sandpaper, cotton, and sponge may be used for differentiating feeling things through touch.

*Drawing:* To learn the words *fingers, hand, toes, feet,* each child places his hand or foot on a paper while the teacher traces around it. The fingers and toes are counted.

*Bathtub:* A large doll is bathed in a toy bathinette. Each child is given a wash cloth and in turn follows the directions. "Wash the leg." "It's dirty." "The baby is wet." "Dry her."

*Paper Plates:* To review the concepts of *long* and *short,* paper plates are used to make a face. Yarn is stapled on for long hair. Each child is asked to cut some of the hair to make it *shorter*.

*Photographs:* Each child makes a chart which contains photographs of his family members. These charts are placed about the room. Each photograph is discussed regarding age, sex, color of eyes, or whether he wears glasses or she has pigtails. The family members are counted. The pictures may be matched to the family of dolls.

*Dress-Up Clothes:* The children dress up as family members and play house. The mother irons the clothes. Father mows the grass. The baby is a doll and is rocked or put into the crib.

*Household Work-Tools:* A broom, hammer, rake, dish pan, and dishes are brought to the classroom. Each is discussed and questions are asked. "What would you use to sweep?" "What would you do with a broom?" The children play act the use of each tool.

*Picture File:* A sequence of four pictures depict a trip to grandmother's and grandfather's house. The pictures are placed out of order and the children arrange them in correct sequence.

### Basic Vocabulary (B-2)

| | | |
|---|---|---|
| arms | fingers | sad |
| baby | grandma | say |
| back | grandpa | see |
| blow | hair | show |
| body | hands | sister |
| bottle | happy | sleep |
| brother | head | smell |
| comb | hear | talk |
| cry | laugh | teeth |
| daddy | legs | toes |
| ears | mothers | touch |
| eyes | mouth | work |
| family | nose | |
| feel | play | |

### Games, Stories, Songs, and Nursery Rhymes (B-2)

The teacher makes appropriate selections for this unit.

### Home Training Hints for Parents (B-2)

1. Bring out the family albums for purposes of reinforcing the vocabulary learned at school.
2. While bathing the child talk about his body parts. "What shall we wash next?"
3. Talk about body parts as you help the child get dressed. "What goes in this sleeve?" "Does your leg go in this sleeve?"
4. Encourage the children to help at home. Talk about the equipment. "Why do I need a broom?" Provide a different job for each day. At the end of the week talk about the jobs and which pieces of equipment were used.
5. When folding clothes, show a sock and ask, "Where do you wear

this?" "Find something in the basket that you use to dry your hands." Teach the child to fold towels and wash cloths.

6. Discuss actions of family members found in magazine pictures. "What is mother doing?" If the child cannot name the action, encourage him to imitate it.

7. Play "Guess Who" with members of the family. Take turns hiding eyes while someone speaks then the hider guesses who spoke.

# BEGINNING LEVEL (B)

## Unit: Halloween (B-3)

CLASSROOM ACTIVITIES

*Pumpkins:* Paper pumpkins of various sizes are arranged in a play store. The teacher, as clerk, asks the child, "Do you want to buy a *big* pumpkin or a *little* pumpkin?" This activity is followed up by a field trip to buy a pumpkin. On another day a jack-o'-lantern is carved in class emphasizing what is inside the pumpkin and facial parts. A lighted candle may be inserted into the pumpkin and viewed in a closet.

*Costumes:* Each child is assigned a day to bring his costume to class during the week preceding Halloween. The teacher will stress such language as *mask, friendly, scary, ghost, skeleton,* and *witch.* A simple chart of each child's costume will help the class remember what each will be wearing at the Halloween party.

*Paper Dolls:* The teacher makes a variety of Halloween costumes for a large paper doll. The children choose and name the costumes they put on the doll.

*Playhouse:* A playhouse made from a paper box large enough for the children to enter is a good motivational technique to practice trick or treat. One child stays in the box to give out the treats. Another child dons a costume, goes to the door and says, "Trick or treat."

*Mask:* The teacher makes black cat masks from paper and the children paste on whiskers. Each child in turn pretends being a friendly cat or a scary cat.

### Basic Vocabulary (B-3)

| | | |
|---|---|---|
| bag | jack-o'-lantern | ring the doorbell |
| candy | knock on the door | scary |
| costume | mask | tonight |
| gum | pumpkin | top |
| Halloween | refreshments | trick or treat |

*Games, Stories, Songs, and Nursery Rhymes* (B-3)

The teacher makes appropriate selections for this unit.

*Home Training Hints for Parents* (B-3)

1. Parents reinforce vocabulary by purchasing and carving a jack-o'-lantern at home.
2. Seeds from the pumpkin are saved for another activity. Mothers draw an outline of a pumpkin on paper and invite neighbor children in to decorate it with the seeds. Glue is placed on appropriate spots to outline a lantern, to place facial parts on it, or to cover the entire lantern.
3. At home, the children may make jack-o'-lanterns from oranges. Toothpicks hold raisins in place for eyes, nose, and mouth. The finished product is used for a table decoration.
4. The children dress up in their costumes at home. Parents are cautioned about urging their child to wear a mask. Often he will prefer to carry it.
5. Parents may want to take their children to a few houses in the neighborhood for "Trick or treat."

# BEGINNING LEVEL (B)

## Unit: Clothing (B-4)

CLASSROOM ACTIVITIES

*Doll Trunk:* Matching dolls which are large enough for small children to handle, and two trunks with matching doll clothes are placed in front of the class. The teacher chooses a dress for baby to wear. A child chooses the one that matches. Then he chooses an article and asks a classmate to find one that matches. The clothes can be described as to color, and long or short sleeves. When time to put the clothes away, John puts the socks in the bottom drawer, and Mary puts the panties in the top drawer.

*Picture File:* Pictures are selected to show the sequence of a boy getting dressed. The teacher talks about what the boy puts on first, second. Each child has a turn to sequence the pictures.

*Pasting:* The children are given duplicated pictures of a girl or boy doll. They paste the shoes, hat, dress, etc. at appropriate places. Questions are asked, "Where do we wear shoes?" "What do we wear on our feet?"

*Washday:* Doll clothes are washed with soap, rinsed, hung on the line, and ironed the next day. The teacher holds the garment while the child works the clothes pin. *Wet* and *dry* clothes are discussed.

*Dress-Up Clothes:* The teacher presents a piece of clothing and asks "Who wears this?" "Try it on." "It's too big." "It's too little." "It fits." Then the children dress up as Mother and Daddy and participate in role playing, such as "Daddy reading a newspaper," and "Mother feeding the baby."

*Blackboard:* The teacher draws a shirt or a coat on the blackboard. The children take turns drawing a circle for the buttons, and straight lines to represent stripes. This activity can also be done with paper dolls using real buttons and lace trim.

*Home Assignment:* Each child is assigned to bring a suitcase to class with only one piece of clothing in it. He is to describe it to the class. This is a good opportunity to stress seasonal clothes, such as the snowsuit, the raincoat, or the bathing suit.

*Buttons:* Buttons are interesting to children and may be used to teach color words, number concepts, big-little, and "Point to the hand that holds the button."

*Box of Accessories:* A necklace, bracelet, ring, hearing aid, glasses, gloves, tie, belt, pin, and earrings are in a box. The children find "what you wear on your finger," or are asked "Where do you wear a watch?"

*Straws:* Necklaces and bracelets can be made from drinking straws. The children cut the straws and string them on wire or stiff plastic so that they may take them home.

### Basic Vocabulary (B-4)

| | | |
|---|---|---|
| beads | iron | slip |
| belt | jacket | socks |
| button | new | sweater |
| clothes | old | take it off |
| coat | pants | tie |
| dress | petticoat | watch |
| dry | pocket | water |
| glasses | purse | wear |
| gloves | put it on | wet |
| hang it up | ring | zipper |
| hat | shirt | |
| hearing aid | shoes | |

### Games, Stories, Songs, and Nursery Rhymes (B-4)

The teacher makes appropriate selections for this unit.

### Home Training Hints for Parents (B-4)

1. As you assist your child in dressing, tell him which shirt or dress to get. Describe it as to color, buttons in front or back, or sleeve length.
2. Let your child help you rearrange the dresser drawers. "Put the panties on this side and the socks on that side."
3. Teach him to fold the matching socks together. Point out small differences in some of daddy's socks.
4. Take a trip to a clothing store. Ask him to name items of clothing he sees. Draw pictures and rename when you return home.
5. Cut swatches of material and let your child feel velvet for fuzzy, satin for slick.
6. Give your child one set of paper dolls and you take the other. Dress the doll in pajamas and ask him to do the same. Let your child have a turn being teacher.
7. Pack a suitcase with two socks, two dresses, two shoes. (They should not be identical articles.) You select one item and let him find the one that is like it. Name who wears it, when and where it is worn.

# BEGINNING LEVEL (B)

# Unit: Thanksgiving (B-5)

CLASSROOM ACTIVITIES

*Blocks:* With small blocks each child builds a fence to enclose miniature turkeys. Number concepts are developed by asking the children to place *one* or *two* turkeys inside the fence.

*Toy Birds:* For an auditory memory activity a toy turkey, duck, and a bird are placed on a table. The sound each makes is demonstrated and the children imitate. Then a child turns his back and listens while the teacher produces one of the sounds. The child points to the appropriate one.

*Cookies:* One of the mothers is asked to bring turkey cookies to school. The teacher and children make icing from powdered sugar, water, and food coloring. As the decorating takes place vocabulary of body parts is reviewed.

*Paper Turkey:* A large paper turkey with the tail missing is constructed. Red, yellow, blue, and green paper tail feathers are assembled. Directions as to the color and the number are given. "Put on the red tail feather." or "Find a tail feather this color."

*Paper Plates:* Each child receives a paper plate and an envelope which includes pictures of Thanksgiving food. The children are asked to "Paste the turkey on the plate." "Put the cranberries beside the turkey."

## Basic Vocabulary (B-5)

| Holiday | Thanksgiving | turkey |
|---------|--------------|--------|

## Games, Stories, Songs, and Nursery Rhymes (B-5)

The teacher makes appropriate selections for this unit.

## Home Training Hints for Parents (B-5)

1. The concept of Thanksgiving is not stressed but vocabulary concerned with food and turkeys can be increased. Parents collect appropriate pictures from November magazines and from discussions of the pictures, the children help plan the Thanksgiving Day menu.
2. The children in the neighborhood gather to make a table decoration. Turkeys are constructed from apples using toothpicks for legs, "How many legs does a turkey have?" and toothpicks strung with raisins for tail feathers. The mothers will provide a paper head.
3. Children help set the table for Thanksgiving dinner. They count the silverware, fold the napkins, and place all appropriately on the table.
4. When serving the turkey, ask the child which part he would like, wing, leg, or a piece of the body.
5. The following day mother can ask her child if he remembers what they had for Thanksgiving dinner.

# BEGINNING LEVEL (B)

## Unit: Christmas (B-6)

### CLASSROOM ACTIVITIES

*Toys:* A wide variety of toys is placed on a table. In turn the children select according to use, indoors or outdoors, for a girl or a boy, according to function as well as by name.

*Santa's Toy Bag:* A laundry bag is used for Santa's toy bag. The children learn, "It's empty, let's fill it with toys." They experience training in short term auditory memory with such commands as "Put the train and the doll in the bag." Or they practice remembering visual clues as the teacher drops two toys in the bag and asks, "What did I put into the bag?" If they cannot remember, they are given a clue by putting their hands in the bag to feel the toys.

*Letter:* A letter to Santa Claus is written as a group project. The teacher writes "Dear" and places a picture of Santa next to it. Then she writes, "Tommy wants a ——" and in turn the children paste pictures of toys they want. When the letter is finished, it is turned over, and the children are asked to remember, "What does Tommy want for Christmas?"

*Tree Decorations:* The children help decorate the classroom tree. Paper chains are made as a group project. Precut shapes, circles, stars, bells, are colored by the children and strung with colored yarn and hung on the tree.

*Christmas Party:* Parents bring inexpensive gifts which are hidden in the room. "Molly, get the gift that's *under* my desk."

### Basic Vocabulary (B-6)

| | | |
|---|---|---|
| airplane | Christmas tree | pretty |
| ball | jet | ribbon |
| Baby Jesus | push | toys |
| | present | |

### Games, Stories, Songs, and Nursery Rhymes (B-6)

The teacher makes appropriate selections for this unit.

### Home Training Hints for Parents (B-6)

1. Children select from magazines pictures of toys they would like to have for Christmas. They are cut out and placed in envelopes to be brought to school when the teacher requests them.
2. Parents provide their children with a tiny tree which they can decorate and redecorate throughout the holidays.
3. Children may want to visit Santa in a shopping center. Parents explain the procedure before the trip. Insistence that a child sit on Santa's lap should be avoided for just watching may be equally as satisfying.
4. Lotto games concerned with toys may be purchased or made at home. The mother varies the game by asking, "Who can find the one we pull?" "The one we ride in?"
5. Guessing games are played while sitting around the tree. "I see something on the tree that makes a sound when you ring it. What is it?"

# BEGINNING LEVEL (B)

## Unit: Home (B-7)

CLASSROOM ACTIVITIES

*Classroom Furniture:* Using the furniture in the classroom, the teacher asks the children to "Put my pencil *on* the table." *"Push* your chair." "Sit *in* the *big* chair." "Sit in the *little* chair." "Go *to* the door." The children play follow the leader and do as teacher does: sit in a chair, crawl under a table, open a door.

*Making Doll Furniture:* The children make their own doll furniture. A cardboard box, bottom side up with an oven door cut to fold down, becomes a stove. Tables are made from an empty spool, and circles of paper for the top. A small jewelry box which still has the cotton in it becomes a bed.

*Plastic Doll Furniture:* For a tactile activity, about five pieces of plastic furniture are placed in a box that has a hole just large enough for a child to get his hand in. The teacher shows a piece of furniture and a child finds the matching piece by feeling the ones in the box.

*Phonograph Records:* Using a sound effect record the teacher plays a household sound such as the telephone bell, and a child finds the appropriate object (the telephone). Flannel board cutouts may be used in place of the objects. Or, pictures of the sounds to be heard may be drawn on the blackboard and a child erases the picture as a sound is identified.

*Shoe Box:* A doll house may be made from a shoe box. The children are helped to cut wall paper, lay carpets, and make furniture.

*Story Books:* After the story of *The Three Bears* has been read, the teacher draws the different sizes of the chairs, beds, and bowls on the blackboard. The children discuss "big" and "bigger" or "small" and "smaller."

*Large Cardboard Shipping Box:* A playhouse may be made from a large box. Curtains are added to the windows and the door and other accessories are painted. Commands are given such as "Open the door." "Put your head out the window." "Mary and Helen, go inside."

*Playhouse Furniture:* Each day a different set of playhouse furniture is arranged in one corner of the classroom. Activities related to that room are carried out and discussed.

*Large Toy Truck:* In the classroom the teacher places two doll houses, one representing an *old* house and one a *new* house. A large toy truck is used as a moving van. A child is asked to "Take a chair out of the old house and put it into the van." Similar directions are given when unloading furniture at the new house.

*Broom and Dust Cloth:* With these two items prepositions are taught. A child sweeps *in front* of the desk, *behind* the desk, *under* the desk. Another child dusts *on top* of the cabinet, or *under* the desk.

### Basic Vocabulary (B-7)

| | | |
|---|---|---|
| bar stools | dresser | saucer |
| bath tub | dust | sewing machine |
| bed | dust pan | sheets |
| bedroom | family room | sink |
| bed spread | fork | sofa (couch) |
| blankets | kitchen | spoon |
| broom | knife | stove |
| carpet (rug) | lamp | sweep |
| closet | living room | take a bath |
| coat hanger | mirror | telephone |
| coffee table | mop | television |
| davenport | napkin | toothbrush |
| den | pillows | toothpaste |
| dining room | plates | vacuum |
| dishes | radio | wash cloth |
| drawers | refrigerator | washing machine |

### Games, Stories, Songs, and Nursery Rhymes (B-7)

The teacher makes appropriate selections for this unit.

### Home Training Hints for Parents (B-7)

1. Your child can learn more about your home if you include him in your daily activities. Instead of sending him for the broom each time, vary your directions. "I am going to sweep the floor. What do I need to sweep the floor? Go get it for me." Call him to hold the dustpan for you.
2. When it's time to dust, give your child a dust cloth too. As you proceed from room to room, ask him to suggest the next piece of furniture to be dusted. If he cannot name the pieces, give him a choice among three that you name. Place pictures of furniture in a box and ask him to draw one out. This will be the next piece to be dusted.

3. Hide objects around the house and ask him to "Look *under* the bed, *in* the closet, *under* the table, or *on* the couch."
4. While making the bed ask him which to put on first, the sheet or the blanket.
5. Look at magazines together. Ask him to find objects in your home represented by the pictures.
6. Let your child help you put clothes away by deciding in which room they belong; towels in the bathroom, socks in the bedroom.
7. The parents and their child build a shoe box version of their home. They decide where to place the door, what color to paint the house, where to place the various rooms.

# BEGINNING LEVEL (B)

## Unit: Valentine (B-8)

CLASSROOM ACTIVITIES

*Valentines:* Incorporate construction activities in the lesson plans for the week preceding Valentine's Day. Construct a different valentine each day to be kept in a folder and taken home at the end of the week. These will be given to family and friends. Use large red hearts on which are pasted smaller white hearts. In the very center paste a colorful seal. Construct faces with a large heart. With magic marker draw eyes, nose, mouth. Add a bow tie for a boy and a bonnet for a girl. Hearts pasted on lacy doilies which are again pasted on a colored sheet of paper are particularly pretty. A book of punch out valentines provides the children with an opportunity to choose the one they like. When punched out, it is pasted on a folded piece of paper making a card. The teacher asks him what to print on the card, "I love you." or "Be my valentine." Using candy hearts with phrases printed on them, the teacher allows the children to choose one. She reads a message and a child repeats after her before he receives the candy.

*Valentine Box:* Each child helps the teacher decorate the Valentine box for the room. Seals, hearts, glitter and other ornaments are applied by the children. "Put the seal *on the side* of the box."

*Valentine Game:* Two matching sets of valentines may be used for: (1) hiding and finding games, (2) chart lessons for likeness and difference activities, (3) "What is missing?" (4) identifying valentines by description, when the teacher describes, and (5) when the child describes.

*A Party:* At the party the children take turns delivering valentines (wearing the postman's hat). The teacher calls a name, a child selects a valentine and takes it to the child whose name was called.

*Increasing Vocabulary:* This is a good unit for teaching the word "friend." Two children exchange valentines and say, "I like you, you're my friend."

## Basic Vocabulary (B-8)

Valentine                        lace

## Games, Stories, Songs, and Nursery Rhymes (B-8)

The teacher makes appropriate selections for this unit.

## Home Training Hints for Parents (B-8)

1. This is an opportune time to take a child to the post office to purchase a stamp and to mail a valentine to a friend. The mother should ask the friend to show the child the valentine after it has been received.
2. Mother prepares the child to say "I love you" as he gives a valentine to his Daddy and vice versa.
3. Children can help their mothers bake valentine cookies and decorate them.
4. Parents purchase candy hearts of various colors to be used for matching, rote counting, and number concept development.
5. Mother draws several hearts on a large piece of paper and her child outlines the hearts with various colored crayons.

# BEGINNING LEVEL (B)

# Unit: Yard, Playground (B-9)

### CLASSROOM ACTIVITIES

*Doll House:* Several toy items that belong inside and outside the house are placed in a box. The doll house is arranged in an outdoor scene; grass, trees, fence. Each child draws an object from the box and places it appropriately inside or outside the house.

*Plants:* Beans and other fast growing seeds may be planted and kept in the classroom. The children note how they grow. An egg shell may be filled with dirt and grass seed. A boy's face painted on the shell will eventually take the form of a head as the grass grows for hair.

The children may pretend to be flowers while "Mistress Mary waters them." Each child curls up on the floor then gradually "grows taller and taller."

*Stamp Set:* Each child has a sheet of paper with a scene containing house, grass, fence, garage, and tree. The teacher gives a child a flower from the stamp set and says "Put the flower by the garage." Another child may "Stamp the girl under the tree."

*Yard Tools:* Each child is assigned to bring a yard tool to class; rake, spade, toy lawn mower. The function of each is discussed then the children select the appropriate tool when asked, "What would I use to rake the leaves from this yard?" "What would I use to cut the grass?" "What would I use to dig a hole to plant the tree?" "What should I use to carry the weeds?"

*Field Trip:* A trip to the park is planned. Two mothers accompany the teacher. One mother makes a lesson plan around the refreshment period and the other conducts a playground activity.

*See-Saw:* A see-saw is set up in the classroom using a board and a large block. While the children are participating the teacher stresses vocabulary; *up-down, see-saw, seat* and *handle.* Two children may act out the activity by holding hands. One child stands while the other squats. They alternate positions with the words *see-saw.*

*Sandbox:* A sandbox made from a large wash tub is brought to the classroom. Funnels, strainers, cups, pails, and other toys are available. As the children play, the teacher builds vocabulary and encourages appropriate sentence structure; "Bury your feet in the sand." "The pail is empty." "Fill it up." "It's light." "It's heavy."

*Flowers:* Each child is given a piece of paper and with a green crayon he makes vertical lines. Flower seals are given him to paste at the top of each line.

For a young group this activity can be conducted by the teacher who places a piece of paper on an easel. The children take turns drawing lines and pasting flower seals.

Flowers can be made from precut stems and leaves plus cupcake papers as blossoms. Other flowers are created by drawing a large circle on construction paper which the teacher cuts out. The children take turns cutting into the edges of the flower, usually about an inch all around the circle. This makes a fringed edge. A long strip for the stem, and appropriately shaped leaves complete the flower which may be taped to the classroom wall.

*Picnic Basket:* As a group project the children plan what to take on a picnic. Then the items are packed into a basket.

*Wall Mural:* The children make a large mural of things found in a yard. Fringed paper serves for grass, small pieces of paper are cut for leaves on the trees, and paper cup flowers are appropriately situated. This activity is carried out step by step over several days.

### Basic Vocabulary (B-9)

| | | |
|---|---|---|
| basket | gate | porch |
| bench | grass | sand |
| bird | hose | sandbox |
| bugs | ice cream | sandpile |
| climb | kite | sandwich |
| coat | leaves | slide |
| dig | lunch | string |
| dirt | mosquitoes | swing |
| down | park | trees |
| driveway | patio | up |
| fence | penny | yard |
| flowers | pick | |
| fun | picnic | |

### Games, Stories, Songs, and Nursery Rhymes (B-9)

The teacher makes appropriate selections for this unit.

### Home Training Hints for Parents (B-9)

1. Purchase or share phonograph records that require action from the children. Keep in mind that verbs are being stressed in this unit even though some of them may have been introduced in previous units.
2. Use the following suggestions for teaching language related to swinging in a swing at the park. "Hold on to the seat. Your hands get rusty from the chain." "Is the swing too high for you?" "Can your feet touch the ground?" "Shall I push you?" "I'm going to run under you." "Hold tight." "Do you want the middle swing?" "Is the seat made of wood or cloth?"
3. With weather permitting do the following: Fly a kite. Plant flower seeds. Visit a garden shop and ask the child to choose a plant to take home for the yard or his room. Pull weeds and put into a basket. Feed the birds with breadcrumbs or bird seed.
4. In bad weather place a sweet potato or carrot top in water and watch it grow. Bulbs do well indoors during winter months.
5. Visit the amusement park. Retell the trip in sequence and ask the child to retell it to his father when he comes home from work. Use pictures if necessary, but encourage your child to want to communicate his experiences to someone who has not shared them.
6. Take a walk with your child and bring back leaves, twigs, and rocks to show Daddy.

7. Sit in the yard after dark to develop a vocabulary related to things seen after dark; stars, moon, dark, bugs, moths. A night walk with the flashlight is fun.

# BEGINNING LEVEL (B)

## Unit: Easter (B-10)

CLASSROOM ACTIVITIES

*Paper Rabbits:* Easter is a good time of the year to do cutting and pasting activities. The children color dittoed rabbits and then paste cotton balls for tails. "The rabbit's tail is fluffy." or "The rabbit can hop."

*Easter Baskets:* Easter baskets may be constructed from paper and filled with paper eggs. These eggs may be decorated with colorful seals or tiny candies.

*Bunny Hop Dance:* Pin large cotton ball tails on the children for a "Bunny Hop" dance. Children hop as long as the music plays. When it stops, they do one of the following: hop to their homes, find their partners, sit on the floor or back their "tails" up flat against a wall. Tall paper ears may be placed on headbands to be used for the "Bunny Hop" dance.

*Plastic Easter Eggs:* Use plastic Easter eggs that open. Hide a surprise in it and ask the child to "Open the egg." Inside may be a small fluffy chicken, a little rabbit, or some candy.

*Easter Egg Hunt:* Prepare for Easter egg hunt by dying eggs in the classroom. Stress color words and such concepts as "It's wet." "Dip it in the dye." Hide the eggs in the classroom and ask the children to hunt for them. "Find the blue egg. It's under the desk." Count the number of eggs in the basket. Discuss the difference between real eggs and paper eggs.

### Basic Vocabulary (B-10)

| | | |
|---|---|---|
| bunny (rabbit) | dye | egg |
| chicken | duck | hide |
| chocolate | Easter egg | marshmallow |
| church | Easter egg hunt | Sunday School |

### Games, Stories, Songs, and Nursery Rhymes (B-10)

The teacher makes appropriate selections for this unit.

*Home Training Hints for Parents* (B-10)

1. Easter is a good time to expand the children's vocabulary related to clothing. Introduce words such as *vest, bow tie, loafers, cape, bonnet, sandals.*
2. There are many different types of Easter candy and goodies. Parents take their children to shop for chocolate rabbits, marshmallow chickens, or candy eggs. A package may be sent to class the next day.
3. Parents may make Easter baskets at home from oatmeal boxes, plastic containers, milk or ice cream cartons.
4. Invite the children in the neighborhood to participate in an Easter parade.
5. The children color Easter eggs at home. They place an egg in the blue water or match a piece of blue paper to the blue water if they are just learning color words. Faces may be drawn on the eggs with a magic marker pen.

# BEGINNING LEVEL (B)

## Unit: Pets (B-11)

CLASSROOM ACTIVITIES

*Sound Effects Record:* Each child has before him a card with four animal pictures. A recording of the sound made by one animal is played. The children cover the appropriate picture as in lotto.

*Pets:* Parents are requested to bring to school an appropriate pet. It is truly a great day when a child's dog or cat visits school. Arrange for a different pet each week which will allow for concentration on dogs one week, cats the next, and then turtles.

*Pocket Chart:* A pocket chart is placed before the class with pictures of a variety of pets. The children sort them appropriately. Several days later pictures may be arranged on a chart with their respective homes; dog house, bird cage, turtle dish.

*Rhythm Record:* The change in tempo of rhythm records makes them convenient for walking like a turtle, hopping like a rabbit, or flying like a bird.

*Song:* Each child holds a picture of a pet. The teacher sings "Old Mac-Donald Had a Farm." As she names a pet the appropriate child stands. All children join in singing the chorus.

*Picture File:* "Real" and "Not real" may be contrasted by showing pictures of a dog drinking a coke, a horse sitting on a chair, or a bird swimming in the water. The children are encouraged to laugh and see the humor in the pictures.

*Film Strips:* Film strips on pets and their care are available. After viewing the films the children may want to care for a pet in the classroom, perhaps a goldfish or a turtle.

*The Pet Shop:* Arrangements may be made to visit a pet shop. Each child plans to buy a pet, or the class as a whole may purchase one pet for the classroom. Parents should meet at the shop to show all the pets to their children. If someone has a camera, pictures taken can be used later for building sequence stories. What happened first? What happened next?

*Hand Crafts:* Pets can be made from marshmallows and toothpicks. A dachshund has five large marshmallows for his body and one for his head. Two small ones are strung on toothpicks for each leg.

A turtle is made by stapling two pie plates together with a head, tail, and legs between them.

Paper birds can be made from construction paper and hung from the classroom ceiling.

*Flannel Board:* On a flannel board is a picture of a bird with a head missing. The teacher instructs a child to tell "What is missing?"

### Basic Vocabulary (B-11)

| | | |
|---|---|---|
| animal sounds | dog house | pets |
| animal | feed | pony |
| bad | fish | rabbit |
| bark | fish bowl | short |
| bird | in | soft |
| bowl | little | trail |
| dish | long | under |
| dog | on | |

### Games, Stories, Songs, and Nursery Rhymes (B-11)

The teacher makes appropriate selections for this unit.

### Home Training Hints for Parents (B-11)

1. Instead of just teaching the child the names of animals consider names for the type of body covering (hair, scales, skin, feathers, shell); the kind of food they eat; their peculiar method of locomotion; where they live in a natural state (cave, tree, hole in the ground,

ocean); where they live as a pet (large zoo, cave, aquarium, fish bowl, dog house, basket); color; length of tail, ears, legs; and whether they are wild or tame.

2. Because a child uses very simple words and phrases does not suggest that you talk to him on this level. A child's ability to talk is usually less than his ability to understand. Although he may not use the word *animal*, he may know the meaning of the word.
3. Bake gingerbread boy cookies. Ask questions about the story while eating the cookies.
4. With a cookie cutter make gingerbread boys from rolled out clay.
5. Teach the child a sequential routine for feeding his pet.
6. Look through magazines with your child and ask him to identify pets as you name them. Then he names and you identify.

# BEGINNING LEVEL (B)

## Unit: Birthday Parties (B-12)

### CLASSROOM ACTIVITIES

*Invitations:* The child with a birthday brings invitations that he and his mother have made at home. The class opens them in school while the teacher reads the content.

*Peg Board:* Each child has a peg board before him and pretends it is a birthday cake. To present a lesson in number concepts the teacher gives such directions as "Place three candles (pegs) in the cake." "Blow out three candles." (Pegs are removed.)

*Cardboard Cake:* To develop vocabulary and concepts surrounding a birthday party, the teacher and class construct a pretend cake from a paper box. The children decorate it and place an appropriate number of candles.

*Place Cards:* The children fold the place cards according to the teacher's directions. Colorful seals are placed *on the front* of the card.

*Birthday Party:* The party consists of refreshments, favors, opening gifts and several games. Each child may bring a ten-cent gift. The mother of the birthday child furnishes refreshments and favors, and assists the teacher during the party.

### Basic Vocabulary (B-12)

| | | |
|---|---|---|
| cake | gift | present |
| candles | matches | sucker |
| | party | |

*Games, Stories, Songs, and Nursery Rhymes* (B-12)

The teacher makes appropriate selections for this unit.

*Home Training Hints for Parents* (B-12)

1. Parents allow their children to help select an inexpensive gift and teach them how to wrap it.
2. The birthday child helps his mother make his cake. She employs many teaching techniques related to memory, number concepts, and vocabulary.
3. Parents may decide before the party what presents they will buy. The value of the gift giving is in the variety of the objects received and the vocabulary that may stem from the gifts.
4. The gifts are taken home and shown to Daddy and other members of the family. Conversations about the events of the party should be encouraged.
5. The teacher or parent of the birthday child furnishes favors for the other children. The favors should be chosen for reinforcement of vocabulary or specific learning skills that have been taught during that week.

# PRE-KINDERGARTEN LEVEL (PK)
## (*Child Growth and Development Data*)

## 4 to 5 Years

Loves to hear stories, reacts bodily. (43)
Questioning is at a peak but not always interested in answers. (43)
Counts three objects, pointing to each in turn. (43)
Common expression, "I don't know." (43)
Names one color. (43)
Counts to four. (43)
Mean length of response is 5.4 to 5.7 words. (105)
Can skip somewhat, but not hop. (43)
Brushes teeth. (43)
Dresses self but cannot tie. (43)
Washes and dries face. (43)
Alternates feet up and down steps. (43)
Usually will go in examining room without mother. (43)
Likes to choose own menu. (43)
Cooperative play begins. (43)
Fear of dark and such things as roosters, cotton, etc. (43)
Sometimes fabricates. May not know truth from fable. (43)

Plays tag, hide-and-seek, marbles, etc. (34)
Weight: boys, 38.2 to 43.2 lbs.—girls, 37.3 to 42 lbs. (73)
Height: boys, 40.9 to 43.9 in.—girls, 40.9 to 43.6 in. (73)
Sleep 11.75 hours. (71)
Bedtime around 7:55 p.m. (71)
Up to 27% males and 20% females bite finger nails. (117)

## PRE-KINDERGARTEN LEVEL (PK)
### (*Language Skills*)

## I. COMPREHENSION OF ORAL LANGUAGE
### A. RECOGNITION OF OBJECTS
#### 1. By Name
a. Objects such as zoo animals are placed in a "surprise box." Children take turns finding the object named by the teacher.

b. A paper nest with slots for the birds is placed on a large poster board or on a flannel board. A variety of different sized and colored birds are assembled beside the chart. The children are asked to "Put the *red* bird in the nest." or "Put a *big* bird in the nest."

c. A model of a miniature zoo (or any model appropriate to the unit being studied) is constructed in the classroom. The children are asked to locate the tiger, the seal, the zoo keeper, and the cage.

#### 2. By Function
a. A store is the theme with the teacher serving as store-keeper. The children buy objects according to function. "Buy something to cut with." "Buy something to write with."

b. Several familiar objects are placed in a bag and the teacher asks a child to "Find one that you brush your teeth with." He places his hand in the bag and feels for the correct object.

c. During the food unit, cookies may be made in class. The children bring the teacher "What you stir with." "Something to bake the cookies on."

### B. RECOGNIZING PICTURES
#### 1. By Name
a. Place a landscape and ocean scene in an opaque projector. Ask the children to point to the object named such as sailboat, train, bridge, trees, children.

b. Building blocks with pictures on each side are placed on the table. In turn the children "Place the lion on top of the elephant." "The tiger on top of the lion."

c. A picture of a doctor's office is placed on a flannel board. The children "Put the pills in the office." "Put the band-aid in the office."

2. By Function

a. A picture of the nursery rhyme "Little Miss Muffet" is placed in the pocket chart as the teacher says the rhyme. Later the children find "What she sat on." "What she ate." "What frightened her."

b. The children make placemats from construction paper. Cut-outs of the utensils needed for dinner are given to each child who selects the appropriate one when asked to "Paste on the one we drink out of."

c. A mural of a zoo is made by hanging a long piece of white paper along the wall. The children "Paste on one that roars." "One that balances a ball on his nose."

C. CATEGORIZING

1. Several objects are placed on the table: toothpaste, toothbrush, washcloth, soap, shoes, shoelaces. The children "Find what goes with the toothbrush." "What goes with the soap?"

2. On a worksheet are printed objects that are alike and one that is different. (Two cars and one airplane.) The children are asked "To color the ones that are alike." or "To color the one that is different."

3. Scenes of Halloween, Christmas, and Valentine's Day are placed on a table. In turn the children select an individual picture and place it on the correct scene from a group of appropriate pictures related to each holiday.

D. NUMBER CONCEPTS

1. A bus is constructed from a shoe box if a toy bus is not available. Pictures or plastic dolls are arranged so that a specific number are in the bus and others are waiting for the bus. For example, two people may be on the bus and three people waiting for it.

2. A large nest for Easter eggs is given to each child. Before pasting the eggs to the nest, the children practice placing a specific number, e.g., one, four, three.

3. One child with socks on his hands pretends to be a seal. The other children throw him a specified number of fish.

E. SPATIAL AND TEMPORAL ORIENTATION

1. One child leaves the room while the teacher directs another child to "Hide the train under my desk." "Hide the car under Jill's desk." The seeker finds the objects while the children tell him whether he is getting closer or farther away by calling out "hot" or "cold."

2. During a period of exercising the children are asked to "Put your hands over your head." "Put your hands on the floor." "Put your hands behind you."

3. Pictures of trucks are cut into several pieces and given each child. With paper in front of them they are asked to "Put the wheels at the bottom of the paper." "Put the cab in the middle." When loosely assembled, the picture is then neatly pasted together by the children.

F. SERIAL DIRECTIONS

1. A box and several different colored objects are placed on the table. The teacher gives directions such as "Put the blue block in the box." "Put the green car in the box and close the box."

2. The children serve as helpers during refreshment time. "Mary get the napkins and place them on the table." "Susan get the cups and John get the juice."

3. The children play "Follow My Directions." The teacher asks a child to "Walk to the door and hop to the record player." "Run to my desk and tip-toe to your chair."

## II. EXPRESSION OF ORAL LANGUAGE

A. NAMING AND DEFINING

1. Naming

a. Each child brings a vegetable to class which can be cut up for a salad. As the teacher chops the vegetables the children name them.

b. Using a "Put together toy" each child names the part as he attaches it appropriately.

c. During the health unit the teacher places a doctor's kit on the table. The children name the objects that go into the kit as they drop them in.

2. Defining

a. A food store is set up in the classroom. A child buys an item by describing it as to color, shape, size. The teacher may have to provide leading questions.

b. Several valentines are placed on the chart rack. The teacher describes one and a child guesses the correct one.

c. Easter eggs are dyed and decorated in class. Each child describes his favorite egg.

3. Action Agent

a. Several animal masks made from construction paper are placed on the table. By turn the children select a mask and put it on. The teacher says, "Freddie is a frog. What does he do?" If the children gesture the answer, the teacher supplies the word until no longer necessary.

b. The teacher laughs, cries, coughs, or whispers and asks "What was I doing?"

c. Using the melody "Here We Go Round the Mulberry Bush" the children adapt actions to the unit being studied. "This is the way we drive our car." "This is the way we wash our car." "This is the way we row our boat."

B. CATEGORIZING

1. An outdoor scene is placed on the flannel board. The teacher places objects in incongruous places; a bus in the sky, a train on the street, a house in a tree. The children tell what is "silly" about the picture.

2. A restaurant is set up in the classroom. The teacher serves as waiter and first asks the children to order something that could be eaten for breakfast. This may be followed by dinner, or snacks.

3. A picture of an animal is pinned on each child. The teacher gives the command, "All of the animals that live on the farm stand up." "All animals that live in the jungle go to the window."

C. NUMBER CONCEPTS

1. A grocery store is organized in the classroom and each child is given ten pennies. Every item costs from one to ten cents. The storekeeper gives the price of the item and the child pays the appropriate amount.

2. The girls go to one side of the room and the boys to the other. The teacher asks, "How many boys are at school today?" "How many girls are at school?" "Are there more boys than girls?" "How many girls are wearing hair ribbons?"

3. Specific scenes are placed in the opaque projector. If a picture of a zoo is shown, the teacher may ask, "How many animals do you see?" "How many ducks do you see?"

D. SPATIAL AND TEMPORAL RELATIONSHIPS

1. The playhouse is used to teach the following words: *in, on, under, underneath, above, over, beside, on top, inside, outside, in between, upside down, up,* and *down.* The children manipulate the dolls and furniture as the teacher suggests: "Put the doll inside the playhouse."

2. Concepts of today, yesterday, and tomorrow may be taught during the refreshment period. A host and hostess chart designates who will distribute the cups, napkins, and cookies, and on which days. Presenting the chart for the week the teacher asks, "Who will pass out cups today?" "Who passed the napkins yesterday?" "Who will serve cookies tomorrow?"

3. Frequent opportunities occur to present the meaning of the words *first* and *last.* "Who is first in line?" "Name the first picture in the row." "What happened first in the story?"

E. SENTENCE BUILDING

1. Story telling may be accomplished in the following ways:

a. During Show and Tell each child explains what he has, where he got it, what he can do with it, and any other pertinent information.

b. The teacher tells the story of "The Three Billy Goats Gruff" through the use of pictures. The children dramatize the story, in sequence, innovating the story dialogue.

c. Action pictures are shown by the opaque projector. The children take turns telling what is happening in the picture. The stimulus pictures may remind the children of personal experiences which can be related.

2. Syntax

a. Using a lotto game the teacher asks, "Who has a flower?" The child must respond, "I do." or "I have it." or "He has it." When the activity is structured in this fashion such responses as "Me do." or "I got it," are not acceptable.

b. During the refreshment period the children must ask for a cookie or cracker in a well structured sentence. "May I have a cookie, please?" "I want another one, please."

c. Hollow, plastic Easter eggs filled with pictures are given the children. After a child has opened his egg, he names his picture. The teacher asks, "Where was the duck?" to which the child replies, "In the egg." Then he is asked to tell it all, "The duck is in the egg." or "The duck was in the egg."

Demanding complete sentences at all times stifles the child's spontaneity. In certain activities, however, building correct sentences is part of the training program.

## PRE-KINDERGARTEN LEVEL (PK)
### (Avenues of Learning)

### I. MEMORY: SHORT TERM

A. AUDITORY

Goals: To remember at least three auditory signals or commands not necessarily in sequence, and to repeat short sentences.

1. The sounds of zoo animals are played on a tape or phonograph recording. The child points to the pictures of the animals related to the sounds.

2. Two children are given telephones. The teacher tells one child what to say and he repeats it. Then the second child is told what to answer, and he repeats it.

3. Appropriate pictures are given to each child and as the teacher reads "The Little Engine that Could" each child play acts his picture.

Goal: To remember three items in sequence.

1. "Get your school boxes, take out your pencils and place your boxes under your desks."

2. Short stories utilizing pictures are told by the teacher. The children retell them in sequence.

3. The teacher places noise makers on the table and has duplicates in her lap. She sounds three of them while a child's back is turned. He is to select the appropriate ones.

B. VISUAL

Goal: To remember at least three visual events not necessarily in sequence.

1. One child hides his eyes while three others leave the room. The guesser names who is missing.

2. The teacher tells a story with pictures. She removes one picture and places the remainder on the chart rack. The children guess which one is missing.

3. A car with three parts missing is drawn on the blackboard. One child names the missing parts and another child may be chosen to add them to the picture.

Goal: To remember at least three visual events in sequence.

1. The teacher shows three pictures to the children; e.g., a man driving a car; a man changing a flat tire; a man getting into a car. A child is asked to act out what he has seen.

2. A grocery store is set up in the classroom. The teacher selects three items and a child is asked to choose the same items in appropriate sequence.

3. Using a large chart the teacher places a dog on the grass, a child by the house, and a duck in the pond. Someone is asked to repeat the activity.

C. VISUAL-MOTOR

Goal: To remember at least three motor acts in sequence when oral language is not involved.

1. The teacher demonstrates how the paper napkins should be folded for the tea party. The children fold their napkins the same way.

2. The teacher taps a desk, a table and the door. A child is asked to repeat the activity.

3. Someone flies like a bird, hops like a rabbit and falls down. Another child repeats the activity.

## II. VISUAL-PERCEPTUAL-MOTOR

Goal: To perceive a visual image and reproduce it.

1. The children put puzzles together.

2. An animal is cut into five parts and a child is asked to paste the parts in appropriate relationship on a piece of paper.

3. The teacher makes a bracelet from colored macaroni. The children copy the pattern for their own bracelets.

## III. SOCIAL MATURITY

Goal: To teach work habits that are essential to learning in a group situation.

1. The teacher gives simple group instructions, such as, "Now you may start coloring." or, "Children, put a sticker at the top of the paper." Group instructions are often more difficult to follow than individual instructions.

2. The children are taught to sit still while the teacher reads short stories.

3. The children are taught to sit for longer periods of time at their desks.

Goal: To develop independence in self-help skills.

1. The children are taught to remove and put on their coats and sweaters.

2. Before refreshment period each child washes and dries his own hands.

3. The children practice selecting the kind of food they would choose if at a restaurant.

Goal: To teach appropriate situational behavior.

1. The children learn certain routine behavior such as keeping their school supplies in order, and cleaning up after the refreshment period.

2. The principles taught in the Beginning Level are reinforced.


# PRE-KINDERGARTEN LEVEL (PK)
## (Pre-Academic Subjects)


## I. LIKENESSES AND DIFFERENCES

Goal: Through group work the children learn to find one like this and find one that is different.

1. Flannel board one (the teacher's) contains pictures of a house, a bird, and a tree. Flannel board two contains just a bird. Pointing to the second board, the teacher says, "Find one like this on my board." If successful, he places both birds on the teacher's board. Matching may be done with different colors, shapes, and simple pictures.

2. Pictures are hidden in the room, and the children "Find the one like this," as the teacher holds up a matching picture.

3. Several pictures are drawn on the blackboard in a cluster. The teacher draws one of the objects apart from the cluster and says, "Draw a circle around one like this."

4. Three birds and one ball are placed on the flannel board, and the children "Find the one that is different." They take turns being teacher.

5. Three trees and one house are drawn on the blackboard. A child is asked to draw an X through the one that is different.

6. Pictures are placed in the pocket chart, three alike and one different. A child removes the one that is different.

Goal: Through individual work the children learn to find likenesses and differences.

1. Each child has his name card and an individualized seal pasted on the back of his chair. He will remember his chair because he

chose the seal. At a later date the seal is removed to check recognition of name cards.

2. Each child finds his name card when he comes to school. It is placed on the name chart.

3. The teacher places names on sheets of paper which are to be used for an activity. The children find their paper.

## II. PHONICS TRAINING

1. When playing the game "What's missing?" the teacher uses pictures that begin with the same sound, and one that may be omitted or substituted in the children's speech. Although the children are not aware of the phonics training, they do receive special attention in listening and using specific sounds.

2. A group of cards from the card file that start with "f" may be used to play a hiding game. One child tells the teacher which card he wants to hide. Another child finds it and reports what he found.

## III. WRITING READINESS

Goal: The children are expected to draw simple pictures on the blackboard or on large pieces of paper.

1. On a piece of paper the children learn to follow the teacher's instructions to draw a circle for the face and make smaller circles for eyes, and a line for the mouth. Yarn may be pasted around the face to represent hair.

2. A house is made by drawing a square with smaller square windows and a rectangular door with a small circle for a knob. The teacher provides a construction-paper triangle for the roof.

3. The children draw circles to represent flowers and lines for the stems. Precut leaves are pasted to the stems.

4. Ditto copies of a Christmas tree are given each child. They draw circles with their crayons to represent colored lights.

5. The teacher draws an engine on the blackboard. Each child adds a box car.

## IV. NUMBERS

Goal: To teach the children to rote-count to ten and develop number concepts through three.

1. The children count the number of chairs in the circle for story time, the girls and boys when two classes meet together, sheets of paper, paper cups, and crayons.

2. One, two, or three seals are selected for a picture. The same activity applies to rubber stamps, flannel board cut-outs, and crayons.

3. Dots on configuration cards (like dominoes) are counted. For the configuration five, the two at the top, going from left to right are one

and two. The bottom ones are three and four (left to right), and the one in the center is five. Pegs may be inserted in the peg boards in a domino configuration of one through five.

4. The teacher talks about the clock, what it is, and points out the hands and numbers. She introduces the vocabulary "It's *late*." "It's too *early*." "How *long* until refreshment time?"

5. As a group the children keep a weather calendar. They discuss the current weather and find the appropriate picture to place on the calendar.

6. Each child learns his own age. A paper birthday cake chart is placed on the flannel board. In turn each child selects the number of candles appropriate to his age and places them on the cake.

7. Exposure to coin names is accomplished by bringing a specific coin from home, a penny for the gum machine when the grocery store is visited, a nickel for candy at the zoo, a dime for a coke to take on an outing, a quarter to spend on the Christmas gift for mother.

## PRE-KINDERGARTEN LANGUAGE DEVELOPMENT: PROPOSED CALENDAR

September:  School (PK-1).
October:  Dishes (PK-2); Halloween (PK-3).
November:  Food (PK-4); Thanksgiving (PK-5).
December:  Christmas (Toys) (PK-6).
January:  Health (PK-7).
February:  Review; Valentine (PK-8); Transportation (In general) (PK-9).
March:  Transportation (Bus); Transportation (Train); Transportation (Airplane); Transportation (Boat).
April:  Easter (PK-10); Transportation (Cars); Games involving all means of transportation.
May:  Zoo (PK-11).
Extra:  Birthday (PK-12).


# PRE-KINDERGARTEN LEVEL (PK)

## Unit: Zoo

SAMPLE LESSON PLAN

  I. Goals: To teach and/or expose children to:
   1. Recognize their names when spoken within a sentence.
   2. The vocabulary words and short phrases in the zoo unit.
   3. Cutting and drawing skills.

4. Number concepts through three.
5. Rote counting through ten.
6. Concepts of likenesses and differences.
7. Drawing circles and straight lines to form a pattern.
8. Recognize and name the colors *red, yellow, blue,* and *green.*
9. Auditory and visual sequencing of three pictures.

II. Activities

**10:00–10:05** As the teacher calls each child's name he answers, "I'm here." The children may take turns being "teacher."

**10:05–10:20** The teacher introduces the "seal" through a variety of pictures. She discusses his body parts, where he lives, how he moves about, and what he eats. Then each child receives a large simple drawing of a seal and is asked to draw in the eyes. (Visual-Motor-Perception.) When completed, they cut out the picture. (Cutting skills.)

**10:20–10:40** Large blocks are arranged in a circle to represent the seal's cage, and a cardboard box in the middle represents a rock. (Concepts of circle and middle.) One child with paper flippers taped to his hands pretends to be a seal. (Concept of pretend.) The other children stand around the cage and throw fish to the seal. (Questions and answers as, "What does the seal eat?")

**10:40–10:50** Each child receives a picture of a seal's cage. Using the stamp set, each child in turn places *one, two,* or *three* seals in the cage. (Learning number concepts to three.)

**10:50–11:00** A picture of a seal is pasted on the school calendar. The children count the number of days until the class visits the zoo to see the seal. (Rote counting to ten and exposure to time concepts.)

**11:00–11:20** Pictures of zoo animals are hidden in the room. The teacher with a matching set shows one picture and asks a child to "Find one like it." (Likenesses and differences.)

**11:20–11:45** A picture of a balloon man is drawn on the blackboard. For seat work, each child is given a large sheet of paper and instructed to draw three circles. (Number concepts.) Then they add straight lines to represent the strings. (Visual-Motor-Perception.) When completed, the teacher says, "Go get your supply box and take out a red crayon." (Auditory memory sequencing.) When they have colored one balloon, she says "Put the red crayon back, and get your blue one." The activity continues in this manner.

**11:45–12:00** The teacher shows and explains three sequence pictures depicting a trip to the zoo. The pictures are placed on the table, and as the teacher describes one picture, the children take turns selecting the appropriate one. Then the pictures are arranged in the correct order. (Visual sequencing.) The next step would be to tell the story. (Auditory sequencing.)

# PRE-KINDERGARTEN LEVEL (PK)

## Unit: School Routine (PK-1)

CLASSROOM ACTIVITIES

*School Tools:* To review the names of school tools and teach new vocabulary, the teacher places several objects (stapler, eraser, chalk, scissors) in a row. One child wears a blindfold while the teacher removes one of the objects. The blindfold is removed and the child names the object taken. Questions are asked, "What's missing?" "Who found it?"

*Construction Paper:* A large tree with detachable leaves is made from construction paper. Each child's name is printed on a leaf. During roll call, the child selects his name and pins the leaf to the tree.

　　Additional leaves, flowers, or fruit appropriate to the season may be made from different colored paper. Numbers and colors may be taught by having the children follow the teacher's directions in placing the leaves on the tree. "Place two leaves on a branch." "Put two red flowers under the tree."

*Class Members:* The game of "Call Somebody" is played to teach the children names of classmates and an orderly way to leave the room or come to the "talking circle." At dismissal time, for example, the leader stands by the door and responds to the teacher's command, "Call somebody who has a clean desk." Bill is called, goes to the door and the leader leaves the room. "Call somebody who is wearing a red jacket." Joe is called and Bill leaves the room. The game continues until all children have been dismissed.

*Bean Bags:* To teach numbers and colors various colored bean bags are placed in front of the children. In turn they throw them into a box according to the teacher's instructions. "Karol, throw two green bags."

*Boxes:* Have the children trace around boxes of graduated sizes then discuss "Who drew the *largest* box?" "The *middle sized* box?" "The *small* one?"

*Look and Tell Game:* Action words are reviewed and new ones learned by playing the game of "Look and Tell." One child pantomimes an action (climbing a tree, skipping rope, sweeping the floor) and the others take turns guessing the action. If the children cannot think of an action they may choose from a group of pictures.

*Blackboard:* A circle is drawn on the blackboard, and the children think of objects that can be made from it (a face, apple, lollipop). The children draw a big circle on their sheet of paper and make a picture of their choice.

*Refreshments:* The teacher presents two varieties of juice and two of cookies. The children make a choice when asked, "What kind of juice do you want?" "Do you want a chocolate or a vanilla cookie?" This procedure avoids "Yes" and "No" answers.

*Objects:* To teach comparative adjectives the teacher selects objects appropriate to her questions. "Bring me the *short* pencil." "Bring me the *largest* book." "Bring me the one in the *middle*."

*Puzzles:* The children make puzzles by coloring a simple picture and pasting it on cardboard. The teacher cuts it into four or five parts which are counted then assembled. The puzzle can be placed in an envelope and mailed as a greeting card.

### Basic Vocabulary (PK-1)

| | | |
|---|---|---|
| all | easy | orange |
| ask | eraser | paper cutter |
| black | fast | purple |
| blackboard | flannel board | puzzle |
| brown | give | count |
| chalk | keep | sing |
| chalk board | kind of | skip |
| chart | later | slow |
| child | leave | song |
| children | leave it alone | stapler |
| circle | line | tape |
| climb | look | tell |
| do | middle | use |
| don't | now | what |
| drop | off | white |

### Games, Stories, Songs, and Nursery Rhymes (PK-1)

The teacher makes appropriate selections for this unit.

### Home Training Hints for Parents (PK-1)

1. In preparing to do activities at home, take out just one thing at a time, so that you will have the child's undivided attention. If a new storybook is being introduced, let your child look through the book before you begin, so he can become familiar with the pictures and will be ready to listen when you begin reading. On the first presentation (or even the first few) don't read the story word for word. Tell

it using the new language to be introduced. Have some props ready so that the story can be acted out; ask other family members to help in acting out the story. Ask questions about the story such as: "What did _____ do first?" "What did he do next?" "What happened next?" "Who was last to do ____?" or "What happened last?" If a page of the book gets torn, teach your child to mend it with tape.

2. If the child has puzzles at home, remove a piece representing a specific object that can be identified by name. Ask "Which puzzle piece is missing?" or "Is the shoe or the face missing?" The missing part must be something the child can name.

3. Keep a *chart* of rainy, sunny, and windy days. This is not to be an actual calendar though it will look like one. Let your child help draw the *lines* to form a box representing each day. Use *yesterday, today,* and *tomorrow* in describing the weather. For example, "Is it rainy or sunny today?" "Did the sun shine yesterday?" "If it doesn't rain tomorrow, you can play outside." "Today it's raining." "It's raining now." "It's raining. You may go outside later."

4. After the laundry has been folded, let your child help put away his own clothing by following directions to place items in *top, middle,* or *bottom* drawer.

5. After dinner, ask your child to help clear the table, putting objects *on* the counter, or on *top, middle,* or *bottom* shelves.

6. Using a blackboard or paper, teach your child to follow up to three directions. First teach him the language to be used (line, circle, small, middle) and then present a single command, "Draw a *line.*" Once the vocabulary is learned, ask him to "Draw a line and draw a small circle." "Draw a short line in the middle of the blackboard."

7. Draw simple objects like a box for your child to cut out.

8. To teach colors ask your child to "Get your green dress." "Your white socks." "Bring me your red dress, your white socks and your black shoes."

9. When looking at pictures in a magazine, your child may "Count all the _____ on the page." "How many children are in the picture?"

10. To teach the words *ask* and *tell,* instruct your child to "Ask Daddy if he wants a coke." "Tell Johnny that supper's ready."

## PRE-KINDERGARTEN LEVEL (PK)

### Unit: Dishes (PK-2)

CLASSROOM ACTIVITIES

*Silverware:* As an introduction to the dishes unit, the children set a table each day for refreshment period. In turn they follow such directions as "Put the spoon and knife on the table."

*Dishes:* At the completion of the refreshment period, one child washes the dishes, one dries, and one puts them away. The one who puts them away must place pieces of silverware together. Three plate sizes are used. In turn the children find the "largest plate, the smallest plate, and the middle-sized plate."

*Placemats:* Cut placemats from large rectangular pieces of paper and have the children cut out circles for plates. Paste the plate along with the plastic silverware, napkins, and paper cups on the placemats. The finished product may be taken home on a piece of sturdy cardboard.

*Nursery Rhymes:* The children are taught to act out "Hey Diddle Diddle." Later they paste a paper bowl and spoon on tagboard, and draw stick arms and legs to represent "and the dish ran away with the spoon."

*Tea Party:* Mothers and siblings are invited to a tea party. In advance, the children have fringed placemats by snipping into construction paper, folded napkins, decorated cups, and set the table according to directions given by the teacher. As the mothers gather behind the door the teacher calls out "Whose mother is Mrs. Smith?" That child comes forth to seat his mother. This helps to teach children their own and their parents' last name.

*Cups:* The teacher assigns each child to bring in a designated cup. They might bring a mug, a tin cup, a plastic cup, a paper cup, a tall cup, a short cup, etc. When it is time for refreshments, each child is served using his own cup. All children see the differences or likenesses and discuss them. At the end of the refreshment period, they decide which are disposable and which can be washed to be used again.

*Doll Dishes:* Serve lunch to dolls. Set the table and serve play food on the doll's dish. Have the children tell the doll how *not* to eat. For example, "Don't put your fork in the soup." or "Don't eat out of the pan."

*Table Cloth:* In advance the teacher cuts a large paper table cloth into squares of sufficient size to cover the tops of the children's desks. Each child chooses a picture from a large selection representing the words on the "dishes list." He must decide where his object goes by matching it to the place setting on a demonstration desk. The teacher may need to provide hints such as "The knife goes on the right of the plate. The right side is by the window."

*Dishes:* Arrange a variety of dishes, pans, and silverware on a shelf representing a cupboard. In turn the children respond to the teacher's commands, "Bring me something to fry bacon in," ". . . to cut with." If a child cannot perform, he is shown an appropriate picture. This activity is excellent for teaching children the function of objects.

*Nylon Net:* Cut several squares of nylon net. Help children punch holes through the centers of four different sized squares. Insert a pipe cleaner through the holes, form into a circle and draw up into a bunch. Use these for pretend games involving dish washing and pot scrubbing.

### *Basic Vocabulary* (PK-2)

| | | |
|---|---|---|
| barbecues | kettle | salt shaker |
| (cook, grill, | oven | set |
| charcoal) | pan | silverware |
| burn | pepper shaker | soak |
| butter dish | pitcher | sugar bowl |
| can opener | plate | table cloth |
| freezer | platter | |
| glass | pot | |

### *Games, Stories, Songs, and Nursery Rhymes* (PK-2)

The teacher makes appropriate selections for this unit.

### *Home Training Hints for Parents* (PK-2)

1. Parents help their children set up a lemonade stand with pitcher and paper cups. Neighborhood children purchase the drinks for a nominal sum.
2. Organize a tea party with your child for the neighborhood children.
3. Teach your child to set the table for breakfast. Provide serial directions and teach the function of objects, "Get cups for the coffee." "Glasses for the milk." Later in the week say, "Get something to drink from."
4. Children should learn to wash dishes and put them away in appropriate places.
5. With your child select magazine pictures of cooking utensils and food. Teach him to match the appropriate food with the utensil; eggs and frying pan, hot vegetables and sauce pan, muffins and muffin tins.

# PRE-KINDERGARTEN LEVEL (PK-3)

## Unit: Halloween (PK-3)

**CLASSROOM ACTIVITIES**

*Bed Sheet:* Halloween begins to take on more meaning at this level. The children should be introduced to owls, witches, and ghosts as well as the meaning of *real* and *pretend*. Each child in turn dons a ghost costume made from a white sheet with holes cut for the mouth and eyes. The teacher shows pictures of *scary* ghosts and friendly ghosts. Have the children play act the two kinds of ghosts: friendly and scary.

*Paper Napkins:* Children can make ghosts in the classroom. Stuff one facial tissue into the center of a white paper napkin. Tie with a string to form a head. Cut black paper eyes, nose, and mouth and paste on the face or draw the parts of the face with a magic marker.

*Headband:* The children wear owl headbands made from an 18 inch strip of black construction paper about 1½ inches wide. Make a moon and sun from construction paper, and while the children are wearing their owl headbands, hang the sun or moon in the classroom. Have the children go to sleep when the sun comes up; have them awaken and make the owl sound Oo-oo-oo-oo when the moon is up.

*Paper Bags:* Each child brings a paper bag to class to be made into masks. For a cat mask, draw a big grin for the cat's mouth, add paper ears to the bag, and glue on a few broom straws for the cat's whiskers. Tie a bright bow around the child's neck to hold the mask in place.

*Trick or Treat Bags:* Paper bags can also be brought by the children to make trick or treat bags. They draw ghosts, owls, jack-o'-lanterns on the bags or paste on figures cut from construction paper.

*Tape Recorder:* Make a tape recording of Halloween noisemakers. Have the children match the sounds they hear with the noisemakers that are placed on a table in front of them.

### Basic Vocabulary (PK-3)

| | | |
|---|---|---|
| sack | whistle | ghost |
| horn | rattle (shaker) | owl |

### Games, Stories, Songs, and Nursery Rhymes (PK-3)

The teacher makes appropriate selections for this unit.

### Home Training Hints for Parents (PK-3)

1. When the child is to wear a special Halloween costume, let him practice wearing it at home before he wears it to the school party. Go over the special parts. Ask questions such as "How do you know you are a _____?" Go over the identifying areas of the costume such as a cotton tail or long ears or sharp claws. Remember that the trick or treat bag is often part of the costume. You might want to make one at home or buy one.

2. On Halloween night, let the child answer the door when "trick-or-treaters" come. Help them guess which neighbor child is behind the mask. Discuss each "trick-or-treater's" costume.
3. A project for all children in the family might be to cut up a real pumpkin, help cook it, help mash it, watch Mother add the different spices and flavorings, and put it into the oven. The children will enjoy this activity as well as learn how a pie is created.
4. Before you go to the store to buy the child's costume, look at a catalogue with pictures of different costumes. Let the child decide what he wants to be on Halloween. If you sew, make him a special costume of his choice.

# PRE-KINDERGARTEN LEVEL (PK)

## Unit: Food (PK-4)

CLASSROOM ACTIVITIES

*Field Trip:* A field trip to the grocery store will set the stage for this unit. Before going, decide on something for which ingredients must be bought, such as instant pudding, and to cover costs have the parents send money with each child. Prepare the children by playing "checker" and letting them buy the ingredients from you.

When you return from the store, have the children help reconstruct the outing. Using the hectograph or a ditto, they can be encouraged to tell what to draw, and write. The stories can then be duplicated and taken home to retell to mother and daddy.

*Instant Pudding:* Using ingredients bought at the store, the children help make instant pudding. Let them tell you what to do or what utensil you need for each step as well as which dishes will be needed for serving. A sequence story can be written about the preparation of the pudding.

*Simple Foods:* Other foods which can be prepared in the classroom using a hot plate and refrigerator are: jello, lemonade, cocoa, applesauce, sandwiches, deviled eggs, bacon, popcorn, candy, and icebox pie with cookie crust.

Ask one mother to send a pie shell to fill with pudding mix and another mother to send baked cup cakes to ice. A different food can be prepared each day for refreshment period.

*Pretend Grocery Store:* Grocery store play is fun. Set up the store with a different goal for each day's activity.

As the children stack the food on shelves, some attempt can be made to put categories of food together. Meat, vegetables, and cereal categories can be taught in a casual way if the children are told to "Put the cereal on the top shelf." Pretend that one area of the store is the refrigerator and let the children help decide which food goes into the refrigerator and which may stay on the shelf without spoiling.

The store man needs a helper to sack groceries. He must put objects into the bag according to directions; for example, first the cereal, then milk, then eggs.

*Play Money:* Groceries cost 1, 2, or 3 cents each. The children count out the pennies as they buy food.

*Canned Food Labels:* The children bring canned food labels to be pasted in rows on a chart. They decide which row to select; corn goes with vegetables and pears go with fruit. The children are not expected to know the categories of food at this age, but much incidental learning may take place through such an activity.

*Fresh Fruit:* The fruit unit may extend for a week, a different fruit being served each day. Discuss whether you eat the peeling or not, what the seeds look like, pictures of trees or vines on which it grows, and the color of the fruit. After the fruit is eaten, a picture of it can be drawn, colored, or painted. A chart of the seeds may be constructed followed by a discussion of which seed is larger or smaller.

*Jelly:* At some point during the food unit, dinner rolls or bread may be brought to school as well as different flavors of jelly or jam. The children try to match the taste of the jelly with the fruit from which it was made.

*Toy Milk Bottles:* Teach numbers by letting the children take turns being the milkman and delivering milk. The "housewife" asks for the number of bottles needed and the milkman gives that number.

*Opaque Projector:* Use an opaque projector for pictures of Daddy barbecueing on the patio. Discuss what is seen in the picture, as well as aspects of the picture that make them think the fire is hot, which food is warm or cold, if the weather is hot or cold.

*Restaurant:* A culminating activity involves a trip to a restaurant or cafeteria where the children do their own ordering and practice good table manners. Prior arrangements with the restaurant manager should be made. Ask for a menu so the children can decide beforehand what they will order, and the cost. You can practice being the waitress and taking orders before you go. A simple undertaking such as a sandwich and ice cream may be best for this age.

## Basic Vocabulary (PK-4)

| | | |
|---|---|---|
| apple | frozen | pepper |
| bacon | fruit | pie |
| banana | grapefruit | pineapple |
| beans | grapes | plum |
| bread | grocery store | popsicle |
| butter | ham | pork chop |
| buy | hamburger | potato chips (fritos) |
| can | hot dog | pudding |
| carrots | ice | salt |
| cash register | jello | shelf |
| checker | jelly | shopping |
| check out | lemon | sour |
| cherry | lettuce | steak |
| coffee | lots | sweet |
| corn (cob) | nickel | tea |
| cost | peach | tomatoes |
| dessert | peanut butter | vegetable |
| dollar | pear | weigh |
| flour | peas | wiener |

### Games, Stories, Songs, and Nursery Rhymes (PK-4)

The teacher makes appropriate selections for this unit.

### Home Training Hints for Parents (PK-4)

1. For a home project, help your children set up a model grocery market in the basement or in the bedroom. Use blocks, cartons, orange crates, or pieces of furniture—such as bedroom dressers to form the enclosure for the store. Place a toy cash register or compartmented cash box on a chair for the child who is playing "Cashier." Open all canned goods upside down, wash the cans, but leave the labels on. These cans will look just as real on the model shelves as they do at the market. Invite the children in the neighborhood to help, but ask each child to bring from his home not more than six grocery items at a time. Soap boxes, frozen food packages, and dry packaged foods may be taped shut after the contents are removed. When you take your children to the real grocery store, point out to them how the merchandise is separated into departments, so they may organize their own grocery store in the same manner. Help the children label the shelves with prices (1, 2, or 3 pennies only), and print signs directing the customers to the various departments. Demonstrate how to play store with pennies so that they will not need to make change.

The store lends itself not only to the needs of the children who like to plan and build, but also to those who enjoy dramatic play. One can be the cashier, several the customers, one the store manager.

This kind of home activity provides fun, introduction to reading, counting, and dealing courteously with other people.

2. Let your child plan a Sunday breakfast or Saturday lunch by helping him decide which foods are appropriate for that meal.

# PRE-KINDERGARTEN LEVEL (PK)

## Unit: Thanksgiving (PK-5)

CLASSROOM ACTIVITIES

*Paper Plates:* Turkeys are constructed from paper plates (the body) with paper head, feathers and feet appropriately pasted to the plate.

*Leaves:* Fresh leaves which have been collected and pressed are used to form the tail of a cardboard turkey.

*Paper Feathers:* A "Pin the Tail on the Turkey" game is played with colored feathers. The children are asked to select a feather, designated by color, and when blindfolded, pin it to the turkey.

*Toy Turkeys:* The children construct a turkey farm and later take the birds to market. First show a picture of a farm scene including turkeys, then make a fence from small blocks to enclose the miniature turkeys. Next, show a picture of turkeys being loaded onto a truck to be taken to market. Using a toy truck, the children respond to such requests as, "Put three turkeys on the truck." To conclude, the children tell the story in sequence using the pictures.

*Opaque Projector:* Using the opaque projector and a picture of Thanksgiving dinner, the teacher asks the children to point to the foods according to directions. "Find the turkey." "Show me the mashed potatoes and pumpkin pie."

*Plastic Food:* Toy plastic foods are used to improve visual memory. The teacher selects three foods and places them on her plate. After a few seconds she removes them and asks a child to repeat her choices. The children then take turns being teacher.

### Basic Vocabulary (PK-5)

| | | | |
|---|---|---|---|
| Thanksgiving | favor | dinner | serve |

*Games, Stories, Songs, and Nursery Rhymes* (PK-5)

The teacher makes appropriate selections for this unit.

*Home Training Hints for Parents* (PK-5)

1. Take a Sunday drive to a poultry farm. Discuss what the birds eat, how eggs are gathered, and the fact that we eat the birds.
2. Your child can help you plan Thanksgiving dinner by participating in menu making, shopping, and decorating the table.
3. Talk with your child about the many things for which he can be thankful. Explain why we say "Thank you" when we receive something.

# PRE-KINDERGARTEN LEVEL (PK)

## Unit: Christmas & Toys (PK-6)

CLASSROOM ACTIVITIES

*Cardboard Trees:* Using green paper draw a circle the size of a quarter and make seven more a little larger than the preceding one. The children arrange the circles according to size, punch a hole through the center of each and slip them on a paper straw (the smallest at the top and the largest at the bottom). The straw is placed in a small piece of clay and the finished product is covered with snow spray.

*Christmas Cards:* Christmas cards are made in class and the children go to the post office to buy stamps and mail the cards. Parents open the cards in the child's presence.

*Jewelry Box:* The children "cut on the line" to make felt squares to fit the bottom of a plastic sandwich box. The top can be decorated with stars, seals, or artificial flowers to complete the jewelry box for mother. A paper weight can be made for father by painting a flat rock and gluing to it marble chips used in fish bowls.

*Wrapping Paper:* The children can help make decorative wrapping paper. Draw a tree, flower, or any design on a piece of paper then outline with indelible pencil. Press the cut surface of a potato against the design then outline with a knife. Tempera paint or ordinary office stamp pad with red or green ink is used on the potato to stamp the design on wrapping or shelf paper.

The children by following teacher's suggestion may draw red and green stripes on paper going left to right or top to bottom to make attractive gift paper.

*Ornaments:* Children often become very creative in making Christmas tree decorations, and these experiences provide good hand skill activities.

Appropriate Christmas shapes (bells, stars) are cut out by the teacher from various colored construction paper, and children decorate with glue and glitter.

The children place toothpicks into a styrofoam ball which is later sprayed and hung on the tree.

"Star Men" are created by using each point of a star to represent a body part; head, arms, legs.

An auditory memory game is played when a child places the ornaments on the tree as the teacher directs.

### Basic Vocabulary (PK-6)

| | | | |
|---|---|---|---|
| wrap | decorate | shining | to |
| bow | bright | star | from |

### Games, Stories, Songs, and Nursery Rhymes (PK-6)

The teacher makes appropriate selections for this unit.

### Home Training Hints for Parents (PK-6)

1. Take your child to the Christmas tree lot when you purchase your tree. Later show him how it is like other trees. Make a sequence story to include how a tree is chopped down, taken to the store, bought by a family, and finally decorated for Christmas.
2. Before visiting Santa Claus, talk about the toys your child will request. Some children are fearful about sitting on Santa's lap, but enjoy watching from a distance. It may be just as interesting to talk about the toys other children request from Santa.
3. From a catalogue of toys let your child pick out several favorites to paste on a chart. Have him categorize the toys according to toys for boys, and toys for girls, toys that have wheels, toys that are for dolls, and toys that fly.
4. Stress thoughtfulness and good manners around Christmas time by having the children in the family perform good deeds for one another.
5. Children love to give gifts as well as receive them. Help your child shop for small gifts for other family members, and teach him how to wrap them in covered boxes or colored sacks. This age is too young to wrap with paper and ribbon.

# PRE-KINDERGARTEN LEVEL (PK)

## Unit: Health (PK-7)

### CLASSROOM ACTIVITIES

*Doctor Kit:* To introduce this unit, discuss what happens at the doctor's office. The children take turns playing doctor and nurse with medical kits available at the toy store. While a child examines the sick doll, the teacher directs the procedure, "Nurse, take her temperature," "Doctor, look at her throat." Simple costumes are used such as a tie for the doctor, and a hat for the nurse.

*Health Chart:* Use the Ivory Patrol or similar health chart for daily inspection; clean fingernails, combed hair, clean socks. Children take turns being the nurse by wearing the uniform and examining classmates as the teacher calls out the areas to be checked.

*Dress Up:* One child dressed as a nurse helps the teacher obtain the height and weight of each class member. The figures are entered on a class height-weight chart that will show who is tallest and who is heaviest. The children may paste on index cards pictures of a ruler and a scale. The teacher fills in each child's height and weight and the card is taken home.

*Health Pictures:* Good health rules are discussed when appropriate pictures are shown; a child brushing her teeth, combing her hair. Then one child imitates an action while the others "Guess what I'm doing." If they cannot say what he is doing, they may point to the appropriate picture. This game may be played as a memory activity, too. Show a picture, hide it, then a child pantomimes the action.

*Cafeteria Tray:* The children sort food pictures into meats, vegetables, salads, bread, drinks and desserts, then arrange them on a long table. With a tray they go through the cafeteria line selecting a well-balanced dinner as the teacher asks "What meat do you want?" "What vegetables do you want?"

*Paper Doll:* Weather pictures, a paper doll and her clothing are placed before the class. The children select a picture, appropriate clothing for the picture and dress the doll.

*Posture and Exercise:* Children practice good posture by balancing a sheet of paper on their heads or by imitating the manner in which soldiers stand. They can march to music while maintaining good posture.

As the teacher tells a story the children produce the actions while standing in place: "We were walking in the woods and we saw a snake, we turned and ran until we came to a river. We swam across the river to the other side. We had to climb on rocks to get out."

*Grooming Aids:* The children decide from a large group of objects which two go together; toothbrush and toothpaste, wash cloth and soap, comb and brush, kleenex and nose.

*Picture File:* The teacher shows pictures of hospitals in the city and people who are sick in bed. A discussion of hospitals and their purpose follows.

*Dentist Kit:* With a toy dental kit, one child is the dentist and another the patient. Packing and unpacking the kit will teach the object names. The teacher provides the instructions commonly heard in a dentist's office.

### Basic Vocabulary (PK-7)

| | | |
|---|---|---|
| ache | faucet | shampoo |
| aspirin | fever | shot |
| band-aid | fingernails | shower |
| barber shop | hair dryer | slip |
| bathe | hair oil | sneeze |
| beauty shop | hospital | stomach (tummy) |
| cavity | hurt | stopper |
| chest | medicine | strong |
| clean | messy | teeth |
| cold | neat | thermometer |
| cough | nurse | throat |
| curlers (rollers, | office | tonsils |
| bobby pins, nets) | operation | toothbrush |
| dentist | runny nose | toothpaste |
| dirty | scratch | why |
| doctor | sick (ill) | |

### Games, Stories, Songs, and Nursery Rhymes (PK-7)

The teacher makes appropriate selections for this unit.

### Home Training Hints for Parents (PK-7)

1. Emphasize clean hands and fingernails by giving the child his own emery board and an orange stick for cleaning under his nails.
2. Keep kleenex handy at home. Tour your house to decide where the boxes should be kept. Emphasize when kleenex should be used and how to dispose of them.

3. Your child should be acquainted with a dentist's office by this age. Let him accompany you on a routine check-up to see the equipment used and the reason for going.
4. Plan a visit to the doctor while this unit is being taught. Have your child weighed and measured.
5. Provide a place in the child's room for recording the weekly record of height and weight that has been sent from school. At the conclusion of the Health Unit, make monthly entries.
6. Discuss foods in terms of "good" and "good for you." Help your child limit quantities of gum and candy.
7. By observing the weather every morning, let your child decide what to wear for that day. He chooses from a prepared selection of appropriate and inappropriate clothing.

# PRE-KINDERGARTEN LEVEL (PK)

## Unit: Valentine (PK-8)

CLASSROOM ACTIVITIES

*Construction Paper:* Make various kinds of valentines. Discuss the materials used and color, texture, and shape of the finished product. Suggestions are:

a. Paste a red heart in the center of a paper doily.

b. Trace on white paper around a cardboard heart shape. Cut out the heart, fold in the middle and stick on seals according to teacher's directions.

c. Cut out a large heart on which the children will draw in the facial parts and paste on a hat.

*Valentine Cards:* Each parent may be assigned a day to come into the classroom to teach. His assignment is to bring materials and demonstrate the step by step construction of a valentine card. Parents may need some help in deciding an appropriate activity, how much should be prepared at home, or how many steps the children can remember at one time. Some suggested activities are: a heart face with yarn for pig tails, precut cupids pasted on red paper, a man constructed with big, little, and middle-sized hearts for body parts, lace doily cards.

*Hiding Game:* Hide a large and small heart or colored hearts and give directions, such as "Put the large heart on the counter and put the small heart under your chair." The child who was asked to leave the room returns to find the *large* and *small* heart.

*Valentine Candy:* Several different colored boxes are placed on a table.

While the children are not looking, the teacher hides a candy heart under one box. By turn each child guesses which colored box hides the candy.

*Heart Puzzle:* Paste a valentine picture on tagboard and cut into several pieces. The children use it as a puzzle.

### Basic Vocabulary (PK-8)

| | | |
|---|---|---|
| friend | hearts | love |

### Games, Stories, Songs, and Nursery Rhymes (PK-8)

The teacher makes appropriate selections for this unit.

### Home Training Hints for Parents (PK-8)

1. Set aside a time each day for a few days before Valentine's Day to make cards for family members and special friends. Since elaborate cutting and pasting is difficult for this age child, purchase a "Punch-out" valentine card book. He can assemble the cards, place in envelopes and watch you address them. Later he will go with you to mail them or he will personally deliver to neighborhood friends.
2. Decorate a shoe box with valentine stickers. Let this be his box for school where he can put all the valentines he receives.
3. Plan a special dinner for Valentine's Day. Help your child paste candy hearts on small pieces of paper for place cards, and have him assist you in baking a cake with red frosting.
4. Your child can decorate his room for Valentine's Day. Help him cut large paper hearts from construction paper and hang them with string from the ceiling.

# PRE-KINDERGARTEN LEVEL (PK)

## Unit: Transportation (PK-9)

CLASSROOM ACTIVITIES

*Automobile:* The children are introduced to this unit with an inspection of the teacher's and later the parents' car; steering wheel, brakes, lights, trunk, spare tire are pointed out and named. As a home assignment, parents and child make a "car" from a cardboard box that is large enough for him to stand in. The top and bottom of the box are removed and cardboard wheels and headlights are assembled. The finished product is colored or painted. The cars may be brought to class on a day the teacher has planned to teach STOP and GO signs. The children "drive" their cars on pretend streets.

*Pictures:* Each child has a mimeographed picture of a winding road and is asked to paste his paper cars according to directions; at the beginning of the road, at the end of the road. During the last few days of this unit the children are given a landscape scene and asked to paste the car on the road, train on the tracks, boat in the water, airplane in the sky.

*Field Trip:* Field trips may include the bus station, railroad station, service station, and airport. The children are prepared for what they will see and when they return the outing is reconstructed. They are encouraged to tell the teacher what to write, first by supplying the ideas, then finally someone generating sentences to be printed on the hectograph and taken home.

*Boxes:* Parents are asked to help their child construct one train car from a box to be brought to school (approximately the same size boxes). The train is assembled in class where it can be loaded with appropriate freight.

*Sponge:* Each child brings a sponge from home to form the base for a sailboat. The children fold a square diagonally and cut to form a sail. Holes are punched at the top and bottom through which a pipe cleaner is threaded and then inserted into the sponge. They can float in a portable swimming pool or two boats can be blown across the pool for a race.

*Play Money:* Various vehicles are placed about the classroom. Using play money, the children buy rides for one, two, or three cents. One child who is conductor or boat captain collects the tickets and counts them.

*Tagboard:* A large tagboard chart is constructed and placed on the bulletin board. The children bring pictures from home of things to ride in and give descriptions according to size and color. Then the picture is mounted on the chart and several days later the children try to remember who brought each picture.

*Blackboard:* An unfinished vehicle such as a train, airplane, or bus is drawn on the blackboard. The teacher asks a child to add a wheel, draw a wing, or a square for a window.

*Fishing Pole:* The children fish with a pole that has a magnet attached for "bait." A specified number, size, or color of paper fish with paper clips attached are caught by each child.

*Transportation Toys:* Sets of toys and cardboard figures (airplane and pilot, boat and sailor, tank and soldier) can be utilized in a variety of ways. "Who flies the airplane?" "What does the sailor ride in?"

## Basic Vocabulary (PK-9)

*Airplane*

airport
far
fly
high
large
loud
noise
pilot
play-like (pretend)
real
rocket
seat
small
tickets
tray
trip
uniform
wings

*Train*

caboose
cars
depot
engine
engineer
hook
signal
suitcase
track
whistle (verb)

*Bus*

aisle
brake
bus stop
driver
enough
fare
key
many
money
much
sign
start
street (road)
highway (freeway)
tire
too
wheel

*Car*

air conditioner
ash tray
brakes
drive
fasten
filling station
    (service station)
front
gasoline
honk

restaurant (cafe,
    cafeteria)
station wagon
steering wheel
trunk
windshield
wipers

*Boat*

bait
bay
boat house
captain
deep
ferry
fishing
floats
hook (noun)
icebox
lake
motor
net
oars
reel
rod
sail
sailor
shallow
string
trailer

## Games, Stories, Songs, and Nursery Rhymes (PK-9)

The teacher makes appropriate selections for this unit.

## Home Training Hints for Parents (PK-9)

1. Different types of transportation should be discussed in their natural situations. While driving in the car, talk about the parts of the car: front and back seat, steering wheel, and gauges.

2. Take your child to a service station to watch and learn about the procedures of filling with gasoline, checking tires, and checking under the hood.
3. Let your child help wash the car at home while giving directions: wash the back fenders, the front bumper.
4. Plan a bus trip explaining the procedures to your child. Let him be responsible for handling his own money.
5. Visit the airport to watch planes take off and land. Discuss general activity at the airport.
6. Construct paper dolls and appropriate uniforms for the pilot, stewardess, bus and truck drivers.
7. Boats can be made from bars of soap and used in the bath tub for racing: the pink one was first, the white one was last.
8. Visit the library and check out books about trains, buses, trucks, airplanes.

# PRE-KINDERGARTEN LEVEL (PK)
## Unit: Easter (PK-10)

CLASSROOM ACTIVITIES

*Plastic Eggs:* Using pictures and plastic eggs with miniature chickens, expose the children to the concept of a chicken hatching from an egg. The children may play act "hatching" by hiding under a basket.

*Clay:* Roll eggs from clay and insert a string into one end. Decorate and hang them on a large twig to resemble an Easter egg tree.

*Bunny Costume:* One child, dressed as an Easter Bunny delivers a decorated egg to each child. By turn they describe their eggs: "My egg has pink stripes." "My egg has three blue circles."

*Jelly Beans:* A nest made from artificial grass is placed in the teacher's desk. From a bowl of jelly beans the children select according to directions; "Put five eggs in my nest." "Place a red, yellow, and blue egg in my nest."

*Grass:* Go outdoors and gather grass to bring to the classroom. Contrast the *real* grass with the *pretend* grass.

### Basic Vocabulary (PK-10)

See Beginning Level: Foods, Easter, and Pets.

### Games, Stories, Songs, and Nursery Rhymes (PK-10)

The teacher makes appropriate selections for this unit.

*Home Training Hints for Parents* (PK-10)

1. Plan a visit to an egg farm and make a four-part sequence story with snapshots. The first picture is a snapshot of the family driving to the egg farm. The second is a chicken sitting in her nest. The third is a snap of a truck taking the eggs to market and the last picture is of mother buying eggs at the store. Your child may take the photos to school.
2. Decorate a straw basket with plastic or real flowers and fill with artificial or real grass to cushion the eggs. Introduce the word *breakable* and discuss other *breakable* items.
3. Set aside an afternoon before Easter to dye eggs, explaining each step and encouraging questions: Why do we use hot water? The eggs may be decorated with decals or names of family members.
4. Plan an egg hunt on Easter morning and after the children have found all the eggs, they count them and name colors.

# PRE-KINDERGARTEN LEVEL (PK)

## Unit: Zoo (PK-11)

CLASSROOM ACTIVITIES

*The Zoo:* At the start of this unit take a field trip to the zoo for an over-all view which will give a common reference point for subsequent activities. Additional trips to the zoo may be made to emphasize specifics: food animals eat, contrasts of fur, feathers, and skin.

*Notebooks:* Ditto sheets are used to assemble a zoo notebook to be taken home at the end of the unit. Each sheet should emphasize a language or learning skill. A square with lines from top to bottom is drawn for the lion's cage. The monkey is cut into four pieces to serve as a classroom puzzle and later reassembled for the notebook. An animal behind a cage made of bamboo sticks or toothpicks may appear on the front cover.

*Marshmallows:* Animals are made from large and small marshmallows and toothpicks. The giraffe has a large marshmallow for the body, seven small ones for the neck, one small one for the head, toothpicks for legs, raisins for ears, dots for eyes, and a string for the tail.

*Animal Crackers:* Large animal crackers can be used as follows:
    a. Break off a part of the body and ask, "What is missing?"
    b. A cookie is placed in an envelope and the teacher describes it until a child guesses correctly.

    c. Play games matching the crackers to pictures of animals.

    d. Paste the cookies on a zoo chart.

*Opaque Projector:* The opaque projector may be used to show pictures of zoo animals and teach vocabulary. "Which one is *tallest?*" "Point to the one with the longest neck."

*Picture Stamps:* Prepare a large chart depicting a zoo scene. Using an animal stamp set, the children stamp pictures in appropriate places. "Which animal goes in the pond?" "Which animal lives in a cage?"

*Picture File:* Matching animal pictures are used for: hide and find games, pocket chart matching, and what's missing?

*Cardboard Food:* Animal feeding games help develop number skills. One child pretends to be a seal and the others throw him 4 paper "fish."

*Picture Cards:* Prepare two sets of picture cards to teach vocabulary words, *wild* and *tame:* animals that are pets and those that are seen at the zoo.

*Film Strips:* Show film strips related to the zoo and zoo animals.

### Basic Vocabulary (PK-11)

| | | |
|---|---|---|
| balloon man | growl | shell |
| bars | hay | snake |
| bear | heavy | snow cone |
| beg | horns (deer) | spots |
| bite | kangaroo | stripes |
| cage | lion | swim |
| camel | locks | tall |
| claws | monkey | tame |
| cotton candy | peanuts | tiger |
| dangerous | pop | trunk |
| deer | popcorn | wild |
| elephant | rhinoceros | zebra |
| feathers | roar | zoo keeper |
| fur | rocks | |
| giraffe | seal | |

### Games, Stories, Songs, and Nursery Rhymes (PK-11)

The teacher makes appropriate selections for this unit.

### Home Training Hints for Parents (PK-11)

1. Give your child color books and magazines from which he may select and cut out zoo animals. Tack them to your bulletin board or paste into a notebook.

2. When discussing the animals, go beyond naming and include: what they eat, types of cages they live in, habitats they come from, and physical descriptions.
3. Visit the library and check out books concerning the zoo and zoo animals.
4. Purchase phonograph records about zoo animals.
5. Buy animal crackers to be used for counting, matching, and describing.
6. Help your child construct a cage from a shoe box. You can place a toy animal in it and add bars.

## PRE-KINDERGARTEN LEVEL (PK)

### Unit: Birthday Party (PK-12)

CLASSROOM ACTIVITIES

*Photographs:* The teacher prepares a birthday calendar and pastes on appropriate dates, a snapshot and printed name of each child. As the pages are removed, the children observe whose birthday is next.

*Chair:* The birthday child is host or hostess for his party and greets the guests. As a special treat, he sits in a decorated chair, and wears a button with his age imprinted.

*Presents:* When opening presents, the teacher should emphasize the concepts of *"to"* and *"from."* After presents have been opened, the children may sort according to things you *play with, wear.* A "What's missing?" game can be played by removing one present and guessing which one it is.

*Styrofoam Disks:* Each child is given a styrofoam disk and candles. Number configurations are made depicting appropriate ages.

*Noisemakers:* Birthday noisemakers such as paper horns, snappers, rattlers, are used for sound discrimination and auditory memory games.

### Basic Vocabulary (PK-12)

See Beginning Level: Birthday Unit.

### Games, Stories, Songs, and Nursery Rhymes (PK-12)

The teacher makes appropriate selections for this unit.

### Home Training Hints for Parents (PK-12)

1. Plan a special shopping trip to purchase the birthday child's present, but before going, discuss things a boy would like and things a girl would like. Help your child decide on three or four possible gifts,

then allow him to make the choice at the store. Discuss the cost of the gift, help him wrap it and sign the card to _____ from _____.

2. After the party, discuss gifts the birthday child received, games played, and refreshments served.

3. Help your child plan for his own birthday party. Begin with the calendar and count the weeks and days until his birthday is due. Let him go with you to buy the invitations, favors, and refreshments. Discuss how many and who will be at the party. Teach him to draw a birthday cake with the correct number of candles.

## KINDERGARTEN LEVEL (K)

### (Child Growth and Development Data)

### 5 to 6 Years

Can carry a tune. (43)
Can tell his age. (43)
Can give names of penny, nickel, and dime. (43)
Can identify or name four colors. (43)
Counts ten objects pointing to each in turn. (43)
Fairy tales confuse him. (43)
Gives a descriptive comment while naming the objects in a composite picture. (43)
Mean length of response is 5.7 to 6.6 words. (107)
Can fold a triangle. (108)
Learns to point to simple words as his own first name. (34)
Can skip smoothly and jump well. (43)
Can comb hair, brush teeth, etc. well. (43)
Shows interest and competence in dish washing. (43)
When drawing he makes each stroke meaningful. (43)
Distinguishes left and right hand in self, not others. (43)
Tricycle is a favorite outside toy. (43)
Balances on tiptoe. (43)
Plays table games as dominoes, tiddlywinks, etc. (34)
Can make purchases. (34)
Likes to complete what he starts. (43)
Dependable and obedient in household. (43)
Protects younger playmates. (43)
Plays with 2-5 in a group, also with imaginary playmate. (43)
Likes to play dress-up. (43)
Social conformability. (43)
Can put toys away in an orderly manner. (43)

Likes to dramatize everyday functions: business, kitchen, transportation, etc. (43)

Talkative during meals. (43)

Realizes that peers cheat in play so he may have mild deceptions and fabrications. (43)

Weight: boys, 43.2 to 47.6 lbs.—girls, 42 to 46.4 lbs. (73)

Height: boys, 43.9 to 46.1 in.—girls, 43.6 to 45.8 in. (73)

Sleeps 11.25 hours. (71)

Bedtime around 7:59 P.M. (71)

29% males and 31% females bite nails. (117)

At six years draws twice as many details as five years. (43)

Draws simple but easily recognizable forms. (43)

## KINDERGARTEN LEVEL (K)
### (*Language Skills*)

## I. COMPREHENSION OF ORAL LANGUAGE

A. RECOGNITION OF OBJECTS

1. By Name

a. A toy fire engine, police car, and ambulance are placed before the class. By turn the children "Remove the ladders from the fire engine." "Push the police car." "Open the ambulance doors."

b. A toy fireman, policeman, and ambulance driver are placed with the cars. The children "Put the fireman on the fire engine." "Place the policeman in the police car."

c. Sweaters, scarves, ear muffs, mittens, and other winter apparel are used for dress up clothes. The children learn the name of each article of clothing.

2. By Function

a. Using various Halloween objects such as a mask, trick or treat bag, and pumpkin, the teacher asks the children to "Show me something that holds your Halloween treats." "What glows in the dark?" "Put on something that covers your face."

b. While decorating the Christmas tree, the teacher asks the children to "Find something that is shiny." "Give me something that goes on top of the tree." "Which one lights up?"

c. When seeds are ready for planting in the window box, the children are directed to "Find something that grows." "Something to water the plants." "Something to dig a hole."

B. RECOGNITION OF PICTURES

1. By Name

a. Around the classroom are placed pictures of a variety of

workers. The children form a line and as the teacher names a worker, the first child stands by the appropriate picture.

b. Pictures of circus animals are hidden in the classroom. Upon request the children find the pictures.

c. Pictures from a storybook are projected on a screen, and the children point to the characters in the story as the teacher names them.

2. By Function

a. Packages of flower and vegetable seeds are distributed among the children. The teacher asks, "Who has something that makes the yard look nice?"

b. A picture of a circus animal is given to each child to hide behind his back. The teacher requests, "I want something that jumps through a hoop." "I wonder who has an animal that balances a ball on his nose?"

c. Pictures of various toys; a sand bucket, ice skates, and a scooter are placed in the chart rack. The teacher asks, "Which one would I use at the beach?" "What do I need to go ice skating?" "Which one could I use on the sidewalk?"

C. CATEGORIZNG

1. From pictures of workers and vehicles children find "what goes together." (A postman drives a mail truck. A policeman rides a motorcycle.)

2. After having talked about objects that start with a certain sound, for instance *b*, the teacher places three pictures on the flannel board: *ball, bed,* and *scissors.* She asks "Does *bed* start like *ball?*" "Does *scissors* start like *ball?*" "Which ones start with the same sound?"

3. On the chart rack are pictures of dogs performing various activities, such as eating from a dish, running, and bringing the master the paper. Included are some absurd pictures such as a dog wearing glasses or playing a guitar. The children are asked, "Can a dog run?" "Can dogs eat?" "Do dogs wear glasses?"

D. NUMBER CONCEPTS

1. The child whose turn it is to be helper for the day may be told, "There are nine children in class today. We will need nine cups for refreshment time. Get nine cups, please."

2. Four firemen are placed on the toy fire engine. The teacher makes one jump off to attach the hose, then asks, "How many firemen are on the truck now? Three or four?"

3. Eight flowers are arranged in a domino configuration on the flannel board. The children place honey bees in a matching configuration on their desks.

E. SPATIAL AND TEMPORAL ORIENTATION

1. The preposition *between* can be taught during "Show and Tell." "The person who is sitting *between* Bill and Kathy will be next."

2. The "Simon Says" game is played. The teacher tells the children "Simon says put your hand *on* your head." "Simon says put your hands *behind* your back." If the command is not preceded by "Simon Says," they don't have to follow the command.

3. Time is discussed as it relates to *bedtime, time to go home, time to get up in the morning, time for school.*

F. SERIAL DIRECTIONS

1. The teacher says, "Let's pretend we're trapeze artists. Let's climb up the ladder, grab the trapeze, and swing." The children imitate the necessary steps.

2. How to report a fire to the fire department is discussed. Then the children with a play telephone dial the number, tell the fireman there is a fire, and the address of their home.

3. The sequence of preparing to mail and mailing a letter is discussed. The children compose a general letter to their parents which is run off on the duplicator. Each child receives a letter, an envelope, and a stamp. When appropriately assembled and addressed, the letters are taken to the mail box or post office.

## II. EXPRESSION OF ORAL LANGUAGE

A. NAMING AND DEFINING

1. Naming

a. A collection of hats depicting various community helpers: fireman, policeman, nurse are given to the children. The teacher asks, "Who is Mary?" "Who is John?"

b. Each child receives a picture of a circus performer or circus animal. In turn they dramatize the action in their picture. The other children guess which performer is represented. (A seal balancing a ball on his nose, a ringmaster with a whip, a juggler.)

c. Pictures of objects depicting various seasons of the year are placed in a box. By turn the children select a picture, name it, and paste it to a large chart of the four seasons. (The snowball on the winter scene, the red leaf on the fall scene, the beach ball on the summer scene.)

B. DEFINING

1. The teacher presents a set of matching pictures of workers and the tools they use in performing their jobs. The children take turns describing a certain tool, and the rest of the class guess which worker uses that tool. One child might say, "I have something that shoots water on a fire." (Fire hose.)

2. The children bring to class pictures starting with a certain sound. A guessing game which also becomes a phonics activity is played. The teacher gives an example of how to play the "guessing game." "Bobby brought a picture of something that is yellow, and can be eaten. What is it?" The children in turn describe their pictures for others to guess.

3. One child selects an object from a box and hides it behind him. He is asked questions about its size, shape, color, and function. Questions could be "What color is it?" "Is it big or little?" "Is it round or square?" "What does it do?"

C. ACTION AGENT

1. The teacher presents pictures depicting action verbs, and asks questions, "Who's crawling?" "What's hopping?" or "Who's hitting the ball?" The children should answer in full sentences by saying, "The baby's crawling." "The rabbit's hopping." "The boy's hitting the ball."

2. A guessing game with nursery rhyme characters is played. The teacher says, "I'm thinking of someone who fell down and broke his crown. Who was it?" Then the children dramatize the rhyme.

3. The children look at a series of pictures: fireman, policeman, mailman, and whisper to the teacher which one he would like to be. Then he describes himself, "I want to be someone who helps us when we are sick. Who am I?" The class provides an answer.

D. CATEGORIZING

1. The opaque projector is used to show a picture of a beach scene. The children are asked "What do we eat at the beach?" "What do we wear at the beach?" "What are the things we play with at the beach?"

2. Objects in the classroom are categorized as *heavy* or *light*. Commands are given, "Kathy, pick up the stapler. It's easy to pick up. It's *light*." "John pick up my desk." The child might respond, "No, it's too heavy."

3. Pictures of a bird, airplane, and kite are presented and the class tells how they are alike.

E. NUMBER CONCEPTS

1. In preparation for a field trip to the park to ride the train, the children work on number concepts: "All the members of the class want to ride the train. How many tickets should we buy?" "How many cars are on the train?" "How many children will fit on each seat?"

2. When dyeing Easter eggs, the children put three in the red dye. The teacher removes them one at a time and says, "I took one egg out. How many are still in the dye?"

3. After roll call the teacher says, "There are usually nine children at school. Ellen is absent. How many came to school?"

F. SPATIAL AND TEMPORAL

1. In the beginning of February the teacher marks Valentine's Day with a red heart, and the children count each following day until the holiday.

2. The children are told that "Show and Tell" will be on Tuesday. On Monday the teacher asks, "Is Show and Tell today?" The children are taught, "No, it's tomorrow."

3. After the children have collected their Easter eggs they are asked questions as to where they found them. "Did you find it? *Under* the tree or *in* the drain pipe?"

G. SENTENCE BUILDING

1. The children are taught to describe pictures by being asked "What do you see in the picture?" "What are they doing?" "Where are they going?" Complete sentences are expected: "I see a boy, a car, and a dog. The dog is jumping in the car. They are going to the park."

2. During refreshment period, the children are asked to respond with more than one word. "What do you want?" "I want a cookie."

3. After a field trip to the post office, the teacher helps the children build a sequence story. Questions are asked, "What was done first?" "Whom did you see?" "How did you get to the post office?"

# KINDERGARTEN LEVEL (K)
## (*Avenues of Learning*)

## I. MEMORY

A. AUDITORY

Goal: To remember three or four auditory signals or commands in sequence.

1. A number of objects associated with a policeman are placed on a table. The children follow such directions as, "Put the hat on the policeman, blow the whistle, and shoot the gun."

2. When a child learns his telephone number, he repeats it to the teacher who dials his mother. (This activity is discussed in parent conferences before it occurs.)

3. The teacher reads a circus story. By turn the children relate the events in sequence.

B. VISUAL

Goal: To remember three or four visual events not necessarily in sequence.

1. A large circus scene is placed before the class. The teacher points to four items in the picture, then covers it. A child is asked to select the correct item from duplicate picture cards on a table.

2. Use a flannel board stick figure, and after removing several parts such as an arm, two legs, and an ear, ask the children to tell what is missing.

3. Several Christmas toys are placed before the children, three are removed, and the children name the missing ones.

Goal: To remember three or four visual events in sequence.

1. Using pictures and gestures the teacher presents the story of

"Three Billy Goats Gruff." Then she places a picture on the chart rack and asks a child to find the picture of what happened next.

2. After attending the circus, discuss which act was first and which acts followed.

3. The teacher draws three designs on the blackboard, a circle, a star, and a square. From a set of cards containing designs drawn in series of three and four, the children (with their backs to the blackboard) select the appropriate card.

C. VISUAL-MOTOR

Goal: To remember motor acts in sequence when oral language is not involved.

1. The teacher constructs a pattern from large blocks. The children copy the pattern.

2. The children draw pictures for a classmate who is ill. The teacher demonstrates how to fold the picture, place it in the envelope, seal it, and address it. The children follow the directions.

3. Pantomimes such as a baseball player getting his bat, hitting the ball, and running to the base are demonstrated by the teacher. The children imitate what they have seen.

## II. VISUAL-PERCEPTUAL-MOTOR

Goal: To perceive a visual image and reproduce it.

1. The children copy the drawing of a fireman's ladder which the teacher has drawn on the blackboard. (Parallel lines *down* and horizontal lines *across*.)

2. A Hopscotch game is made on oilcloth to be spread on the floor. Squares one, two, and three are to the left. Four parallels three, five parallels two and six is across from one. The teacher demonstrates a jumping pattern and in turn the children imitate. (Jump on 1, off the oilcloth to the left, then jump on 2 and off again to the left.)

3. With a real clock for a sample, the children construct *make-believe* clocks from cardboard pie plates.

## III. SOCIAL MATURITY

Goal: To teach the childen good work habits and acceptable behavior in the classroom.

1. The teacher makes a simple assignment such as "Bring a milk carton to school. We will make a circus cage with it." Each child should be reminded as he leaves the room, and only has to remember it as far as the waiting room. If too difficult at first, the teacher draws a picture as a reminder and clips it to his shirt. If a child does not bring a carton, he cannot construct a cage.

2. The children are taught to work individually at their desks. They learn to "stay with the teacher," follow instructions, and be neat.

3. Courtesy is taught by suggesting that a child hold the door for another child who has his hands full, or asking a child to share his paste with another. All instances of a child using good judgment should be mentioned and labeled with such words as *generous, kind, thoughtful.*

## KINDERGARTEN LEVEL (K)
### (*Pre-Academic Subjects*)

### I. LIKENESSES AND DIFFERENCES

Goal: To categorize things that are alike and things that are different. Individual Work: The following activities are stenciled on unlined paper. The teacher presents only one row the first week and adds rows during the subsequent week. The activities involve left to right and top to bottom progression. Some children may need to cover the rows not being worked on until they become adept at moving from top to bottom.

1. "Find one like this." To the left is a chair; to the right is a ball, chair, and door.

2. "Put an X on the one that is different." In sequence are two balls a chair and a ball.

3. "Draw a circle around the two that are alike." To the left is a chair and a ball; to the right are two balls.

Group Work: As a group the children participate in the following activities at the blackboard, flannelboard, or with charts.

1. "Find one like this." To the left is the letter C; to the right are letters K, O, and C.

2. "Draw an X through the one that is different." In sequence are the words chair, chair, ball, and chair.

3. The *Non-Oral Series* (51) is used for word-matching. (Refer to the following charts: 1, school objects; 4, color words; 2, action words; and 3, number words.) Other activities to be used with the *Non-Oral Series* are suggested by Rister (93).

### II. PHONICS

Goal: To prepare the children for basic skills in reading and spelling.

1. Three by five picture cards are filed according to the initial letter. The children learn that certain words have the beginning sound in common. (Group work is recommended until the latter part of the school year.)

A different sound is presented each day and a picture of the key word (which starts with the sound) is placed in a conspicuous place in the classroom. If the picture is *table*, then games using the *t* pictures are devised for that day's activities.

A. *Questions.* "What is it that starts like table and you can spin?" (Top.) "It lives on a farm and says gobble, gobble." The children may take turns being the teacher.

B. *What's Missing?* Six or seven *t* cards are placed on the chart rack. A child hides his eyes while one picture is removed. He guesses which one is missing. Later several pictures may be removed.

C. *Discrimination Games.* All children stand if the teacher says words which start like *table,* and sit down if the word does not start like *table.*

D. *Gossip.* New words such as *ostrich* can be taught in a game similar to gossip. The first child watches and listens to the teacher as she says the word and hands him the picture. He turns to the person behind him, repeats the word, and passes the card. If not repeated correctly, the previous child must repeat the word.

E. *Home Assignment.* Parents help children collect pictures which start like *table.* These pictures are brought to school and pinned on the bulletin board. They are used for a review game. If a new sound is taught each day, it takes a month to six weeks to complete them. The method of teaching a new sound four days a week and using the fifth day to contrast the four sounds has been successful.

## III. WRITING

Goal: To introduce the Spalding (101) approach to writing in combination with phonics games.

1. Teaching time concepts with a clock is accomplished with cardboard clocks for each child. Numbers which correspond to the teacher's clock are located. The two o'clock position should be stressed because it will be used later in the writing program.

2. At the blackboard the children are taught the meaning of *go down, across to the right,* etc.

3. Using the Spalding approach the children write letters on the blackboard. Later the teacher prints large colored letters on unlined paper for the children to trace. (The children always begin at the correct place to start the letter and proceed in the proper direction.) Accuracy should be taught in the beginning of the program.

## IV. NUMBERS

Goals: Rote counting one through thirty, number concepts through ten, and the concept of one-half.

1. Rote counting through thirty may be accomplished by daily use of the calendar.

2. Configuration cards (domino figures) assist in teaching number concepts. Six is domino five and one more. Drawing a line down the middle of the card helps the children learn that the first group is five and one more is six.

3. The concept of one-half may be taught in every unit.

4. Vocabulary words such as *more than, fewer than, less than,* and *one more* are taught.

5. Coin names may be taught by playing "Button, button, who has the button?" by substituting a coin for the button, "Nickel, nickel, who has the nickel?"

## KINDERGARTEN LEVEL (K): PROPOSED CALENDAR

September: School (K-1); Fall (K-2).
October: Circus (K-3); Halloween (K-4).
November: Circus; Thanksgiving (K-5).
December: Christmas (K-6); Winter (K-7).
January: Winter; Workers (K-8).
February: Workers; Valentine (K-9); Workers (postman).
March: Workers (policeman); Workers (policeman); Spring (K-10).
April: Easter (K-11); Family Fun (Park) (K-12); Family Fun (Beach).
May: Family Fun (Picnic); Review Workers & Transportation; Summer (K-13).
Extra: Birthday (K-14).

## KINDERGARTEN LEVEL (K)

### Unit: Workers (Fireman)

**SAMPLE LESSON PLAN**

I. Goals: To teach and/or expose children to:

1. Know their first and last name.
2. Names of their classmates.
3. Their address and phone number.
4. Rote counting through thirty.
5. Number concepts through 10.
6. Concepts of time.
7. The days of the week and the months of the year.
8. Visual and auditory memory for four items or activities.
9. Visual-motor-memory tasks.
10. Gross motor-skill activities.

11. Hand skills.
12. Spontaneous oral expression.
13. Correct sentence structure.
14. Verbal absurdities.
15. Social maturity skills.

II. Activities:

**1:00–1:10** Roll call, calendar, and news of the day. The teacher calls each child's name, varying the order from day to day, and the child responds "I'm here," adding any news which he cares to contribute. Discussion follows regarding the name of the day of the week, the number of days of the week that have passed, and the number remaining. The teacher directs rote counting by pointing to each day of the month and asking the class to count. This activity is child-directed once the idea is established. Forthcoming holidays and birthdays are marked and the number of days until these special events are counted.

**1:10–1:30** Sequence Story. The teacher prepares a simple five-picture story which she shows visually with no verbal comments. It is presented slowly and repeated at least once. All children take turns arranging the shuffled story into proper sequence (short term visual memory). The verbal counterpart is then added to the pictorial sequence, retold, and the children take turns retelling in proper sequence. (Short term visual and auditory memory.)

Example for story:

1. The fireman is sleeping.
2. The fire alarm rings.
3. The fireman awakens and dresses.
4. The fireman slides down the pole.
5. The fireman gets into the fire truck.

**1:30–1:50** General Discussion. The children are encouraged to use more than one word responses and correct sentence structure in structured discussion.

Topics for discussion:

1. Reasons to call the fire department.
2. What to say when calling the fire department. "I want to report a fire." "I live at (child's address)." "Hurry" or "Come quickly."
3. How to report a fire using an alarm box.
4. Hazards of playing with matches.
5. What is absurd about this picture? (A bear lighting a fire. A dragon breathing fire.) Discuss verbal absurdities such as "Would a fireman ride a bike to a fire?" "Do forest animals freeze when there is a forest fire?"

**1:50–2:00** Refreshments. The children read the helper chart for the day to see who will pass out cups, cookies, napkins, and pour the juice. The children count the number of each item needed (visual recognition of names, and number concepts). Good manners are emphasized, "Please," "Thank you," and "May I?"

**2:00–2:05** Follow the Leader. This exercise period allows for energy expenditure before seat work is started. (Gross motor skills.)

**2:05–2:20** Number and Color Concepts. The children are given a mimeographed picture containing a fireman, fire truck, and ladder (without rungs). The children draw specified number of rungs on the ladder. (Left to right.) Then the teacher gives directions for coloring the pictures. Questions are asked, "Is a fireman's hat red or black?" "Is a fire-truck red or orange?" The fireman's uniform and the fire truck are colored according to the teacher's directions. (Number and color concepts, and auditory memory.)

**2:20–2:30** Hand Skills. The children cut strips of black paper which are rolled and pasted to make a long paper fire hose. The teacher asks, "Would water go through this hose?" (Verbal absurdity.)

**2:30–2:55** Dramatization. Using paper fire hose and fire chief's hat, a child dramatizes extinguishing a fire. The teacher draws a burning house on the blackboard, then tells one child to call the fire department. He makes the appropriate call giving his phone number and address. Directions are given to another child to "Put on the fireman's hat." "Climb on the fire truck." "Attach the hose to the hydrant." "Put out the fire." (Auditory memory for four serial directions.)

**2:55–3:15** Show and Tell. The children take turns telling about something they brought from home. (Oral expression.) The teacher encourages appropriate sentence structure by providing carrier phrases, "I brought a _____." or "I have a _____." At the completion of the activity the teacher asks questions related to what will burn and what will not burn.

**3:15–3:30** Motor Activities. Kindergarten blocks are used to build the walls for a fire station. Plywood board is used for the roof of the station. A large opening is left for the fire trucks to enter. The building is pushed over and the children reconstruct it. (Visual-motor-memory.)

## KINDERGARTEN LEVEL (K)

## Unit: School Routine (K-1)

CLASSROOM ACTIVITIES

*Scissors:* Skill in using scissors is accomplished by developing motor coordination and motivation. Left handed scissors are used when indicated.

If necessary, the teacher assists the child by helping him move the scissors or by holding the paper while he cuts. Precut circles are given to the children who fringe the edge by cutting into the circle about one-half inch. The finished product becomes the blossom of a flower. A heavy black line is drawn for the stem and if necessary the teacher helps the children cut on the line. The stem is stapled to the flower.

*Cookie Cutters:* Cookie cutters provide a simple method of tracing an object.

*Cardboard Shapes:* Basic shapes such as circles, squares, triangles, and cones may be cut from heavy cardboard or plywood and used for tracing. The children are asked, "What object can I make from this square?" If no answers are forthcoming, she may show pictures of a window, television set, or a handkerchief. Then they are asked to think of other objects.

*Blackboard:* On the blackboard the teacher draws a square and asks the children what they would like to make. If they select a television, they draw one like the teacher's which is on the blackboard (slant lines are drawn for the legs and antennae and two circles for the knobs).

*Paste:* Children select precut shapes to paste together, for example, a cone and a circle to represent the ice cream.

*Manikin:* Precut shapes for constructing a manikin are given each child. "Find a circle. Paste it near the top of your page. This will be a head. Paste the blue rectangle under the circle for the body." If a child cannot follow verbal directions, he is given a sample picture to copy.

*Construction Paper:* The children cut shapes such as a large triangle, square, small rectangle, and two small squares. These are assembled according to directions to make a house. Each child's house has a number with a street sign, and all finished products are used to decorate the bulletin board.

*Bulletin Board:* The child who can repeat his address by "reading" it from the house numbers and street signs on the bulletin board may be first in line to leave the classroom at the end of the day.

*Beads:* Beads of different colors but with the same shape are given to the children. The teacher selects three beads which she strings and holds horizontally before the class. The children look for a few seconds then after the teacher hides her string, they make one like it. When finished, each child hides his string and waits until he hears "time's up." In unison they count to five then show their strings of beads.

*Pencil and Paper:* The preceding activity is transferred to seat work where the children draw a horizontal line, a round bead, a horizontal line, a square bead, etc.

## Basic Vocabulary (K-1)

| | | |
|---|---|---|
| absent | helper | ruler |
| address | hole-punch | second |
| afternoon | last night | seven |
| arrow | lavatory | seventeen |
| artificial | left | shade |
| because | letter | six |
| behind | light (lighter) | sixteen |
| between | morning | squeaky |
| calendar | music | strawberry |
| chalk tray | name (first, last) | street |
| chocolate cookies | nine | ten |
| chocolate ice cream | nineteen | third |
| dance | noisemakers | thirteen |
| dark (darker) | number | trace |
| eight | o ("oh") | twelve |
| eighteen | phonograph | twenty |
| eleven | pink | vanilla |
| fifteen | pointer | weather |
| fourteen | race | why |
| gentle | right | yardstick |
| gray | rough | |

## Games, Stories, Songs, and Nursery Rhymes (K-1)

The teacher makes appropriate selections for this unit.

## Home Training Hints for Parents (K-1)

1. Using artificial flowers or fruit, parents may teach their child the concept of *artificial*. The child smells the real flowers and the artificial flowers. Questions are asked, "Which smells better?" "Can you smell an artificial flower?"
2. To teach *rough* and *gentle* parents talk about the way to treat a baby or a family pet.
3. *Right* and *left* may be taught during bath time. "Wash your right arm first." "Wash your left leg." The directions may be reinforced by setting the table with the fork on the left side of the plate and the knife and spoon on the right.
4. A calendar similar to the one used in the classroom may be drawn with the help of a parent. This calendar is hung over the child's bed

and each evening he crosses out the current day, counts the number of days left in the month, and the days until the next holiday.

5. Parents bring their child's attention to the various shades of color in his clothing. One sweater is light blue and another is dark blue.
6. Cookies with different shapes are purchased and the children learn to identify and name the shapes.
7. While shopping at the grocery store, ask the child which *flavor* ice cream or jello he wants you to buy.
8. Parents and siblings can help a child learn his first, last, and middle name.
9. To teach a child his address, parents may walk with him down their street making note of the different house numbers yet the same street. A drawing of the street may be made on his blackboard or a large piece of paper.
10. Periodically parents turn the calendar to the child's birthdate and tell him the date and month. Some children, through this method, learn to say their birthdate at an early age.

# KINDERGARTEN LEVEL (K)

## Unit: Seasons (K-2)

CLASSROOM ACTIVITIES

*Poster:* A large tree with branches is painted on a poster. Using material that will stick to the poster, the children "Put 7 leaves *on* the tree." "Put an orange, yellow, and brown leaf *on* the tree." "Put a leaf *on the top* branch." "Put a leaf on the *longest* branch."

*Magazines:* From magazines the children cut pictures of a fall scene and bring them to school. Each child describes his favorite picture.

*Leaves:* The children bring real leaves to class for various activities; making a "leaf man," painting leaves, discussing the various colors. To make a leaf silhouette, place a leaf on construction paper, spray the paper with paint, and remove the leaf.

*Acorns:* During a walk through the park, the children look for fall leaves, cones, acorns, and other signs of fall. They bring back real acorns and trace around them to make paper acorns to be used to teach number concepts. One child pretends he is a squirrel (use props such as paper ears and a bushy tail) and the teacher tells him to "Put eight acorns in the tree."

*Picture File:* Pictures of ripe pumpkins and other vegetables are introduced to the class. The children dramatize "harvesting the vegetables." One child is the farmer who goes into the field to gather the ripe vegetables. He is asked to "Put 2 pumpkins in the wagon and all of the corn in the box."

*TV Screen:* Cut a frame for a TV set from a cardboard box. Glue thread spools on for dials. Each day, a different child gives fall weather forecast.

*Felt Scraps:* Discuss colors associated with fall by sorting felt scraps cut into leaf shapes. Select scraps so that there is a predominance of yellow, orange, and brown.

*Buttons:* Make an owl ditto into a three dimensional picture by pasting on buttons for eyes and twigs for a limb on which to stand.

*Felt Paper:* Each child has one dittoed chipmunk which he can color light brown and then paste strips of felt paper for the stripes on his back.

*Seed Field Trip:* Walk just outside the school area and pick up as many different types of seeds as can be found. Each child pastes these on his own chart which can be added to at home.

### Basic Vocabulary (K-2)

| | | |
|---|---|---|
| calendar | days of the week | September |
| change | hurricane | storm |
| clouds | lightning | thunder |
| cloudy | month | turn |
| day | November | weather |
| | October | |

### Games, Stories, Songs, and Nursery Rhymes (K-2)

The teacher makes appropriate selections for this unit.

### Home Training Hints for Parents (K-2)

1. Father may organize a leaf-raking party. He invites the neighborhood children and his own to rake the leaves, place them in the wheelbarrow, and dispose of them in the usual way. When the job is completed, the children may be served cider and doughnuts and perhaps make a leaf man from special leaves that were saved.
2. When parents and children are out driving, they may stop by a fresh fruit and vegetable stand. Here they look at and talk about fruits and vegetables which are harvested in the fall and how they reached this particular food stand.

# KINDERGARTEN LEVEL (K)

## Unit: Circus (K-3)

### CLASSROOM ACTIVITIES

*Picture File:* Circus pictures are presented to the class and they answer in unison the following questions. "What do you see?" "Where is it?" "What is he doing?" "How many do you see?" "How did it get there?"

On a subsequent day the activity is repeated with individual children expected to answer specific questions.

*Opaque Projector:* Three different circus acts are shown with the opaque projector. When the projector is turned off, the children recall the pictures. Another day, the same activity is repeated with one child describing the pictures.

*Story Book:* A circus story is read to the children who recreate the story in sequence by selecting appropriate pictures. Magnetic clips attach the pictures to the blackboard. The teacher then asks, "What happened first?" "What happened next?"

*Bingo Cards:* Circus pictures are dittoed on sheets, cut into individual squares, and mounted on construction paper to form bingo cards. Each child is given bottle tops, circles of construction paper, chips, or some type of marker. They listen as a group and cover the object *described* by the teacher. "Cover the acrobat." "Cover the acrobat balancing on one foot." "Cover the high wire." Number concepts may be incorporated into the activity as the teacher reminds each child to say "Circus Bingo" when he has covered five of his pictures.

*Toy Circus:* A toy circus may be purchased for motivational material and used in the following activities:

1. The teacher sets up a specific act, allows the children time to view it carefully, then takes it apart. One child is asked to reconstruct what he has seen while a "Ringmaster" checks for errors.

2. One child constructs a specific act while the Ringmaster tells the class step by step what is being constructed.

3. The teacher constructs an act and purposefully makes an obvious error by placing an elephant on the high wire. She asks "What's wrong with this?" The child who answers appropriately corrects the error.

4. The teacher places all of the circus people and animals in a row on a table. She asks, "Give me all of the things that perform in the air, things that climb ladders, things that have four legs, or things that can stand on one leg."

*Construction Paper:* Each child cuts a large circle out of construction paper to be used as a circus ring in the following activities: "Place a bear, dog, and horse in the ring." "Put three different acts in the ring."

Using the rubber stamp set, the children stamp specific numbers of animals in the circus ring. Spatial vocabulary may be taught through directions. "Put 3 lions next to the *edge* of the ring." "Put the Ringmaster *behind* the line."

A maze is drawn for each child who finds the path of the lion from his line to the center of the ring.

*Dress-up Clothes:* Dress-up clothing and very simple make-up for the children, enhances dramatizing. Charcoal, lipstick, flour, and other forms of make-up are used for clown faces. Each child may be made-up differently; a happy clown, a sad clown. Cardboard tubes are cut and painted red to make noses; yarn is used for hair. The children visit other classrooms and describe what is on their faces.

The teacher says, "Happy clown with white nose, shake hands with a very sad clown."

The children are taught clown tricks. One clown blows up a balloon, accidentally lets go, and tries to find it in the air. Another child follows his balloon and accidentally sits on it, popping it in the process. The teacher asks "What funny thing did clown Bill do?"

*Dress-up Clothes:* The children form teams and perform a circus act. One is lion tamer and another his trained lion. The participants introduce their act and explain it as they perform. "I'm climbing to the top of the ladder and now I'll dive into the tank."

*Trapeze:* Two long strings are hung from the ceiling and tied to a stick that forms a trapeze bar. A stuffed doll is used to demonstrate a flip and somersault. Each child observes then copies what he has seen.

*Blocks and Board:* A board is laid over two large blocks and the children take turns walking across. The audience is encouraged to respond with "Be careful." "Don't fall." "What happens if he loses his balance?" "What happens if a real tightrope walker loses his balance?" (The purpose of the net is discussed.)

### Basic Vocabulary (K-3)

| | | |
|---|---|---|
| acrobat | bareback rider | flat |
| announcer | cannon | flip |
| audience | circus | loud speaker |
| balance | coliseum (tent) | midway |
| band | dime | parade |

| peanuts | safety net | thin |
|---|---|---|
| popcorn | sawdust | tightrope |
| program | somersault | trainer |
| quarter | souvenir | trapeze |
| ringmaster | spot light | trick |

### Games, Stories, Songs, and Nursery Rhymes (K-3)

The teacher makes appropriate selections for this unit.

### Home Training Hints for Parents (K-3)

1. Parents observe the newspapers for pictures or advertisements concerning a circus that might be coming to town. These are shown to the child and discussed.
2. If the class does not attend the circus, parents should take their children. What to wear, money for tickets, refreshments, and what will be seen are discussed.
3. Parents help build a circus ring in the backyard; blocks and a board for the tightrope, a trapeze for the dolls, a hoop for the lions, and a circus ring from building blocks.
4. The children take a trip to the zoo to find which animals are also circus animals.

# KINDERGARTEN LEVEL (K)

## Unit: Halloween (K-4)

CLASSROOM ACTIVITIES

*Stencils:* From stencils the children trace bats, cut them out, and hang them from different string lengths attached to the ceiling. A paper moon and sun are constructed to explain when bats fly.

*Toothpicks:* Toothpicks are assembled to form a skeleton.

*Paper Sacks:* In turn the children describe an object in their trick or treat sacks and ask classmates to guess what it is.

*Soap Suds:* A "haunted" house is made from a cardboard box, pointed roof, with whipped soap suds covering all. Figures of a skeleton, scarecrow, devil, goblin, witch, and bat are placed inside the house. The teacher describes one of the figures and the child who guesses correctly removes the original.

*Construction Paper:* The children cut out several large, medium, and small pumpkins. These are used to set up a "pretend" pumpkin stand. With toy money the children buy a pumpkin, each size priced differently.

### Basic Vocabulary (K-4)

| | | |
|---|---|---|
| bat | fairy | scarecrow |
| carnival | goblin | skeleton |
| devil | mess | witch |

### Games, Stories, Songs, and Nursery Rhymes (K-4)

The teacher makes appropriate selections for this unit.

### Home Training Hints for Parents (K-4)

1. Parents should help their child purchase and cut a jack-o'-lantern from a pumpkin.
2. The children make a scarecrow from a mop, yardstick, and rags, and learn why farmers use scarecrows.
3. The story of "The Wizard of Oz" should be read to the child.
4. A small Halloween party for the neighborhood children may serve as a review of many vocabulary words and previously discussed activities.

# KINDERGARTEN LEVEL (K)

## Unit: Thanksgiving (K-5)

### CLASSROOM ACTIVITIES

*Calendar:* The November month of a large calendar is placed in a conspicuous spot in the classroom. The teacher has a collection of small turkey feathers. They are pinned over each date which also has the "helper for the day" printed beside it. Each day a feather is removed, the helper is notified and the class counts the number of days until Thanksgiving (designated by a turkey). The child whose name is under the feather wears it during the day. Before going home he places' it appropriately for a tail feather in a clay turkey. As the children are looking at the feathers on the calendar, the teacher generalizes concepts by asking, "What has feathers?" "For what do we use feathers?" The answers lead into a discussion of pillows, feather beds, quills for writing, feather hats, and feather flowers.

*Mural:* The children make a class mural to include things for which they are thankful. Each day the children bring a picture representing something for which they are thankful. The teacher could have a large supply of pictures available from which the children may choose. The teacher asks questions such as "Do you have this at home?" "Do you wear it?" "Who uses this most?" "Why do we need this?"

*TV Dinner:* The class begins to plan for their Thankgiving dinner at school very early in the month. On the chosen day the children bring TV dinners or utilize the school cafeteria. Each child makes his own placemat. Material brought from home may be fringed. The children may draw designs on appropriate size construction paper, or seals may be pasted on the mats. The children make place cards: each name is printed with dots to be filled in by the child. The day before the dinner, all place cards are put into a box. The leader for the day, who has already placed his name card on the table, says to a classmate, "Choose the name of the person who will sit beside you." The child covers his eyes, draws a name, and places it next to his own seat at the table. The next day the children are asked to remember where they are to put their place cards when setting and decorating the table. Pine cones are used to make turkeys for the place card holders. Colored construction paper feathers are used for the tail and a bent red pipe cleaner for the head. A horn of plenty made from cardboard or construction paper is the center piece. Each child is responsible for providing real items for the horn of plenty: nuts, uncommon fruits or vegetables, or decorative squash.

*Book:* Stories on "manners" are read to the children. The Thanksgiving unit provides an opportune time to teach good table manners. If table blessings are said, the children may be taught:

> "Thank you for the world so sweet,
> Thank you for the food we eat,
> Thank you for the birds that sing,
> Thank you God for everything."

### Basic Vocabulary (K-5)

special                    manners                    horn of plenty

### Games, Stories, Songs, and Nursery Rhymes (K-5)

The teacher makes appropriate selections for this unit.

### Home Training Hints for Parents (K-5)

1. The children help plan the Thanksgiving dinner and accompany mother to the store to purchase the food.
2. Mother makes a pumpkin pie with the help of her child.

3. As a family activity the children help make place cards.
4. The children learn how to polish apples and arrange fruit in a bowl. A discussion where the fruit grows is carried on during this activity.

# KINDERGARTEN LEVEL (K)

## Unit: Christmas (Toys) (K-6)

CLASSROOM ACTIVITIES

*Calendar:* The teacher constructs a large December calendar from tagboard. Weekends contain red squares and week days have green squares mounted so the top edge is pasted and bottom may be lifted. The name of the leader for the day is listed on each schoolday. The children count the days to Christmas then to New Year's. "Which day comes *first?*"

*Santa's Toy Shop:* Parents are asked to provide toy catalogues. As a group the children follow the teacher's directions: "Circle two boy-toys with your red color." "Circle three girl-toys with your green color." "Cut out, on the green or red line, the circled toys."

Santa's work shop is divided into several sections; girl-toys, boy-toys, games, elves or Santa helpers, broken toys, baby toys, and toys for older children.

Pictures of toys are cut into several pieces depicting a broken toy. The children fit the pieces together.

A specific part of the toy is cut off; wagon wheel, doll arm, gun handle. The teacher asks "What's missing on this one?" If the child cannot tell her, she gives him a choice from a collection of parts.

The teacher mixes up all the toys and asks two children to race. "John, put all of the baby toys under your desk and Judy put all grown up toys by the door." There should be an equal number of objects for the race. The class judges the selection of the items.

*Gifts:* Early in the month the children draw names for exchange of gifts. Parents are asked to supply tags. These presents should arrive three weeks prior to the Christmas party. The teacher places all gifts in a large box, talking to the group as she does so, about the wrappings. The children help wrap the big box in plain brown paper, tie it with heavy string, and address it to the teacher at the school. On a field trip to the post office the children mail the box.

When the box is delivered to the school, the children are asked to remember which package was theirs (without seeing the name tag) and also to whisper its contents to the teacher. The gifts are placed under the tree to await the party day.

*Miniature Toys:* Number configuration cards using miniature toys are placed on the bulletin board for daily reference. Card number one, showing the beginning configuration of one, might contain a toy car, while card two has two doll shoes, and card three, three jacks.

For variety, the children play an "I am thinking" game by describing something they see on the configuration cards. When a child guesses, he says, "He is thinking about the card with four guns."

*Field Trip:* After the children have had many experiences with names of toys and their function, the teacher plans a field trip to see Santa Claus, sit on his lap, and tell at least 3 things he wants for Christmas. After the visit with Santa, the children tour the toy department, but the focus is not on what the individual child wants. The teacher directs their interest to quantity, sizes, materials such as plastics, and breakable or nonbreakable objects. The sporting goods department could be visited to introduce gifts for parents: fishing rods and reels, bowling supplies, baseball equipment, and golf equipment.

During the field trip a Christmas tree for the classroom is selected. The teacher leads the children to a choice of two favorite trees and the group votes for the one they like best.

On the same day or the next day, a stick figure sequence story of what happened is drawn by the teacher on a ditto as the children tell the story. When the ditto is run off, it is cut into squares, mixed up, and a child reassembles it in appropriate sequential order.

### Basic Vocabulary (K-6)

| | | |
|---|---|---|
| angels | Mary | silver |
| carols | narrow | walnuts (other nuts) |
| gold | ornaments | wide |
| Joseph | shiny | |

### Games, Stories, Songs, and Nursery Rhymes (K-6)

The teacher makes appropriate selections for this unit.

### Home Training Hints for Parents (K-6)

1. The parents take their child to select the Christmas tree and allow him to help decorate it.
2. A day is selected to take the children to see Santa. A discussion of what will be asked, Santa's clothing, and other details is held in preparation for the visit.
3. The child accompanies mother to the store to purchase inexpensive gifts for the family. He is taught how to wrap them and decorate with seals.

4. Christmas cards are made with colored paper and seals to be given each family member.
5. A large December calendar is placed in a convenient location in the home. Pictures are appropriately placed to identify the following dates: dressing the Christmas tree, baking cookies, the school Christmas party, the evening mother and father are invited out, etc.

# KINDERGARTEN LEVEL (K)

## Unit: Winter (K-7)

CLASSROOM ACTIVITIES

*Picture File:* Winter and summer are contrasted with pictures. The children sort and describe them.

*Paper Dolls:* The children dress paper dolls appropriately for the weather. New vocabulary is introduced: *mittens, scarf, hood.* Several directions are given, "Put the scarf and boots on the paper doll." Articles of clothing are placed on the table. Two are removed and the children tell what is missing.

*Picture File:* Pictures of animal homes during the winter are discussed: bear in a cave, snakes and ants under the ground, the caterpillar in a leaf. Paper birds are arranged in an appropriate pattern and a discussion follows regarding their flight to the south.

*Tongue Depressor Sticks:* Toy sleds are constructed from tongue depressor sticks and paper. The children learn the names of the parts and directions for guiding: "Turn to the right." "Turn to the left." "Go straight."

*Artificial Snow:* A mountain made from rocks, papier mâché, or crumpled paper is covered with a sheet of cotton. Place a house and artificial trees in the scene and mold snowballs from thick soap mixture. Spray the scene with artificial snow. Styrofoam balls may be used for a "snowball fight."

### Basic Vocabulary (K-7)

| | | |
|---|---|---|
| bare | heater | scarf |
| cool | hood | snowman |
| December | January | warm |
| February | mittens | year |

### Games, Stories, Songs, and Nursery Rhymes (K-7)

The teacher makes appropriate selections for this unit.

*Home Training Hints for Parents* (K-7)

1. Pictures depicting winter scenes are cut from magazines and pasted into a scrapbook.
2. The family plays a "Trip Game" naming objects to be taken to a cold climate. Each person repeats the two previously mentioned items, then adds another.
3. Parents can plan to do something special on a cold winter evening which should be a family project: make popcorn or candy, look at slides of last summer's vacation, play simple table games.

# KINDERGARTEN LEVEL (K)

## Unit: Workers (K-8)

CLASSROOM ACTIVITIES

*Opaque Projector:* This unit is introduced by placing pictures of "community helpers" on the bulletin board. An opaque projector is used to present pictures of various workers; the type of clothing each wears (nurse—white uniform, fireman—red hat), tools symbolic of their profession (farmer—tractor, postman—mailbag, policeman—gun, whistle), where each one works (cowboy—ranch, nurse—hospital), what each rides on (policeman—motorcycle, milkman—milk truck, pilot—airplane).

*Toy Airport:* Following a field trip to the airport, the children construct a toy airport. "Put the *small* plane near the *large* silver planes."

The children take turns role playing. The stewardess says "Fasten your seat belts." "Do you want a magazine?" "The man at the front of the plane wants milk." "The man in the back wants coffee." "Put the coat on the shelf and give the lady a pillow."

Questions and answers are prepared for a conversation between the pilot and the man in the control tower. The teacher reads them and asks two children to play the roles.

*Scrapbooks:* The class discusses various things that could catch on fire and whether or not a fireman should be called. The children make a scrapbook of fire hazards. Each day one child is assigned a fire hazard to investigate in his home.

One child calls the fire station—"Help, help. My house is burning, come to _____ (child gives his own address)." Another child plays the fireman's role: puts on his boots, slides down the pole, and climbs on the fire truck.

*Policeman:* A policeman is invited to the class to discuss: how to ride a bike carefully, hazards of talking to strangers, and the purpose of his uniform.

The children play the role of a policeman; directing traffic, going to an accident, catching robbers, helping a lost child, stopping a speeding car, and giving the person a ticket.

Pretend driver's licenses are made and filled in by the teacher as each child repeats his name, address, and phone number.

*Invitations:* As a group, the children compose an invitation for mother to come to school for a party. Hectograph copies are made for each child who signs his name, folds the letter, puts it into an envelope, and tells the teacher his parents' name, address, and city.

The class may go to the post office, buy the stamps, and mail the letters. The children report to the class when the letters arrive.

One child plays the role of a postman. He carries a bag of letters and make-believe packages to each child's mail box (cardboard shoe box).

*Stamps:* With real coins the children purchase stamps from the teacher (values up to ten cents). Then a child is chosen to sell the stamps.

*Milk Cartons:* Prepare to go on a train trip. Pack a suitcase following directions by remembering three and four things to include each time. The children help construct a train from milk cartons and pipe cleaners for people: engineer, conductor, porter, passengers. The children follow directions, "Put the engineer in the first car." "Put three passengers in the dining car."

The children line up to form a train. The engineer (first child) follows the teacher's instructions. "Turn your train to the right." "Back up your train."

*Paper Dolls:* Armed service paper dolls and war equipment are assembled. The children match the paper doll with the appropriate equipment. The children describe clothing, mode of transportation, and equipment then ask, "Who am I?"

*Picture File:* Pictures of all workers studied in the unit, plus others, are placed on the left side of 5 by 7 cards. From a box of pictures the children select the things that go with the pictures (fire hose, fire truck) and clip them to the right side of the card. Included in this game are the baker and bread, the druggist and medicine, and other workers not already discussed in the unit.

*Toy City:* Using a set of blocks to depict buildings in a city, the children assemble a shopping area.

*Mural:* The children help construct a mural of a shopping area which contains a department store, bakery, drug store, restaurant, etc.

### Basic Vocabulary (K-8)

| | | |
|---|---|---|
| address | fireman | patrol |
| Air Force | fire plug | pistol |
| alarm | garbageman | pole |
| ambulance | glue | policeman |
| Army | golf | porter |
| arrest | gun | postman |
| attic | holster | post office |
| ax | hose | radio |
| badge | jail | rifle |
| baggage | jeep | robber |
| bank | label | roof |
| bullets | ladder | sea |
| butcher | letter | seal |
| chief | lever | scooter |
| conductor | library | siren |
| cross | lick | slick |
| deliver | luggage | slot |
| department | mail | smoke |
| directs | mail box | speed |
| driver's license | mailman | stamp |
| drop | mail truck | stewardess |
| drug (other stores) | meat market | tank |
| envelope | motorcycle | ticket (speeding) |
| extinguisher | Navy | traffic |
| fire | ocean | war |
| fire engine | package | wreck |

### Games, Stories, Songs, and Nursery Rhymes (K-8)

The teacher makes appropriate selections for this unit.

### Home Training Hints for Parents (K-8)

1. Any trips taken by the family, relatives, or friends should serve as topics for broadening concepts of transportation and workers.
2. Pictures of members of the Armed Forces are clipped from newspapers and magazines. Parents discuss the pictures with their child and then ask him to sort them according to the branch of service and the work being done.

3. Parents take their child to an army surplus store to look at the equipment and discuss its function.
4. A home fire hazard check list may be obtained from the local fire department or insurance company. A parent and his child make an inspection trip of their home discussing possible fire hazards.
5. A list of incidents records the times a child might need a policeman. The child role-plays what he should do and say in a specific situation such as being lost downtown.
6. Help your child collect stamps from your mail. Each time a different stamp appears it is cut from the envelope and saved. When ten different stamps are collected, he places them in the configuration of ten on a card and brings it to school for "Show and Tell."

# KINDERGARTEN LEVEL (K)

## Unit: Valentine (K-9)

CLASSROOM ACTIVITIES

*Construction Paper:* The children trace hearts, cut them out, and use them to develop number concepts. "Give me five valentines." "There are six children in our class. How many valentines do we need so that each child has one?"

*Candy Hearts:* Using valentine candy, the teacher gives sequence directions, "Put four pink hearts and two yellow hearts in the cup."

*Bow and Arrow:* The teacher draws a large heart on the blackboard. A toy bow and arrow set are used to shoot at the heart.

*Valentine Cards:* Valentine cards are cut in half. Each child receives a half and finds the counterpart in the classroom.

*Branch of a Tree:* Paint a tree branch white and place it in a clay base. The children make small valentines to hang on the "Valentine Tree."

### Basic Vocabulary (K-9)

Review vocabulary from previous units.

### Games, Stories, Songs, and Nursery Rhymes (K-9)

The teacher makes appropriate selections for this unit.

### Home Training Hints for Parents (K-9)

1. Mother discusses the number of valentines to be purchased for each member of the family, the cost, and the day to purchase them. She

takes her child to the store and assists if necessary in the purchase. The children copy from mother's example: "To _____ From _____."

2. The children help their mothers make cupcakes. Red candy hearts are placed in configuration when the cakes are iced.

3. Colorful valentine pictures are cut from magazines and pasted in a scrapbook. The children and other members of the family tell stories about the pictures.

4. Help child make valentines for members of the family. Have each valentine in an envelope with name and address on it. Have the child copy his name on the card. When Valentine's Day arrives, have the cards in a shoe box that has been decorated like a mail box. Have every member of the family go to the mail box to get their valentines.

5. Count the members of the class and get punch-out valentines. Write "To _____ From _____" to give child practice in copying and writing name.

# KINDERGARTEN LEVEL (K)

## Unit: Spring (K-10)

CLASSROOM ACTIVITIES

*Construction Paper:* Demonstrate the concept of a windy day with pictures of trees swaying, windmills, sailboats, and kites. On construction paper each child traces a kite pattern. The kite is cut out, a string and a tail are attached, and the children fly them in the classroom or outside. Umbrellas may be traced, cut out, and decorated when the concept of rainy weather is taught.

*Sequence Story:* Sequence pictures are used to teach the concept of *planting*. The first picture shows the boy digging a hole, and the second putting in the seed. The third and fourth pictures depict sun and rain influencing the growth of the plant, and the last scene shows the roots, leaves, and growth of the plant.

*Flowers and Vegetables:* An assignment is made for the children to bring flowers to school. They learn the names of them, then the teacher makes simplified drawings of each flower on the blackboard. The children "draw like the teacher's" and color appropriately.

Beans, seeds, and bulbs are planted in glass and the class watches them grow. Digging, planting, growing, watering, fertilizing, pot, and egg shells are talked about.

Sweet potatoes and carrot tops are placed in water. The children observe daily changes.

*Paper Objects:* Each child is given a paper bird nest, a male and female bird, six eggs, and three baby birds. They follow such directions as "Place three eggs in the nest with the mother bird on top of the eggs." "Place three baby birds in the nest and have the father feeding them."

*Insects:* An assignment is made for each child to bring an insect to school in a glass jar. How and where the insect was captured is explained by each child. A discussion of body parts and diet follows.

### Basic Vocabulary (K-10)

| | | |
|---|---|---|
| April | bud | robins |
| bird | March | shower |
| bird house | May | windy |
| bloom | nest | |

### Games, Stories, Songs, and Nursery Rhymes (K-10)

The teacher makes appropriate selections for this unit.

### Home Training Hints for Parents (K-10)

1. Parents assist their child in planting a vegetable garden. The child should assume responsibility for caring for the garden.
2. On a windy day, help your child construct and fly a kite.
3. When riding in the car, ask the child to find signs of spring: trees budding, grass turning green, and baby animals with their mothers.
4. Build a bird house and put it near the child's window. Observe and discuss what is seen: birds building nests and feeding their young.

# KINDERGARTEN LEVEL (K)

## Unit: Easter (K-11)

**CLASSROOM ACTIVITIES**

*Blackboard:* The teacher proposes the question, "What are some things you see at the park?" The teacher draws items on the blackboard as the children name them: trees, grass, flowers, benches, and tables. She gives a command: "Hide a pink egg under the bench." A child draws it with colored chalk in the correct place. After the eggs have been hidden, they are found by erasing.

*Oatmeal Box:* Paint oatmeal boxes with dripless liquid tempera paint. This forms the body of a rabbit. Cotton balls for tails, construction paper for ears, and felt cut outs for facial parts are appropriately assembled according to the teacher's directions, "Put the cotton ball on the bottom of the box."

*Bunny Puzzles:* Silhouettes of a bunny are prepared by the teacher. Each one has a major body part missing. The children choose the missing part from a large assortment of pieces.

*Easter Cards:* To construct Easter cards, the class is directed to: "Fold your paper like mine." "Draw a circle like mine." (A rabbit can be drawn on the card using different sized circles.) The cards are mailed to the parents.

*Eggs:* The children make puppets from dyed and decorated egg shells. A stage can be made from a shoe box. The teacher directs an Easter morning play for all "eggs."

### Basic Vocabulary (K-11)

| | | |
|---|---|---|
| contest | most | winner |
| free | prize | |

### Games, Stories, Songs, and Nursery Rhymes (K-11)

The teacher makes appropriate selections for this unit.

### Home Training Hints for Parents (K-11)

1. Mother helps her child purchase candy Easter eggs to be placed in a paper Easter basket which has been made at home and filled with artificial grass. The child copies from mother's writing "To _____ From _____" cards filling in the name of each family member to receive a basket.
2. The children help mother make a bunny cake. New vocabulary and serial directions are given.
3. Colored Easter eggs are used to teach new vocabulary and to generalize concepts the week following Easter: hard cooked, soft boiled, raw, chopped eggs, egg salad.
4. To prepare a salad, fill empty egg shells with jello. When firm, remove the shell and place the "egg" on coconut that has been colored green to represent grass.

# KINDERGARTEN LEVEL (K)

# Unit: Family Fun (K-12)

**CLASSROOM ACTIVITIES**

(This unit might be titled "Places to Go." Some of the following suggestions may be incorporated into other units or used in a summer program.)

*Library:* The class visits a local library and each child selects a book to be checked out on the teacher's library card. A small library is set up in the classroom and the children play-act library activities. When the books have been read, the class returns them.

*Book Shelf:* A poster depicting a book shelf is placed on the bulletin board. The children report the names of books that have been read to them at home and the teacher prints these titles on one of the hand drawn books to be pasted on the poster.

*Original Book:* The children compile a book with the help of the teacher. A simple topic is suggested, the story is developed by the group, each child illustrates a page, and the teacher duplicates the material. The children make a cover and take the book home.

*Zoo:* The zoo unit was studied in the Pre-Kindergarten Level. A review is used to broaden concepts. The children visit the zoo and later categorize the following: those who eat vegetables and those who eat grass, those who live in cages and those who do not, those who live in daylight and those who live in the dark. Which cages are appropriate for each animal, bird, or reptile is illustrated by a large poster of various cages placed before the class. The children are given a picture to paste on an appropriate cage. Discussions consist of "Why is there a top on the bird cage, but not the alligator pond?"

*Playground:* Parents are asked to familiarize their children with playground equipment. Subsequently they construct a playground in the classroom. Make a child's see-saw with a wooden box and board, or make a smaller version which will hold stuffed animals or dolls. To make a slide, the children are given a drawing of a slide with no rungs on the ladder. From a variety of lengths of toothpicks, they select appropriate pieces to paste on the picture. A swing is made by pasting straws on paper for the rope and a piece of tongue depressor for the seat.

The children walk the length of a plank that is on the floor. Then the plank is placed on blocks. Blue paper may be used to simulate water and the plank is raised higher than before to make the task more difficult.

*Picnic:* The children plan a pretend picnic by selecting pictures of things to be placed in the picnic basket. Foods such as olives, pickles, and potato chips that were not presented in the Food Unit are included. Later an experience story is written about a picnic, each child contributing a sentence.

*Ice Cream:* Ice cream is made at school. The recipe is discussed and each child brings an assigned item: one *quart* of milk, two *packets* of ice cream mix. With the help of the children, the teacher makes the ice cream and encourages conversation: "Let me pour." "Let me stir." Each takes a turn at the freezer which is then given to the parents to finish. The ice cream is served with syrup to teach *chocolate, butterscotch, strawberry,* and to help the children learn to make choices.

*Beach:* A sandpile is kept in the classroom for a week. The children take turns building sand castles, tunnels, mountains, and lakes. The class guesses what has been built.

A beach picture is made by gluing sand and pieces of shell macaroni on blue paper.

*Lake:* A tub filled with water is identified as a lake. The children, portraying the wind, blow sailboats across the surface. In an empty tub, cardboard fish, each with a picture, are placed in the bottom. With a magnet at the end of the fishline the children hook the fish (paper clip attached). They describe their picture.

*Movie:* The children plan to take a field trip to the movies. Bring the movie page from the newspaper. Discuss what is on at the movies, which are suitable for children. Act out: arrival at the theater, waiting in line to buy tickets, giving them to the doorman, buying candy and popcorn at the refreshment counter, letting the usher show them to their seat, being quiet so that they will not disturb others.

The children make a movie with a shoe box, sticks, and a roll of paper the width of the box. Use magazine pictures to develop a sequence story. A flashlight can be used to light the screen.

### Basic Vocabulary (K-12)

| | | |
|---|---|---|
| baloney | handle | potato salad |
| baseball game | hardens | salad |
| beach | jelly fish | salt water |
| bleachers | jetty | sand dollar |
| camp fire | lettuce | sculpture |
| camping | life guard | sea wall |
| careful | lotion | shell |
| celery | mayonnaise | sleeping bag |
| clam | molds | snail |
| clay | movies | star fish |
| cot | museum | sun burn |
| crab | mustard | swim |
| damp | olives | theater |
| drive-in | painting | tomato |
| film | park | touchdown |
| football game | pickles | tuna fish |
| gather | picnic | waves |
| ground | pier | wood |

*Games, Stories, Songs, and Nursery Rhymes* (K-12)

The teacher makes appropriate selections for this unit.

*Home Training Hints for Parents* (K-12)

1. Since this unit lends itself to going places, parents should plan many special outings to reinforce classroom activities.
2. Teach safety rules at the park; "Stay away from the swings." "Stay on the merry-go-round until it stops moving."
3. Teach theater manners before attending the movie. "Sit quietly." "Save talking until after the movie."

# KINDERGARTEN LEVEL (K)

## Unit: Summer (K-13)

CLASSROOM ACTIVITIES

*Wiener Roast:* Plan a wiener roast at a nearby park. When the class returns, make a pretend fire in class. Tell the children "Put 9 sticks on the fire." Paper wieners on a hanger are roasted over the fire.

*Swimming Pool:* Make a pool out of cut styrofoam boards covered with plastic so that it will hold water. Add a diving board. Dress a doll in a bathing suit and give directions: "Make the doll dive into the water and then swim on his back."

*Tub of Water:* Get a small tub of water. Put various objects in the tub and see which ones float and which ones sink.

*Sand:* Have a tub of sand in the room. Bury objects in the sand and give directions, "Find the penny, dime, and quarter."

*Picture File:* Supply the class with pictures of the four seasons. Let a child draw a picture from the stack and place it in an appropriate spot. Use holiday pictures with appropriate seasons.

### Basic Vocabulary (K-13)

| | | |
|---|---|---|
| August | mountains | trip |
| company | plains | toll road |
| June | rest stop | vacation |
| July | swimming pool | visit |
| life jacket | travel | |

*Games, Stories, Songs, and Nursery Rhymes* (K-13)

The teacher makes appropriate selections for this unit.

*Home Training Hints for Parents* (K-13)

1. Plan a family picnic. Your child helps you prepare the food and pack the picnic basket. Discuss what foods would be appropriate for a picnic and which ones are not.
2. A camping trip can be planned or let the child "camp-out" in the backyard. Put up a tent, sleep in the sleeping bag, and cook a hot dog on the open fire to illustrate how camping is different from living at home.
3. Set up a wading pool in the backyard. Discuss wading, floating, swimming, diving, and dunking. You might also discuss which animals swim, other places to swim such as the lake, ocean, stream, and swimming safety.

# KINDERGARTEN LEVEL (K)

## Unit: Birthday Party (K-14)

CLASSROOM ACTIVITIES

*Calendar:* At the beginning of the school year, the teacher directs the production of a calendar that will serve to teach birthdates. Each child's birthday is appropriately represented by his photograph.

*Birthday Cards:* Presents brought to a birthday party should include a birthday card. The words "To _____" are printed on the outside of the envelope and a card inside is signed "From _____." Opening the cards should be a teacher-directed activity; "Who receives this card?" "Who sent this card?"

*Menu:* The birthday child plans the menu for his party. He may ask his classmates for preferences. "All of those who want chocolate cake raise your hands. All those who want white cake raise your hands."

*Theme:* The child is assisted by teacher and parent to choose a theme for his party. A theme in keeping with a unit recently studied should be considered.

*Ditto Pictures:* The teacher provides a series of ditto pictures pertinent to a birthday party but ones which represent absurdities; the candles on the cake are upside down, the hats are on the chairs and the children are on the floor, the children are sad and crying, the children are dressed in their pajamas.

### Basic Vocabulary (K-14)

The teacher selects pertinent vocabulary of her choice.

### Games, Stories, Songs, and Nursery Rhymes (K-14)

The teacher makes appropriate selections for this unit.

### Home Training Hints For Parents (K-14)

1. To parallel the classroom activity of teaching birthdates, plan for two weeks to check off on the calendar each day preceding your child's birthday.
2. Look through the calendar and circle other family member's birthdays. At the appropriate time talk about them, then go shopping for presents and wrap them.
3. After the classroom party determine if your child can recall who gave each present. The present and giver should be recorded for later thank-you notes.
4. Have your child sit with you while you print thank-you notes. He helps decide what to say, signs or copies his name and address, and finishes with stamping and mailing.

# READINESS LEVEL (R)

### (Child Growth and Development Data [1])

### Humble Independent School District
### Humble, Texas

### Before Entering First Grade

Many items are listed as being desirable for children about to start school for the first time, but the following suggestions are especially recommended by the Humble First Grade teachers. Experience has proved to teachers that young children will likely get off to a better start in school if they have some help and encouragement in these various areas before September.

1. Your child should be prepared and eager for school to begin. He should not fear or dread this new phase of life. He should understand that he is to be away from home and parents for several hours during the day.

[1] Humble Independent School District, Humble Elementary School, Harris County, Texas.

2. He should come to school knowing that his teacher and others who work with him will love him and help him at all times.

3. He should know how to keep up with his personal belongings such as money, pencils, coats, caps, shoes, socks, and so on.

4. Be able to speak his words plainly with no baby talk.

5. Be cooperative and eager to learn to read.

6. He should have already learned to listen to directions and to follow instructions.

7. Should have had some experience with hand work such as cutting with scissors, using paste, and coloring.

8. He should continue to get plenty of rest and sleep at night.

9. He should eat a nourishing breakfast if he is to do his best school work each day.

10. Should have a complete physical check-up by a physician before September.

11. He should be able to tie his shoes and dress himself.

12. He should be able to use the bathroom properly.

13. Should be careful and practice safety habits.

14. Should be able to make up simple stories about pictures and tell the stories to others.

15. Know his age and the month of his birth.

16. Should know his complete name and be able to print his first name.

17. Be able to count 10 to 20 objects without help from others.

18. Know enough about money to recognize a penny, a nickel, a dime, and a quarter.

19. Have the ability to complete a simple task suitable to age.

20. Be able to take part in a group discussion and wait his turn to talk.

21. Generally is polite and courteous to adults and other children.

22. Should have many books of simple stories and pictures. Parents or other adults should read some stories to him every day.

## READINESS LEVEL (R)

*(Child Growth and Development Data [2])*

Spring Branch Independent School District
Spring Branch, Texas

Minimum Standards of Achievement for First Grade

I. READING—Upon completion of the first grade, a child's progress in reading should be considered satisfactory if the child:

[2] Spring Branch Independent School District, Houston, Texas.

A. Mastered the basic vocabulary in context of the first grade reading program of the three preprimers; *Jack and Janet* and *Up and Away.*

B. Reads by phrases rather than words.

C. Has word attack skills.

D. Has acquired skills through listening.

E. Has acquired skills through reading.

F. Has good reading habits.

G. Handles seat work or workbook independently.

H. Has read assigned supplementary readers.

II. ARITHMETIC—Satisfactory progress for a child completing first grade should be judged on the child's ability to:

A. Read and write numbers by 1's, 2's, 5's, and 10's to a hundred.

B. Have an understanding of the meaning of two-place numbers and to read and write the two-place number.

C. Learn ordinals first through tenth.

D. Tell time to the even hour.

E. Know addition and subtraction facts.

F. Understand the value of money and to count money up to one dollar.

G. Have some knowledge of measurements such as: day, week, month, yard, foot, ruler, clocks, calendar, etc.

H. Be able to make own oral problems using concrete materials to show the meaning.

III. SPELLING—To be progressing satisfactorily in the area of spelling the child should be able to:

A. Spell all the words on the basic list.

B. Write simple sentences from dictation.

C. Make new words by substituting consonants on known words.

D. Spell his first and last name.

E. Add simple endings to known words.

# READINESS LEVEL (R)

## (*Language Skills*)

## I. COMPREHENSION OF ORAL LANGUAGE

A. RECOGNITION OF OBJECTS

1. By Name

a. The teacher presents objects concerned with a farm (barn, corral, tractor) and the children select them as named by the teacher. A farm scene is built as the teacher gives directions, "Put the barn here." "Put three horses in the corral."

b. A drawing of a farm scene is given each child who stamps (using a stamp set) as directed by the teacher. "Put the horse in the corral. Place the sheep in the pen. Let's have a bird in a tree."

c. Shape names may be taught by playing the game, "Button, Button, who has the Button" using a different shape each day. "It" gives the shape to one person then says, "Square, square, who has the square?" The "guesser" becomes "It" if he is correct the first time.

2. By Function

a. Several objects are placed in a "feel box" which has a hole in the back. By turn, each child puts his hand into the box and brings out the objects described "Find something you cut with (scissors)." "Find something you write with (pencil)."

b. At the conclusion of a birthday party all gifts are collected and placed in a box. The teacher asks, "Who brought something that will float (boat)?" "Who brought something that you can shoot (gun)?"

c. Schoolroom objects are assembled on a table (tape, hole-punch, thumb tacks, stapler). The teacher says, "I have pictures to put on the bulletin board. What do I need to make them stay on the bulletin board (tacks)." "I want to mend my torn page. What do I need (tape)?" If a child does not comprehend, the torn page is shown to him. Carry-over is tested on another day.

B. RECOGNITION OF PICTURES

1. By Name

a. New vocabulary is easily taught through the Kindergarten issue of Weekly Reader (86). Each week the new vocabulary list in the teacher's edition accompanies the children's list. Pictures of words such as desert, jungle, and oasis are introduced.

b. To teach the fact that one word may mean more than one thing, the teacher makes a chart and adds two pictures each day such as, *pear* and *pair* of shoes.

c. Each child brings to school a picture of a farm scene. Using an opaque projector, the teacher names the objects in a scene as the child who brought the picture points with the ruler.

2. By Function

a. Flannel backed pictures of farm tools are distributed to the children. The teacher asks, "Who has something the farmer would haul his feed in (truck)?" If a child can not answer the question, the teacher presents a picture of grain growing in the field and relates it to feed. From a series of pictures such as scissors, knife, and combine, the children choose which would be used to cut the grain.

b. As a homework assignment in phonics, the children bring pictures which begin with the initial sound in "fish." The pictures are tacked to the bulletin board and the teacher asks, "Who brought something which would make you cool (fan)?" "Who brought something to eat with (fork)?" After the correct response, the teacher points to the picture to reinforce learning for all the children.

    c. Assignments such as found in Reading-Thinking Skills, Level I (72, p. 15) can be used to teach function. "What would you use to repair a flat tire (jack)?" "What would you use to hit the baseball (bat)?" As a group teaching device, the children take turns finding the correct precut picture to go with the flat tire and baseball. As an individual hand skill activity each child completes a page.

  C. CATEGORIZING

    1. What goes together? Pairs of pictures such as toothbrush and toothpaste, hat and coat, table and chair, mop and broom, apple and orange are collected and mounted separately on tagboard and one picture is given to each child. By turn they are told "Find your partner." The partners hold hands until all pairs are found.

    2. Charts labeled with category words such as toys, fruit, vehicles, and furniture contain two sample pictures. The children find additional pictures in magazines appropriate for the chart of the day. These charts are used later for a review of category words.

    3. A top for toys, a saw for tools, a hat for clothes, an orange for fruit are placed in separate open shoe boxes. Each child draws a card from a stack of pictures and places it in the appropriate box. On another day one child may sort all the pictures.

  D. NUMBER CONCEPTS

    1. For children who can match configurations one through six, a modified domino game is presented. Each child receives three dominoes and the remainder are in a box. The child with a "double" starts the game. The teacher calls out the possibilities and the child on the left continues if he can. The children may count the dots one by one if they do not recognize the total configuration. The first child without dominoes is the winner.

    2. Two or three charts containing groups of objects such as 4 chairs, 5 boys, 4 beds, 5 balls are placed before the class. Each child is given a smaller card containing groups of different objects such as 4 shoes, 5 trees, 3 dogs and they try to determine to which chart their card belongs.

    3. Cards with seals or stamped pictures are constructed to look like domino "doubles." The "doubles" are cut apart in a zig-zag fashion so that each looks different. The separate pieces are distributed to the children who are requested to "Put your

puzzle together." Each child must find the child whose piece fits his to make a double.

E. SPATIAL AND TEMPORAL ORIENTATION

1. To teach the "passage of time" the teacher removes her watch and any clocks from the classroom. Periodically a child is asked to go to the clock in the hall and when he returns he sets the toy clock like the one in the hall. The teacher announces the time then follows up with such statements as "One more hour until we hear the story," or "Soon it will be time to go home." "In ten minutes it will be time to go home."

2. The calendar is used to teach passage of time. The leader for each day is marked on the calendar at the beginning of the month. It is then easy to discuss "Who is the leader today?" "Who was leader yesterday?" "Who will be the leader tomorrow?" "How many days until we go to the Rodeo?" "How many weeks until Easter?" The children refer to the calendar for answers. Rote and rational counting are also practiced.

3. Chart 12 of the Houston Speech and Hearing Center *Communication Charts* (9) or Chart 6 of the *Non-Oral Reading Series* (51) teaches concepts of in, on, under, beside, etc. A child is asked to place a ball in front of the chair. If he does not understand, the "in front of" pictures from the charts are shown. Objects are drawn on the blackboard and the children "Draw a ball *on top of* the tree."

F. SERIAL DIRECTIONS

1. Serial directions are given for constructing a circus ring [Kindergraph Workbook (66)]. Key words for each step are written on the blackboard such as color, cut, paste, write your name, put it on the table. If written words are not known, the teacher enumerates orally as she prints the words. "First color them. Second, cut them out. Third, paste them on the stars to make a ring." This age group should be responsible for at least one activity a day which involves remembering a sequence of directions.

2. A story is told such as "A boy was going to the barber shop. On his way to the barber shop, he passed a cow eating grass, a dog barking loudly, a fire truck going fast, and a girl flying a kite. Then he came to the barber shop." The children recreate the story by placing in sequence premounted pictures. Errors can be demonstrated by referring to the back of each card which has been numbered sequentially. Other stories may be found in *We Read More Pictures* (48).

3. Pictures in the *Kindergraph* Workbook (66) depicting "The Farmer in the Dell" are arranged in appropriate order.

Each child holds a picture. As the song progresses, the wife goes to the right of the farmer, etc. Later the pictures may be arranged in sequence on any metal surface with magnetic clips. Left to right progression is always observed with the farmer at the left.

## II. EXPRESSION OF ORAL LANGUAGE

### A. NAMING AND DEFINING

1. Naming

a. The mothers are asked to bring a variety of boxed cookies. During refreshment time the children ask for the cookie they want by name: vanilla wafer, chocolate chip cookie, ginger snap.

b. To teach the names of shapes such as circle, square, rectangle, and triangle, the teacher draws them on the blackboard. She asks, "Who can find a rectangle?" After an appropriate selection, the teacher asks, "How can you make the rectangle into a door?" (The child draws a door knob.) A roof is added to a square to make a house and a line to a circle for a hearing aid cord and receiver.

c. Children learn to name parts of objects by telling what is missing from drawings on the blackboard; the knob from the door, the handle from the wagon, the dial from the telephone.

2. Defining

a. For "Show and Tell," the assignment is to bring something from home in a closed box. By turn each child describes his object and the teacher guesses what it is. If she is unable to guess because of poor clues, the child cannot show his object to the class until it is again his turn and he gives a better description.

b. Using the chart of opposites (Chart 8 in the *Non-Oral Reading Series* [51] or the *Communication Charts* 8 and 9 [9]), the teacher says to a child, "These are both apples. You may put one in the pocket chart. Which one will you choose?" He must respond with "The good apple," or "The bad apple." If he replies "apple" the teacher again says, "These are both apples," but gives some clues. The same approach applies to the round and square button, the long and short pencils.

c. The game of "clues" is played any time a few spare minutes occur in the daily program. From a box of hidden objects, a child selects one and hides it in a paper sack. As he describes it as to color, function, or where it can be seen, the children guess what it is. At first the teacher may have to ask questions such as, "What color is it?" "What is it used for?" "Where would we see it?" Later the game can be varied by asking the children to tell only two things about the object.

3. Action Agent

a. For a break in the class routine, the children play "How will I go to the window?" Each child chooses a different way. "I will crawl like a baby." "I will jump like a kangaroo." "I will hop like a rabbit." When he tells it correctly, he may perform.

      b. Chart 2 of the *Non-Oral Reading Series* (51) or Charts 3, 5, 7, 11, 15, 22, 27, 28 from the *Communication Charts* (9) are used to teach verbs. The children pull a picture from a stack of pictures and make sentences with the verb. "A dog cannot fly." "A bird can fly." "A boy can run." "A table cannot run."

      c. Using a box of objects, the children play "What can you do with it?" Each child in turn puts an object in his sack, then tells one thing he can do with it. "You can cut with it (knife)." The children name things that cut until the correct answer is given. When an incorrect answer is stated, the teacher or child says "It could be, but it isn't." If an answer such as bread is given, the teacher demonstrates the absurdity.

  B. CATEGORIZING—SORTING

    1. Noun picture cards are sorted differently from day to day. One day they are sorted according to the material they are made from such as wood which includes chairs, tables, and desks; leather which includes purses, shoes, and belts. Another time the children distinguish what goes in the kitchen such as glasses and pots from objects found in the bedroom such as clothes, sheets, and pillows. The child who is sorting tells the class, "The pillow would be in the bedroom." "The glasses would be in the kitchen."

    2. Using charts 20, 16, 18, 22, and 23 from the *Non-Oral Reading Series* (51), the children question each other by calling out "Which chart has the cow?" The child who answers "The farm" takes his turn as teacher.

    3. Seals or stamp-set pictures are arranged on "likenesses and differences" cards. For instance, one card has three flowers and a vegetable, consequently a child names the rose, the lily, and the violet and states, "They are alike because they are flowers." "The radish is different because it is a vegetable."

  C. NUMBER CONCEPTS

    1. The children take turns counting anything which is needed for the classroom activities. For example, one child counts the cups for refreshment time. If he did not have enough, the teacher asks him to count the children without cups, then asks, "How many more do you need?"

    2. Small crackers are lined up on the refreshment table. The teacher asks one child to count *eight* crackers and to eat the *eighth* one. Or, the teacher may point to a cracker and ask a child which number (in line) it is. If he succeeds, he eats the cracker. If he fails he goes to the end of the line and the teacher gives him an easier number on his next turn.

3. This game may be played with two groups of cookies or crackers to teach the concept of "more, less, many, few." The children choose what they want by stating "more" and pointing to the group with 3 instead of the group with 2. The next day, he may say he wants "less" and gets his cookies if he points to the group with 4 instead of 10.

D. SPATIAL AND TEMPORAL ORIENTATION

1. Using Thinking Skills, Level One (72, p. 21), for a group activity the children discuss "What's missing?" The teacher asks, "If I gave you a ladder, where would you place it?" The child who answers "Under the painter," pastes it on the picture. Each child receives an individual sheet when he correctly names where to paste each of the missing items.

2. The *Kindergraph* (66) has a work sheet showing how vegetables grow, and how a sand box is used for the garden. Small construction paper vegetable cut-outs are planted in the sand. A discussion follows as to the part of the vegetable that is edible and which part grows under the ground.

3. A daily weather calendar is kept in the classroom. Periodically weather conditions such as rain, snow, cloudy, foggy, and sunshine are discussed. Pictures are used to help teach weather concepts such as clothing on a boy to illustrate temperature. Small additional pictures like clouds and rain are pasted appropriately on the calendar. Each day the weather pertaining to "yesterday" or "last Sunday" is mentioned.

E. SENTENCE BUILDING

1. The children take turns role playing the weatherman. A cardboard box is cut to represent a television screen. Each day the "weatherman" describes the atmospheric conditions. At first he may need to be prompted to "tell about the sky" or "What kind of clothes did you wear to school?" The teacher encourages a series of sentences.

2. Simple stories such as "Three Billy Goats Gruff" are acted out, and the children take turns being each character. The teacher often has to tell a child (by soft voice or whisper) what to say, but by the time the last child has a turn, the "lines" will have been learned. The play is presented to the parent group another day.

3. The children are given practice in using sentences at refreshment time. The teacher or leader asks, "What do you want?" The child receives a cookie only if he makes a sentence. He is complimented if he makes a sentence different from the child before him. This same approach may be used whenever paper, paste, books, or pegs are passed out to the class.

# READINESS LEVEL (R)

## (Avenues of Learning)

### I. MEMORY: SHORT TERM

A. AUDITORY

Goal: To follow at least five directions, to remember at least three sound effects and to listen carefully for story content.

1. Packets of seeds are placed on the table. In turn the children select the ones named: corn, beans, peas, radishes, cucumbers.

2. Tape recordings of farm animal sounds are played and the children are taught to identify them. The sounds are replayed to test memory.

3. The teacher tells a short story. "The farmer walked to the tree. He pulled the carrot from the tree. He put it in his basket." The children tell which part does not belong.

Goal: To follow in sequence at least four directions, to retell a story, and to relate an experience.

1. On planting day each child is told to follow directions in a specific sequence: dig a hole, put the seeds in, put the fertilizer in, cover the hole with dirt, water it. If he cannot retell the directions before planting the seed, pictures are supplied and placed in sequence on the chart rack.

2. Events that are easy to retell in sequential order are "Raising rodeo calves," "Trees that bear fruit," "From the sheep to the sweater."

3. After a field trip to the farm, the children are asked to tell in chronological order what they did and what they saw.

B. VISUAL

Goals: To remember without stressing sequence eight objects or pictures previously seen, to recognize the missing part of a series of pictures, and to recall the missing printed word.

1. Pictures of farm tools are placed on the table, the children view them, and the teacher covers them with a piece of tagboard. One child names as many as he can remember, and as he calls the names, the teacher takes the appropriate picture from under the tagboard.

2. The teacher shows the children a picture of a tractor, then out of their vision, cuts off a wheel. As a group the children call out the missing part. The various pictures and their parts are later given to the children to assemble.

3. The names of all children in the class are placed in the pocket chart. One child hides his eyes while one or more name cards are removed. He must supply the missing name(s).

Goals: To remember the following in sequence: a full length story with four objects or pictures, and to supply the missing number or letter that has appeared in a series.

1. The story of Cinderella is told with pictures. The children tell what happens next by locating the appropriate picture.

2. The teacher places in a row five pictures of Christmas presents. She shuffles them and hands them to a child to resequence.

3. A series of numbers are placed in the pocket chart. The teacher removes one number while a child hides his eyes. He is responsible for naming the missing digit.

C. VISUAL-MOTOR

Goal: To copy patterns from memory.

1. As the children observe her, the teacher builds an outline of a barn with toothpicks on a colored sheet of paper. The children return to their seats and construct one like it. If correct, they may paste the sticks in position.

2. The children learn to dramatize the rhyme "One, Two, Buckle My Shoe."

3. The children make lacy patterns from paper by observing the steps demonstrated by the teacher.

## II. VISUAL-PERCEPTUAL-MOTOR

Goal: To perceive a visual image and reproduce it.

1. Each child receives a piece of paper with two rows of round balls drawn on it. Their assignment is to color theirs like the teacher's which has red and blue in a specific pattern.

2. The teacher presents to the class a picture of a barnyard scene with a specific number of chickens and cows in it. With appropriate equipment, the children make one like the teacher's. (Right and left is emphasized by placing the chickens to the left of the barn and the cows to the right of the barn.)

3. The children make necklaces from colored macaroni in a design presented by the teacher.

## III. SOCIAL MATURITY

Goal: To gain more independence in self-help skills and to cooperate with adults in both work and play activities.

1. The children at this level should be capable of working independently at their seats. Assignments are made and the children instructed that they will receive no help.

2. Each week a child with the help of his parents selects and pays for the juice to be brought to school for refreshment periods.

3. The children learn to conform to rules and demonstrate good sportsmanship when playing games.

# READINESS LEVEL (R)

## (*Pre-Academic Subjects*)

Goal: Readiness for academic work in the areas of reading, writing, spelling, and arithmetic are strongly emphasized on this level.

## I. LIKENESSES AND DIFFERENCES

INDIVIDUAL WORK

A. From four pictures the child selects the one that is different.

B. A child is given a card containing a letter (f) and is asked to find it from a series of four letters; d, e, f, t. He proceeds to a more complex task of finding d in a series of b, q, d, p.

C. Activities related to matching words may be found in the *Non-Oral Reading Series* (51) charts one through six. Similar activities may be created from the *Communication Charts* (9).

GROUP WORK

Group activities may be organized from charts seven through twenty-six from the *Non-Oral Reading Series* (51).

## II. PHONICS TRAINING

GROUP WORK (Later done as individual work)

A. The children continue to learn the Spalding (101) approach to learning sounds the letters make and how to write each phoneme. The following symbols are used b＿＿＿＿ the words that start like boy; ＿＿＿b＿＿ the sound in the middle of the word; ＿＿＿＿b the sound at the end of the word. Then activities may be varied by introducing Mike and Cindy Stories (18), Listening For Speech Sounds (123), Let's Play Hide and Seek (39), Hear, See, and Tell Stories (89), and performing the activities found in Phonetic Keys to Reading (99).

B. When all phonemes have been learned, introduce rhyming words. (The ends of the words are the same, but the beginning sounds are different.) Three pictures, two that rhyme and a third that does not, are attached to the blackboard with magnetic clips. The children say them aloud then decide which one does not belong.

C. Activities from the Kindergarten Level are expanded to the Readiness Level.

INDIVIDUAL WORK

A. Any of the group work may be translated to individual work.

B. Give a child three pictures and ask him to place the two that rhyme in the chart slot.

C. The children complete the work sheets made from the book *Rhymes to Color* (69).

## III. WRITING

A. The teacher continues to teach from Spalding (101) using primary writing paper.

B. "Draw like mine" activities may be found in the *Fun to Draw Book* (68). The children develop better spatial orientation and the ability to utilize a step-by-step approach to pencil and paper tasks.

C. Activities from the Frostig Program (41, 42) have been used successfully at this level.

## IV. NUMBERS

A. The children are taught number concepts through ten. They change the domino five to a line of five things and learn that the patterns still represent five.

B. A birthday calendar is constructed and the children are taught during the year to remember their own birthdates.

C. From number workbooks such as *Happy Ways to Numbers* (2) the children learn to count by 2's, by 5's, by 10's, and by 1's to 100; and the value of coins.

### READINESS LEVEL (R); PROPOSED CALENDAR

September: School (R-1); Fall (R-2).
October: Farm (R-3); Halloween (R-4).
November: Farm and Food (R-3); Thanksgiving (R-5).
December: Christmas (R-6); Christmas; Winter (R-7).
January: Winter; Rodeo (R-3).
February: Valentine (R-8); Valentine; Rodeo (R-3); Rodeo.
March: Farm (Planting) (R-3); Spring (R-9).
April: Easter (R-10); Easter; Safety (R-11); Safety.
May: Safety; Summer (R-12).
Extra: Birthday (R-13).

# READINESS LEVEL (R)

## Unit: Farm

**SAMPLE LESSON PLAN**

I. Goals:
1. Expand vocabulary related to the farm.
2. Increase short term auditory memory to following three compound directions.

3. Teach the scientific concept of growth.
4. Reinforce calendar terms and ordinal words which were introduced in the School Routine Unit.
5. Sort and categorize through the sense of taste.
6. Teach the Spalding (101) sound of "t."
7. Teach material from the *Non-Oral Chart*, number 24 (51).

II. Activities:

**1:00–1:10** *Pledge to the Flag and Star-Spangled Banner.* This is a daily routine at which time one child holds the flag while the children place their right hands over their hearts, repeat the pledge, and sing the song. (Left-right discrimination and sentence building through auditory memory.)

**1:10–2:00** *Planting.* Each child is asked to select "three different *seeds*" (category word) which are taken to his desk. The teacher asks, "What shape is your seed?" (Defining.) "What happens to a seed?" (Naming from action.)

With the help of the teacher the children plant three different types of seed, each type being placed in a separate container. To demonstrate plant growth, place one container in a dark closet, one by the window, and the other which contains only water, by the window. "Take the pot with the grass seed to the closet and place it in a dark place." (Auditory memory with two directions.) "Take the pot with the dry soil to the window ledge." (Auditory memory for one direction.) "Fill the pie pan with water, drop several bean seeds into it, and place the pan on the window ledge." (Auditory memory for three directions.)

A schedule for routine watering of the plants is posted and contains the names and days when a specific child is assigned the task. On his day, the child must remember his job without being reminded. (Long term memory and independent work habits.)

**2:00–2:20** *The "T" Sound.* The Spalding (101) sound of "t" is introduced. Each child says the key word then writes it on the blackboard according to the teacher's directions. The following activity involves selecting pictures from the "t" picture file and asking questions. "What starts like table that you can spin?" "What lives on a farm and says 'gobble, gobble?'" The children provide answers. (Identifying words by beginning sound, and comprehension of sentences.)

**2:20–2:30** *Writing.* The class is asked to "Take out your tablets (primary writing paper) and place your fingers on the top right-hand corner." (Auditory memory for two directions and left-right orientation.) At this spot the children are asked to write their initials. (Phonics training and writing.) Next, according to the teacher's directions, the children write several "t's" across the page. At the completion of the activity, papers are checked and mistakes are pointed out. When corrections are made, the children may choose a vegetable seal (Naming) to paste on their papers.

**2:30–2:50** *Refreshments.* The teacher places small pieces of pickles, lemon, potato chips, ham, apple, and candy on a plate. The children sample and decide which is sweet, sour, or salty. (Categorizing and vocabulary building.) Pictures of the various foods are placed in appropriate categories on a "Taste Chart."

**2:50–3:10** *Word Cards.* Using the *Non-Oral Reading Chart* 24 (51), the teacher instructs the children to match the word card to the chart and then generate a sentence. (Likenesses and differences and sentence building.)

**3:10–3:30** The children make a sample page for their personalized story book. Each draws a picture of his house (Visual memory) and prints his address by copying or from memory.

# READINESS LEVEL (R)

## Unit: School Routine (R-1)

CLASSROOM ACTIVITIES

*School Supplies:* The children are required to remember the school supplies listed by the teacher and to ask their mothers to help them purchase the necessary items. The teacher shows a sample box of the items she wants them to bring: a cigar box, a primary pencil, scissors, large primary crayons (eight to a box), paste (in a plastic jar), and a small package of kleenex. Several times during the day the children review aloud the items they are to bring.

*School Supply Box:* A guessing game called "Clues" is played. A child describes an item (from his school supply box) by its function. The one who guesses has the next turn of describing.

*Classroom Tools:* When the teacher needs a tool during the day, she asks a child to obtain it for her. "I want to draw a long straight line on the blackboard. What do I need, Johnny?" He answers and brings it to the teacher.

*Storybook of Myself:* Over a period of time the children construct a storybook which is about themselves. Pages may include:

A picture of himself. I am a _____. My name is _____ _____.
A picture of the school. I go to _____ school.
A picture of the teacher. My teacher is _____.
A picture of a birthday cake with the correct number of candles de-

picting his age. I am _____ years old now. My birthday
is _____.

I will be _____ years old on my next birthday.

A picture of his house. My address is _____.

A picture or map of the city. The city I live in is _____.

A map of the state. The state I live in is _____.

A picture of a telephone. My telephone number is _____.

At the completion of one day's efforts, the teacher may shuffle the pages
belonging to the class and ask, "Who lives at _____?" If the child cannot recognize his address, he is shown his picture.

*Scales:* The children are weighed on one day and measured on the next.
A picture of the scales may be placed on a sheet with "I weigh _____
pounds" and inserted in the "Storybook of Myself."

The names of the children in the class are arranged according to
their weight rank. A similar one ranks them according to height. Questions are asked, "Is Charlie taller than Joe?" "Does Mary weigh less than
Caroline?"

*Calendar:* The teacher constructs a chart containing: Yesterday was
_____, Today is _____, Tomorrow will be _____. Each
morning the children choose an appropriate word card (by matching if
necessary) that fits the blank. The class generates sentences regarding
something that happened yesterday, something that happened today,
and something that will happen tomorrow.

*Refreshments:* At refreshment time the teacher asks the children, "What
do you want?" They are asked to answer with a sentence. Emphasizing
the vocabulary word *sentence* is the basis for future instruction that will
require the children to "Use the word in a sentence."

*Homemade Movies:* The teacher reads a familiar story such as "The
Three Pigs." The important scenes are drawn by different class members and the children arrange them in sequence. Next they are pasted
together (from left to right) on a roll of shelf paper. Two sticks are
placed through the sides of a box which is wide enough to hold the shelf
paper roll. The beginning of the roll is glued to the stick and the roll
is slipped on the bottom stick. The children take turns manipulating the
sticks so the class can view the movie. They take turns telling pieces of
the story as the pictures are presented.

*Puzzles:* One part is cut from each of ten pictures (back of a chair, handle
of a wagon, leg of a table). Both the picture and the parts are distributed
to the class members. "Who has the picture of the chair?" "What is missing?" "Who has the missing part?" The children answer in sentences.

A part from an animal cookie may be broken off, and the child who
can name the missing part receives the cookie.

*School Picture:* On a previously prepared ditto sketch of the school, the children draw stick figures to depict the correct number of classmates and teachers in their room.

## Basic Vocabulary (R-1)

| | | |
|---|---|---|
| beginning | leader | tablet |
| check | letter | tens |
| city | measure | tomorrow |
| company | oval | twelve o'clock |
| crescent | plant | twenty-one |
| cross | pocket chart | week |
| dictionary | question | weekly reader |
| dotted line | rectangle | weight |
| end | rhyming | when |
| factory | roll | word |
| fourth through tenth | salute | workbook |
| half-dollar | sentence | write |
| hour, half hour | shape | yesterday |
| inches | sound | 0 = zero |
| job | sounds | |

## Games, Stories, Songs, and Nursery Rhymes (R-1)

The teacher makes appropriate selections for this unit.

## Home Training Hints for Parents (R-1)

1. The parents make a height and weight chart of family members and discuss "Who is heaviest?" "Who is the tallest?"
2. Go for a walk with your children. Observe the neighbors' homes to learn the following: What materials are used to make the houses? Are the addresses the same? Where is the street name written? Who lives to the right of your home as you face it, and who lives to the right of it when you face the street?
3. Help a child select his "Show and Tell" object and assist him, in formulating descriptions: Who gave it to him? On what occasion? Its specific purpose. Does it run on batteries? Is it a game or is it an indoor or outdoor toy?
4. When parents are working on an activity at home which is designed to reinforce learning that has taken place at school, they should ask themselves three questions: (1) What did I do to secure interest in this activity? (2) What new thing did my child learn from this activity? (3) What did I do to encourage my child to talk about the activity?

5. To understand how children learn to talk and for games to play at home, read *Helping Children Talk Better* (112).

# READINESS LEVEL (R)

## Unit: Fall Season (R-2)

CLASSROOM ACTIVITIES

*Seeds:* Each child carries a paper sack on a field trip where he gathers acorns and other seed pods. After returning to the classroom, a discussion of the findings ensues. Then the children paste the items on a paper plate according to the teacher's directions or they create their own pattern. An adhesive picture hanger is placed on the back of the plate and the picture is taken home for mother.

*Nuts:* To teach number concepts, the teacher assumes the role of mother squirrel and the children pretend to be baby squirrels with paper nests and real nuts. Directions are given, "Baby Squirrel Darlene, place five nuts in your nest."

*Ditto Pictures:* Each child receives three dittoed pictures: a tree with green leaves, a night scene with Jack Frost painting the tree, and the tree with leaves falling to the ground. The teacher tells the story and the children place their pictures in sequence. Later they tell the story and then color their pictures.

*Fall Objects:* Ten fall objects such as a rake, a nut, a yellow leaf, and a pine cone are placed in a line on the table. As each child's name is called he finds the fifth object that is common to the fall season. Using a sentence he tells what he found and its numerical position: "The leaf was seventh."

*Berries:* The children bring a variety of frozen or fresh berries to school. (The parents decide in the group conference which berries will be brought by whom.) At refreshment time the children sample the different berries. Labels cut from the containers or made by the children are pasted on a chart according to where they grow: on a bush, or on a vine.

### Basic Vocabulary (R-2)

| | | |
|---|---|---|
| acorn | Jack Frost | seed |
| berries | pecans | seed pods |
| | rake | |

*Games, Stories, Songs, and Nursery Rhymes* (R-2)

The teacher makes appropriate selections for this unit.

*Home Training Hints for Parents* (R-2)

1. Take your children to the library and check out books related to fall activities.
2. Take walks around your yard or through the park to find fall grasses and seed pods for flower arrangements. Spray the delicate hairs found on some plants that have gone to seed with inexpensive spray net.
3. Allow your children to help you put away the summer clothes and decide which clothing will be needed for the fall season.

# READINESS LEVEL (R)

## Unit: Farm (R-3)

CLASSROOM ACTIVITIES

*Picture File:* The children learn to sort pictures of edible plants from nonedible plants.

*Beans:* Beans are placed in a flat dish with water. The children make daily observations to study how the beans crack and the sprouts emerge.

*Carrots and Radishes:* Select carrots and radishes which still have the green tops intact. Plant in a can of soil to demonstrate how they grow.

*Storybook:* After a trip to the bakery and retelling of the story of the bakery visit, the teacher reads the story of "The Little Red Hen." The children dramatize the story.

*Fruits and Vegetables:* During a field trip to the Farmer's Market, the children purchase fruits and vegetables to be brought back to the classroom. The next day they categorize the food according to whether it is eaten raw or if it is better cooked.

Field trips may also be made to a dairy farm, a chicken farm, a rodeo, and a fat stock show.

*Category Charts:* The children bring a wide variety of pictures of fruits, vegetables, milk products, and meat from home. They are pasted on appropriate charts. If there is a question as to whether the picture is a fruit or a vegetable, the teacher may introduce the dictionary and read the description to the class.

*Toy Farm Tools:* When the children recognize the farm tools by name, they engage in auditory memory drills; place the hoe against the door, give the rake to Susie, and take the shovel to your desk.

*Butter:* If a hand churn cannot be obtained, use a fruit jar to turn whipping cream to butter.

*Incubator:* Fertile eggs are purchased and placed in an incubator made from a cardboard carton and warmed by a light bulb. The children observe the hatching process.

*Cotton:* Using slides or an opaque projector, the teacher shows pictures of cotton fields and individual plants. Then she makes a large chart which represents a field. The children draw plants and glue bits of cotton to the pictures.

The teacher discusses the process required to make cloth from cotton and shows pictures or movies depicting the process.

## Unit: Rodeo (R-3)

*Plastic Animals:* The teacher presents a box of plastic animals and asks the children to place the zoo animals in the cage and farm animals inside a farm yard.

*Roll Call:* Cowboy language such as "Howdy, pardner," "Ride 'em cowboy," may be woven into the daily roll call.

*Rope:* Use a soft cotton rope to "rope and tie" a chair for the calf.

*Brands:* Let children see a variety of brands and how they are constructed. Then help them design their own brand from their initials.

### Basic Vocabulary (R-3)

| | | |
|---|---|---|
| above | farm | lift |
| apricot | farmer | lime |
| barn | flour | machine |
| below | gather (harvest) | milk (verb) |
| "bring in the crops" | goat | mud |
| bush | goose | nylon |
| calf | grind | orchard |
| chop | grow | pasture |
| colt | hatch | pen |
| corn | hen | pick-up truck |
| cotton | hen house | plum |
| creamery | hoe | raise |
| dairy | kill | rice |
| dress | lamb | rooster |

| roots | *Rodeo* | jeep |
|-------|---------|------|
| stem | barrel | lasso (rope) |
| tractor | bull-dog (verb) | leather |
| vine | calf-scramble | ranch |
| weeds | chaps | saddle |
| well | corral | sheared |
| wheat | cowboy | skin |
| wool | hide | steer |

*Games, Stories, Songs, and Nursery Rhymes* (R-3)

The teacher makes appropriate selections for this unit.

*Home Training Hints for Parents* (R-3)

**FARM**

1. The children should develop the concept that a farm is a large place where certain animals and crops are raised. You can help teach this concept by setting up a farm scene in a sand box with a commercial farm set or by constructing one from boxes and pipe cleaners or clay animals. Let him play with the set by telling you where each animal belongs; in the pen, in the pasture, in the chicken house, in the barn.
2. Try to visit a farm, (if this is not possible, at least slow down if you pass a farm on the highway). Discuss the animals: what they eat, what product they give the farmer, relative size to other animals, noise they make. Discuss the crops: what can be made from each crop, when it is planted, when it is harvested.
3. Let him go to the grocery store with you occasionally. Name foods you seldom buy (fresh asparagus, artichokes, etc.) and show him what part of the plant you eat. Discuss whether you eat it raw or cooked. Point out fruits and vegetables. Ask him to classify one that you point out as to whether it is a fruit or a vegetable. When you are preparing food, discuss what part of the plants you eat and which part you discard. Talk about the meat you serve. Discuss what animal it is from.

**RODEO**

1. Discuss the events you will see before you attend the Rodeo. Talk about the timed activities; the winner will be the fastest person.
2. Discuss the calf-scramble. Try to teach the concept that the calves were donated; the boy will feed it until it is ready to sell, etc.
3. Talk about the winners of the Fat Stock Show. They win Blue Ribbons. Relate them to medals, loving cups, prizes, etc., won at other contests.

# READINESS LEVEL (R)

## Unit: Halloween (R-4)

CLASSROOM ACTIVITIES

*Disguise Kit:* Make a simple disguise kit: eye glasses out of 2 paper circles; black paper moustache; brown paper eyebrows; white paper teeth; triangle for a nose (folded in half to make a point), and an old hat. Disguise each child differently. Teach different ways to disguise who they are.

*Song:* Children can sing a song for Halloween such as "The Old Witch in the Sky" to the tune of "Farmer in the Dell" with verses such as "The witch takes a goblin," etc. Pictures of Halloween figures can be pinned on the children while they play this game.

*Musical Chairs:* Place different Halloween pictures on the floor. The teacher has matching pictures in a box. The children walk around the pictures while the music is on. When it stops, the children see if they are standing on the picture that the teacher has drawn. If they are, they make up a full sentence to describe the picture.

*Halloween Items:* Have eight Halloween objects such as a shaker, jack-o'-lantern, black cat, witch, hobo, pirate, fairy, and devil on the table where the children are sitting. Place a matching set on another table in back of the room. Show each child 3 objects that you want him to find on the table in the back of the room.

*Neighborhood Map:* Each child is assigned to bring in a map of his own neighborhood and talk about where he will go trick or treating by using such phrases as: across the street, 2 blocks away, next door, and opposite corner.

## Games, Stories, Songs, and Nursery Rhymes (R-4)

The teacher makes appropriate selections for this unit.

## Home Training Hints for Parents (R-4)

1. Prepare a chart (made out of the top of a very large box) of things that can be gathered in a Halloween bag. Pictures or the exact object may be taped to the chart. When all the items are placed on the chart, present the language for flavors: fruit, mint, chocolate, sour,

etc. When trick or treat night has passed, check the contents of his sack against the items on the chart.

2. Work out some kind of trick to be played on a family that may not want to treat: place leaves behind the screen door or a tin can on the doorstep. Let your child practice some tricks on his own family before going out to trick or treat others. Discuss the types of tricks that are bad, dangerous, or destructive. The day after Halloween, drive around your neighborhood and past a few stores to see what types of tricks have been played and let the child classify them in terms of good and bad.

3. Let your child decorate his room with items appropriate for Halloween. These may be things he made at school, at home, or bought at the store. Help him make up a sequence story about a ghost or skeleton which he can tell to some other member of the family, or invite other children into his room for story telling time.

# READINESS LEVEL (R)

## Unit: Thanksgiving (R-5)

CLASSROOM ACTIVITIES

*Opaque Projector:* Introduce the Thanksgiving unit by showing pictures on the opaque projector and reading books about the Pilgrims and Indians. Find out what the children know about it and proceed from there. Discuss the planting of the corn, harvest, the friendliness of the Indian, and why the Pilgrims wanted to "give thanks."

*Crepe Paper:* Act out the first Thanksgiving with simple crepe paper hats and costumes. The parents or younger children might be invited to see your performance.

*Chart:* Make a chart of things "we are thankful for." Encourage each child to add a sentence which is different. Use this as the Thanksgiving prayer. Duplicate it for the children to take home in an appropriate cover for a Thanksgiving card to his parents. He will be able to "read" it to them because of the repetition in class.

*TV Dinners:* Plan to have a Thanksgiving dinner at school. TV dinners featuring turkey and dressing can be bought by each mother and warmed at the home of one mother. Have each child bring one different piece of fruit to go in the cornucopia for the centerpiece. The children prepare in advance for the dinner by making the placemats and place cards, folding the napkins, and making a favor for the table. It might be a Pilgrim or Indian made from pipe cleaners, or paper dolls cut out and glued to clothes pins so they will stand up.

*Centerpiece:* On the day of the dinner party the children set the table with their art work and arrange the fruit for the centerpiece. The Thanksgiving prayer previously worked on can be said from memory with each child providing a different sentence of what "I am thankful for." As they eat, discuss what they are eating and encourage them to use the good table manners that they have practiced in class.

At the end of the meal, have a "tasting party" with the fruit. Pass each piece of fruit so that the children can discuss if the skin is "rough or smooth," if it should be peeled before eating, the color of the outside and inside, a guess as to the size of the seeds. Cut small portions of the fruit to be put on a paper plate and passed for tasting (or just feeling if the child does not want to taste it). Examine the seeds and save them to make a seed chart for use in the room the following week.

### Basic Vocabulary (R-5)

| | |
|---|---|
| grateful | sharing |
| Pilgrim | Thanksgiving |

### Games, Stories, Songs, and Nursery Rhymes (R-5)

The teacher makes appropriate selections for this unit.

### Home Training Hints for Parents (R-5)

1. Let your child go through magazines to find pictures of things for which he can be thankful. Suggest things such as furniture, food, clothing, toys. Paste these things on a chart.
2. Send a note to the teacher a week before Thanksgiving stating your plans for the Thanksgiving season which your child will tell at a special "Show and Tell" time. The note should include: how far you will travel for Thanksgiving dinner (or will be staying at home), who and how many people will be there, manners to be used, clothing to be worn, time of day when dinner will be eaten, and events to take place after dinner, if known.
3. When you are driving to and from school, have the child locate sign boards appropriate for the Thanksgiving season.
4. While watching television, let the child see some of the Christmas parades which are televised on Thanksgiving Day. Be sure to in-

corporate new vocabulary for him such as float, twirlers, costume, balloons, etc.

# READINESS LEVEL (R)

## Unit: Christmas (R-6)

CLASSROOM ACTIVITIES

*Evergreen Needles:* A field trip can be taken which will focus on securing needles from several different evergreen trees. On a ditto page with a tree, the children tape various types of needles taken from the trees.

*Ditto Pages:* Prepare a ditto page which shows objects of various sizes and shapes on the left side and various sizes and shapes of boxes on the other. The children draw lines from the object to the box that would hold it appropriately.

There may be a page for matching names and addresses.

*Picture Story:* The children make up a story from pictures: Visiting Santa, Going to the Post Office, Buying Presents for Friends.

*Song Book:* All new Christmas songs should be presented in picture form with words added below the pictures. Make these into a Christmas songbook.

*Christmas Pictures:* Outline any item from a regular Christmas coloring book with liquid glue then sprinkle colored glitter over the outlined areas.

*Holiday Notebook:* Prepare several Christmas ditto pictures; number the pages, and give each child the pages in random order. After he has numerically arranged them, explain that this book is for him to color and enjoy over the holiday period.

*Gift Purchase:* Use the day you visit Santa as a time to purchase a special present for grandmother, an aunt, cousin, or even baby sitter. Mothers discuss in advance what Aunt Betty likes to do best in the kitchen and what she might need. The children bring $1.00 to school and all go shopping for their own gift. Each child watches the others purchase, listens to his reasons for it, and then observes how he gets change. This should be a teacher directed and controlled activity since many things may be unfamiliar to the children. Parents help the child wrap, tie, seal, and deliver the gift.

*Christmas Tree:* The Christmas tree for this age group should not be purchased by the mothers but picked out and brought to school by the class. Discussion includes: how full this one is, this one has a flat side, this one is too dry, etc. When the selection has been narrowed down to two trees, then the class must vote for the one tree to be used at school.

*Decorations:* The children make all decorations for the school tree. Included are stars, paper cup bells, popcorn, and cranberry strings. The decorations are taken home after the party to be used on a tree in the child's play room.

*Construction Paper Santa:* Build a Santa, part by part. Introduce each segment as a clue to the Surprise Visitor. Start with boots, then legs, tummy, arms, hands, chest, and finally, head. Precede each new part with this poem:

> Tromp, tromp, tromp
> I hear a fellow coming.
> Clomp, clomp, clomp
> He's heavy as can be.
> Tramp, tramp, tramp
> You can soon begin your guessing.
> Bump, bump, bump
> Don't tell! Just wait and see!

### Basic Vocabulary (R-6)

| | |
|---|---|
| carol | pageant |
| hearth | spangle |
| toll | |

### Games, Stories, Songs, and Nursery Rhymes (R-6)

The teacher makes appropriate selections for this unit.

### Home Training Hints for Parents (R-6)

1. The children send Christmas cards to each other. You will need to supply the teacher with the requested envelopes, stamps and cards. Do not try to pick out the card for the child. Let him go into the store with you and choose the ones which he would most likely want to send to his friends. Select cards which are sold singly rather than boxed.
2. Help your child prepare for the holiday season by decorating his own room. Supply him with the materials which he might use and let him decide where to place the decorations. These decorations should not be ones which break easily or are of much value since your child may spend much of the holiday time decorating and undecorating his room. Include: a Christmas tree which can be a limb from your own tree, a place to mount or hang his own Christmas cards, a box of Christmas tree decorations, and a large box of scrap materials which can be

colored, cut, pasted or torn apart for the special gifts he may want to make for his family.

3. Let your child assume the responsibility for decorating and supplying a Christmas tree in the yard for the birds, small animal friends or his pet. He should keep this tree supplied with crackers, seeds, bread and water. Remind him about the weather for the day and how it may affect his friends' ability to find food.

4. Set aside some time for special Christmas baking when your child can help you. While baking cookies, let him help decorate. When friends drop by, he serves his cookies to his friends in his room while the "grown-ups" are entertained in another area of the house. Keep a supply of paper cups, napkins, and plates for him to use for serving his guests.

5. At the beginning of December, mother and child can remove toys from his toy chest, drawers, or closet and decide which ones are broken beyond repair, which ones he would like to give to poor children, and those he would like to keep. The toys to be given away are boxed and taken to the Fire Department, a church, etc. Deliver the toys in person so that your child grasps the meaning of sharing before entering the Christmas season.

6. Basic instruction of your particular religion may begin at this level. Secure printed information from your church office to be used for daily reference or story telling.

7. A number of small inexpensive Christmas story books are published and available at Christmas. Purchase a few of these and set aside reading time during vacation. Be sure to emphasize the work he has had in phonics, number concepts, and vocabulary. Many times you can read a book without looking at the written text but rather making up a story to fit the picture. Choose a book for this purpose and let the child create the story.

8. Allow your child to help with gift wrapping. Give him a box similar to yours and one that is simple to wrap. As you fold the paper around your box, he imitates. When you fold the ends over, do so a step at a time, or do two things and wait for him to catch up. When the package is wrapped, decorate it without the use of ribbon, but rather by using assorted flowers, glitter, colored tape, etc. He labels his package by copying the appropriate name.

9. Prepare a calendar at home which will designate the following: school Christmas party, church parties, nights when the child will have a baby sitter, day the tree will be purchased, time when the tree will be decorated, time when he can go shopping with mother for daddy's present, or vice versa. Children who are celebrating Chanukah can use their calendar for identifying the day that starts the season, and how many candles to be lit on the pertinent days.

# READINESS LEVEL (R)

## Unit: Winter (R-7)

CLASSROOM ACTIVITIES

*Snowflakes:* The children fold and cut paper to make lacy snowflakes to hang in the room.

*Picture File:* The teacher uses a set of winter pictures such as skis, sled, skate, and another set of rhyming pictures. As the teacher holds up a picture of a *ski* the child finds the picture of a *bee*.

*Map:* Using a simple map of the United States, the teacher divides it into North, East, South, West. Each day an aspect of winter in different parts of the country is discussed and pictures are appropriately pasted on the map (a winter scene or winter clothing for the North, boating in the South, etc.).

*Creative Dramatics:* A play can be organized by giving each child a picture of what he is to be: a tree laden with snow, an ice skater, a skier, a rock, etc.

*Thermometer:* A large ditto thermometer is hung on the wall. Each day the temperature is observed on an outdoor thermometer and the children decide if the weather is above or below freezing. The teacher uses a variety of colored lines on the ditto sheet to indicate the daily change in weather.

### Basic Vocabulary (R-7)

Refer to Kindergarten, Pre-Kindergarten, and Beginning Level Units.

### Games, Stories, Songs, and Nursery Rhymes (R-7)

The teacher makes appropriate selections for this unit.

### Home Training Hints for Parents (R-7)

1. On a typical winter day take your children on a tour around the yard and show them what happens to the flowers, trees, and grass in the winter. Discuss winter weather in colder and warmer climates.
2. Consult the weather report in the morning newspaper. Talk about the temperature expected and appropriate clothing that can be worn that day. Make comments such as "It will be 40° today." These comments will introduce the concept that higher numbers mean warmer weather.

# READINESS LEVEL (R)

## Unit: Valentine (R-8)

CLASSROOM ACTIVITIES

*Hearts:* Each child traces around various sized hearts and cuts them out. From a variety of patterns (man, animals, flowers) the children choose one and copy it.

*Mosaic:* A mosaic heart is made from drinking straws. The children cut the straws into short lengths and glue them inside a heart that has been drawn on heavy paper.

*Candy Hearts:* The children paste candy hearts on paper to form a number configuration which the teacher has drawn on the blackboard.

*Potato:* Carve a heart shape in a potato as you would a linoleum block print. Dip the potato in tempera paint and stamp heart designs on paper. Let the children elaborate by adding stems to produce flowers, seaweed to make an underwater scene, or arms and legs to make a man.

*Valentine Box:* Each child brings a decorated shoe box with a slot in the cover. The teacher provides a large decorated box to serve as a central mail box where the children deposit their valentines. One child who is postman retrieves the valentines from the central office, another child assists in sorting them into the children's shoe boxes. A third child may deliver these boxes to the appropriate children.

### Games, Stories, Songs, and Nursery Rhymes (R-8)

The teacher makes appropriate selections for this unit.

### Home Training Hints for Parents (R-8)

1. Help your child copy on an envelope the name of a sick school or neighborhood friend. Place a homemade or store bought card in the envelope and have the child deliver it.
2. Purchase a box of valentines well in advance of the party day. Each day choose two or three and read the verse helping the child interpret the humor in the written lines. Let them make up simple stories about the pictures on the card or to whom it will be given.
3. Send valentines to grandparents and let your child sign them personally.
4. Through observation of the advertising in magazines and on bill boards, help your child see what colors are associated with Valentine's

Day. For example, black and orange belong to Halloween while red and white are valentine colors. The child can choose clothing appropriate to wear to the party in terms of color combinations.

# READINESS LEVEL (R)

## Unit: Spring (R-9)

**CLASSROOM ACTIVITIES**

*Picture File:* A beautiful sunshiny spring day is a good time to talk about signs of spring that can be seen from the window. Show pictures of winter and spring with the opaque projector. Point out differences in the trees, grass, games to play, holidays, and clothing to be worn in the spring as opposed to winter.

*Spring Chart:* Make a spring chart as a group activity. Each child brings a recent issue of a magazine and cuts out pictures which illustrate spring. Before pasting a picture on the chart, he must answer the question, "Why does this picture represent spring?"

*Windy Day:* On the blackboard illustrate the effects of wind on several different objects. Then the children look out the window to observe the things illustrated on the board.

*Seeds:* The children make flower or vegetable gardens at home and bring some of the seed they have planted to school. A seed chart (using transparent tape) is made to illustrate categories of seeds.

*Butterfly:* The Kindergraph workbook (66, p. 37) has a large butterfly which can be cut, painted on both sides, and hung by string from the ceiling of the classroom. The metamorphosis of the butterfly is discussed.

### Basic Vocabulary (R-9)

See Kindergarten, Pre-Kindergarten, and Beginning Level Spring Units.

| | |
|---|---|
| bloom | cocoon |
| bud | tad poles |
| worms | |

### Games, Stories, Songs, and Nursery Rhymes (R-9)

The teacher makes appropriate selections for this unit.

*Home Training Hints for Parents* (R-9)

1. The concept that spring reawakens with new life in trees, flowers, grass, and animals can be emphasized.
2. As you talk about animals and birds, discuss how they are born.
3. Let the children have a flower garden even if it is just a pot. Show them how to plant the seeds, and discuss the need of water and sun for growth.
4. Be sure to talk about weather when the day is hazy, overcast, foggy, drizzling rain, windy, or stormy. Talk about wind and its benefits: dries the clothes, flies the kite, turns the windmills, and carries seeds.
5. Show the children nesting places for birds. Talk about the role of the mother and father bird; how each kind of bird makes a different nest, how the birds keep cats away from their baby birds, and how the mother bird teaches her babies to fly.
6. Many seasonal and science concepts can be taught to your child by activities suggested in workbooks such as *Do You Know* (116).

# READINESS LEVEL (R)

## Unit: Easter (R-10)

**CLASSROOM ACTIVITIES**

*Easter Parade:* Ask mothers to help their children create some type of special Easter bonnet to wear in the school Easter parade. Encourage the use of vivid imagination in the creation of the hat. It should be one that utilizes flowers, lace, straw, grass, etc. The teacher gives prizes to each child: the tallest ears, the biggest hat, the most colorful hat, the tiniest one.

*Cardboard Rabbit:* As a group project, the class can make and decorate from cardboard a life-sized rabbit to be used for a ring-throwing game. Each child is given 5 fruit jar rings to throw over the rabbit's ears. After the game, discuss who has the "most" or "least" points.

*Plastic Eggs:* The children hide plastic Easter eggs in the room. Two and three sequence directions are given such as "Hide the blue egg behind the record player, and hide the white one under the table." Similar directions are given when searching for the eggs.

*Decorated Eggs:* Compare two decorated Easter eggs, stressing the questions, "How are they alike?" and "How are they different?"

*Stained Glass Window:* Make stained glass windows by shredding wax crayon on a piece of wax paper. Fold over and iron so that the crayon melts. Cut a church window from black paper and insert the "stained glass window."

### Basic Vocabulary (R-10)

| | |
|---|---|
| egg white | stained glass |
| egg yolk | symbol |

### Games, Stories, Songs, and Nursery Rhymes (R-10)

The teacher makes appropriate selections for this unit.

### Home Training Hints for Parents (R-10)

1. Plan a week of menus which will utilize eggs in unrecognizable form (custard, cake, etc.). Have your child assist in the preparation.
2. Decorate a branch with Easter symbols.
3. Prepare for Easter Sunday by discussing where you will go and what will be expected of the child while he is there.
4. Take your child to your garden or to some garden center prior to Easter and "predict" which plants will be blossoming by Easter.
5. Point out all signs of springtime growth such as budding trees, grass turning green, buds on vines or bushes.

# READINESS LEVEL (R)

## Unit: Safety (R-11)

**CLASSROOM ACTIVITIES**

*Construction Paper Streets:* Each child is given a piece of construction paper on which he will draw straight lines that will resemble streets. Each child has a car and drives it on his paper (streets) according to the directions of one child who portrays the policeman. "Go to the right." "Go to the left." "Stop." "Go up hill."

*Film Strip:* One of Walt Disney's public school film strips presents Jiminy Cricket riding a bicycle correctly and incorrectly.

*Chart:* Prepare a safety chart using written words or stick figures. Safety rules include: pick up broken glass and place in a trash can; do not run with a candy stick in your mouth.

*Traffic Lights:* Make a city traffic light from construction paper and place on an imaginary street in the classroom. Thumbtack an arrow to the light in such a manner that it will indicate a left and right turn as well as straight ahead. One child being policeman directs the traffic (the class) by manipulating the arrow.

*Highway Signs:* Teach form recognition with highway road mark signs. The children copy them on the blackboard or on paper.

*Book:* "Mr. Pine's Mixed Up Signs." (64) is the story of a sign maker who becomes confused. The majority of the signs in the book are those which are found on roads and highways.

*Notebook:* The children make their own notebook of schoolground safety by drawing stick figures. New figures are added when a new safety rule has been experienced.

*Tongue Depressors:* Each child makes his own set of schoolground or highway safety signals by pasting appropriate paper signs on tongue depressors.

*Sacks:* The children, each carrying a paper sack, tour the playground to locate and pick up harmful objects. A discussion follows as to why they are harmful.

*School Tools:* The teacher demonstrates an unwise activity such as holding the scissors by the cutting edge. A child is selected to correct the error through a demonstration of how scissors should be carried.

### Basic Vocabulary (R-11)

| | | |
|---|---|---|
| bicycle | flat | rule |
| blunt | handlebars | safe |
| brakes | lane | safety |
| buddy | lost | shallow |
| chain | luggage rack | sharp |
| corner | pedestrian | shock |
| disturb | plugs | spoke |
| dive | points | stand |
| electricity | reach | strangers |
| emergency | rubber | traffic |

### Games, Stories, Songs, and Nursery Rhymes (R-11)

The teacher makes appropriate selections for this unit.

### Home Training Hints for Parents (R-11)

1. Help your children see the reason for good safety rules at home, in school, and while playing. Point out what happens when the bathroom floor gets wet. Show them how toys left in the middle of the floor may cause someone to be injured.

2. Demonstrate the use of seat belts in the car and show the children how to use these without getting their fingers pinched. Discuss behavior in the car such as standing, being off balance, or being on the edge of the seat.
3. When the children are watching TV, make it a point to bring safety rules to a conscious level (insurance company commercials or American Safety Council programs).
4. Many local police departments offer bicycle inspections which include license plates for the bike and ownership cards for the children. Accompany your child and bring his bike for such an inspection.
5. Take your child on a tour of your home to observe electrical outlets and their plug guards.
6. Discuss safety with strangers: the man who stops his car to ask a question, the person ringing the doorbell when mother is in the shower.

# READINESS LEVEL (R)

## Unit: Summer (R-12)

CLASSROOM ACTIVITIES

*Vacations:* Summer as a season can be taught the last month of your school year, either May or June, and introduced as the vacation months. Discuss forthcoming trips that the class members and their parents are planning. Show pictures and talk about the games and various recreational activities that the children will enjoy in the summer.

*Opaque Projector:* Use the opaque projector to show pictures of summer on the farm, yards with summer flowers in bloom, clothing for the summer, trees with the full green foliage. Contrast them with the winter, spring, and fall scenes.

*Picture File:* Use this unit to sum up the four seasons. Use a symbolic picture of an apple tree to depict all four seasons: without leaves for winter, with blossoms for spring, green leaves for summer, and apples for fall. All accumulated season pictures are sorted appropriately by the children.

*Calendar Months:* The four seasonal pictures of your tree (or whatever you choose for your symbolic pictures of the seasons) are used for the categories: fall, winter, spring, and summer. Pictures, objects, or the children's birthdates (use their name cards) are placed under the appropriate season.

*Objects:* Place objects depicting holidays in appropriate season labeled boxes.

*Basic Vocabulary* (R-12)

See Pre-Kindergarten, Kindergarten, and Beginning Language Units.

*Games, Stories, Songs, and Nursery Rhymes* (R-12)

The teacher makes appropriate selections for this unit.

*Home Training Hints for Parents* (R-12)

1. Keep an experience book or diary before a trip. Write in it before you go, write in it when you come back, but let the children supply sentences.
2. Visit the library every two weeks. Choose books you want to read to your children and allow them to choose books.
3. Visit the fire station, post office, bank, airport, train station, etc.
4. Take a short train trip. Have another mother drive to the nearest town where the train stops and pick you up.
5. Take a bus trip to a small town close by. Have someone meet you. Walk through the little town.
6. Ride a ferry if one is in your area. You'll see the light house, islands, ships, docks, harbors, etc.
7. Buy food at the farmer's market.
8. Visit the Natural Science Museum and the Museum of Fine Arts.
9. Ask about recreation classes at city parks. Enroll your child if a suitable class is available.

# READINESS LEVEL (R)

## Unit: Birthday Party (R-13)

**CLASSROOM ACTIVITIES**

*Birthday Cake:* Draw a picture of a birthday cake, with the appropriate number of candles. At the beginning of the school year use these pictures for the birthday list, and write each child's initials and birthdate on his cake. Each child on his birthday places his picture on the bulletin board with other special interest objects for that month.

*Height and Weight Chart:* Keep a chart of each child's height and weight throughout the year. As a child's birthday approaches, weigh and measure him. Discuss how much taller he is, and how much he has gained or lost since school started.

*Party:* The birthday child and his mother have the complete responsibility for planning the one hour birthday party in the classroom. The mother plans at least one game and comes into the room to take charge of it and the refreshments. A few days before the party, the birthday child gives his invitations to his classmates.

Party favors may include the following:

*Nut Cups.* The birthday child traces a pattern of an animal, toy, etc., cuts out the figures, and pastes or tapes them to cup cake liners. He fills the cups with nuts or candy and presents them as favors.

*Pin Wheels.* Stick a pinwheel made from a square of paper to the eraser of an unsharpened pencil.

*Felt Pins.* The birthday child cuts figures from felt (for example, a star, an animal, a flower). Mother sews a safety pin on the back of each and the children wear them as lapel pins at the party.

Each child in the class brings the birthday child a gift not to exceed 10¢. A discussion of appropriate gifts for this sum of money precedes the purchase. The child shops for or makes his own gift, wraps it, and addresses the birthday card. The children should be encouraged to make gifts at home such as a crayon can made from an empty tin can trimmed with rickrack and felt cut-outs, then filled with crayons and wrapped.

The child presenting the gift gives "clues" as to what it is. The one who guesses is next in turn to present his gift.

### Basic Vocabulary (R-13)

See Pre-Kindergarten, Kindergarten, and Beginning Level Units.

### Games, Stories, Songs, and Nursery Rhymes (R-13)

The teacher makes appropriate selections for this unit.

### Home Training Hints for Parents (R-13)

1. Since mothers have the responsibility for planning the child's birthday party at school, much teaching can be accomplished at home. The child assists in constructing party favors, nut cups and center piece, all related to a prechosen theme. Vocabulary and sentence structure as well as number concepts are stressed during the preparation of cake, cookies, etc.

2. When a relative's or friend's birthday is near, allow the child to take a specific sum of money to the store, select an appropriate card, purchase it, and return to the car without your help. Help him address it and have him deposit it in the mail box.

3. Discuss the people whose birthdays have been declared National Holi-days, such as Washington and Lincoln.

4. When a child is notified by invitation that he is invited to a birthday party, help him plan for the part he will play at the party. If the type of party is known, mother should discuss clothing he should wear, the selection of the gift, and manners. Some of the best gifts are those which the child makes, especially if it is for an older person or member of the family.

*Appendix*

## QUESTIONNAIRE FOR PARENTS

Date ...................................................
Child's name ............................... Birthdate ......................... Case No. ..............
Information given by ................................... Relationship ..............................
What do you feel is the child's problem? ..................................................

...................................................................................................................

Note: The following questions are asked so that we can better understand your child. Please read them carefully and answer as fully as possible. If you are not sure how to answer some of the questions, please tell us and we will discuss them. If you need more space, use the back of the sheet.

## SECTION I

1. Is mother Rh negative?...........Did mother have any illnesses during her pregnancy with this child?...........Did mother have to stay in bed?...........
Take medications (other than vitamins)?...........Almost have a miscarriage?...........If yes to any of these, explain ..............................................

   .................................................................................................................
   Has mother had previous miscarriages?...........
2. Was labor very long or especially short?...........If yes, estimate time...........
Was the birth of this child normal?...........If not, explain.....................

   .................................................................................................................
   How much did child weigh?...........
3. Did child have any trouble breathing after birth?...........Was child kept in an incubator or airlock over 12 hours?...........Why?.............................
Did child look blue or yellow after birth?...........For how long?...........
Did child come home from hospital with the mother?...........If not, why?...........
4. Is child adopted?...........How old was he when he was adopted?...........

## SECTION II

1. At what age did child sit alone?...........Crawl?...........Walk by himself?
...........Was child very active as a baby?...........
2. Was feeding the child a problem?...........Why?...................................
When was he taken off the bottle?...........Was weaning a problem?...........
3. Is child a "picky" or fussy eater now?...........Does he seem to have any trouble swallowing?...........Chewing?...........Will he eat meat, caramels, etc?...........Does child eat with a spoon?...........Fork?...........Both?...........
Is he messy?...........Can he spread butter?...........Cut his own meat?...........

4. Was toilet training a problem?...........When was child completely trained? ...........Does child wet the bed at night now?..........How frequently?...... ......Does child wet or soil himself during the day?...........How often? ............

5. Does child dress himself completely?...........Partially?...........Does he completely undress himself?...........Partially?...........Does he button?...........Tie shoes?...........

6. Does child fall frequently?...........How well can he climb?...........Throw a ball?...........Hit a ball?...........Ride a trike?...........Ride a two wheel bike?...........Run?...........

7. Which hand does child use to eat with?...........Draw or write?........... Throw a ball?...........

## SECTION III

1. Has child been back in the hospital since birth?...........If so, explain (operations, accidents, etc.) and give his age at the time........................ .................................................................................................................. ..................................................................................................................

2. Has child had other serious illnesses?...........If so, describe........................ ..................................................................................................................

3. Has child ever fainted or passed out?...........Has he ever had a convulsion?...........How many?...........Describe.................................................... ..................................................................................................................

4. Does child complain of frequent headaches, stomachaches, leg cramps? ..................

5. Does child have any problem hearing?...........Has he had ear infections, running ears, ears lanced?...........If so, explain.......................................... .................................................................................................................. Has he ever worn a hearing aid?...........

6. Does child see normally?...........Does he have glasses?...........

7. Is child allergic?...................................................................................................

8. Does child take any medicine regularly except vitamins?...........Why?...... ..................................................................................................................

9. Has child been seen by a neurologist?...........Psychologist?...........Had an EEG?...........Has his speech or hearing been tested before now?........... Has child had training in a speech, hearing, and language center?...........

## SECTION IV

1. Was child very quiet as a baby (did not babble and coo as much as most babies)?...........Did he cry excessively?...........

2. How old was child when he began to say words?...........How old was child when he began putting 2 or 3 words together in a phrase?............
3. How much does child talk now?.................................................................
4. How much of this speech can mother understand? All.........Most...........
   Some...........How much can other adults understand? All...........Most...........
   Some............None............
5. How much does child use gesture to help others understand?............
6. Has child learned to say nursery rhymes?............Prayers?............Sing songs?
   .............
7. Do parents feel child stutters or stammers?.....................................................
8. Does child's voice sound like other children's voices?............If no, describe.
   Very soft...........Very loud...........Hoarse...........Nasal...........Other............
9. Have parents done anything to help child with his speech?...........If so, explain...........................................................................................................

## SECTION V

1. Did child attend Nursery School?...........Kindergarten............Did he have any problems in Nursery School or Kindergarten?...........If so, explain.
   ..............................................................................................................
2. What grade is child in at present?...........Has he repeated any grades?
   ...........Which grades?...........What grade is he now making in reading?
   ...........Spelling...........Arithmetic...........Writing...........Conduct............
3. Does child like to go to school?...........Does he seem to have many friends at school?...........Does he seem to remember school assignments?
   ...........Can he follow directions in school?............

## SECTION VI

1. Below is a list of words which describe children's personality and behavior. Please circle those which you feel tend to describe your child.

| | | | |
|---|---|---|---|
| sad | leader | happy | follower |
| moody | quiet | even tempered | very active |
| friendly | independent | prefers to be alone | dependent |
| hard to discipline | | has trouble sleeping | |
| has temper tantrums | | is unusually fearful | |
| how often?............ | | | |
| affectionate | | sucks thumb | |

2. Describe any behavior which is a problem to parents...............................
   ..............................................................................................................
   ..............................................................................................................

3. Does child enjoy books (being read to or reading)?...........
Does he like to watch TV?...........For how long?...........
4. What are child's favorite activities?.........................................................
............................................................................................................................
............................................................................................................................
5. How well does child play alone?...........With younger children?.........
With children his own age?...........With older children?...........With his
brothers and sisters?...........

## SECTION VII

1. Are parents now separated?...........Divorced?...........If so, how old was
child when this occured?...........Has either parent been married previously?
...........Which one?...........Is either parent deceased?...........
2. Father's occupation .......................................................................................
Father's level of education ...........................................................................
Mother's occupation .......................................................................................
Mother's level of education .........................................................................
If mother works, who takes care of child?................................................
How old was child when mother went to work? .....................................
3. Give name and ages of other children in the family..............................
............................................................................................................................
4. Are there persons living in the home other than the parents and chil-
dren?...........Who?.........................................................................................
5. Is any language other than English spoken at home?.............................
6. Are there relatives, on either side of the family, who have had:
   Trouble speaking clearly or who have been late to learn to talk?...........
   Trouble with their hearing?...........
   Trouble learning in school so that they left school or failed several
      grades, or who have had real trouble learning to read?...........
   Problems like epilepsy, mental retardation, cerebral palsy, etc?...........
If so, describe the problem..............................................................................
............................................................................................................................
............................................................................................................................

## GENERAL CASE HISTORY FORM

Name ................................................
Birth date ........................................
Date of Interview ............................

Case Number ....................................
Examiner ..........................................
Informant ........................................
Reliability ........................................

Chief Complaint:

---

Key: (+)  significant
     (-)  not significant
     (?)  lack of information

### BIRTH HISTORY
Previous pregnancies
Miscarriages
Mother's health, attitude
Rh problems, other
Gestation period
Labor
Delivery
Birth weight
Trouble breathing, sucking
Cyanosis, jaundice
Oxygen

### MOTOR DEVELOPMENT
Sat alone
Crawled
Fine and gross motor coordination
Feeding, sucking, chewing
Drooling
Self-help skills
Toilet Training
Enuresis
Handedness

### MEDICAL HISTORY
Convulsions
Convulsive equivalents
Fever
Childhood diseases

Cerebral disease, meningitis, poisoning
Other cerebral problems
Glandular disturbances
Excessive sweating
Allergies
Drug Therapy
Tonsils, adenoids, palate
Otological-audition problems
Vision
Operations
Accidents
Congenital deformities, dysplasias
Amputations
Name of physician(s)

### LANGUAGE
Comprehension
Jargon
Gestures
Echolalia
Perseveration
Onset of words
Current number of words
Onset of sentences
Examples of sentences
Child's awareness of problem
Previous assessments

Previous training

**SPEECH**
Loudness
Pitch
Rate
Rhythm-stress
Non fluencies
Oral mechanism, palate, tongue,
   jaw
% understood by parents
% understood by other adults
% understood by siblings
% understood by peers
Child's awareness of problem
Previous assessment
Previous training

**SCHOOLING**
Play school
Pre-academic
Academic
Grades failed
Achievement scores
Time spent at school
Attitude toward school
Name of teacher

**INTER-PERSONAL RELATIONSHIPS**
General disposition
Playmates and play habits
Parent-child relationships
Other adult relationships
In contact with environment
Discipline
Affectionate
Aggressive
Compulsive
Cries easily
Daydreamer
Fears

Hyperactive
Hypoactive
Jealousy
Leader or follower
Perservation
Sleep habits
Social perception
Tantrums
Psychological assessments
Psychological treatment
Psychiatric assessments
Psychiatric treatment

**FAMILY**
Parent's age, health
Parent's occupation
Parent's education
Parent's income
Marital status
Is child adopted
Siblings; age, health
Others in home; age, health
History of learning problems
   in family
Other problems
Language spoken in home
Transportation

**ADDITIONAL COMMENTS**

## LANGUAGE AND LEARNING ASSESSMENT: For Training
### Worksheet

Name.................................................

Date.................................................

Age .................................................

KEY:   + passed

        − failed

        0 did not attempt

        blank did not administer

---

### RECOGNIZING OBJECTS
*By Name*

........ 2   (2-0 or below)

........ 5   (2-0 or below)

........ 10  (2-0 to 2-6)

........

*By Function*

........ 9   (2-0 to 2-6)

........ 11  (2-6 to 3-0)

........ 14  (3-0 to 3-6)

### RECOGNIZING PICTURES
*By Name*

........ 1   (2-0 or below)

........ 3   (2-0 or below)

........ 6   (2-0 to 2-6)

........ 7   (2-0 to 2-6)

........ Ammons or Peabody

*By Function*

........ 17  (3-6 to 4-0)

........ 18  (3-6 to 4-0)

........ 20  (4-0 to 4-6)

### NAMING AND DEFINING
*Naming*

........ 27  Binet vocabulary

........ 28  (word combinations)

........ 29  (2-0 or below)

........ 30  (2-0 to 2-6)

........ 31  (2-0 to 2-6)

........ 32  (2-0 to 2-6 gives name)

........ 33  (2-6 to 3-0)

........ 37  (3-0 to 3-6)

........ 54  (4-6 to 5-0)

........ 55  (4-6 to 5-0)

*Action Agent*

........ 34  (2-6 to 3-0)

........ 35  (3-0 to 3-6)

........ 40  (3-6 to 4-0)

........ 44  (4-0 to 4-6)

........ 50  (4-6 to 5-0)

*Defining*

........ 36  (3-0 to 3-6)

........ 38  (3-0 to 3-6)

........ 39  (3-6 to 4-0)

........ 41  (4-0 to 4-6)

........ 46  (4-0 to 4-6)

........ 47  (4-0 to 4-6)

........ 48  (4-0 to 4-6)

........ 49  (4-0 to 4-6)

........ 51  (4-6 to 5-0)

........ 52  (4-6 to 5-0)

........ 60  (5-0 to 6-0)

........ 61  (5-0 to 6-0)

........ 69  (7-0 to 8-0)

........ 74  (9-0 to 10-0)

### CATEGORIZING
*Comprehension*

........   Pictorial Identification

........   Pictorial Association

**CATEGORIZING (Continued)**
.........         Pictorial Analogy
.........21    (4-0 to 4-6)
.........22    (4-0 to 4-6)
.........24    (4-6 to 5-0)
.........25    (4-6 to 5-0)

*Expression*
.........42    (3-6 to 4-0)
.........45    (4-0 to 4-6)
.........56    (5-0 to 6-0)
.........57    (5-0 to 6-0)
.........62    (6-0 to 7-0)
.........63    (6-0 to 7-0)
.........65    (6-0 to 7-0)
.........67    (7-0 to 8-0)
.........68    (7-0 to 8-0)
.........70    (8-0 to 9-0)
.........71    (8-0 to 9-0)
.........72    (8-0 to 9-0)
.........76    (9-0 to 10-0)

**NUMBERS**
*Comprehension*
.........23    (4-0 to 5-0)
.........26    (5-0 to 6-0)

*Expression*
.........43    (3-6 to 4-0)
.........53    (4-6 to 5-0)

.........59    (5-0 to 6-0)

**SPATIAL**
*Comprehension*
.........12    (2-6 to 3-0)
.........15    (3-0 to 3-6)
.........16    (3-0 to 3-6)
.........19    (4-0 to 4-6)

**SERIAL DIRECTIONS**
*Comprehension*
......... 4    (2-0 and below)
......... 8    (2-0 to 2-6)
.........13    (3-0 to 3-6)
.........Three commissions (4-6)

**SENTENCE BUILDING**
.........58    (5-0 to 6-0)
.........64    (6-0 to 7-0)
.........73    (8-0 to 9-0)

**MEMORY FOR STORIES**
.........66    (7-0 to 8-0)
.........77    (9-0 to 10-0)
.........75    (9-0 to 10-0)

**JARGON**
**ECHOLALIA**
**GESTURE**
**COMMENTS**

## LANGUAGE ASSESSMENT

*Scoring*

Sub-test items are scored according to the principles set forth in the Stanford-Binet Intelligence Scales (107, 108). In the Stanford-Binet, six items are included within each six months level and every correct item receives one month credit. (For example, six items correct at year 2-0 to 2-6 provides an M.A. of 2 years 6 months.)

The following language segments from the *Language and Learning Assessment: For Training* battery include several six month levels that contain less than six items. Prorating is necessary (Any credit of one-half month or greater is interpreted as one month.)

*Examples:*

5 items correct at 2-0 to 2-6, scores 5 and 4/5 months or the 2 year 6 month level.

2 items correct at 2-0 to 2-6, scores 2 and 2/5 months or the 2 year 2 month level.

The total months credited become the *Mental Age* for each segment, namely *Language Comprehension* and *Language Expression.*

### LANGUAGE COMPREHENSION

*Year 2-0 and below*
( 1) ....... 1. "Picture Cards" (43), pp. 217-220.
( 2) ....... 2. "Identifying Objects By Name" (108), p. 75.
( 3) ....... 3. "Identifying Parts Of the Body" (108), p. 76.
( 4) ....... 4. "Obeying Simple Commands" (107), p. 77.
( 5) ....... 5. "Identifying Objects By Name" (107), p. 135.
............... Months Credit.

*Year 2-0 to 2-6*
( 6) ....... 1. "Picture Identification" (43), pp. 217-220.
( 7) ....... 2. "Identifying Parts of the Body" (108), p. 70.
( 8) ....... 3. "Obeying Simple Commands" (108), p. 71.
( 9) ....... 4. "Identifying Objects By Use" (108), p. 69.
(10) ....... 5. "Identifying Objects By Name" (107), p. 80.
............... Months Credit.

*Year 2-6 to 3-0*
(11) ....... 1. "Identifying Objects By Use" (107), p. 140.
(12) ....... 2. "Discriminates Prepositions" (43), pp. 233-234.
............... Months Credit.

*Year 3-0 to 3-6*
(13) ....... 1. "Obeying Simple Commands" (107), p. 83.
(14) ....... 2. "Identifying Objects By Use" (107), p. 84.
(15) ....... 3. "Comparison of Sticks" (108), p. 76.
(16) ....... 4. "Comparison of Balls" (108), p. 74.
............... Months Credit.

*Year 3-6 to 4-0*
(17) ....... 1. "Pictorial Identification" (108), p. 77.
(18) ....... 2. "Pictorial Identification" (107), p. 146.
............... Months Credit.

*Year 4-0 to 4-6*
(19) ....... 1. "Discriminates Prepositions" (43), pp. 233-234.
(20) ....... 2. "Pictorial Identification" (108), p. 80.
(21) ....... 3. "Aesthetic Comparison" (108), p. 79.
(22) ....... 4. "Pictorial Similarities and Differences I" (108), p. 79.
............... Months Credit.

*Year 4-6 to 5-0*
(23) ....... 1. "Number Concept of Three." (107), p. 151.
(24) ....... 2. "Pictorial Similarities and Differences II" (108), p. 82.
............... Months Credit.

*Year 5-0 to 6-0*
(25) ....... 1. "Pictorial Likenesses and Differences" (107), p. 96.
(26) ....... 2. "Number Concepts" (108), p. 84.
............... Months Credit.

## LANGUAGE EXPRESSION

*Year 2-0 to 4-0*
(27) ....... 1. "Picture Vocabulary" (108), p. 68.
............... Months Credit.

*Year 2-0 and Below*
(28) ....... 1. "Word Combinations" (107), p. 77.
(29) ....... 2. "Naming Objects" (107), p. 137.
............... Months Credit.

*Year 2-0 to 2-6*
(30) ....... 1. "Naming Objects" (107), p. 79.
(31) ....... 2. "Naming Objects" (107), p. 138.
(32) ....... 3. "Gives Full Name" (43), pp. 220-221.
............... Months Credit.

*Year 2-6 to 3-0*
(33) ....... 1. "Naming Objects" (107), p. 141.
(34) ....... 2. "Action-Agent Test" (43), pp. 223-224.
............... Months Credit.

*Year 3-0 to 3-6*
(35) ....... 1. "Action-Agent Test" (43), pp. 223-224.
(36) ....... 2. "Comprehension I" (107), p. 144.
(37) ....... 3. "Response To Pictures: Level I" (108), p. 75.
(38) ....... 4. "Comprehension I" (107), p. 85.
(39) ....... 5. "Tells Sex" (43), pp. 228-229.
............... Months Credit.

*Year 3-6 to 4-0*
(40) ....... 1. "Action-Agent Test" (43), pp. 223-224.
(41) ....... 2. "Comprehension II" (108), p. 78.
(42) ....... 3. "Opposite Analogies I" (108), p. 77.
(43) ....... 4. "Number Concept of Two" (107), p. 147.
............... Months Credit.

*Year 4-0 to 4-6*
(44) ....... 1. "Action-Agent Test" (43), pp. 223-224.
(45) ....... 2. "Opposite Analogies I" (108), p. 79.
(46) ....... 3. "Definitions" (107), p. 149.
(47) ....... 4. "Materials" (108), p. 79.
(48) ....... 5. "Comprehension III" (108), p. 80.
(49) ....... 6. "Materials" (107), p. 90.
............... Months Credit.

*Year 4-6 to 5-0*
(50) ....... 1. "Action-Agent Test" (43), pp. 223-224.
(51) ....... 2. "Definitions" (108), pp. 81-82.
(52) ....... 3. "Comprehension II" (107), p. 152.
(53) ....... 4. "Counting Four Objects" (107), p. 93.
(54) ....... 5. "Knows Coins" (43), p. 235.
(55) ....... 6. "Names Red, Yellow, Blue, Green" (43), p. 235.
............... Months Credit.

*Year 5-0 to 6-0*

   (56) ....... 1. "Opposite Analogies II" (108), p. 85.

   (57) ....... 2. "Differences" (108), p. 84.

   (58) ....... 3. "Response To Pictures Level II" (108), p. 86.

   (59) ....... 4. "Counting 13 Pennies" (107), p. 155.

   (60) ....... 5. "Distinguishes Morning and Afternoon" (43), p. 235.

   (61) ....... 6. "Vocabulary" (108), p. 83.

   ............... Months Credit.

*Year 6-0 to 7-0*

   (62) ....... 1. "Opposite Analogies III" (108), p. 87.

   (63) ....... 2. "Similarities – Two Things" (108), p. 86.

   (64) ....... 3. "Sentence Building I" (107), p. 157.

   (65) ....... 4. "Picture Absurdities I" (108), p. 86.

   ............... Months Credit.

*Year 7-0 to 8-0*

   (66) ....... 1. "Memory For Stories: The Wet Fall" (108), p. 89.

   (67) ....... 2. "Similarities and Differences" (108), p. 90.

   (68) ....... 3. "Verbal Absurdities I" (108), p. 90.

   (69) ....... 4. "Vocabulary" (108), p. 88.

   ............... Months Credit.

*Year 8-0 to 9-0*

   (70) ....... 1. "Rhymes: New Form" (108), p. 93.

   (71) ....... 2. "Similarities and Differences" (107), p. 162.

   (72) ....... 3. "Verbal Absurdities II" (108), p. 92.

   (73) ....... 4. "Dissected Sentences I" (107), p. 161.

   ............... Months Credit.

*Year 9-0 to 10-0*

   (74) ....... 1. "Vocabulary" (108), p. 94.

   (75) ....... 2. "Word Naming" (108), p. 96.

   (76) ....... 3. "Finding Reasons I" (108), p. 96.

   (77) ....... 4. "Memory For Stories I: The School Concert" (107), p. 164.

   ............... Months Credit.

## SPEECH, HEARING, AND LANGUAGE CENTER
## LANGUAGE AND LEARNING ASSESSMENT: For Training
## (LLAT)
### Diagnostician's General Report Form

Name .................................    Date ........................................

Examiner ...........................    Birth date ...............................

I.    *Description of child or adult*
     A.   Chief complaint as given by parent
     B.   Summary of reports from other agencies or physicians
     C.   Dates and comments of previous assessments
     D.   Past and current class placement

II.   *Behavior during the assessment*
     A.   Cooperation
     B.   Work habits
        1.   Profits from instruction
        2.   Recognizes errors – corrects them
        3.   Gross and fine motor skills
        4.   Handedness

III.   *Hearing*

IV.   *Oral Communication* (see Language and Learning Assessment Worksheet)
     A.   Comprehension
     B.   Expression
        1.   Language
        2.   Speech – agnosia, apraxia, dysarthria, voice, stuttering, etc.

V.   *Written communication*
     A.   Reading
     B.   Writing
     C.   Spelling
     D.   Arithmetic

VI.   *Avenues of Learning*
     A.   Memory (short term)
        1.   Auditory
        2.   Visual (for pictures)
        3.   Visual-motor
     B.   Visual-motor-perception

VII.    *Social Maturity*
    A.    Self-help skills
    B.    Social perception and participation with familiar persons and strangers.
VIII.   *Impressions*
    A.    Summary of this assessment
    B.    Comparison with previous assessments (including teacher's report)
IX.     *Recommendations*

**SPEECH, HEARING, AND LANGUAGE CENTER**
Diagnostic Division

January 9, 1963

Re: Richard Bartell

Dr. T.R. Castle (Pediatrician)
710 Main Street
Houston, Texas

Dear Dr. Castle:

We have completed our speech, hearing, and language assessment for your patient, Richard Bartell (see enclosed report).

Mrs. Bartell will be enrolled in a five day Pre-Training Class which is designed to provide her with basic information related to language and learning, and to define Richard's and her role in the class to which he will be assigned.

Thank you for the referral and if you would like further information, please let us know.

> Very truly yours,
> **Speech and Language Diagnostician**

## SPEECH, HEARING, AND LANGUAGE CENTER
### Diagnostic Division

Name: Richard Bartell                     Date:      1962 12 13
Examiner: Joan Lynch, Diagnostician       Birth
                                          date:      1959  1  2
                                          C.A.:      3 - 11

Mrs. Bartell brought her son to the center with the complaint that "He is not talking on his age level and does not seem to understand much of what is said to him." Richard, a very good looking boy, accompanied the examiner and his mother to the test room without any fear or apprehension. His cooperation was quite good, but he preferred to string beads and manipulate the toy cars.

### Hearing

Although standard audiometric procedures were not possible, hearing appeared to be adequate for the development of oral communication. Richard responded to soft, high and low frequency sounds as well as the human voice. A complete audiological study will be scheduled in the near future.

### Oral Communication

*Comprehension:* During this assessment Richard demonstrated no comprehension of single words or connected discourse. Mother reported that he does not follow any of her oral directions at home.

*Expression:* Although this boy has a five or six word vocabulary it is not functional. His six or seven words are usually used inappropriately. He communicates primarily through gesture; taking a person's hand and leading him to the object apparently desired.

### Learning Skills

All tasks which did not require Richard to understand oral directions or to give oral responses were passed between the two and three year level with the exception of a block design activity which did not require memory. On this item he scored between the 3 year 6 month and 4 year 6 month level.

**Social Maturity**

With mother as the reporter, Richard scored at the three-year level in self-help skills, motor development, etc.

**Impressions**

This child is delayed in most of his learning skills and performs below the twelve month level in oral communication. It would not be possible at this time to predict this boy's progress in the areas of language and learning.

**Recommendations:**

1. Mrs. Bartell asked about the advisability of a neurological study and we suggested she discuss this matter with you.
2. Richard will be enrolled in a pre-academic class at this center, subsequent to mother's enrollment in the Pre-training Language Class.
3. A language and learning re-assessment will be made at the end of the school year.

Speech and Language Diagnostician

## SPEECH, HEARING, AND LANGUAGE CENTER
### Diagnostic Division

September 23, 1964

Re: Gary Simonson
C.A.: 7 yrs. - 1 mo.

E.A. Crosby, M.D. (Otologist)
1692 Main Street
Center, Texas

Dear Dr. Crosby:

We saw your patient, Gary Simonson, on September 18, 1964. Although he was a very difficult child to assess, I believe we have obtained a good picture of his assets and deficits.

### Hearing

Pure tone audiometry demonstrated a bilateral, sensori-neural hearing impairment with a possible conductive component in the left ear. There appears to be no explanation for the depressed bone conduction responses in the right ear. Repeated trials failed to obtain any better results. On his better ear, the right, Gary understood connected discourse at approximately 30 dB (ASA). Discrimination was good. On the left ear he was not aware of anyone talking until the 50 dB level was reached. Discrimination was poor. Test reliability was judged good (audiogram enclosed).

It is our impression that part of Gary's oral language delay may be related to hearing impairment during his language development years. With this concept in mind we took Mr. and Mrs. Simonson into the sound treated room and demonstrated, via free field, the level at which Gary responded. In addition, we talked to them at approximately 50 dB to demonstrate the loss of acuity in the left ear. We pointed up the significance of making use of the right ear in all learning situations, and that distance from the speaker was an all important factor.

If a hearing aid were to be tried, and this is questionable, it should be used in the right ear because discrimination in the left ear was very poor. Continued middle ear infection may cause periods of reduced hearing which, of course, might enhance the need for an individual aid. Getting this boy to tolerate a hearing aid may be a difficult task. If an aid is contraindicated, parents must talk to him at close range and the teacher must be appraised of his communication problems.

## Oral Communication

*Language:* Gary's ability to understand what is said to him, to answer questions, complete statements, and define words is no better than the four year level. He has number concepts to two, only.

*Speech:* A phonetic inventory was administered and revealed sound substitutions that are typical of four year old children. In light of his language scores, I would interpret his speech as being commensurate with his language development. Although speech therapy might be helpful, the primary concern should be language development.

## Written Communication

This boy is enrolled in a second grade where he is doing poorly. Mother stated that her son was reading on a second grade level, but after questioning her, it was apparent that he is calling words on that level, but has no reading comprehension.

The results of the language and learning assessment indicate Gary is in need of pre-academic work in preparation for first grade. He will need a great deal of stimulation in oral communication such as good TV programs, being read to, and a planned language development program.

## Learning Skills

On tests which involve auditory and visual memory, he performed between the five and six-year level. His best skills are in the area of visual-motor-perception when memory is not involved. It is interesting to note that the parents say he does a good job of copying letters.

## Social Maturity

With mother as informant, her son scored at the six-year level on the Vineland Social Maturity Scale.

Gary has a very short attention span for work that is difficult for him. He apparently recognizes his inability to cope with the problem, therefore moves on to something easier and more interesting to him — cars or objects around the room. His attention for "non-intellectual" play is extremely long and takes on a perseverative pattern. The parents say he will sit for hours, if allowed, turning the wheel on a tricycle or bicycle which is upside down. He will also pick up an object and twirl it with his hand until someone distracts him.

Although I could discipline Gary during the assessment, I found that I needed to continually motivate him for his attention. If I "pushed" him too far, he would withdraw and refuse the task at hand.

Gary demonstrates some pieces of the autistic syndrome, but I would not be in agreement with a diagnosis of autism. He relates very well to people and appears to enjoy them as long as they do not expect more from him than he can do.

I suggested to the parents that they not pressure Gary beyond his capabilities or they may find a tremendous amount of emotional disturbance in addition to his immature behavior.

**Impressions**

Gary impresses us as being a slow learning child with an added deficit in oral language which is probably related to hearing impairment.

At your suggestion we called the neurologist whom you recommended. He would have been pleased to see Gary the following day but scheduling EEG studies was not possible. He recommends Dr. Karl Smith of your city. I did not give the parents this name for I felt you may have someone of your own choice.

Thank you for referring this boy to us. He was a challenge to assess, to say the least, and I do feel we have a baseline for his present skills. I would like to have him return in a year for a re-evaluation which will tell us more about his learning rate. Both parents would like you to review with them our findings.

Very truly yours,

Speech and Language Diagnostician
Audiologist

**SPEECH, HEARING, AND LANGUAGE CENTER**
**Diagnostic Division**

May 1, 1951

Re: Mr. Karl H. Engle

Mr. J.L. Burns, President
A.B.C. Manufacturing Company
Lansing, Texas

Dear Mr. Burns:

At the request of Mr. Karl Engle, we are providing a report of our findings concerning his daughter, Karen Lou Engle.

Karen Lou was first seen at this Center in February, 1951, because of suspected hearing impairment. An audiometric assessment revealed severe hearing loss on both ears, but no deficits in the areas of learning. Mrs. Engle and Karen Lou were enrolled in a three week Pre-Training Class during which time a hearing aid was recommended and purchased by the parents.

This little girl at fourteen months is wearing her aid during all waking hours. We have checked the community in which this family lives and find there is no appropriate training center available to them. It has been our experience that parents and children need professional guidance in these early years of language development. If such can be provided, many of them will enroll in regular first grade classes rather than schools for the deaf.

If at all feasible, we would hope that Mr. Engle and his family could be transferred to this city where we would be able to enroll Karen Lou until she is of school age. We feel strongly that this little girl has a good chance to live a normal life in a hearing world if her training is started at this early age.

Please feel free to contact us if more detailed information is needed.

Very truly yours,

Associate Director

## SPEECH, HEARING, AND LANGUAGE CENTER
### Training Division

Date.....................................

Dear...................................

There is an opening in the training program for your child. If you wish to register for the designated class, please sign the enclosed form and return it with your registration fee.

Since the Speech, Hearing, and Language Center is supported by the United Fund of Harris County, patients living within this county may apply for fee reduction if they are unable to pay full tuition. If you wish to request a reduction in fees, obtain a financial and budget form from the main office.

If I have not heard from you by......................, another child will be assigned to the class.

Please contact me if you have further questions.

Very truly yours,

Supervisor of Training Program

## SPEECH, HEARING, AND LANGUAGE CENTER
### Training Division
### Registration Form

Name.............................................................Case No. ................Date.....................
Classes meet...................Time ...........Beginning...............through....................
Scheduled conferences ....................................................................................
Charges for the semester............. payable........................, a month in advance.
Registration fee...................................
Total due now.................................

---

*Enrollment:*            I wish to complete enrollment procedures for this class.
                         My charge of..............................is enclosed.

                         Signed ..................................................................
                         Current address ....................................................
                         City...................................Zip...........................
                         Phone ..................................................................

---

*Field Trip:*            My child may participate in class sponsored field trips.
                         Signed ..................................................................

*Photograph Release:*    This authorizes the Houston Speech and Hearing Center
                         to release photographs of the enrollee in any manner
                         they consider advisable.
                         Signed ..................................................................

---

*Information Release:*   The Houston Speech and Hearing Center is hereby autho-
                         rized to release information in regard to the enrollee
                         when a request for such information is received from
                         professional persons.
                         Signed ..................................................................

*In Case of an Emergency:*    Contact Dr. ...................................................

## PARENT-TEACHER CONFERENCES
### Topics for Discussion

1.  The *Handbook of Information For Parents.* This booklet prepared by the supervisor and teacher-clinicians presents the rules and regulations of the Speech, Hearing, and Language Center.
2.  An outline of selected topics to be discussed during the school year.
3.  The role of the teacher.
4.  Definition or review of such terms as language, speech, learning, deaf, hearing impaired.
5.  Developmental data and individual differences.
6.  Handedness.
7.  The importance of working with the child outside of class hours.
8.  Assessments and re-assessments of the child: language, learning, speech, and hearing.
9.  Basic principles of training at the Speech, Hearing, and Language Center as well as other schools in the vicinity.
10. The importance of teaching a child to understand before he talks.
11. How to communicate with the child: if the parents do not understand him or if he does not understand the parents.
12. The importance of every day living experiences and special experiences.
13. The value of playing games, singing songs, finger play, television.
14. Teaching words which express emotions, morality, sound.
15. Generalizing concepts of individual words or phrases.
16. The importance of teaching colloquial language.
17. Proper methods for reading a story and telling a story from pictures.
18. The importance of the father and other family members in the training program.
19. Goals for each unit as it is introduced.

## SPEECH, HEARING, AND LANGUAGE CENTER
### Training Division
### Teacher-Clinician's General Report Form (Worksheet)


Name ........................................ Case No ...................... Date ............................
Teacher-Clinician ...................... Class ........................... B.D. ............................
This report covers the period from ............................... to ...............................
First entered the training program ...................................................................

(NOTE: The number in parenthesis is the approximate age level for that activity)

I. **Description of child**
   A. The problem
   B. Physical findings
      Size: (if significant) small, large, average, tall, short.
      Defects and corrections.
      Central nervous system dysfunction: diagnosis, medication.
      Sensory:   Hearing impairment, "This child has a bilateral sensorineural hearing impairment and wears his aid in his..............ear. He has an aided threshold for noun word pictures at..............dB (ASA or ISO).
      Visual impairment: glasses, functional vision.
      Others: Heart, breathing (asthmatic), muscular.
      Oral mechanism: structure (cleft, teeth), mobility (tongue, jaw, lips), drooling.
   C. Length of time in the training program.
   D. Gross and Fine Motor Abilities.
      Walking on tiptoe (2-1/2).
      Running in stiff propulsive gait (1 - 2), smoothly (3 - 4).
      Climbs stairs with help (1-1/2), without help (2), alternates feet (4-1/2).
      Throws ball (1-1/2), well directed (3 - 4).
      Catches ball with stretched arms (3 - 4), with flexed arms (4 - 5).
      Skips fairly well (4 - 5).
      Eating with spoon (1-1/2), fork (2-3), pours from a pitcher (3 - 4).
      Bead stringing of four beads in two minutes (3).
      Puzzles.

Draws by scribbling on and off paper (1-1/2), scribbles on paper
(2), undifferentiated drawing but names it (3 - 4), recognizable shapes (5 - 6), colors inside the lines, holds pencil correctly (5 - 6).

Pasting.

Peg boards.

Pointing to objects while counting them (through 13, 5 - 6 to
6 - 0).

Scissors can be used to cut into paper (2 - 3), cut around a
picture easily, with difficulty.

E. Handedness:   right, left, mixed.

## II. Participation and Work Habits in Class

A. Attention to the task at hand.
B. Cooperation.
C. Profits from instruction.
D. Recognizes errors and corrects them.
E. Attention span for listening, working, watching the speaker.
F. Distractable.
G. Organization in attacking work: Initiative, ability to shift activ-
ities, finish work on time, finish work but not on time, cre-
ative, rigid, neat.
H. Learning rate when taught a new skill.

## III. How well does he organize information without oral or written clues?

A. Matching: forms, colors, objects to objects, picture to picture,
picture to object, letters, words, phrases, sentences, five balls
to five boxes.
B. Patterning: peg boards, beads, blocks, number configurations.
C. Puzzles: easy, difficult.
D. Sorting: colors, forms, quantities, toys, food, people, furniture.
E. Categorizing: sees relationships such as all have feathers, all make
noise.
F. Likenesses are observed (6).
G. Differences are observed (5 - 6).
H. Picture absurdities are identified.
I. Missing parts are identified.

## IV. Oral Communication

A. Comprehension (How well he understands what is said to him
when he does not have to give an oral response).

Identifies by name: objects, pictures, parts of body.

Understands simple commands: Will do four different activities with a ball (2).

Identifies objects by use.

Understands through listening alone, or lip reading and/or listening at specified distances.

Understands questions.

Number concepts through two (3), through three (4-1/2).

Discriminates among prepositions: in, on, under (3 - 4), in front of, behind (4+).

Adjectives: longer and shorter, big and little (3 - 6).

Verbs: (What hops?).

Likes to hear stories (4 - 5).

Follows individual instructions.

Follows group instructions.

Knows left and right on self (6).

B. Expression (How well he answers questions, completes statements, defines, relates events).

    1. Language.

    Gesture.

    Babbling.

    Jargon.

    Words: singly, combination of two or more (2).

    Nouns.

    Verbs.

    Pronouns: may be incorrect (2 - 3).

    Adjectives, adverbs and prepositions.

    Generating sentences: scanning, awkward or bizarre expressions. (Give examples).

    Spontaneous verbalization is projective.

    Asks questions (3 - 4).

    Answers questions: full name (2-1/2), age (5 - 6), birthday (6), address, phone.

    Describes a picture: enumerates three objects (3 - 3-1/2), more detail (5 - 6).

    Rote counting: three objects while pointing (4).

    Number concepts of two (3-1/2 - 4), of four (4-1/2).

    Penny, nickle, dime, and quarter are identified: three out of four (4-1/2 - 5).

    Color words: knows four (4-1/2 - 5).

    Defines: such as, What is a pencil? (4 - 4-1/2), What is mother's purse made of? (4 - 4-1/2), How two things are alike (6 - 7), How two things are different (7 - 8).

Verbal absurdities are described: such as "I saw a chair flying" (7 - 8).

Rhymes words (8 - 9).

2. Speech.

Voice quality: hoarse, nasal, breathy, "typical voice of the deaf."

Pitch: high, low.

Duration: rate too fast, too slow, not rhythmical.

Loudness: inappropriate at times, too loud, too soft, inaudible.

Rhythm: stuttering, cluttering, other.

Stress: sing-song, monotone, stress on wrong word or syllable.

Articulation: intelligibility of words, phrases, sentences, conversational speech (as heard by parent, teacher or other): discription of phonemic aspects as heard in unstructured speaking situations.

## V. Written Communication

A. Reading:

Single letters.

Single words.

Short phrases.

Sentences.

Stories.

B. Writing: manuscript, cursive.

C. Spelling: can write and spell single letter beginning a word, single words, sentences from dictation, sentences from his own experience, stories.

D. Arithmetic: rote counting, number concepts.

## VI. Avenues of Learning

A. Memory (short term):

Auditory: follows one oral direction (2), two directions (3), three directions (4 - 4-1/2), repeats nine word simple sentence (3-1/2 - 4), remembers sound effects in or out of sequence.

Visual: How many objects pictures or word symbols or events can he remember in or out of sequence?

Visual: tapping, folding paper, drawing or constructing, supplying the missing part, writing name.

B. Perceptual-Motor (Visual): copies circle, cross, square, diamond; copies a four block tower (2), a bridge (2-1/2 - 3), his name.

C. Spatial Orientation: remembering which way to go in a circle game; "Draw like mine"; finding on paper the top, bottom, middle, this corner; reversals in writing.

VII. **Social Maturity**
A. Self-help skills: washing and drying hands (3 - 4), use of handkerchief, in the bathroom, dressing.
B. Social perception and inter-personal relationships with familiar persons and strangers.
   Play: alone, parallel (1-1/2 - 2), cooperative (3 - 4), takes turns (3 - 4), group games as tag and hide and seek (4 - 5), tea-party and drop the handkerchief (3 - 4), table games as dominoes and cards (5 - 6).
   How he relates to the group: hits, works with group, plays with group.
   How he relates to others: teachers, parents, strangers.
   Withness: eye contact, social perception.
   Emotionality: reaction to frustrating experience; sense of humor; feelings of pity, shame, self esteem; compulsive; inhibition; sucks thumb or masturbates; obedient (3 - 4); responsibility as feeding pets and dusting (3 - 4); participates in Show and Tell.

VIII. **Summary: Assets and Deficits**

IX. **Impressions**
A. Current status.
B. Summary of progress.
C. Parent or relative participation.

X. **Recommendations**
A. Further testing.
B. Class placement as recommended by teacher and supervisor: class level, seating arrangements, size of class.
C. Where child was placed if parents did not follow above recommendations.

## SPEECH, HEARING, AND LANGUAGE CENTER
### Training Division
### Progress Report Form

Name ............................................ Case No. ................ Date ...............................
Teacher-Clinician ...................... Class ...................... B.D. ...............................
This report covers the period from ...................... To ...............................
First entered the training program ...............................................................

I. **Description of child or adult**
   A. The problem.
   B. Physical findings.
   C. Length of time in training.
   D. Gross and fine motor skills.
   E. Handedness.

II. **Participation and work habits in class**
   A. Attendance.
   B. Cooperation.
   C. Profits from instruction.
   D. Recognizes errors and corrects them.

III. **Oral Communication** (See work sheet for **Language and Learning Assessment: For Training**)
   A. Comprehension.
   B. Expression.
      1. Speech, agnosia, apraxia, dysarthria, other.

IV. **Written Communication**
   A. Reading.
   B. Writing.
   C. Spelling.
   D. Arithmetic.

V. **Avenues of Learning**
   A. Memory (short term)
      1. Auditory.
      2. Visual.

   B. Perceptual-Motor (no memory involved)

**VI.** **Social Maturity**
  A. Self-help skills.
  B. Social perception and participation with familiar persons and strangers.

**VII.** **Impressions**
  A. Current status.
  B. Summary of progress.
  C. Parent, spouse, or relative participation.

**VIII.** **Recommendations**

## SPEECH, HEARING, AND LANGUAGE CENTER
### Training Division
### Progress Report

Name ..Richard Bartell............. Case No. ...9730..... Date ...11-12-1965.........
Teacher-Clinician... Lucinda Young..... Class Pre-Kindergarten.. B.D... 1-2-1959..
This report covers the period from .....9-3-1965............to .......12-10-1965.......
First entered training program .........1-13-1963.................................................

## DESCRIPTION OF CHILD

Richard is a tall, five and one-half year old with a marked delay in oral language comprehension and expression. His hearing acuity is within normal limits and his oral mechanism appears adequate for speech.

In the spring of 1964 his neurologist stated "This leaves us with the last diagnosis—brain damage involving the language centers—which is not valid by neurological examination." Richard has had numerous changes in drug therapy, both anti-convulsants and tranquilizers. His behavior at school this semester has noticeably improved. Recently, however, Mrs. Bartell reported that her son was becoming more hyperactive and clumsy at home. Neither mother nor teacher have noticed any change at school.

## PARTICIPATION AND WORK HABITS IN CLASS

Work habits are improving but remain poor. Short attention span for listening is noted and often he does not watch the speaker. He attends better when there is physical contact between the teacher and himself. For example, if the teacher puts her arm on his chair or his shoulders, his attention improves. Richard is learning to stay with a task when the teacher reminds him to "look" and to "listen." Once his attention is focused, he usually learns the task quickly and performs it well.

## ORGANIZATION INFORMATION WITHOUT ORAL CLUES

Richard can match pictures, objects, and number configurations through five. Puzzles are worked quickly. He can sort materials into groups such as food and dishes and sees relationships well enough to categorize in a task such as "all are birds because they have feathers."

## ORAL COMMUNICATION

*Comprehension.* Comprehension of oral language has improved greatly in the classroom although it is still below age level. He identifies many objects and pictures by name and use, understands simple commands, knows common action verbs, and discriminates several prepositions and comparative adjectives. His understanding of complex questions is improving although at times he still responds with echolalia. He enjoys hearing stories and comprehends them better than earlier in the semester.

*Expression.* Oral expressive language has improved noticeably although it remains below age level. He still has difficulty naming objects and pictures, but, here again, there has been improvement. He is beginning to ask questions and to answer the questions of others. Describing pictures and relating events is much better.

The greatest improvement has been in the use of spontaneous language. Emotions are frequently expressed verbally and he finds enjoyment in giving explanations to other children. Samples of his expressive language are: "I'm sorry. I be good and not sit in corner." "Little children not use steel knife. It too dangerous. Only big people cut with knife."

Richard has started to use five and six word sentences fairly consistently. Sentence structure is better although he still confuses pronouns, verbs, and omits many of the function words. When word confusions occur he often verbalized them, for example, he can be heard saying to himself, "*He* is a boy. *She* is a girl."

His language is usually projective and meaningful. At times he still perseverates on a sentence or an idea. This usually occurs when he is relating an event, but the pattern may be broken by discussing the subject with him. He can give you his full name and age, and can name some coins and many color words.

Speech is characterized by several consonant substitutions and omissions as well as distorted vowels. His conversational speech is usually understood by all.

## WRITTEN COMMUNICATION

Richard expresses an interest in learning to print his name and numbers.

## AVENUES OF LEARNING

*Short-term auditory memory.* Simple directions are followed in a one to one relationship but he has considerable difficulty following group instructions. Short term auditory memory is his greatest deficit. He has followed three oral directions but is not consistent in this type of performance. He is able to repeat three numbers and a short sentence, but cannot re-tell a sequence story adequately.

*Short-term visual memory for pictures, objects, events.* Richard appears to be on age level in this modality.

*Short-term visual memory for hand-eye coordination tasks.* This ability varies with the activity. It is difficult to know if the problem is memory, coordination, or both.

*Spatial orientation.* The left hand is used for most activities. He is poorly oriented in space and has difficulty finding locations on paper. It appears that he consistently understands top, bottom, and middle in reference to positions on a sheet of paper. There is improvement in his ability to use directions in games, but he often becomes confused.

*Visual-motor-perception.* Richard is better than age level in his ability to copy block patterns and geometric designs. He usually scribbles when drawing and has difficulty cutting on lines.

## SOCIAL MATURITY

Good habits of personal hygiene are always present.

He relates well to the teacher and seeks her affection through conversation and physical contact. Attempts to relate to classmates are sometimes accomplished by inviting conversation with them, or engaging in cooperative play. He does not like too close physical contact with the children and is sensitive to the praise they receive from the teacher. When feeling crowded or jealous, he may react by hitting or pushing another child. He is expressing his feelings verbally and meaningfully at this time. For example, he will often hug the teacher and say, "I love you," or when reprimanded, "I hate you." Gains have been noticed in his ability to inhibit some of his undesirable traits in the classroom and to be obedient when reproached.

## SUMMARY

| *Assets* | *Deficits* |
|---|---|
| 1. Organization of information. | 1. Understanding and answering questions. |
| 2. Comprehension and use of oral language is improving. | 2. Sentence structure |
| 3. Conversational speech is usually intelligible. | 3. Short term auditory memory. |
| 4. Remembering what he sees. | 4. Hand skills. |
| 5. Doing a motor task from remembering what he has seen. | 5. Social maturity. |

*Assets (Cont.)*

6. Some improvement in spatial
   orientation.
7. Classroom behavior has shown
   good improvement, and work
   habits are steadily improving.

## RECOMMENDATIONS

1. Remain in his present class until the end of the semester.
2. Staff at the end of the semester to determine placement in the summer program. Mrs. Bartell has been informed that we will dismiss Richard from our training program after July, 1966. Steps are being taken to find appropriate placement in public school.

## PRE-TRAINING CLASS FOR HEARING-IMPAIRED CHILDREN AND THEIR PARENTS' GOALS

This program consists of classes which meet five days per week for fifteen one hour sessions. It is designed: (1) to assist the audiologist in selecting appropriate wearable hearing aids for the children, and (2) to provide their parents with basic information they will need to understand and manage the problems of hearing impairment. The classes are not designed to teach the children to talk, only to prepare them and their parents for subsequent training in language and speech development.

### CHILDREN'S SESSIONS

#### Equipment

Six stations of a commercial group auditory training unit are mounted to a table that will accommodate seating arrangements for six children. The master control unit that contains the turntable, tape playback, and master attenuator is situated in a convenient location to be controlled by the audiologist or an aide.

#### Objectives

**First Objective**

*To persuade the children to wear the earphones.* Initially many youngsters reject the phones by pulling them off or by demonstrations of loud crying. Suggested techniques for overcoming the rejections are:
1. Each parent sits on a chair in front of a station and holds her child in her lap.
2. The audiologist wears the phones and is animated at all times.
3. The parents wear the phones indicating it is a pleasurable experience.
4. One phone is placed over the child's ear while the parent listens with the other phone.
5. In each hand the child holds a flag or any interesting objects which will distract attention from the phones.
6. When the sound signal is presented, all mothers and the audiologist indicate a pleasant surprise.
7. Patience and a positive attitude is maintained: all children *will* wear the earphones. Only occasionally will five to ten sessions of persuasion be needed.

## Second Objective

*To help the children become aware of the presence and absence of sound.* If old enough, the children may be conditioned to wave a flag when the sound is presented and stop waving when the sound is not presented. Starting and stopping activities such as placing pegs in a board and rings on a stick may also be employed.

## Third Objective

*To obtain audiometric thresholds for each child on individual ears.*

## Fourth Objective

*To teach each child to accept a wearable hearing aid.* Using a hearing aid (on loan) the audiologist will find the following suggestions helpful in accomplishing this objective.

1. A positive pleasant attitude is maintained as the ear insert and hearing aid case are appropriately placed on the child. A parent must assume that her child will wear the aid just as he wears his diapers, shoes, or sweater.
2. As the audiologist or parent assembles the hearing aid on the child, interesting objects are placed in his hands.
3. To prevent very young children from pulling at the receiver, the parent places a bonnet over the child's head and ties the ribbons securely.
4. Children must be disciplined for mishandling their hearing aids just as they must be disciplined for other unacceptable behavior. The vast majority of children under four years of age willingly accept a wearable hearing aid. The older the child, the greater the likelihood of rejection.

## Fifth Objective

*To recommend one or a variety of hearing aids which meet the child's needs.* The parents are referred to appropriate hearing aid dealers.

## Sixth Objective

*To make an appropriate referral for training.*

## Class Time

The length of time spent with the children during each class hour will be dependent upon their cooperation. If the audiologist obtains the first two objectives with a child in two or three days, that child is ready for an audiological assessment and hearing aid on loan. He may remain with the group on subsequent days either using the phones or the wearable aid.

If the audiologist obtains good cooperation from the class on a specified day, and is accomplishing his objectives, he may spend forty minutes with the children and the remainder of the hour with the parents. As the days pass by more time is given over to the parent group.

## Aides

A volunteer or teacher aide serves a two-fold purpose in the program: (1) at the direction of the audiologist she controls the presentation of the auditory signal, and (2) she cares for the children while the audiologist meets with the parents.

## PARENTS' SESSIONS
### First Day

### Announcements

1. Looseleaf notebooks are to be brought to class each day for purposes of recording lecture information and retaining printed materials.
2. Attendance is important.
3. Questions may be submitted in writing to the audiologist at the beginning of each class.

### Lecture

1. Copies of the goals and general outline for the course are given each parent and a discussion follows.
2. The audiologist anticipates the many questions that parents wish to ask during their first day in class; Will my child learn to talk? Will he always have to wear a hearing aid? How much will an aid cost and can it be bought on time? Such questions are answered in generalities assuring the parents that detailed information will be presented during the following weeks.

**Recommended Reading**

From time to time printed material will be given to parents and pamphlets and books will be recommended as supplementary information. Use of the school library is explained.

**Question and Answer Period**

Written as well as oral questions are answered by the audiologist and the parents during a specified time.

**Supplies for the Day**

1. Copies of the goals and general outline of the class procedures.
2. Copies of any school forms which have not previously been filled in by the parents: release of information sheet, intake forms, etc.

**Preparation for Subsequent Days**

1. Schedule dates for audiological assessment of each child.
2. Schedule audiological test suites for demonstration to parents of pure tone and speech signals under varying conditions.

### Second Day

**Announcement**

Pertinent announcements are made.

**Lecture**

Each parent receives a printed vocabulary list, each word defined in language that is meaningful to the parents. The audiologist discusses the definitions in generalities, indicating that specific information will follow in future lectures.

**Recommended Reading**

Mildred Groht, *Natural Language for the Deaf.*

**Question and Answer Period.**

**Supplies**

1. Mildred Groht's book.
2. Printed vocabulary lists. Suggested terms are:

| | |
|---|---|
| aided threshold | hearing aid |
| amplification | language |
| audiogram | language of signs |
| audiometer | learning |
| auditory training | lipreading, speech reading |
| auditory training unit | schools for children with |
| conductive hearing loss |    hearing impairment |
| deaf | sensorineural hearing loss |
| decibel | speech |
| ear canal | teachers of children with |
| hard of hearing |    hearing impairment |

## Third Day

**Announcements**

1. Dates and hours for each child's audiological assessment are given to parents.
2. Methods of making ear impressions and cost to parents are discussed.

**Lecture**

In lay language, the teacher describes the anatomy and physiology of the hearing mechanism and the transmission of sound.

**Question and Answer Period**

**Supplies**

1. A printed illustration of the hearing mechanism.
2. A model of the ear.
3. Human bones from the ossicular chain.

## Fourth Day

### Announcements

"I want to tell you about an experience you are going to have very soon. A woman or man whom you have never seen is going to walk up to you in the grocery store. He or she will tell you about a cure for hearing impairment or give you the name of a doctor who lives 1000 miles from here who can improve your child's hearing. Be cautious — check with your otologist and audiologist before you seek the magic cure."

### Lecture (May be given by a local otologist)

1. Types of hearing impairment.
2. Causes of hearing impairment.
3. Treatment of hearing impairment.

### Recommended Reading

### Question and Answer Period

### Supplies

1. Printed illustration of the hearing mechanism.
2. Appropriate reprints.

## Fifth Day

### Announcements

Pertinent announcements are made.

### Lecture and Demonstration

How to determine the presence of hearing impairment.

1. Medical examination.
2. Case history information.
3. Diagnostic training program.
4. Audiological testing. A portable audiometer is used to demonstrate an audiometric test. Each parent is given several audiograms for plotting the patterns described by the audiologist.

**Question and Answer Period**

**Supplies**

1. Portable audiometer.
2. Audiogram forms.
3. Audiogram board or blackboard, chalk, and eraser.

## Sixth Day

**Announcements**

Parents are reminded of dates and hours of audiological assessments.

**Lecture**

The parents visit the audiometric suite to listen to pure tone and speech signals under varying conditions of loudness and filtering.

**Question and Answer Period**

**Supplies**

Audiogram board or blackboard, chalk, and eraser.

## Seventh Day

**Announcements**

Pertinent announcements are made.

**Lecture and Demonstration**

A recording of attenuated and filtered speech is played for the parents.

**Question and Answer Period**

## Supplies

1. Tape Recorder.
2. Extension Cord.
3. Tape.
4. Pick-up reel.

## Eighth Day

### Announcements

Pertinent announcements are made.

### Lecture and Demonstration

With the aid of a variety of hearing aids, the audiologist lectures on the following topics:

1. Historical development and use of hearing aids.
2. The modern hearing aid.
3. Why very young children will wear hearing aids and many older children and adults reject them.

### Question and Answer Period

### Supplies

1. Early model hearing aids.
2. Several current instruments representing the following models: body-worn, behind the ear, and temple.

## Ninth Day

### Announcements

Parents are to bring the handout sheet, "Troubleshooting Chart"    to the next day's class.

1. How a hearing aid is chosen for a specific child.
2. Cost and financing of hearing aids.
3. Care of the hearing aid.
4. A harness for the hearing aid.

**Recommended Reading**

Hallowell Davis, "Troubleshooting Chart."

**Question and Answer Period**

**Supplies**

1. Reprint of "Troubleshooting Chart".
2. A commercial harness for hearing aids.
3. Printed diagram of a harness for hearing aids.

## Tenth Day

**Announcements**

Vocabulary lists should be brought to the next day's class.

**Lecture**

1. A detailed discussion of the "Troubleshooting Chart."
2. How to check your child's hearing aid each morning.
3. Parents assemble hearing aids (battery, cord, receiver), listen to them, and trouble shoot when indicated.

**Question and Answer Period**

**Supplies**

1. "Troubleshooting Chart."
2. Several aids which the parents can assemble, listen to, and troubleshoot if indicated.

## Eleventh Day

**Announcements**

On the last three days of the course there will be no need to bring the children.

**Lecture**

A lecture on language, speech, learning, and emotional overlay.

**Question and Answer Period**

**Supplies**

Vocabulary sheet.

## Twelfth Day

**Announcements**

Pertinent announcements are made.

**Lecture**

Methods of training preschool children with hearing impairment. Facilities in the community and the approach of each to training. Selecting the training program in which parents have confidence and remaining with it.

**Recommended Reading**

"Helping Your Hearing Impaired Child."

**Question and Answer Period**

**Supplies**

Reprint of "Helping Your Hearing Impaired Child."

## Thirteenth Day

**Announcements**

The parents are given the number of the observation booth where they will observe the Toddler's Class.

**Lecture and Demonstration**

1. The audiologist presents the purpose and a brief description of the Toddler's Class before the parents leave for observation.
2. The parents return ten minutes before the close of the hour to discuss the class which they have just observed.

**Question and Answer Period**

**Supplies**

    1. Key to the observation booth.

<h2 style="text-align:center">Fourteenth Day</h2>

**Announcements**

The parents are given the number of the observation booth where they will observe the Readiness Class.

**Lecture and Demonstration**

    1. The audiologist presents the purpose and a brief description of the Readiness Class before the parents leave for observation.
    2. The parents return ten minutes before the close of the hour to discuss the class which they have just observed.

**Question and Answer Period**

**Supplies**

Key to the observation booth.

<h2 style="text-align:center">Fifteenth Day</h2>

**Announcements**

Parents not enrolling their children in the training program may leave twenty minutes before the close of the class.

**Lecture and Demonstration**

    1. The recording of the attenuated and filtered speech is replayed.
    2. The course is summarized including the importance of: annual audiometric retests or more frequently when indicated; language, learning, and speech assessments and reassessments.

3. Parents receive copies of the "Parents Handbook" which is concerned with the rules and regulations of the training center.

## Question and Answer Period

## Supplies

1. Tape recorder
2. Extension cord
3. Tape
4. Pick-up reel
5. Parent handbooks

## TROUBLESHOOTING CHART*

| *Symptoms* | *See Paragraphs* |
|---|---|
| Hearing aid dead: | 1, 2, 3, 4, 5, 7, 10, 14, 15 |
| Working, but weak: | 1, 2, 3, 4, 5, 6, 7, 8, 9, 10, 13 |
| Works intermittently or fades: | 1, 3, 4, 5, 10, 15, 16 |
| Whistles, continuously or occasionally: | 6, 9, 11, 12, 13, 15, 17, 18 |
| Sounds noisy, raspy, shrill: | 1, 3, 4, 5, 8, 9, 10, 11, 12, 17 |
| Sounds hollow, mushy, muffled: | 1, 2, 7, 15, 16 |
| Other kinds of bad quality: | 1, 7, 10, 15, 17 |
| Noise when the wearer moves: | 19, 20, 21 |

### Causes, Tests, and Remedies

1. *Cause*--Dead, run down, or wrong type of battery. *Test*--Substitute new battery. *Remedy*--Replace battery.
2. *Cause*--Battery reversed in holder so that (+) terminal is where (-) terminal should be. *Test*--Examine. *Remedy*--Insert battery correctly.
3. *Cause*--Poor contacts at receiver-cord plugs due to dirty pins or springs. *Test*--With hearing aid turned on, wiggle plugs in receptacles and withdraw and reinsert each plug. *Remedy*--Rub accessible contacts briskly with lead-pencil eraser, then wipe with clean cloth slightly moistened with Energine or similar cleaning fluid. Inaccessible contacts usually can be cleaned with broom straw moistened with cleaning fluid.
4. *Cause*--Break or near break inside receiver cord. *Test*--While listening, flex all parts of cord by running fingers along entire length and wiggling cord at terminals. Intermittent or raspy sounds indicate broken wires. *Remedy*--Replace cord with new one. Worn ones cannot be repaired satisfactorily.
5. *Cause*--Plugs not fully or firmly inserted in receptacles. *Test*--While listening, withdraw and firmly reinsert each plug in turn. *Remedy*--Obvious.
6. *Cause*--Eartip too small or not properly seated in ear. *Test*--With the fingers press the receiver firmly into the ear and twist back and forth slightly to make sure that the eartip is properly positioned. *Remedy*--Obvious.

---

*Hallowell Davis and Richard Silverman, <u>Hearing and Deafness.</u> Holt, Rinehart and Winston, Inc., New York, 1960, pp. 347-349.

7. *Cause*--Eartip plugged with wax, or with drop of water from cleaning. *Test*--Remove eartip, examine visually, and blow through it to determine whether passage is open. *Remedy*--If wax obstructed, wash eartip in lukewarm water and soap, using pipe cleaner or long-bristle brush to reach down into the canal. Rinse with clear water and dry. A dry pipe cleaner may be used to dry out the canal, or blowing through the canal will remove surplus water.

8. *Cause*--Loose receiver cap. *Test*--Examine. Shake. *Remedy*--If cap is of the screw type, turn tight with fingers. If cap is cemented on or crimped, and has become loose, it can be repaired only by the manufacturer.

9. *Cause*--Insufficient pressure of bone vibrator on mastoid. *Test*--While listening press the bone receiver more tightly against the head with the fingers. *Remedy*--Bend the bone-vibrator headband to provide greater pressure. This is preferably done by the dealer, who is more skilled in maintaining conformation with the head.

10. *Cause*--Battery leakage (resulting in poor battery connections) or corroded battery contacts. *Test*--Examine battery and battery holder for evidence of leakage in the form of a powder or corrosion. *Remedy*--Discard the battery and wipe the holder terminals carefully with cloth dampened (not wet) in warm water to remove loose powder. Then clean with pencil eraser.

11. *Cause*--Receiver close to wall or other sound-reflecting surfaces. *Test*--Examine. *Remedy*--Avoid sitting with the fitted side of the head near a wall or other surface. Such surfaces close by tend to reflect the sound from the receiver so that it is more readily picked up by the microphone, thus causing whistling.

12. *Cause*--Microphone worn too close to receiver. *Test*--Try moving instrument to provide wider separation between it and the receiver. *Remedy*--Avoid wearing microphone and receiver on same side of the body, or close together.

13. *Cause*--Microphone facing the body. *Test*--and *Remedy*--Obvious.

14. *Cause*--Telephone-mike switch in wrong position. *Test* and *Remedy*--Place switch in desired position.

15. *Cause*--Faulty receiver. *Test*--Examine receiver for possible breaks, cracks, etc. *Remedy*--Replace with a new receiver.

16. *Cause*--Collapse of tubing. *Test*--Check to see if tube bends (either when head is in a satisfactory position or is moved.) *Remedy*--Shorten or replace tube.

17. *Cause*--Volume control turned too high. *Test*--Reduce volume until speech sounds clearer. *Remedy*--Obvious.

18. *Cause*--Air leak between earmold and receiver. *Test*--Check ring, retainer of earmold, receiver nozzle, and plastic seal washer. *Remedy*--Replace defective part.

19. *Cause*--Clothing noise from loose clothing clip. *Test*--Check. *Remedy*--Tighten or replace clip.

20. *Cause*--Clothing noise from improper placement of aid. *Test*--Experiment by placing aid in different positions on the body. *Remedy*--Obvious.

21. *Cause*--Clothing noise because garment bag is not used. *Remedy*--Obvious.

If the above tests do not disclose the source of trouble, the difficulty is probably internal in the receiver, microphone, or amplifier and the instrument should be serviced by your dealer.

## A Word to the Wise

No one but an expert should ever open the case of a hearing-aid amplifier. Even opening and closing it may cause trouble, and to poke around inside may cause severe damage that will be expensive to repair. If you must satisfy your curiosity and see the inside, your dealer will be glad to show it to you. Remember, if you do damage through opening up the case (and don't think your dealer will fail to detect it), it is liable to void your service guarantee!

## HELPING YOUR HEARING-IMPAIRED CHILD*

Following is a condensed list of suggestions for parents who wish to help their hearing impaired children acquire oral language.

1. Make it possible for your child to receive an appropriate hearing aid early in life, keep it in excellent working order, and, except on obvious occasions, have him wear it every waking hour.
2. Teach him that he always must watch your face when you talk. By so doing he will learn to lip read in a very natural way.
3. You, your family, and friends must talk to him frequently and include him in family conversations. In the early stages of training it is important to use short (two to five word) phrases which are meaningful to him.
4. Talk to him during all daily, routine activities such as dressing, bathing, eating, or shopping. This is the only way he will learn to understand and to talk.
5. Repeat phrases, using the same words, until you feel sure your child understands.
6. Help the child recognize his own name (through listening alone, if possible).
7. Create many new experiences for your child, for he must have something to talk about.
8. Attempt to understand your child even though he may not be clearly articulate.
9. Accept your child's gesture language when he does not have the words to express himself, but use gesture yourself only when necessary.
10. Stoop to talk with your child as frequently as possible in order that your face may be on a level with his. Or, sit him on the counter top while you are washing dishes or preparing vegetables. Lip reading is much easier for him if he is on your level.
11. Use clearly articulated speech, but do not over-emphasize mouth movements.
12. Do not speak to him in "baby talk" or more than one national language.
13. Keep a weekly diary of your child's language progress.
14. Enroll your child in a language development program with a trained teacher.
15. Select a training program where the methods are made clear to you, and a program in which you have confidence. Do not shop from one method to another.

*Compiled by Paul Caillet, audiologist, Houston Speech and Hearing Center, Houston, Texas.

## Addendum to Non-Oral Reading Series ( 93 )

The teacher of language-delayed children with or without hearing impairment, faces one of her most difficult tasks when she decides that they are ready for a formal reading program. She asks herself which series to use only to find that the majority of reading series are designed for children with a normal background in language experience. Therefore, she is faced with the tasks of adapting the series of her choice to her class and finding the time to prepare the innumerable charts that are necessary to teach the words in the series.

One answer to this dilemma is the Non-oral Reading Series.
The entire kit consists of 57 charts, each of which is accompanied with matching picture and word cards. The manual and the charts are so prepared as to lend themselves well to all children who have language deficits regardless of etiology. In addition, homework can be prepared easily, work sheets can be duplicated as each lesson is completed, and the children can work at their own rate with seatwork. It is important to note that before beginning the non-oral reading series, a child must be able to (1) match uncolored pictures and printed words, (2) match groups of objects such as five dots to five stars, and (3) to trace a word from beginning to end.

The reviewer of the method presents the following suggestions for adapting the lessons to language delayed children.

**Lesson 1.** Two sets of name cards are made for each member in the group and games are played until each child can recognize his name card by matching it to the name card on his desk.

**Lesson 2.** To begin this lesson use the last four words, table, door, window and chair, for the following reasons: they look and sound different to the children, they appear in the classroom so that the teacher may illustrate the object, they are in the home for mother to use when reinforcing a lesson, and each object can be drawn easily. In order to proceed, the teacher selects her name card, the picture of the chair and moves over to touch a chair. Then she holds up a child's name card, gives him a picture and he is expected to touch the corresponding object in the room. When there is an error, either the teacher or another child shows the correct response. Word cards are presented in like manner with the addition of tracing the word on the chart and writing it on the blackboard. Each student should have a turn at tracing and writing the words as well as matching them to the correct pictures. For further reinforcement, the picture of a chair can be drawn and the child asked to write the appropriate word under it. Or, the word may be written and he is asked to draw the correct picture by consulting the dictionary chart. Seatwork similar to the group work can be assigned and those who finish first may take turns being the teacher.

**Lesson 3.** When introducing the number chart it may be wise to start first with numbers one through five. Several sessions on matching the word cards to the configurations are needed. Work sheets may be devised which contain pictures of four chairs, two doors, and five tables, all in configuration. The children are expected to write the correct number under each grouping. By the same token, "3 doors" may be written and the child asked to draw the correct number of doors in configuration. Learning seems to be reinforced best when a child gets to be teacher.

**Lesson 4.** Chart 2, the first verb chart, may be introduced by employing the words walk, hop, run, ride, fly, and jump. The teacher touches the picture and performs the action, then writes the word and completes the action. Finally, when the children become skilled, they may write the word for a classmate to demonstrate.

**Lesson 5.** The following sentence is written on the blackboard, "Joe, hop to the door." When a child cannot perform, the teacher demonstrates. Charts 1 and 2 should be used to enable the children to see how an action word and a noun can be related in a sentence.

**Lesson 6.** When learning to match printed words to written words, the children may cut matched words from newspapers and magazines that correspond to the written words on the blackboard. It is important to point out differences in such phonemes as "a" and "g." One added feature is to type a list of words with the same scrambled list in written form in a second column. The children draw a line from the typed word to the matched written word.

**Lesson 7.** Capitalization may be introduced by showing the words found on the back of the verb cards. They will find the "Hop to the door." requires a capital H for "hop" but a small h when they say "Joe, hop to the door." Seatwork may involve drawing lines to the words or letters that are the same regardless of whether they are small or capitalized.

**Lesson 8.** It is motivating for the teacher to show a name card, write on the blackboard, "Run to the door." and then ask the child who completes it to write another sentence.

**Lesson 9.** With the introduction of the color chart, the teacher may label the chairs on the seatwork sheet with color words. The children, then, are instructed to color the objects by matching the color word to the color chart.

**Lesson 10.** The words "draw and color" from Chart 2 may now be introduced and are easily taught through the use of colored chalk. "Draw a door. Color the door red."

**Lesson 11.** The color word can be placed in its proper place in the sentence by instructing the children to "Draw a yellow chair." and "Draw a blue door and a red table."

**Lesson 12.** With the use of Charts 1, 2, 3, and 4, numbers and colors may be integrated into a sentence. "Draw 2 green doors. Draw 4 yellow tables."
**Lesson 13.** It follows, that by using charts 1, 2, 3, 4 and the big and little chart that the children are now ready to "Draw 2 little blue chairs. Draw 4 little green doors and 3 big blue doors."
**Lesson 14.** The remainder of Chart 1 can be expediently introduced at this time since the children now have become adept at matching. Magazine pictures may be labeled with appropriate words.
**Lesson 15.** One of the most difficult lessons is the one which deals with the concept of "can" and "cannot." The children may be instructed to fill in the blank in sentences such as "A boy............hop. A table...........hop."
**Lesson 16.** The "doing" form of Chart 2 may be introduced as late as lesson 17. The sentence "Barbara, ran." is written on the board and she is told to do so and is expected to do so until told to stop. While she is running the teacher may write, "What is Barbara doing?" At this point the "doing" chart is presented and the class chooses the word "running." At this point the teacher writes "Barbara is running." This is not an easily learned lesson and may have to be supplemented with seatwork involving a written description of magazine pictures depicting persons in action.
**Lesson 17.** Lesson 16 is repeated and Barbara is told to "stop" and another child is asked to write what she did. The "did" chart will complete the story with "Barbara ran." Noun and verb charts as well as where and which charts are presented in a similar manner.

The aim of the Non-oral reading series is not directed toward teaching children to memorize words before going on to the next lesson, but rather to teach them the skills involved in looking at a chart for purposes of finding the correct word. As one might expect, the words do become memorized because of so much repetition, and at this point the children are ready to begin the reading series used in the "regular" classroom. They will have learned the majority of words that appear in the pre-primers.

The Non-oral Reading Series presents language as a unified subject teaching the following almost simultaneously, reading, writing, spelling, colors, numbers, oral language (comprehension, ideation, and usage) and speech. There is no limit to the variety of practice lessons, and the teacher has at her command an orderly sequence of lesson plans and materials for teaching language.

## PICTURE FILE AND OTHER TRAINING MATERIALS

I. PICTURE FILE (Pictures related to specific motivational techniques)
  A. Units within the curriculum guide
    1. Pictures related to linguistic systems
      a. Phonemic structure
        (1) Rhyming words
            Example: cat, bat, rat.
        (2) Phoneme recognition
            Pictures filed behind beginning sounds.
            Example: "b" boy, bat, bug.
      b. Semantic structure
        (1) Recognizing and naming pictures
            Pictures of the vocabulary presented with each unit.
            Example: Clear cut pictures of a tie, shirt, coat, etc., for the clothing unit.
        (2) Recognizing and naming pictures by function
            Example: A picture of an outdoor yard scene elicits responses such as "Which one do we use to rake leaves?"
        (3) Defining
            Example: Pictures of tables depicting various sizes, shapes, materials, places found, and use.
        (4) Describing
            Example: A picture of a birthday party showing children "pinning the tail on the donkey."
      c. Syntactic structure
        (1) Declarative sentences
            Example: Any of the above pictures such as the outdoor yard scene may be used to assist in generating sentences. "Daddy is raking the leaves," "Billy is mowing the lawn."
        (2) Questions
            Example: Using the outdoor yard scene, the child is the teacher and asks "Who is mowing the lawn?" or "Who is watering the grass?"
      d. Morphologic structure
        (1) Tense
            Example: Action pictures such as a boy running, "The boy *is running*"; a broken glass to elicit "He *broke* the glass"; a man carrying a paint brush and paint from the garage, "He *will paint* the house."

(2)    Number

Example: Pictures of people including 1 man, 3 men; 1 child, 4 children; 1 boy, 2 boys; 1 woman, several women.

(3)    Case

Example: The possessive case; a picture including a boy and the boy's clothing along with a girl and the girl's clothing. The teacher asks "Whose hat is this?" to obtain the answer, "The boy's." The teacher, who has family photographs for each child, asks "Whose brother is this?" The child answers "It's mine." Other children might say "It's hers" designating the appropriate child.

(4)    Person

Example: Using a picture of a Halloween party, the teacher asks "Who is at the party?" If the answer is "boys and girls," the teacher changes the answer to *"They* are." or, "Who is holding the balloon?" *"He* is."

2. Pictures related to avenues of learning

   a. Memory (short term)

     (1)    Auditory

Example: Matching pictures accompany noisemakers. The teacher rings the bell, blows the horn, and hits the drum while the children have their eyes closed. One child is asked to select from five pictures the three which represent the sounds heard.

     (2)    Visual

Example: Five pictures are placed in a pocket chart and one is removed while the children have their eyes closed. One child names the missing picture.

Example: A picture of a string of colored beads is presented. After it is removed, the child duplicates the pattern with his beads.

   b. Perceptual-Motor (no memory involved)

Example: Step by step pictures illustrating how to draw a wagon.

Example: (1) rectangle, (2) circles, (3) line, (4) cross for a handle.

        c. Integration

                Example: (1) pictures of incongruities such as a boy picking a dollar bill from a tree, (2) a bicycle without a seat, "What's missing?"

      3. Pictures related to social perception.

                Example: A picture showing a big brother taking candy from his younger sister. "What's wrong with this picture?"

  B. Communication charts

  C. Non-Oral Reading Series

  D. Writing Road to Reading

II. Ditto stencils, mimeographs etc. for each unit in the curriculum guide.

III. Patterns for hand skill activities related to each unit.

IV. Toys and other motivational materials.

  A. Toys for each unit (in storage boxes)

  B. Work books

  C. Weekly Readers

V. Children's books

VI. Recordings, film strips, and other audio-visual aids

VII. Parents' library

VIII. Parent handouts

# Bibliography

1 Allodi, P., *Building Blocks For Speech*. Evanston, Ill., Northwestern Speech Clinic, 1964.

2 Ambrose, M. N., *Happy Ways to Numbers*. Philadelphia, The John C. Winston Co., 1960.

3 Ammons, R. B., and Ammons, H. S., *Full Range Picture Vocabulary Test*. Missoula, Montana, Psychological Test Specialists, 1948.

4 Amoss, H., *Ontario School Ability Examination*. Toronto, The Ryerson Press, 1936.

5 Anderson, R. C., and Ausubel, D., eds., *Readings in the Psychology of Cognition*. New York, Holt, Rinehart and Winston, Inc., 1965.

6 Arthur, G., *A Point Scale of Performance Tests*. New York, The Psychological Corporation, 1947.

7 Bangs, J. L., *A Clinical Analysis of the Articulatory Defects of the Feebleminded*. Unpublished Master of Science Thesis, University of Washington, 1941.

8 Bangs, J. L., *A Comprehensive Historical Survey of Concepts Regarding Congenital Language Disabilities*. Unpublished Doctoral Dissertation, University of Iowa, 1948.

9 Bangs, T. E., Rister, A., Bowman, E., and Shoenholtz, B., *Communication Charts*. Houston Speech and Hearing Center, Houston, Texas, 1965.

10 Bangs, T. E., "Evaluating Children With Language Delay." *Journal of Speech and Hearing Disorders*, Vol. 26 (February, 1961), p. 6.

11 Baruch, D., *New Ways in Discipline*. New York, McGraw-Hill, Inc., 1949.

12 Bellefleur, P. A., and McMeniman, S. B., "Problems of Inductance Loop Amplification." *The Volta Review*, Vol. 67, No. 8. (1965), p. 559.

13 Bellugi, U., and Brown, R., eds., "The Acquisition of Language." *Monograph of the Society for Research in Child Development*, Vol. 29, No. 1 (1964).

14 Bender, L., "Childhood Schizophrenia." *American Journal of Orthopsychiatry*, Vol. 17 (1947).

15 Berko, J., "The Child's Learning of English Morphology." *WORD*, Vol. 14 (1958), p. 150.

16 Berry, M., and Eisenson, J., *Speech Disorders*. New York, Appleton-Century-Crofts, 1956.

17 Birch, H. G., ed., *Brain Damage in Children*. Baltimore, Williams and Wilkins Co., 1964.

18 Boland, L. C., ed., and Jones, M. J., illustrator, *Mike and Cindy Stories*. Central State College Press, 1965.

19 Bridgman, P., *The Logic of Modern Physics*. New York, The Macmillan Co., 1927.

20 Brown, R., and Bellugi, U., "Three Processes in the Child's Acquisition of Syntax." *Harvard Educational Review*, Vol. 34 (1964).

21 Brown, R., and Fraser, C., "The Acquisition of Syntax." *The Acquisition of Language Monographs of The Society for Research in Child Development*, Vol. 29 (1964), p. 43.

22 Brown, R., *Social Psychology*. New York, The Free Press, 1965.

23 Brown, R., *Words and Things*. New York, The Free Press, 1958.

24 Buros, O. K., ed., *Mental Measurements Yearbook*. 5th ed. Highland Park, N. J., Gryphon Press, 1959.

25 Calvert, D. R., Reddell, R. C., Donaldson, R. J., Pew, L. G., "Comparison of Auditory Amplifiers for the Deaf." *Exceptional Children*, Vol. 32, No. 4 (1965), p. 274.

26 Cattell, P., *The Measurement of Intelligence of Infants and Young Children*. New York, The Psychological Corporation, 1947.

27 Chomsky, N., *Syntactic Structure*. The Hague, Mouton and Co., 1957.

28 Cruikshank, W. G., *The Teacher of Brain-Injured Children*. Syracuse, N. Y., Syracuse University Press, 1966.

29 Cruikshank, W. G., et al., *Perception and Cerebral Palsy*. Syracuse, N. Y., Syracuse University Press, 1957.

30 Darley, F. L., *Diagnosis and Appraisal of Communication Disorders*. Englewood Cliffs, N. J., Prentice-Hall, 1964.

31 Dasaro, Michael J., and Vera, J., "A Rating Scale for Evaluation of Receptive, Expressive, and Phonetic Language Development in the Young Child." *Cerebral Palsy Review* (September-October, 1961).

32 Davis, H., and Silverman, S. R., *Hearing and Deafness*. New York, Holt, Rinehart and Winston, Inc., 1960.

33 Décarie, T., *Intelligence and Affectivity in Early Childhood*. New York, International Universities Press, Inc., 1965.

34 Doll, E., *Vineland Social Maturity Scale*. Circle Pines, Minn., American Guidance Service Inc., 1947.

35 Dunn, L. M., *Peabody Picture Vocabulary Test*. Nashville, Tenn., American Guidance Service, 1959.

36 Ewing, A. W. G., ed., *Educational Guidance and the Deaf Child*. Manchester, Manchester University Press, 1957.

37  Ewing, I. R., and Ewing, A. W. G., *Opportunity and the Deaf Child.* London, University of London Press, 1947.

38  Fairbanks, G., *Voice and Articulation Drillbook.* New York, Harper & Row, Publishers, Inc., 1960.

39  Fitzsimons, R. M., *Let's Play Hide and Seek.* Magnolia, Mass., Expression Co., 1963.

40  Flavell, J., *The Developmental Psychology of Jean Piaget.* A Series in Psychology. Princeton, N. J., D. Van Nostrand Co., 1963.

41  Frostig, M., and Horne, D., *The Frostig Program for the Development of Visual Perception,* Teacher's Guide. Chicago, Follett Pub. Co., 1964.

42  Frostig, M., "Perceptual and Motor Skills." *Monograph Supplement Perceptual and Motor Skills,* Vol. 19 (October, 1964), p. 463.

43  Gesell, A., et al., *The First Five Years of Life.* New York, Harper & Bros., 1940.

44  Gesell, A., et al., *Gesell Developmental Schedules.* New York, The Psychological Corporation, 1949.

45  Glaser, G., ed., *EEG and Behavior.* New York, Basic Books, Inc., 1963.

46  Gleason, H. A., *An Introduction to Descriptive Linguistics.* New York, Holt, Rinehart and Winston, 1965.

47  Goodenough, F. L., *Measurement of Intelligence by Drawings.* Chicago, World Book Co., 1926.

48  Gray, W. S., Artley A. S., Monroe, M., *We Read More Pictures.* Chicago, Scott Foresman and Co., 1951.

49  Griffith, E., *The Abilities of Babies, A Study in Mental Measurements.* London, London Press, 1954.

50  Groht, M., *Natural Language for Deaf Children.* Washington, D. C., The Volta Bureau, 1958.

51  Guibor, C., *Non Oral Reading Series.* Chicago, Primary Educational Series, 1963.

52  Hebb, D. O., *The Organization of Behavior.* New York, John Wiley and Sons, Inc., 1948.

53  Heber, R. F., "A Manual on Terminology and Classification in Mental Retardation." *American Journal of Mental Deficiency,* Vol. 64, Monograph Supplement, 1959, Revised edition, 1961.

54  Hejna, R. F., *Developmental Articulation Test.* Ann Arbor, Speech Materials, 1963.

55  Higgins, D. D., *How to Talk to the Deaf.* Newark, N. J., Mount Carmel Guild, 1959.

56  Hiskey, M. S., *Hiskey-Nebraska Test of Learning Aptitude.* Lincoln, Nebraska, 1966.

57  Hiskey, M. S., *Nebraska Test of Learning Aptitude.* Lincoln, Nebraska, 1941.

58   Hunt, J., *Intelligence and Experience.* New York, The Ronald Press Co., 1961.

59   Ilg, F., and Bates, L., *Child Behavior.* New York, Dell Publishing Co., 1955.

60   Jackson, R. L., and Kelly, H. G., "Growth Charts for Use in Pediatric Practice." *Journal of Pediatrics,* Vol. 27 (September, 1945), p. 215.

61   Jerger, J., ed., *Modern Developments in Audiology.* New York, The Academic Press, 1963.

62   Johnson, W., Darley, F. L., and Spriestersback, D. C., *Diagnostic Methods in Speech Pathology.* New York, Harper & Row, Publishers, 1963.

63   Kanner, L., *Child Psychiatry.* 3rd ed. Springfield, Ill., Charles C Thomas, 1957.

64   Kessler, L., *Mr. Pine's Mixed Up Signs.* New York, Wonder Books, Inc., 1961.

65   Kimball, B. D., "Audio-Visual Aids: Addendum to Previous Article." *Asha, A Journal of the American Speech and Hearing Association,* Vol. 6 (December, 1964), p. 500.

66   Kindergraph. Chicago, Follett Publishing Co., 1960.

67   Kirk, S. A., and Weiner, B., ed., *Behavioral Research on Exceptional Children.* Washington, D. C., The Council for Exceptional Children, 1963.

68   Krehbiel, Becky & Evans, *Fun to Draw.* Racine, Wisc., Whitman Pub. Co., 1965.

69   Krehbiel, Becky & Evans, *Rhymes to Color.* Racine, Wisc., Whitman Pub. Co., 1965.

70   Lee, L., "Developmental Sentence Types." *Journal of Speech and Hearing Disorders,* Vol. 31 (November, 1966), p. 311.

71   Louttit, C. M., *Clinical Psychology.* New York, Harper and Bros., 1947.

72   Maney, Ethel S., *Thinking Skills.* The Continental Press, Elizabethtown, Pa., 1958.

73   Martin, W. E., *Basic Body Measurement of School Age Children.* Washington, D. C., U. S. Department of Health, Education and Welfare, Office of Education, 1953.

74   McCarthy, D., *The Language Development of the Pre-School Child.* Institute of Child Welfare Monograph Series, Minneapolis, University of Minneapolis Press, No. 4 (1930).

75   McCarthy, J. J., and Kirk, S. A., *Illinois Test of Psycholinguistic Abilities: Examiner's Manual.* Urbana, Ill., University of Illinois, Institute for Research on Exceptional Children, 1961.

76   Mecham, J. J., *Verbal Language Development Scale.* Minneapolis, American Guidance Service, 1959.

77  Melton, A. W., ed., *Categories of Human Learning.* New York, The Academic Press, 1964.

78  Menyuk, P., "Comparison of Grammar of Children with Functionally Deviant and Normal Speech." *Journal of Speech and Hearing Research,* Vol. 7 (1964), p. 109.

79  Menyuk, P., "Syntactic Rules Used by Children From Preschool Through First Grade." *Child Development,* Vol. 34 (1963), p. 407.

80  Meredith, H. C., "A Chart on the Eruption of the Deciduous Teeth for the Pediatrician's Office." *Journal of Pediatrics,* Vol. 30 (April, 1951), pp. 482-483.

81  Metraux, R. W., "Speech Profile of the Preschool Child—18-54 months." *Journal of Speech Disorders,* Vol. 15 (March, 1950), pp. 37-59.

82  Miller, G. A., *Language and Communication.* New York, McGraw-Hill, Inc., 1951.

83  Miller, W., and Erwin, S., "The Development of Grammar in Child Language." *The Acquisition of Language Monograph of The Society for Research in Child Development,* Vol. 29, No. 1 (1964).

84  Myklebust, H., *Auditory Disorders in Children.* New York, Grune and Stratton, Inc., 1954.

85  Myklebust, H., *The Psychology of Deafness.* New York, Grune and Stratton, Inc., 1960.

86  *My Weekly Reader.* American Education Publication, Columbus, Ohio, Wesleyan University Press.

87  Newby, H. A., *Audiology.* New York, Appleton-Century-Crofts, Inc., 1964.

88  Penfield, W., and Roberts, L., *Speech and Brain Mechanisms.* Princeton, N. J., Princeton University Press, 1959.

89  Perritt, M. F., *Hear, See and Tell Stories.* Northport, Ala., Colonial Press, 1964.

90  Piaget, J., *The Language and Thought of the Child.* New York, Harcourt, Brace and World, Inc., 1926.

91  Piaget, J., *The Psychology of Intelligence.* London, Routledge and Kegan Paul, 1950.

92  Richardson, H. A., *Games for the Elementary School Grades.* Minneapolis, Minn., Burgess Publishing Co., 1963.

93  Rister, A., "Non-Oral Reading Series. An Addendum." *Asha, A Journal of the American Speech and Hearing Association,* Vol. 6 (May, 1964), p. 174.

94  Robinson, H. B., and Robinson, N. M., *The Mentally Retarded Child.* New York, McGraw-Hill, Inc., 1965.

95  Rosenberg, P. E., "*Modern Trends in Auditory Misdiagnosis.*" *Asha, A Journal of the American Speech and Hearing Association,* Vol. 16 (October, 1964), p. 411.

96  Russell, W. R., *Brain, Memory, Learning: A Neurologist's View.* New York, Oxford University Press, 1959.

97  Saporta, S., ed., *Psycholinguistics: A Book of Readings.* New York, Holt, Rinehart and Winston, Inc., 1961.

98  Sataloff, J., *Hearing Loss.* Philadelphia, J. B. Lippincott Co., 1966.

99  Sloop, C. B., Garrison, H. E., and Crickmore, M., *Phonetic Keys to Reading, A Basic Reading Series.* Oklahoma City, The Economy Co., 1958.

100 Smith, M. E., *"An Investigation of the Development of the Sentence and the Extent of Vocabulary in Young Children."* University of Iowa Studies in Child Welfare, Vol. 3, No. 5 (November, 1926).

101 Spalding, R. B., and Spalding, W. T., *The Writing Road to Reading.* New York, Whiteside, Inc., and William Morrow and Co., 1957.

102 Spearman, C., *The Abilities of Man: Their Nature and Measurement.* New York, The Macmillan Co., 1927.

103 Strauss, A. A., and Lehtinen, L. E., *Psychopathology and Education of the Brain Injured Child.* New York, Grune and Stratton, Inc., 1950.

104 Tape Recording: *Stimulating the Auditory Percepts of Children with Hearing Impairment.* Houston Speech and Hearing Center, Texas.

105 Templin, M. C., *"Certain Language Skills in Children: Skill Development and Interrelations."* Institute of Child Welfare Monograph Series, Minneapolis, University of Minnesota Press, 1957.

106 Templin, M. C., and Darley, F. L., *The Templin-Darley Tests of Articulation.* Iowa City, University of Iowa Bureau of Education Research and Service, 1960.

107 Terman, L., and Merrill, M., *Measuring Intelligence.* Boston, Houghton Mifflin Co., 1937.

108 Terman, L., and Merrill, M., *Stanford-Binet Intelligence Scale.* Boston, Houghton Mifflin Co., 1960.

109 Thurstone, L. L., *Primary Mental Abilities.* Chicago, University of Chicago Press, 1938.

110 Travis, L. E., *Handbook of Speech Pathology.* New York, Appleton-Century-Crofts, 1957.

111 Trese, L. J., *"Your Child Needs Praise."* *This Week Magazine* (October 25, 1959), p. 15.

112 Van Riper, C., *Helping Children Talk Better.* Chicago, Science Research Associates, 1954.

113 Van Riper, C., *Speech Correction: Principles and Methods.* Englewood Cliffs, N. J., Prentice-Hall, Inc., 1963.

114 Van Riper, C., and Irwin, J. V., *Voice and Articulation.* Englewood Cliffs, N. J., Prentice-Hall, Inc., 1963.

115   Vigotsky, L. S., *Thought and Language*. Cambridge, Mass., The M.I.T. Press, 1962.

116   Ware, K. L., and Hoffsten, G. B., *Do You Know?* Austin, Texas, The Stick Co., 1963.

117   Wechsler, D., "The Incidence and Significance of Finger Nail Biting in Children." *Psychoanalytical Review*, Vol. 18 (1931), p. 201.

118   Wechsler, D., *Wechsler Intelligence Scale for Children*. New York, The Psychological Corporation, 1949.

119   Wepman, J. M., and Heine, R. W., ed., *Concepts of Personality*. Chicago, Aldine Publishing Co., 1963.

120   West, R., Ansberry, M., and Carr, A., *The Rehabilitation of Speech*. New York, Harper & Row, Publishers, 1957.

121   Whatmough, J., *Language: A Modern Synthesis*. New York, St. Martin's Press, 1956.

122   Wood, N. E., *Delayed Speech and Language Development*. Englewood Cliffs, N. J., Prentice-Hall, 1964.

123   Zedler, E., *Listening for Speech Sounds*. New York, Harper & Bros., 1955.

# Index